The Sound of Bells

The Sound of Bells

The Episcopal Church in South Florida

1892 - 1969

Joseph D. Cushman, Jr.

Foreword by Allen Tate

A University of Florida Book

The University Presses of Florida

Gainesville / 1976

Library of Congress Cataloging in Publication Data

Cushman, Joseph D.
    The sound of bells.

    "A University of Florida book."
    Bibliography: p.
    Includes index.
    1. Protestant Episcopal Church in the U.S.A.
South Florida (Diocese) 2. Protestant Episcopal
Church in the U.S.A.—Florida. 3. Florida—
Church history. I. Title.
BX5918.S65C87   283'.759'3   75-30946
ISBN 0-8130-0518-3

PRINTED BY THE ROSE PRINTING COMPANY, INCORPORATED
TALLAHASSEE, FLORIDA

I dedicate this book to the two who made it possible

MARY SUSAN LIVINGSTONE CUSHMAN
Uxori Dulcissimae Meae

and

JEAN FLAGLER MATTHEWS
Historiae Floridianae Fautrici Fideli

Preface

THE SOUND OF BELLS IS THE SUCCESSOR TO MY FIRST VOL-
ume, *A Goodly Heritage: The Episcopal Church in Florida,
1821–1892.* It records the history of the Diocese of South Florida
from the time it broke off from the old diocese in 1892 until it
was divided into three new jurisdictions in 1969. Those who are
looking for a chronological catalogue of their respective parishes
and missions will be disappointed, for this book is written with a
broader view in mind. Although it touches on parochial life and
history, it also describes the interaction of the ecclesiastical establishment with the social, political, and economic forces abroad in the
state during a period of conflict and change. In addition, an attempt
is made to portray the bishops of the diocese and to assess their roles
as the leaders and spokesmen of the Church.

I am indebted to Bishop Henry I. Louttit for the time he took
from his busy diocesan schedule to give me interviews, suggestions,
and encouragement. I must also thank Bishops James L. Duncan
and William H. Folwell for their interest and help. But I am
particularly grateful to my old friend and fellow Brevardian,
Bishop William L. Hargrave. It was he who conceived the idea
of histories of both the Florida dioceses and he who assisted most

in its execution. I would be remiss if I did not express my gratitude to his wife, Minnie, too, for her warm hospitality during my several trips to St. Petersburg.

Descendants of the British colonists of the 1880s—and the wives of descendants—provided much valuable material for my research. My thanks go to Mr. W. J. R. Cadman and Mrs. Victor Hill of Orlando; Mr. and Mrs. Alfred Bosanquet of Fruitland Park; Mrs. David Newell and Miss Hilda Budd of Leesburg; and Lady Gillett of Tavistock, Devon, the Florida-born daughter of Granville Chetwynd Stapylton, who opened the Stapylton Papers to me and gave my wife and me warm hospitality during our stay in England. The Rev. Charles Paddock of Fruitland Park allowed me the use of the rich records of Holy Trinity Church.

The staffs of the DuPont Library of The University of the South, the Strozier Library of Florida State University, the P. K. Yonge Library of Florida History at the University of Florida, the Magazine Division of the British Museum, and the Lambeth Library, London, offered helpful assistance, as did Mr. William Werts and Mrs. Cecelia Storjohan of the Diocesan Office in Winter Park.

Ten of my colleagues at The University of the South, Professors Charles Binnicker, Hugh Caldwell, Arthur Dugan, Wallace Katz, Edward King, Eric Naylor, Douglas Paschall, William M. Priestley, Bayly Turlington, and Herbert Wentz, read portions of the manuscript and offered many suggestions that have improved the style and organization of the book. Professor Allen Tate, Brown Lecturer at Sewanee, read and commented on the collected poetry of Cameron Mann. His criticism was very helpful to a historian in evaluating the bishop as both a poet and a man. Dean Stephen E. Puckette and the Ford Grant Committee provided money to hasten the preparation of the manuscript for publication.

It is fitting that Jean Flagler Matthews should share the dedication of this volume. She has long been interested in the work of the Church and in the preservation of the state's heritage. All Episcopalians and all Floridians owe her a great debt. I, however, owe her a special one. She not only provided a grant for the research of this work, she also gave most of the funds for its publication.

I must also mention my sons, David and Claybrooke, who during the lengthy preparation of *The Sound of Bells* bore with patience and good humor the demeanor of a sometimes irascible father; and lastly I must thank my wife, Mary Susan, who edited, typed, and helped me in so many ways with the first draft of the manuscript.

JOSEPH D. CUSHMAN, JR.

Contents

Foreword

PROFESSOR CUSHMAN HAS WRITTEN A SCHOLARLY AND eminently readable history of the Episcopal Diocese of South Florida. I am not an Episcopalian but I have the warmest sympathy for the Anglo-Catholic position and great admiration for the author's biographical and historical talents. From his account of the diocese it seems that its theological stance has been something near the moderate Catholicism of Thomas Aquinas and the reasonable Protestantism of Richard Hooker. If we look upon the union of Aquinas and Hooker as Aristotelian rationalism tempered by the sense of the actual church, Rome and Canterbury can be seen as having the same end in view. The bishops of South Florida used the two traditions not only in a missionary sense, but as an expression of Christian concern for all men. Long before such terms as "relevance" and "minority groups" came into general use, Bishop Gray began working with the Seminoles in the Everglades and Bishops Mann and Wing with the blacks along both coasts. But it was Bishop Louttit, using the labors of his predecessors as a foundation, who brought thousands of newly settled Floridians into the fold of Canterbury—northerners, southerners, West Indians, and Cubans.

From reading Mr. Cushman, I gather that there was a wide divergence in ceremonial in the diocese but a common liturgical bond in the use of the Book of Common Prayer. The blending of the Catholic and Evangelical traditions, together with this diver-

xiii

gence and uniformity in ceremonial and liturgy, may have played an important part in making South Florida one of the fastest growing dioceses in the American Episcopal Church. As a Roman Catholic, I have long admired the beauty of the Prayer Book liturgy, and I had hoped that the Episcopal Church would set a standard of language for other Christian bodies (like my own) who are struggling to put their liturgies into English. I have been as disappointed with the products of the Episcopal Liturgical Commission as I have been with those of the Roman Catholic. Many years ago the poet W. H. Auden agreed with me that a vernacular Roman Mass would be very bad. He then said: "Why don't you adopt Cranmer?" Well, why didn't we? There may be many things wrong with the Episcopal Church, but the language of its liturgy is not one of them.

The Plutarchan biographies of Bishops Gray, Mann, Wing, and Louttit are very skillfully done. But the most moving of all is the life of Bishop Gray, the pattern of whose vocation is not unlike that of a medieval saint. *The Sound of Bells* is not merely a pious tribute to the bishops of South Florida. It is complete social history at the hand of a trained historian. There is at least one feature which may entitle this book to a certain uniqueness in the religious history of our time. For example, we get as background, from the labors of the bishops, clergy, and laymen of South Florida, the social conditions, the economic problems, and the racial tensions of their several generations. The chapter dealing with the British immigraton may well deserve further investigation by Florida historians.

My own interests led me to give unusual attention to the life of Bishop Cameron Mann, whose avocation seems to me to have been more English than American. Bishop Mann not only compiled a concordance of the seventeenth-century poet George Herbert; he was himself an accomplished minor poet.

One wishes that the dominant literature of our day were not exclusively secular and that we could expect this excellent book to be read beyond the orbit of the Episcopal Church.

ALLEN TATE

Introduction

THE SOUND OF BELLS IS A GLORIOUS PART OF THE CHRISTIAN heritage. The first bell I can recall hearing was the one in the little board-and-batten Church of St. Gabriel in Titusville, where I grew up. If I could put an inscription on that bell, it would be one that I later read in Dorothy Sayers's novel *The Nine Tailors*:

> When mirth and pleasure is on the wing
> I ring;
> At the departure of a soul
> I toll.

I cannot, however, remember hearing the bell toll, for the practice was abandoned in the early decades of this century. Hence my memories of its sound concern only happy occasions.

I clearly recall sitting as a small child on the coping of the churchyard and being utterly fascinated by the great bell as it called us inside to church school. I also remember my Sunday-school teacher, Edith Crannell, telling us that bells could talk. "Listen," she said, pointing to the steeple. "Come to Church! Come to Church! Come to Church!" I had such a burning desire to ring that bell that I arrived by stealth the next Sunday planning to gratify the craving. I vividly recall being caught by the vicar, Charles Bascom, a huge, brisk, Pickwickian Britisher from the Islands, as I struggled with the gigantic rope. To my amazement he did not reprimand me but came to my assistance. The steeple soon erupted with joyous dissonance. Up and down went the vicar's massive shoulders; up and down I rode on the rope. Finally, exhausted, my hands blistered, I ran outside to watch the bell at work. Bim bam, bim bam, rang the bell, lifting its great bronze mouth to the rhythm of the pull. At last the bell ceased and the vicar appeared, red-faced and rubbing his hands, to join me on the coping. "God is gone up with a merry noise," he cried, gazing at the bell tower contentedly.

Not all my campanological memories are so parochial. One summer evening, just as I was coming in from a sail with my cousin George Cooper, the bells of the town began to ring for evening services. The river was calm. A light wind from the northwest carried their ringing over the water to us. We tried to identify each bell as it came in: the Baptist, the Methodist, the Presbyterian, the Roman Catholic. Soon these were joined by the more distant peals of the two Negro churches farther west. Tin tan, din dan, bom bam. The shore was alive with jubilee. Finally a deeper voice (we thought) joined the others, reluctantly at first, but it soon caught up with the rest. "That's our bell," exclaimed George with relieved satisfaction. The chorus was growing, the sound soaring over the great oaks and pines and orange trees along the shore. I imagined the brazen tongues of a dozen clamoring bells, their wide mouths rising and falling, dancing to their leaping ropes. The mixture of these joyful Christian voices blended into a spontaneous ecumenical song.

As I write these words I fancy I can see old Archdeacon Brown sailing down the Indian River from Titusville in the closing decades of the last century, the bells of his missions in Courtenay, Merritt, and Cocoa calling their congregations together at the sight of his sail; or Parson Mulford of Palm Beach being received with the same dissonant welcome as he visited the settlements along Lake Worth in his launch. The priests who served the interior missions of Central Florida from their base at the Cathedral were saluted by bells as well. Because of the uncertainty of the rail schedule the sexton often did not begin to ring the church bell until he heard the whistle of the train coming into the station.

In those early days of the Church, bells were important heralds of the Word and the sacraments. It is not merely fanciful to say that the growth of the Church in South Florida was accompanied by the jubilant clamor of the sound of bells.

I

The Partition

THE GROWTH OF THE EPISCOPAL CHURCH IN THE DIOCESE OF
South Florida should not be approached as an isolated ecclesiastical development. It is inseparably tied to the growth of the
peninsula as a whole. Not only did Church and Churchmen play
their parts in building the religious institutions of the pioneer state,
but they also participated in, and indeed often led, the social, economic, and political movements of their time.

In the last two decades of the nineteenth century the peninsula
of Florida was the scene of an amazing and varied pattern of population growth and economic expansion that would have seemed
impossible during the disastrous Civil War and crippling Reconstruction. In addition to the social and political revolutions which
came in the wake of war and reconstruction, the financial affairs of
the state were plunged into utter chaos. State debts had reached
gigantic proportions, and creditors, Northern and foreign, were
pressing the government in Tallahassee to place its one remaining
asset, fourteen million acres of state land, on the auction block to
satisfy their claims. These claims had accrued mainly through the
sale of bonds by the Internal Improvement Board of Florida to
finance badly needed railroad construction during the closing years
of the antebellum period. The inability of the state to pay the

interest on these bonds, much less retire the principal, was the source of continuous financial embarrassment. New railroad construction was at a standstill all through the 1860s and 1870s, and as a result the expansion of business and agricultural enterprises was retarded. Florida's unsettled financial affairs drove prospective investors from the state and slowed down the immigration of new settlers.

To transport himself and his belongings, the traveler in the peninsula had to rely upon a primitive and at times unusable network of sand roads and the steamboat services which operated sporadically on both coasts and on the few navigable rivers. The settlement of the peninsula could not seriously be undertaken until transportation was greatly improved, yet the state government could not come to grips with the transportation problem until it could satisfy the avaricious appetites of its creditors.

Three men, more than any others, helped to change the atmosphere of postwar Florida from the gloom and pessimism of the sixties and seventies to the brightness and optimism of the eighties and nineties—Hamilton Disston, Henry B. Plant, and Henry M. Flagler.

In 1881 Hamilton Disston, a rich and successful Philadelphia industrialist, with other Northern capitalists purchased 4,000,000 acres of land from the almost bankrupt state at the ridiculous price of twenty-five cents per acre. The Disston land deal embraced parcels all over the peninsula, and the question of the wisdom of the sale has been argued until this day. It is incontrovertible, however, that the purchase allowed the state to liquidate the most pressing claims of the bondholders and put fiscal affairs into the soundest condition achieved since the war. Disston's drainage projects in the Kissimmee Valley and Lake Okeechobee area opened that wilderness to agricultural development, and his real estate promotions and sales brought in a large amount of outside capital, both Northern and British. This financial transfusion provided the economic base for the rapid changes that took place in the closing decades of the nineteenth century.

The two other members of the triumvirate, Henry B. Plant and Henry M. Flagler, solved the transportation problem and provided the peninsula with an elaborate system of hotels that laid the foundations for a lucrative tourist trade. Plant connected the feeble and isolated North Florida railroads to the national rail system and constructed or absorbed rail lines running through Jacksonville, Palatka, Sanford, Orlando, southwestward through Kissimmee to Tampa. Almost simultaneously Plant connected St. Petersburg and the Lake Country to his network, and by 1892 he had extended his line southward to Punta Gorda on Charlotte Harbor. This feat opened Central Florida and the west coast to an unprecedented period of growth and development.

Henry Flagler began the construction of the Florida East Coast System by purchasing and extending the Jacksonville, St. Augustine, and Halifax Railroad in 1886. With dogged determination he pushed his tracks southward through coastal swamps, sandy rises, and tiny villages. By 1890 the line had reached Daytona; by 1892, Titusville; and by 1894 the tracks were at the Palm Beaches, ready to take tourists to the palatial hotels that Flagler was building on the beach, and pioneers to the Lake Worth area. Several years later Henry Flagler extended the road to Biscayne Bay, an event which heralded the transformation of the tiny hamlet of Fort Dallas into the great tourist metropolis of Miami.

The presence of the new railroads brought on a frenzy of economic development: villages along the tracks grew into towns, hamlets sprang up where before there was only wilderness, citrus groves were planted as the roads moved south, the phosphate industry prospered with this new form of transportation, and each winter thousands of tourists arrived by rail to spend a portion of the season at the hotels in a variety of recently established towns. As a result of such prosperity, the population of Florida increased by almost fifty per cent, from 269,493 to 391,422, in the decade of the 1880s.[1]

The boom in Florida offered the Church an unprecedented opportunity to grow and develop with the state, especially in the peninsula, where the growth of population was even more remarkable

1. U.S. Bureau of Census, *Tenth Census*, 1880, 2: 20; also *Eleventh Census*, 1890, 1: 152. Short titles only are used in the footnote citations from public documents, diocesan publications, and General Convention publications. See Bibliography for full information.

than that in the northern part of the state. Within the confines of the Diocese of South Florida the population increased from 57,104 in 1880 to 121,769 in 1890, a growth of 113 per cent. The increase in the number of Episcopalians within the same area is even more phenomenal. In 1880 there were only 321 communicants in the diocese, but by 1890 the number had grown to 1,420, an increase of 342 per cent. In the same decade the number of missions increased from seven to forty-nine and the clergy from three to twenty-seven.[2]

Since its creation in 1838, the Diocese of Florida had maintained a steady but unspectacular growth until the Civil War. During the war years, however, the Church suffered a series of setbacks. Three churches were burned as a result of Federal military activity, all of the coastal parishes were abandoned as their congregations scattered in the wake of Federal occupation, and the health and strength of the first diocesan, the Rt. Rev. Francis Huger Rutledge, was so taxed that he could not perform his ecclesiastical or administrative duties. Death took the bishop in November 1866, leaving the Church in Florida to face the rigors of Reconstruction without the direction of a chief shepherd.[3]

In 1867 this chaotic condition was remedied by the election of John Freeman Young, assistant rector of Trinity Church in New York, to the episcopate in Florida. Under this enormously energetic prelate, the older parishes of the diocese were reopened and strengthened, efforts were begun to win back some of the Negroes who had wandered into the more fundamentalist evangelical African sects, and attempts were made to reestablish a number of parochial academies. The most enduring monuments to the labors of Bishop Young, however, were the numerous missions that he founded and succored during his dynamic episcopate. The bishop and his missionaries planted the seeds of Anglicanism on the banks of the Indian River, in the upper reaches of the St. Johns, in the Lake Country, and on the Gulf coast. The Episcopal Church was often the first Christian body established in the newly settled areas.

2. Diocese of Florida, *Journal of the Proceedings of the Annual Council*, 1891, p. 30. This publication is cited hereafter as *Diocesan Journal* (Florida), with year.

3. *Diocesan Journal* (Florida), 1967, pp. 23–25.

Because of the bishop's almost prophetic vision, Episcopal missions drew a larger proportion of new settlers than usual simply by being there first. In order to have readier access to the Church's southern missions, Bishop Young moved his residence from Tallahassee to Fernandina and then to the bustling rail center of Jacksonville.

In addition to his prodigious missionary effort among his own people, the bishop established several missions for Cuban immigrants in Key West and later traveled to Cuba itself, where he laid the foundations of the missionary district of that island. During the last year of his episcopate, Bishop Young was pressing the missionary board of the National Church to take over his Cuban work.

The many and varied activities of this pioneering apostle were almost unbelievable, and it was inevitable that Bishop Young's health should break under so great a strain. Fatigued by his labors, he succumbed to pneumonia in November 1885. His successor, the Rt. Rev. Edwin Gardner Weed, in his first diocesan address recognized Bishop Young's unconquerable spirit: "How great were the labors and trials of my predecessor. . . . I knew him but slightly before I came to Florida[;] now[,] however, I feel I know him well, for his words speak, *though he sleepeth.*"[4]

Bishop Weed was as mission-minded as Bishop Young and in the same address vowed to press the Church even farther into what he called "the *terra incognita* of the southern portion."[5] Just thirty-nine at his consecration in August 1886, at St. John's Church, Jacksonville, the new bishop brought to his see not only the youth and vigor sorely needed for the arduous work of the diocese, but also a broad outlook nurtured by his travel and education abroad. As a young man from Savannah he had first matriculated at the Uni-

4. Edwin Gardner Weed, *Episcopal Address*, 1887, bound with *Diocesan Journal* (Florida), 1887, p. 69. The published version of the address appears to have been made from a listener's transcript (unedited). In quotations from this and similar publications, punctuation is supplied where necessary, within brackets.

5. Weed, *Episcopal Address* (Florida), 1887, p. 71. In subsequent footnotes, a bishop's address to the annual convocation of the Church in a missionary jurisdiction, or to the annual convention of a diocese, will be cited as *Episcopal Address,* with the name of the bishop, the name of the missionary jurisdiction or diocese, and the year.

versity of Georgia, but after an interlude as a member of the Confederate Signal Corps, he continued his work at the University of Berlin, an experience which, by its broadening influence, later enhanced his ability to work with the various immigrants of his diocese, especially with the cosmopolitan British who settled in the Orange Belt of Florida.[6] The young prelate came to Florida with sound preparation from General Theological Seminary fortified by the fifteen-year experience of guiding the Church of the Good Shepherd at Summerville, Georgia, from a struggling mission into one of the largest parishes in the diocese. In the six years that he retained supervision of the whole Diocese of Florida, he wore himself out trying to provide for the needs of his huge and growing domain.

Within a year of Bishop Weed's consecration, new churches were erected in Winter Park, Cocoa, Melbourne, and Thonotosassa (east of Tampa), as well as at a number of places in the northern part of the state. A score of congregations were organizing in the rich Orange Belt in the central portion of the peninsula and along the booming Gulf Coast.[7] Each of them had to be supplied with clergymen, and each new congregation taxed the limited financial resources of the diocese and the already overstrained capacity of the bishop.

Annually Bishop Weed traveled the entire length and breadth of the state. When possible he used the new rail lines which were working their way southward. Frequently he journeyed by river steamer. Sometimes he traveled by buggy or ox cart, but many times he was forced to penetrate the more primitive areas on foot. The journey from Jacksonville to Pensacola took fifteen hours by train; the sea voyage from Jacksonville to Key West took twenty-eight hours in good weather; the trip from Jacksonville to Lake Worth took forty-eight hours by train and steamer; and a similar journey from Jacksonville to Apalachicola took thirty-six hours,

---

6. E. L. Pennington, "The Episcopal Church in South Florida, 1764–1892," *Tequesta*, March 1941, pp. 85–87; Joseph D. Cushman, *A Goodly Heritage* (Gainesville: University of Florida Press, 1965), p. 176.

7. *Diocesan Journal* (Florida), 1887, pp. 71–73.

with luck. In 1891 the bishop reported that he had made one hundred twenty-seven episcopal visitations and confirmed eighty-nine candidates. To accomplish this he traveled 20,000 miles and was away from the diocesan office and his home in Jacksonville for three hundred thirty-five days.[8] The tempo of growth accelerated year by year. It was evident to all that the election of a suffragan was a compelling necessity. This simple solution, however, was impossible. The financial structure of the predominantly missionary diocese could not bear the added strain of maintaining another bishop. It was the same old story: the lack of funds which prevented the election of an assistant bishop to help the exhausted Bishop Young also deprived his successor of a suffragan.

When the Diocesan Council met at Christ Church, Pensacola, in 1891, the problem of efficient episcopal supervision was high on the agenda. All of the delegates, clerical and lay, realized that the demands of the whole state were too great for one bishop to fulfill. This frank assessment led Bishop Weed to appoint a committee to consider the division of the diocese. The committee was composed of three priests and two laymen: the Rev. Messrs. Albion W. Knight of St. Andrew's, Jacksonville, and J. H. Davet of St. James's, Zell-wood, Archdeacon John H. Weddell of Trinity, Thonotosassa, and Messrs. W. H. Hyer of Christ Church, Pensacola, and D. A. Finlayson of Christ Church, Monticello.

After a year of intermittent study and discussion, the committee recommended to the next diocesan council, which met in St. John's, Jacksonville, in May 1892, a solution to the vexing problem. It moved the adoption of a memorial to the General Convention of the Protestant Episcopal Church which, if adopted by that body, would divide the diocese. The point of partition was to be the south boundary lines of Levy, Alachua, Putnam, and St. Johns counties. (St. Johns County at this time included Flagler County.) All of the territory south of this line would be ceded to the General Con-

---

8. *Memorial of the Diocese of Florida for the Cession of Territory to the General Convention of the Protestant Episcopal Church* (Baltimore: Printed for the Convention, 1892), p. 264. Cited hereafter as *Memorial*.

vention of the Church for the creation of a missionary district under a new bishop.[9]

A spirited debate broke out on the floor of the meeting over the committee's proposal. The strong opposition aroused by such a revolutionary solution was understandable. Traditionalists opposed the motion on the grounds that the boundaries of the state and the diocese had been identical since the diocesan structure was organized in 1838 and that the division would be followed by a great deal of unpleasant haggling over the distribution of such ecclesiastical loaves and fishes as the real properties and meagre endowments of the diocese. The traditionalists held out in the hope that a suffragan might still be procured and maintained with the help of the National Church.

Many South Floridians opposed the partition because of their fondness for the young bishop. In the six years of his episcopate he had become a much beloved figure for many reasons— for his piety and learning, for his ceaseless labors and travels in the mission field, and for the courage and devotion he exhibited in ministering to the sick and dying during the great yellow fever epidemic of 1888. It was only natural to be unwilling to sever ties with such a man. Then, too, many of the delegates, clerical and lay, had long associations with each other on the Diocesan Council and disliked the prospect of separation. The partition motion passed the council narrowly (with thirty-one "ayes" and twenty-four "nays"), but only after the delegations from the five self-supporting parishes in the south had been canvassed and had consented, somewhat reluctantly, to the proposal.[10]

In recent years there has been an increasing tendency to surmise that the partition of the Diocese of Florida was based in part on differences in Churchmanship, the thesis being that more Anglo-Catholics were concentrated in the southern part of the state and more Evangelicals in the north. There are absolutely no grounds for this assumption. During the vigorous episcopate of Bishop Young, the complexion of the entire diocese changed from

9. *Diocesan Journal* (Florida), 1892, pp. 37–38. Also see *Memorial*, p. 264.

10. *Diocesan Journal* (Florida), 1892, p. 38.

an Evangelical hue to a rosy High Church coloring, but the Evangelical tradition continued to exist and even thrive in most areas of the state. When Bishop Weed took the crozier in 1886, a balance between the two extremes was encouraged and a strong stand in either camp was considered unreasonable. At the time of the partition the whole diocese retained a moderate Anglo-Catholic flavor, one tolerant enough to permit a broad range of ecclesiastical practices. There is no evidence in the journals, the newspapers, the bishop's diary, or the Fairbanks collection[11] that Churchmanship was even discussed during the council debates.

On the first day of the General Convention of the Protestant Episcopal Church which convened in Baltimore, October 5, 1892, Florida's veteran delegate, Major George R. Fairbanks, presented the Memorial of the Diocese of Florida. The document was referred to the Committee of New Dioceses for its consideration, and on October 13 the committee reported favorably on the proposal. When both the House of Bishops and the House of Deputies concurred, the division of the work of the Episcopal Church in the State of Florida was ratified.[12] Thus the Missionary Jurisdiction of Southern Florida was born.

Speaking before the Convocation of the Missionary District of Southern Florida years after the partition had taken place, Bishop Weed reflected the bittersweet thoughts in the minds of all Florida Churchmen at the time the momentous decision was made, but perhaps most particularly those in the heart of the man who had given so much of himself to help establish and maintain the Church in the southern portion of the diocese. "During the six years the Lord entrusted to my care the whole State, fifty-six churches were built. The Diocese of Florida became twice as strong as it was in 1886, the year I was consecrated. I need not

11. A collection of Florida letters, manuscripts, and articles, now located in the Strozier Library, Florida State University, Tallahassee, belonging to Major George R. Fairbanks, C.S.A., prominent layman, author, co-founder of the Florida Historical Society and of The University of the South.

12. *Journal of the General Convention of the Protestant Episcopal Church: House of Deputies*, 1892, pp. 176, 264. This publication is cited hereafter as *General Convention Journal*, with year.

tell you the demands in such a rapidly growing Diocese made the administration daily more difficult. Labor as I would or could, there was a sad lack of care, and the future growth of the church became imperiled by my want of capacity to give attention to the numerous details, which called for consideration. Whenever it becomes impossible to keep up with the changes and needs of a work, the daily demands become vexatious. I found myself dreading the erection of a new church, because I knew it meant an additional stipend, another minister, more dissatisfied people, and a greater call on my time. When I tell you I spent eighteen days with my family the last year I had charge of the whole State you can understand why an additional demand on my time was a matter of much serious concern. I think every one recognized the time had come for a change. It was a great trial to give up what appeared to be the most promising part of the Diocese, and what was a still greater trial, was parting from those who had wrought with me, and who by their energy and devotion had so greatly enlarged the Master's Vineyard, and that was paramount."[13]

13. *Journal of the Convocation, Missionary Jurisdiction of Southern Florida*, 1908, p. 40. This publication is cited hereafter as *Convocation Journal*, with year. Similar publications of other missionary jurisdictions are cited as *Convocation Journal*, with name of missionary jurisdiction, and year.

II

The New Jurisdiction

W HEN THE GENERAL CONVENTION OF THE PROTESTANT
Episcopal Church created the Missionary Jurisdiction
of Southern Florida at Baltimore in October 1892, it became the
duty of the upper house of the convention to elect a bishop to
administer the affairs of the new see. For this task the House of
Bishops chose the Rev. William Crane Gray, D.D., rector of the
Church of the Advent, Nashville, Tennessee. Plans were put in
motion at once for the consecration of the bishop-elect, and that
event took place "with all due solemnity" at a "grand and imposing service" in Dr. Gray's old parish in Nashville, December 29
the same year. The Rt. Rev. Charles T. Quintard, Bishop of Tennessee, acted as consecrator representing the Presiding Bishop of
the Protestant Episcopal Church. The coconsecrators were the
Rt. Rev. Edwin G. Weed, Bishop of Florida, and the Rt. Rev.
Thomas U. Dudley, Bishop of Kentucky. Bishops Charles R. Hale
of Springfield and Cleland K. Nelson of Georgia also took part
in the service. As the first bishop of the Missionary Jurisdiction of
Southern Florida, William Crane Gray became the one hundred
sixty-fourth prelate in the American succession.[1]

1. William Crane Gray, *Episcopal Address* (Southern Florida), 1894,
p. 35. See also *General Convention Journal: House of Bishops*, 1892,
pp. 111 and 130.

Bishop Gray's first episcopal function was not performed in his new jurisdiction but in the Diocese of Tennessee. There, at the request of Bishop Quintard, he confirmed a class of twenty-nine candidates which he had prepared while still rector of the Church of the Advent, Nashville.[2]

Bishop and Mrs. Gray and their teenage son, Campbell, arrived in Orlando on January 5, 1893, after a two-day train trip from Nashville. Accompanying the family to the site of the new episcopal residence was the bishop's sister, Miss Emma Gray, a bright soul who was unfortunately deformed, having been born without arms. This extraordinary woman made her home with the Grays for many years, enduring her affliction with such dignity and cheerful resignation that she soon became a favorite among visitors at the Bishopstead and among the people of Orlando as well.[3]

On the day of the bishop's arrival a large group of clergy and laity assembled in St. Luke's Church to greet him. The Rt. Rev. Henry B. Whipple, the venerable Bishop of Minnesota, journeyed from his winter home in Maitland to add his greetings to those of the assembly. At the meeting Bishop Gray made a number of organizational plans and called the first convocation of the missionary jurisdiction for February 21 in the Church of the Holy Cross in Sanford. He also appointed a committee of distinguished lawyers, Louis C. Massey of Orlando, Eleazar K. Foster of Sanford, and H. W. O. Margary of Eustis, to prepare a proper legal charter of incorporation for the approval of the first convocation and of the state legislature.[4]

A series of receptions was held at the spacious home of Mr. and Mrs. Leslie Pell-Clarke on Lake Eola to welcome the bishop and his family to Florida. The Pell-Clarkes, prominent members of the Anglo-American colony in central Florida, entertained successively

2. Gray, *Episcopal Address* (Southern Florida), 1894, p. 35.

3. *The Palm Branch*, July 1897. *The Palm Branch* was the official organ of the Women's Auxiliary of the Missionary District of Southern Florida. It became the official organ of the bishop on the accession of Cameron Mann. (Interview with the Very Rev. Campbell Gray, a grandson of the bishop, July 13, 1967.)

4. Gray, *Episcopal Address* (Southern Florida), 1894, pp. 35–36.

the clergy, the congregation of St. Luke's, and the people of the Orlando area. After these social preliminaries, at which the bishop was able to meet "a large number of church people" as well as "the people of Orlando generally," he departed on his first episcopal visitation to Key West via Tampa and the Gulf coast.[5]

On the morning of February 21, in accordance with the call from the bishop, the clergy and lay delegates from the various parishes and missions of the jurisdiction assembled at Holy Cross Church, Sanford, for the purpose of organizing the Missionary Jurisdiction of Southern Florida. In the quaint little board-and-batten church with its soaring steeple Bishop Gray celebrated the Holy Eucharist before the meeting began.[6]

Within the boundaries of the newly created jurisdiction, there were five self-supporting parishes, forty organized missions, and eleven mission stations, most of which were almost entirely dependent on outside support to maintain the services of the Church. The primary convocation journal lists them as follows:[7]

PARISHES

Key West	St. Paul's
Key West	St. Peter's
Ocala	Grace
Orlando	St. Luke's
Sanford	Holy Cross

ORGANIZED MISSIONS

Arcadia	St. Edmund's
Brooksville	St. John's
Chetwynd (now Fruitland Park)	Holy Trinity
Clearwater	Ascension
Cocoa	St. Mark's
Conway (Orange County)	Holy Trinity
Courtenay	St. Luke's

5. Ibid., pp. 36–37.

6. *Convocation Journal* (Southern Florida), 1893, p. 1.

7. Ibid., pp. iii–iv. For a list of the clergy canonically resident in the jurisdiction at the time of its organization see Appendix I; for a list of lay delegates to the convocation see Appendix II.

Daytona	St. Mary's
DeLand	St. Barnabas's
Dunedin	Good Shepherd
Enterprise	All Saints'
Eustis	St. Thomas's
Fort Meade	Christ Church
Fort Myers	St. Luke's
Key West	St. Alban's
Key West	St. Cyprian's
Kissimmee	St. John's
Lake Buddy (now Dade City)	St. Mary's
Lakeland	All Saints'
Lake Worth (Palm Beach)	Bethesda-by-the-Sea
Lane Park (Lake County)	St. Edward's
Leesburg	St. James's
Longwood	Christ Church
Maitland	Good Shepherd
Merritt (Brevard County)	Grace
Montclair (Lake County)	St. John's
Narcoossee (Osceola County)	St. Peter's
Oaklawn (Marion County)	Trinity
Ocoee	Grace
Ormond	St. James's
Pittman (Lake County)	St. John's
Port Orange	Grace
St. Petersburg	St. Bartholomew's
Tampa	St. Andrew's
Tampa	St. James's
Thonotosassa (Hillsborough Co.)	Trinity
Titusville	St. Gabriel's
Wilhelmsburg (Bradenton)	Christ Church
Winter Park	All Saints'
Zellwood	St. James's

MISSION STATIONS

Bartow	New Smyrna
Cassia (Lake County)	Orange City
Glen Ethel (now Seminole Co.)	Pine Island
Haines City	Punta Gorda
Lake Mary (now Seminole Co.)	Tarpon Springs
Melbourne	

Of the twenty clergymen canonically resident in the jurisdiction, seventeen attended the meeting. About the same number of lay delegates were present, representing mainly the five self-supporting parishes of Southern Florida.[8] Bishop Weed, who had already formally transferred the clergy to Bishop Gray on January 12, was also present to add his prayers and good wishes for the success of the new ecclesiastical organization.[9]

The committee appointed by the bishop to prepare a charter incorporating the jurisdiction presented its report, which was formally approved by the convocation after some discussion concerning legal technicalities. It declared that "the Bishop, Standing Committee, the Chancellor and the Treasurer . . . and their successors . . . are constituted a body politic and corporation under the name, style and title of The Protestant Episcopal Church in the Missionary Jurisdiction of Southern Florida," and that the said corporation had power to receive, hold, and dispose of all property in use by the said church or any institution under the control of it. The Act of Incorporation was passed by the legislature and signed by Governor Henry L. Mitchell in May 1893.[10]

The first convocation decided to adopt the constitution and canons of the Diocese of Florida as a pattern, and the bishop appointed a committee to make the necessary changes in the documents. At the request of the Rev. W. H. Bates of Sanford, the bishop also appointed a Committee on the Endowment of the Episcopate under the chairmanship of the treasurer, Frederic H. Rand. The committee was to formulate and put into operation a plan of raising a fund for the permanent endowment of the episcopate so that the diocese could eventually become entirely self-supporting.

The convocation ratified the bishop's appointments for the required diocesan officers. To the Standing Committee the bishop named the Revs. John H. Weddell of Thonotosassa and C. S. Williams of Sanford as clerical members and Judge E. K. Foster of

8. Ibid., p. iii.

9. Weed, *Episcopal Address* (Florida), 1893, p. 13.

10. *Acts and Resolutions Adopted by the Legislature of Florida, Regular Session*, 1893 (Tallahassee: *Times-Union* Legislative Printers, 1893), p. 188.

Sanford and H. P. Burgwin of Zellwood as lay members. He appointed the Hon. Louis C. Massey of Orlando as his chancellor and Frederic H. Rand of Longwood as treasurer. The Rev. Gilbert Higgs of St. Paul's, Key West, served as the first secretary of the convocation. The Rev. John H. Weddell and Louis C. Massey were elected as delegates to the General Convention of the National Church.

The convocation accepted the invitation of St. Paul's Church, Key West, for its next meeting and adjourned with the blessing of the bishop. Realizing that no money was available in the treasury for publishing a journal of the first convocation, Louis Massey and Henry P. Burgwin provided jointly for the project.[11]

Of the many laymen who served the Church in South Florida during its formative years, Louis C. Massey and Frederic H. Rand were among the most outstanding. Massey, the chancellor, was the chief legal advisor to the bishop and the Standing Committee. A native of Pennsylvania and a graduate of the University of Pennsylvania, he came to Orlando as a young lawyer in 1885. While developing a prosperous practice, Massey also engaged extensively in the cultivation of citrus. He was a lively promoter of Orange County and a founder, and later president, of the State Bank of Orlando. He also served as a county commissioner and represented his district in the state legislature in Tallahassee. His close friendship with the bishop, his position as a frequent delegate to the General Convention, and the many gratuitous services he rendered to St. Luke's Parish, the missionary jurisdiction, and his community gave him a unique position in the Christian society of pioneer South Florida. He was undoubtedly the premier layman of the Church during his long lifetime.[12]

Frederic H. Rand also showed remarkable devotion to the Church in South Florida. Massachusetts-born, Rand immigrated to Florida after graduating from Norwich University in Vermont and serving in the Army of the Potomac. He settled in Longwood

11. *Convocation Journal* (Southern Florida), 1893, pp. 2–3.

12. Rowland H. Rerick, *Memoirs of Florida* (Atlanta: Southern Historical Association, 1902), 2: 622–23.

in 1876 and, like Massey, became an extensive grove owner. His interest in citrus and in real estate led him into the railroad movement. He was a leader in organizing the South Florida Railroad, and when that line was absorbed by the Plant Railroad System in 1887, Rand became the general freight and passenger agent for the whole state, maintaining his central office in Sanford. In addition to his rail interests, he was an incorporator of the South Florida Telegraph Company and general manager of the gigantic Florida Land and Colonization Company, a London-based British corporation which promoted Florida investments. Rand brought much British capital into central Florida, and with General Sanford and several British investors incorporated the First National Bank of Sanford. One of the founders of Christ Church, Longwood, and a liberal supporter of Holy Cross Church, Sanford, Frederic Rand served not only as treasurer of the jurisdiction and chairman of the episcopal endowment committee but also as a trustee of The University of the South.[13] His financial advice to the bishop was invaluable and as unselfishly given as the legal advice of his friend Louis C. Massey.

Of the five parishes represented in the primary convocation, St. Paul's in the port town of Key West was by far the most important. Chartered by the Territorial Legislature in 1832, the congregation grew into the largest parish in the Diocese of Florida. This growth, however, was accomplished in the face of two heartbreaking disasters. The first church building, constructed at great sacrifice, was totally destroyed by the great hurricane of October 1846. It was replaced in 1847 by a frame church which was enlarged and beautified over a span of four decades. In 1886 it too was demolished, in the raging fire which burned half the town of Key West. The persevering parishioners of St. Paul's rebuilt the frame structure in 1886–87 in a more churchly design, and a set of ten bells, the first in the state, was placed in the tower.[14]

One of the great accomplishments of St. Paul's was the founding of a Negro mission, St. Peter's Church, shortly after the Civil War.

13. Ibid., p. 664.
14. *Key West Citizen*, April 13, 1933; also *Diocesan Journal* (Florida), 1839, pp. 7–8; *Churchman*, March 14, 1891.

The older parish nursed the mission to self-supporting maturity, and within ten years it grew into one of the strongest Negro congregations in the South. St. Paul's also fathered two Cuban missions, one white and one colored, for the immigrants who settled in the city. These missions were gradually absorbed by the two established churches, giving them both a Hispanic flavor that made them unique in the American Church.[15] When the Missionary Jurisdiction of Southern Florida came into existence, Key West was the most predominantly Anglican community on the eastern seaboard. The parish register of St. Paul's numbered 600 baptized members, and that of St. Peter's boasted 515.[16]

St. Luke's Church, Orlando, was another promising parish in a rapidly growing town. From a small frontier community of a few stores and about twenty dwellings in the 1870s, Orlando grew in twenty years into the economic and social center of the rich Florida orange belt. In 1890 it boasted a population of 3,500 and a number of urban features—a large modern depot, an iron foundry, a bank, several hotels and newspapers, an opera house, and a number of social and sporting clubs that gave the town a cosmopolitan flavor. In addition to these attractions, there were thousands of acres of productive citrus groves in the vicinity as well as the rail connections necessary to transport the produce to northern markets. In the 1880s the prices on the citrus market generally had held firm, and as a result both the American settlers and the British immigrants had enjoyed an unusually high return on their groves.[17]

Episcopal services were begun in Orlando by Francis Eppes, a grandson of Thomas Jefferson, who immigrated to central Florida from his cotton plantation near Tallahassee. The work begun by Eppes, who was also a founder of St. John's, Tallahassee, and an organizer of the Diocese of Florida (1838), was supported by other settlers, particularly the British. St. Luke's Church was formally organized in 1881. The church kept pace with the growth of the town and within a few years was a thriving parish. In 1893 the

15. Cushman, *A Goodly Heritage*, pp. 143–54.
16. *Convocation Journal* (Southern Florida), 1894, *Abstract of Parochial and Missionary Report*.
17. *Orlando Record* (Supplement), May 2, 1891.

Anglo-American flock numbered 168 persons. St. Luke's was an important adjunct to the life of the English settlers and did much to blend the activities of these people into the life and society of the American community.[18]

Sanford, a town founded in the 1870s by General Henry S. Sanford on the site of old Fort Mellon, was a flourishing place when the new jurisdiction began because of its situation near the head of the St. Johns River and its importance as a center for the Plant Railroad System. Citrus and truck products were shipped from Sanford by rail and by river, and there was every indication that the town was to play the same role at the head of the river that Jacksonville played at its mouth. General Sanford, a man of international connections, not only engaged extensively in citrus cultivation; through the offices of an Anglo-American corporation, the Florida Land and Colonization Company, he also brought much British capital and many British settlers into central Florida.[19] The general, a great benefactor of Holy Cross Church, saw to it that the parish kept pace with the rapid development of the area. The church, built on the plans of Richard Upjohn, the most celebrated architect of his day and the designer of Trinity Parish in New York City, was one of the most beautiful board-and-batten structures in the country. In the 1870s and 1880s it served as headquarters for the missionary activities of the Diocese of Florida. Many of the missions in central Florida and on the Indian River owed their existence to a group of clergy who worked out of Holy Cross.[20] At the time of the partition the parish had 45 families on its register and 195 members.[21]

Grace Church, Ocala, at the northern edge of the jurisdiction, was, like St. Paul's, Key West, an antebellum parish. Organized in 1854, the church did not become self-supporting until the late

18. *Year Book: St. Luke's Cathedral* (n.p., 1935), p. 6; *Diocesan Journal* (Florida), 1882, p. 64; *Convocation Journal* (Southern Florida), 1894, *Abstract*.

19. H. G. Cutler, *A History of Florida, Past and Present* (Chicago: The Lewis Publishing Company, 1902), pp. 535–36.

20. *Diocesan Journal* (Florida), 1873, p. 36; 1881, pp. 35–36; 1883, p. 57.

21. *Convocation Journal* (Southern Florida), 1894, *Abstract*.

1870s.[22] The town, an important citrus and tourist center, was hit hard by a severe freeze in 1886, and many growers abandoned their groves and moved farther south. The development of the phosphate industry in the vicinity in 1889, however, brought in new settlers and new capital, and when the new jurisdiction of Southern Florida was founded, both the town and the church were in a period of prosperous growth.[23] Grace Church numbered 70 families and 347 persons on its rolls. The Rev. Charles Gray, the bishop's brother, was rector of the parish.[24]

Of the forty organized missions in the new jurisdiction, only five had a membership of eighty or more: St. Andrew's and St. James's, Tampa; St. Mary's, Daytona; St. Gabriel's, Titusville; and St.' James's, Leesburg.[25] The field that presented the greatest opportunity for missionary endeavor was the Tampa area. The growth of Tampa had been retarded by the Fort Brook military reservation, which blocked the community's access to the sea until 1883. In that year, however, the reservation was sold by the United States Government, and the town expanded rapidly. It soon became the southern terminus of the Plant Railroad System, an important seaport, and the center of Florida's cigar industry. With the building of the luxurious Tampa Bay Hotel in 1889, the town also became a popular resort for Northern tourists.[26] These activities brought an enormous influx of newcomers into Tampa and Hillsborough County. In the ten-year period from 1885 to 1895 the population of the county grew from 7,973 to 31,362, an increase of almost four hundred per cent.[27]

Unfortunately St. Andrew's Church did not keep pace with the growth of the area, first because of difficulty in finding a permanent priest-in-charge, and then because of the ill health of the man even-

22. *Diocesan Journal* (Florida), 1854, pp. 10–13.

23. Cutler, pp. 543–44.

24. *Convocation Journal* (Southern Florida), 1894, *Abstract*.

25. Ibid. These figures are baptized members only; communicant strength was, of course, much smaller.

26. Cutler, pp. 319–20.

27. State of Florida, *Third Census of the State of Florida*, 1905 (Tallahassee: Capital Publishing Company, 1906), pp. 10–11.

tually appointed. As late as 1893, St. Andrew's numbered only one hundred members. The Negro mission, St. James's, on the other hand, boasted one hundred seventy-seven baptized members and operated the only parochial school in the jurisdiction.[28]

On the east coast the missions at Daytona and Titusville exhibited signs of solid growth. Daytona, with the coming of the Florida East Coast Railroad, became both a winter and a summer resort. Its famous bathing beach, enhanced by several hotels, a golf course, and a yacht club, drew a steady stream of visitors. The church, St. Mary's, was one of the dozen or more charming board-and-batten edifices built during the episcopate of Bishop Young. It possessed a growing congregation of some ninety-two Churchmen.

Titusville, fifty miles south, was an old commercial center before the arrival of the railroad. Located at the head of the Indian River with rail connections to the St. Johns, the town was an important shipping center for citrus, pineapples, and fish. Like its sister mission in Daytona, St. Gabriel's was planned by Bishop Young. Board-and-batten in construction and well-proportioned architecturally, it housed a colorful collection of Victorian stained glass. Through the work of Archdeacon Benjamin F. Brown, for whom the Parson Brown orange was reputedly named, St. Gabriel's staffed, with the help of an occasional assistant, the Indian River missions of St. Luke's, Courtenay; Grace, Merritt; St. Mark's, Cocoa; and Holy Trinity, Melbourne. Parson Brown's register in Titusville held eighty names.[29]

Leesburg, one of the oldest of the settlements in Lake County, was the mercantile center of that area. Surrounded by orange groves and lakes, it was given the appearance of a small city by its commercial and shipping facilities, and as early as 1886 the town boasted a population of 1,500.[30] St. James's Church, like so many of the parishes and missions of the jurisdiction, derived a large portion of its membership of one hundred eight from the ranks of the recently

28. *Convocation Journal* (Southern Florida), 1894, *Abstract.*

29. Ibid.; also see pp. 76–77.

30. Jacksonville *Florida Times-Union,* January 18, 1886; also see J. W. White, *White's Guide to Florida and Her Famous Resorts* (Jacksonville: Da Costa Printing House, 1890), pp. 90–91.

arrived British citrus growers who settled in the vicinity. The priest at St. James's also staffed the Anglo-American missions of Holy Trinity, Chetwynd (Fruitland Park), and St. John's in nearby Montclair.[31]

The parishes and missions of Southern Florida were strengthened annually by the arrival of hundreds of winter visitors. The winter colonies in Winter Park, Palm Beach, DeLand, and Bradenton provided substantial assistance to the local congregations, particularly in their building programs. All Saints', Winter Park, and Bethesda-by-the-Sea, Palm Beach, erected church structures far out of the financial range of their permanent parishioners, and St. Barnabas's, DeLand, and Christ Church, Wilhelmsburg (Bradenton), were also aided in their building plans by the liberal contributions of seasonal guests. The church in DeLand, begun in 1883, was designed by Richard Upjohn.

Just before the separation of the Diocese of Florida, several missions had sprung up in the area south of Tampa Bay. In Fort Myers, St. Luke's Church was assured of its future by the addition of seventeen confirmands, one of the largest classes ever presented by a mission in the jurisdiction. The missionary in charge of St. Luke's also served growing flocks in Punta Gorda, Auburndale, and Fort Meade, as well as scattered Churchmen on Sanibel Island and in St. James City.[32] Some of the mission clergy, particularly the archdeacons, traveled almost as much as the bishop. They came by train, steamboat, sail, and buggy, bringing the Word and the sacraments to the tiny congregations assigned to their cures.

The help of women in the work of the Church in South Florida cannot be overestimated. Not only did they organize in guilds or branches for the benefit of their local parishes and missions; they also took steps to create a Women's Auxiliary to coordinate the labors of these branches on a diocesan level. The Women's Auxiliary in the Missionary Jurisdiction of Southern Florida was established in May 1893 by Harriet Randolph Parkhill of Orlando. The first annual meeting was scheduled to take place at the convocation

31. *Convocation Journal* (Southern Florida), 1894, *Abstract.*
32. *The Churchman*, February 21, March 7, 1891.

at St. Paul's, Key West, in January 1894, but the expense and difficulty of travel prevented the arrival of a quorum. The meeting
was adjourned and convened in St. Andrew's Church, Tampa, the
following week. At the meeting in Tampa eleven delegates were
present from five of the twenty-two branches. One delegate was
present from St. Luke's, Orlando; two from Holy Cross, Sanford;
two from St. James's, Leesburg; one from Trinity, Thonotosassa;
and five from Tampa. Rules of order for meetings and a constitution were adopted, and Mary G. Foster, the wife of Judge E. K.
Foster, was elected the first president. According to a convocation
memorial, "Her wonderful personality, her clear judgment and her
deep spiritual consecration made her a bulwark of strength and
power and an honored and beloved leader in the missionary work of
the district." Mrs. Foster held office until 1901, when she was succeeded by Mrs. Fannie C. Gray, wife of the bishop, who had served
as vice-president until that time. Miss Parkhill served as secretary
from 1894 until 1898, and again in 1912–13.[33]

While still in its infancy the Women's Auxiliary made a contribution of lasting value to the new jurisdiction; it founded the *Palm
Branch*, the official periodical of the Church of South Florida. The
industrious Harriet Parkhill pressured the executive board of the
Women's Auxiliary to undertake the publication of the paper. The
first issue of the *Palm Branch* appeared in Advent 1894 as a tiny
four-page sheet, and its regular publication has been uninterrupted
since that time. The first editor of the paper was Elizabeth Huntington Rand, daughter of Frederic H. Rand of Longwood and
Orlando, treasurer of the jurisdiction. Miss Rand was ably assisted
by her co-workers Mrs. Mary W. Sperry of Tampa and the Misses
Anna Rand, Corinne Robinson, and Harriet Parkhill of Orlando.
Although the paper was started as the official organ of the Women's
Auxiliary and was supported financially by the women, it also contained news of general interest to all Churchmen of Southern Florida. Through its first year the *Palm Branch* was dated for the
Church seasons—Advent, Christmas, Epiphany, and so on. In October 1895 the monthly issues began to appear. The lead article of

33. *Palm Branch*, April 1969.

the first issue, couched in the flowery, optimistic, Victorian style of the period, explained the title and purpose of the publication. "The Palm is the emblem of the Missionary Jurisdiction of Southern Florida. The Palm Branch is modestly chosen by our Women's Auxiliary as their emblem, to wave the banner of the cross in every parish and mission of this fair peninsula. The Palm Branch goes forth to wave in the southern breeze as a token of earnest effort for, and ultimate victory of, Christ's Kingdom in this flower land."[34]

The years immediately following the organization of the missionary jurisdiction saw encouraging signs of life in almost every mission on the peninsula. The new railroad construction, the citrus boom, the steady development of the tourist industry and rapid growth of population offered the Church in Southern Florida an enormous potential for growth. A spirit of optimism pervaded the sessions of the early convocations, and it was reasonable to assume that the new Missionary Jurisdiction of Southern Florida would become the self-supporting Diocese of South Florida within a few years. Neither the clergy nor the laity could forsee that the capriciousness of wind and weather and a national financial depression would delay the realization of this assumption for almost three decades.

34. Ibid.; Advent 1894.

III

The British Immigration

A WELCOME SOURCE OF STRENGTH AND GROWTH FOR THE Episcopal Church in South Florida during the closing two decades of the nineteenth century was the large number of British-ers who immigrated to the state. The presence of these settlers had a profound effect on the development of the Church and of the state as well.

The British immigration was triggered in 1881 when Hamilton Disston, the Philadelphia capitalist, sold two million of the four million acres of land he had purchased from the State Internal Improvement Board to Sir Edward Reed, a British shipping magnate. Sir Edward, it happened, acted as agent for a group of Anglo-Dutch investors, who under the leadership of the Earl of Huntingdon formed themselves into a corporation called the Florida Land and Mortgage Company. The purpose of the company, whose principal offices were in London, was to sell off its land holdings, finance home and business development, and engage in railroad construction and stock speculation. By 1883, the prospects of the Florida Land and Mortgage Company had become so bright that a number of other British companies were formed in imitation. These companies also purchased large tracts of land in Florida and

began to sell off acreages to prospective British and Northern
settlers.[1]

British newspapers were full of lavish praise for the opportunities
available in Florida. The much-traveled Surgeon-General of the
British Army, a Florida investor himself, wrote in *The Times* concerning the state's climate: "After a thorough study of the climate
in different parts of the world, and a stay in Florida of more than
two months, I am prepared to stake my reputation upon the statement, that, in the interior of this state, on the high, dry pine land,
is to be found as pure, balmy, invigorating atmosphere as in any
other part of the globe."[2] Another writer claimed that the state's
climate relieved such maladies as "asthma, hay fever, catarrh, bron-
chitis, rheumatism, Bright's disease, consumption," and even pul-
monary hemorrhages.[3]

The fertility of the soil and mildness of the climate, promoters
declared, offered excellent opportunities for agricultural investments
with attractive profits. Such cash crops as oranges, lemons, pineapples, bananas, tobacco, sugarcane, and winter vegetables could
be grown in abundance. Although it had been difficult to get these
products to market in a salable condition until recently, a frenzy
of railroad construction had solved the transportation problem,
making it possible, a *Times* correspondent predicted, for Florida to
supply "the whole country east of the Rockies."[4] A well-cultivated
orange grove could yield as much as two hundred pounds or one
thousand dollars per acre. Lemons offered an almost equally profitable return, but the most enticing agricultural pursuit, another
writer stated, was the cultivation of pineapples. These tropical
fruits had sold on the London market for as much as twenty-five
shillings, or about $6.50, each.[5]

Other opportunities for investment were ballyhooed also. A

1. *Times* (London), May 21, 1883; April 15, 1884. Also see Chapter I,
p. 5, above.

2. See *Winter Park, Florida, 1888* (Boston: Rand Avery, Printers, 1888),
p. 8.

3. Ibid., pp. 10–11.

4. *Times* (London), January 26, April 14 and April 15, 1884.

5. James W. Davidson, *The Florida of Today: A Guide for Tourists and
Settlers* (New York: D. Appleton and Company, 1889), p. 148.

traveling English correspondent wrote that the "fishing banks along the Gulf Coast are as valuable as those of Newfoundland," and that some entrepreneurs derived as much as $100,000 per year from the sale of sponges and turtles. The same correspondent stated that the cultivation of tobacco also offered excellent investment opportunities, particularly along the shores of Biscayne Bay. Here, he declared, the leaves of the tobacco plants are "comparable to those of the Cuban products."[6] A writer for *Blackwood's Magazine* suggested the hotel and restaurant business as an investment possibility. Florida, he pointed out, was fast turning into the "Italy of America." About one hundred fifty thousand winter visitors came to the state every year. If each visitor spent an average of one pound per day, prospective British hotel investors could expect gratifying returns.[7]

With the state receiving such a favorable press, it was soon apparent that a full-scale Florida land boom was in the making. Thousands of Britishers began to pour into Florida to share in the profits. The immigration reached such proportions that it became almost an invasion. A contemporary authoress wrote that "every train and steamer from the north bears hither its English party. Some come to this *sunland of palm and pine* for pleasure, some for health; some—and these are the majority—come bent on making here the fortune they have failed to make in the old world."[8] The writer took great pride in the successful English settlement: "We have found our own country-people largely represented in all parts of the state, and everywhere they are doing well, and look healthy, happy, bright and contented; and on all sides we see evidence of their thrift, industry, and general prosperity. We inquire to whom belongs some lovely extensive orange grove, or some picturesque luxurious dwelling, and we are told to *some English settlers*, who perhaps began with a shanty in the wilderness, and have transformed it into an earthly paradise of peace and plenty." The writer

6. *Times* (London), October 31, 1883.

7. "Florida: The State of Orange-Groves," *Blackwood's Magazine*, September 1885, p. 318.

8. Iza Duffus Hardy, *Oranges and Alligators: Sketches from South Florida Life* (London: Ward and Downey, 1887), p. 12.

patriotically concluded, "Wherever the Anglo-Saxon spirit stirs, prosperity follows. *When he* [the Englishman] *sets his hand to the plow he doeth it with all his might.*"9 The English did compose the main bulk of the new immigration to Florida which helped people the new settlements. But there were other immigrants from the British Isles—a sizable number of Scots, a smaller number of Welsh, and a few Anglo-Irish. The majority of the British settlers, except for the Scots, were at least nominally Anglican.

The new settlers, roughly speaking, could be divided into three groups. The first group was composed mainly of older professional people with comfortable incomes—retired army officers, civil servants, and doctors. They came to central Florida to invest their static capital in citrus culture in order to increase their incomes as they grew older. They also were attracted by the climate and by the opportunities for sport, particularly hunting and fishing. This group settled mainly in Orange County in the Orlando-Conway area and became leaders in financing and constructing churches in their communities.

The second group were younger settlers, usually second and third sons of the landed and mercantile oligarchy. They were sent to Florida by their parents to invest a certain amount of cash, generally in citrus, from which it was hoped they would derive an income for the rest of their lives. The majority of these young men were just out of public school or university and were often supported by remittances from their parents until the newly planted orange groves could reach maturity. Since the English customs of primogeniture and entail were still in practice during the late nineteenth century, these younger sons could expect little from the family estate through inheritance except a small cash settlement. Many parents felt that if this small inheritance could be invested while their male offspring were still young, the boys might obtain a brighter financial future than they could expect at home. Florida was especially attractive to this class. Citrus culture promised an excellent financial return when the groves reached maturity, and provided a landed way of life in a mild climate where outdoor sports might be

9. Iza Duffas Hardy, *Down South* (London: Chapman and Hall, Ltd., 1883), pp. 222–23.

enjoyed the year round. These younger immigrants settled mainly in colonies of their countrymen or in areas where substantial English communities were already established. They too built churches or supported the existing American missions.

A third group of settlers, composed mainly of working-class people who had saved a small stake, scattered throughout the state. Because of their exceedingly limited capital, they were inclined to go into truck farming rather than citrus. The initial investment was smaller, and they did not have to wait so long for their crops to mature. Unless they were servants of immigrant families, they avoided predominantly English communities where class prejudice prevented them from being accepted as social equals. They did, however, generally attach themselves to Episcopal congregations and support the services of the Church by their attendance.

To the first group of British immigrants, the retired professionals, the Church in Orange County owes much. This group worked closely with American Churchmen to establish St. Luke's mission in 1881 and helped push the mission to parochial status three years later. Three Englishmen—Henry Sweetapple, Charles Lord, and Algernon Haden—played particularly important roles during the formative years of St. Luke's.[10]

Henry Sweetapple had the most varied career of the three. Born in England of Quaker stock, he attended Cambridge University but left that institution in 1849 to take part in the rough-and-tumble California Gold Rush. Later he amassed a considerable fortune mining silver in Nevada. Sometime in mid-life he was converted to Anglicanism. In 1883 Sweetapple retired to Orlando, bought an orange grove on Lake Concord, invested heavily in the Orange Belt Railroad and other local enterprises, and threw himself into the activities of the community and St. Luke's Church. Through the example of his generosity, he helped change the struggling mission into one of the strongest young parishes in southern Florida. One contemporary described this Englishman as "a man of splendid Character,"[11] and a later local historian saw him as a person

10. *Year Book: St. Luke's Cathedral*, 1935, p. 5.

11. E. H. Gore, *From Florida Sand to City Beautiful: A Historical Record of Orlando, Florida* (Orlando: n.p., 1947), p. 136.

who inherited from his Quaker forebears "a quiet devoutness, a simplicity of spirit, and an unparaded generosity." Sweetapple loved his community and his church and unabashedly expressed his affection for both. Unfortunately he was not permitted to serve either long. He died in 1887 and was buried from the parish church that he had helped to build.[12]

Charles Lord, like Henry Sweetapple, was active in church and civic affairs. He came to Orlando in 1885 and founded a large wholesale and retail grocery concern. He was a popular member of the business community, an avid racing fan, and a determined supporter of St. Luke's Church. He was particularly interested in the Church Home and Hospital, an Episcopal institution in central Florida devoted to the care of the infirm and sick. A glance at the convocation journals shows that he was a regular and substantial giver to its program. Charles Lord is also remembered for his unique gift to the city of Orlando. While traveling in England one summer, he secured two pairs of swans and sent them as presents to his adopted town. The swans survived the trip to Florida and fared well in their new surroundings. As the cygnets from these swans grew up they flew to various lakes in the city, where their descendants have been the delight of children and tourists ever since.[13]

Algernon Haden, the third member of the trio, settled in Orlando in the early 1880s after a diversity of careers in India, Burma, the Azores, and the Canary Islands. During the fifty years that he lived in Orlando, he often served on the vestry of St. Luke's Church and had the honor to represent his parish at the Primary Convocation of the Missionary District of Southern Florida in 1893 as well as at several succeeding conventions. Haden's business endeavors were as varied as his former residences. For several years after he came to Orlando he planted pineapples on a large scale, but after the disastrous freeze of 1886 he shifted his investment to citrus. He also founded and headed the successful Artificial Palm Company,

12. William F. Blackman, *A History of Orange County, Florida: Narrative & Biographical* (DeLand, Florida: E. O. Painter Printing Co., 1927), pp. 167–68.

13. Gore, pp. 60, 66.

which shipped his imitations all over the eastern United States. He later bought the Orlando Telephone Exchange and greatly increased both its efficiency and its business. His interest in St. Luke's Church and in the missionary jurisdiction was constant during his long residence in Florida. Haden died while on a visit to his native England and was buried there.[14]

Holy Trinity Church in Conway, an entirely English community several miles east of Orlando, was founded by the same type of professional people as those who helped make St. Luke's a strong parish. Its leaders were two retired army officers—Colonel H. B. Church and Colonel Dudley George Cary-Elwes—and a clergyman, the Rev. Charles W. Arnold.

The Conway community was founded by Colonel Church, who retired from the Indian Army and bought extensive property in the area about 1883. He built a large house on Lake Underhill, enlarged a previously purchased orange grove, and speculated with his substantial real estate holdings. Through his connections in Britain, he interested a number of his countrymen in citrus culture and sold them land on which to plant groves.[15] The Colonel, always a keen sailor, had a small yacht built for sailing on Lake Underhill. His enthusiasm for the sport was so strong that he encouraged a number of the younger settlers to take up his avocation and before long took the lead in organizing the Conway Yacht Club. The Yacht Club was not only famous for its colorful regattas, but also to some extent notorious for its social occasions.[16] This same sporting Colonel wanted to build an Anglican house of worship for the new settlers of his community. The first services of the Church in Conway were held by the Rev. Charles William Arnold, a retired Anglican priest. Mr. Arnold came to Conway in September 1885, to join his son, R. A. Arnold, in the growing of citrus. He brought with him a remarkable entourage: his daughter, six young men who intended to study the cultivation of citrus, and two servants. He built a large frame house with a private chapel

14. Kena Fries, *Orlando in the Long, Long Ago and Now* (Orlando: Ty Cobb's Florida Press, 1938), pp. 39–40.

15. Blackman, pp. 124–28.

16. Ibid.; see also Jacksonville *Florida Times-Union*, March 11, 1886.

and also created a ten-room barracks called Arnold's Court to accommodate his agricultural students.[17]

Before his arrival in Florida, the Rev. Mr. Arnold had spent his entire clerical career in education. Holding both bachelor's and master's degrees from Trinity College, Cambridge, he taught successively in a number of English public schools and ended his Church of England ministry in 1885 as headmaster of Woking College. Mr. Arnold gladly provided the offices and sacraments of the Church for his countrymen in his private chapel at Conway and officiated in St. Luke's, Orlando, as well.[18] Missionary work was such a novel and rewarding experience for the retired priest that he soon left orange-growing entirely to his son. After several years of supply work in Orlando and Cedar Key, Arnold became rector of St. Mary's Church, Daytona, and general missionary to the Halifax River communities, posts he occupied from 1890 to 1906.[19] His services were sorely missed when he left Conway.

Colonel Dudley George Cary-Elwes, a recent settler in the Conway colony, was determined to organize a congregation in the town despite Arnold's departure. Born November 13, 1837, in a Lincolnshire country house that had been in his family for three centuries, Cary-Elwes received an excellent public school education and entered the British army with a commission in Her Majesty's Third Regiment of the Line (The Buffs) in 1857. He served in that regiment in Corfu in 1857, in India in 1858, and in China under General Gordon from 1859 to 1861.[20] In 1862 he retired from active military duty, but continued to rise in the reserve ranks until he attained the rank of colonel. He married Mary Georgina Mangles of Pendell Court, Bletchingley, Surrey, in 1863,[21] and engaged in a number of business enterprises, chiefly in Bedford, for twenty-three years. He also wrote with his friend, the Rev. C. J. Robinson, a historical work on English country houses entitled *Castles, Mansions, and Manors* which was published in 1868. After a successful

17. Blackman, pp. 124–28.
18. *Crockford's Clerical Directory,* 1894 (London, 1894), p. 34.
19. Parish Records, St. Mary's Church, Daytona Beach.
20. Orlando *Daily and Weekly Record* (Supplement), May 2, 1891.
21. *Burke's Landed Gentry,* 1895, p. 700.

business career, in 1886 Colonel Cary-Elwes moved with his family to Conway, where he built a large Victorian house on Lake Fredericka complete with stables and tennis court. He generously entertained the younger settlers of the area, and his famous Wednesday tennis parties became a local institution.[22] As a devout Churchman and mission-minded layman, Cary-Elwes was the natural leader to press for the organization of an Episcopal mission.

He urged that a meeting of the English colonists be held in the spring of 1888. At the meeting a mission was organized, a sum of three hundred dollars was pledged for the stipend of a clergyman, and a fund-raising committee was appointed to obtain subscriptions for the building of a church. Until one could be erected the congregation worshipped in an abandoned store. The first service of the organized mission was held on Trinity Sunday, 1888, with the Rev. E. M. W. Hills of St. Luke's, Orlando, as priest-in-charge. Within a year the building committee under the leadership of Colonel Cary-Elwes and Colonel Church raised $1,800 for the erection of the church, and construction was begun. The church also received about an acre of ground nearby to be used for a cemetery. The first service was held in the new church on June 2, 1889. The following year Bishop Weed confirmed Herbert Cary-Elwes, one of the two sons of the colonel, on his official visitation.[23] The subscriptions and debt on Holy Trinity Church were rapidly paid off, and on January 8, 1892, the *South Florida Sentinel* proudly announced that the church would be consecrated by Bishop Weed the following Sunday. The congregation of St. Luke's, Orlando, was invited to attend the rites and the festivities that followed the service. To facilitate transportation to Conway, the paper stated, "carriages are available from the stables of Coffey and Hyer and Major Foster at reduced rates." On January 10, 1892, amidst a great gathering of people, Holy Trinity Church formally became part of life and worship in the British colony of Conway.[24]

22. Blackman, p. 126.

23. Parish Records, Holy Trinity Church, Conway, now on deposit at Diocesan House, Winter Park, Florida.

24. Orlando *South Florida Sentinel*, January 8, 1892; Weed, *Episcopal Address* (Florida), 1892, p. 15.

Another almost entirely English congregation was Holy Trinity Church in Chetwynd, a settlement near Fruitland Park some six miles north of Leesburg. One of the founders of the Chetwynd colony, Granville Chetwynd Stapylton, eventually took the lead in organizing "Chetwynd Church," as the mission was sometimes called.

Young Stapylton, who came from a family steeped in Anglican tradition, was the son of the Rev. Canon William Chetwynd Stapylton, a former fellow of Merton College, Oxford, and the vicar of Malden and Chessington in Surrey.[25] A graduate of Haileybury College, a school which geared its students for a colonial career, Stapylton arrived in Florida in 1881 at the age of twenty-three with a modest sum of money to invest. After traveling the state, he selected grove property near Fruitland Park (Gardenia) and settled down as an orange-grower.[26] With two other young Englishmen, he formed the firm of Stapylton and Company, which bought a large acreage to be cut up into citrus groves for immigrants. The company induced about eighty Britishers to come to the area to learn citrus culture and buy or set out orange groves. For the settlers who were learning the art of citrus culture, Stapylton and Company built Zephyr Hall, a boarding house on Zephyr Lake. The inmates of "The Hall" were, in the main, fresh from their public schools. Etonians, Harrovians, Wykehamists, and Carthusians could be seen in the company grove picking, packing, pruning, or engaging in whatever work the season required. "They were a happy, care-free group, upon whose shoulders responsibility rested very lightly, and they added much to the pleasure and gayety of what might otherwise have been a dull existence in the new and untried country."[27]

It was one of these former public school men, like so many a master of understatement, who described grove work in the Florida

25. *Crockford's Clerical Directory*, 1894, p. 244.

26. Stapylton Papers, in possession of Lady Gillett, daughter of Granville Chetwynd Stapylton, care of John Gillett, Esq., Gulworthy Farm, Tavistock, Devon, England.

27. Lillian D. Vickers-Smith, *A History of Fruitland Park, Florida* (De-Land: E. O. Painter Printing Co., 1925), p. 17.

summer as "very provocative of perspiration," and another who described an old Florida cracker spitting tobacco with the words "He expectorated afar and quite viciously."[28] When these young men finished their citrus apprenticeship, many purchased land in the area and set out groves of their own. Sometimes they were joined by members of their families—parents, brothers, and even sisters—and it was not long before a sizable English settlement sprang up in the Fruitland Park–Chetwynd area.[29] In December 1885, Granville Stapylton married a sister of one of these settlers, Elizabeth Routledge, at a very festive wedding.[30]

Since these young Englishmen were more interested in the here and now than in life after death, the building of Holy Trinity Parish had to wait until they had founded a number of other equally "English" but more ephemeral institutions. Many of the settlers owned fine horses and, together with some Leesburg businessmen, they formed the A.B.C. (American, British, and Colonial) Racing Association. Although several informal races took place earlier, the first scheduled A.B.C. meet was held on Picciola Island at the association's track on March 15, 1887. Though many of the horses were by no means thoroughbred racers, they and their riders were familiar to all the residents of the vicinity and offered a great deal of amusement and excitement to those who followed the races, which continued to be held at Picciola Island and at the fine course at nearby Montclair.[31] Another activity which absorbed the interests of the English settlers was the formation of a social club in the British town tradition. A member of the colony, G. H. A. Elin, built a large clubhouse east of Spring Lake, which was equipped with a reading room, billiard tables, a bar, and other essentials for recreation and comfort. Apparently the only qualification for membership was the ability to pay the terribly high dues that were necessary to maintain the facilities of the clubhouse. Since its membership was handicapped by a lack of cash, the club was not a success and had to be given up. The building was taken over by the

28. "A Florida Girl," *Cornhill Magazine*, December 1893, pp. 174, 178.
29. Vickers-Smith, p. 18.
30. *Burke's Landed Gentry*, 1885, p. 2128.
31. Vickers-Smith, pp. 17–18.

Bucket and Dipper Club, a more realistic if less ambitious organization, which had been meeting at the houses of its various members. The club was so named because the only refreshment allowed during its meetings was a bucket of water served with a dipper. Its chief object was to promote fellowship and provide social and intellectual entertainments for its members at reasonable cost, entertainments such as concerts, debates, theatricals, and dances. For many years it was the foremost social organization in the colony. The membership was restricted to those of British birth and those with British parents.[32]

The religious life of Chetwynd continued to lag far behind the social life until the arrival of the Rev. J. C. W. Tasker, an English priest, in the summer of 1886. The Rev. Mr. Tasker, a crusty Cantabrigian who had come to Florida to visit relatives and friends, was the retired chaplain of the Bath Mineral Water Hospital.[33] Although not a puritan, the cleric was appalled by the lack of a church in an English community that had managed to support so many secular activities. On July 3, 1886, at his urging a meeting of Stapylton and Company was called at "The Hall," "to discuss what steps [should] be taken to provide the neighborhood with a church and rector." A committee was formed to discuss possible sites for a church and methods for financing its construction. Printed circulars setting forth the needs of the colony were sent back to relatives and friends in England, bringing heartening response. Although a part of the building fund was raised by the young men themselves, the bulk of it was subscribed in England through the untiring efforts of the Rev. Canon William Stapylton, the father of the colony's founder.[34]

All through the fall of 1886 the Rev. Mr. Tasker held services, at first in "The Hall" and later in a barn that was fitted out by the

32. Ibid., p. 19. See also the minutes of the Bucket and Dipper Club, which are in possession of Mr. and Mrs. Alfred P. Bosanquet, Fruitland Park, Florida. Mr. Bosanquet is the son of Louis Bosanquet, a member of the club.

33. *Crockford's Clerical Directory*, 1894, p. 1296.

34. Parish Records, Holy Trinity Church, Fruitland Park; see also *Diocesan Journal* (Florida), 1887, p. 73.

congregation for ecclesiastical use. The work of collecting funds continued, and on December 19 the congregation made a formal application to the Bishop of Florida to become a regular mission. Several weeks later Bishop Weed came personally to Chetwynd to accept the application and to encourage the vestry in its efforts to construct a church.[35] In the meantime, the Rev. Mr. Tasker returned to England, but services were continued by another visiting English clergyman, the Rev. Spencer Fellows, rector of Pulham, Norfolk. On October 30, 1887, that clergyman baptized Granville Brian, the infant son of the Granville Chetwynd Stapyltons. The vestry purchased a lot for the church from Sam Tanner, a freed slave who had homesteaded the desired land after the Civil War, and the church was erected on the outskirts of Chetwynd in November 1888, at a cost of $2,150. The Rev. Joseph E. Julian of St. James's, Leesburg, agreed to accept charge of the new mission in addition to his duties at St. James's. His stipend was set by the vestry at two hundred dollars per annum.

As the new church was very primitively furnished, the vestry decided to remedy the situation. With gifts sent by Mr. and Mrs. Tasker from England, and through the generosity of local parishioners, a number of improvements were undertaken during the Christmas season of 1888. The sanctuary was beautified, choir stalls and a lectern were placed in the chancel, and oil lamps were installed there to permit the choir and clergy to sing the evening service. The vestry minutes also state that pews were put in halfway down the nave and that kneelers were given for the new pews. Outside improvements were also made. The churchyard was fenced, hitching posts were installed, and stabling was constructed to house the horses of the congregation in the event of bad weather. The lych gate, believed by many to be the oldest in the United States, was erected in 1889 and remains one of the distinguishing features of the little church.[36] This covered entrance to the churchyard is used in the burial service as a resting place for the casket and, in the English

35. Parish Records, Holy Trinity Church; see also *Diocesan Journal* (Florida), 1887, p. 79.
36. Parish Records, Holy Trinity Church.

tradition, is where the rector joins the procession into the church proper.

Under the leadership of the Rev. Joseph E. Julian a number of other improvements were made, the debt was retired, and the building was readied for consecration. On July 12, 1889, Bishop Weed visited Chetwynd and solemnly set it aside as a place of Christian worship. There were twelve families and thirty-seven single persons listed on the parochial report. Thus in spite of its slow beginning, more had been accomplished in Chetwynd than in any of the other principally English congregations.[37]

Holy Trinity Church possessed an active ladies' guild, which played an important role in the life of the mission. The women made regular payments to the missionary fund of the old diocese and to the new missionary jurisdiction, decorated the church, cared for the altar, and paid for the maintenance of the churchyard.[38] The president of the guild, Mrs. Granville C. Stapylton, who kept up a voluminous correspondence with relatives and friends in England, described the floral decorations on one occasion: "We had morning service today. Flowers on the altar so pretty—great crimson hybiscious [sic], pretty greenery and lovely poincianias [sic] in smaller glasses." In the same letter Mrs. Stapylton also described the "unsavoury little beasts" which inhabited the churchyard and groves nearby. She asked her correspondent, "Have you ever seen a skunk? They have a horrible smell if attacked. A dog is not fit to come near a house for days after an encounter with one and if anyone has the misfortune to be attacked by one, his clothes have to be burned. They often prowl about at night in search of eggs and other food. The smell wakes one up at night it is so powerful. One ran across the road the other day when we were driving but did not notice us and ran down a gopher hole! They are pretty little creatures—black and dull yellow with a long waving tail which is very bushy and which they carry rather like a squirrel."[39]

A reading of Holy Trinity's vestry minutes shows that the English

37. Weed, *Episcopal Address* (Florida), 1890, p. 10. See *Diocesan Journal* (Florida), 1890, *Appendix,* for statistics.

38. Parish Records, Holy Trinity Church.

39. Letter dated September 13, 1890, Stapylton Papers.

Churchmen were devoted to their American pastor, the Rev. Joseph
E. Julian, who maintained his residence in Leesburg. The Chetwynd vestry combined with the vestries of St. James's, Leesburg,
and St. John's, Montclair, to buy Mr. Julian a horse and buggy
so that he could more easily discharge his pastoral duties. For
nearly four years this conscientious priest rode his circuit in weather
foul and fair, preaching to his scattered flock and bringing them
the sacraments of the Church. In the course of his grueling work,
the cleric's health broke and, not taking a proper rest, he developed
tuberculosis.

The circumstances of his complete collapse and tragic death were
vividly described by the fatherly Bishop Weed before the Diocesan
Council of 1893. "The Rev. Joseph E. Julian, a faithful servant
of the Lord, one who endeared himself to God's people by his acts
of self-sacrifice, took his own life. He had been sick for some time.
He broke down in the chancel and was carried home. While in
bed he severed an artery with a razor which was lying on a table
near at hand." The bishop refused to go into the mental condition of the patient, who was apparently delirious at the time of
his death, nor would he in any way pass judgment. He compassionately told the Council, "His life [Julian's] speaks for itself. It
seems strange that God should have allowed so faithful a servant
to die in such a way. His life was full of good works. His untiring
devotion made people love him. He was always at hand to comfort
and aid the afflicted and distressed. One could write his epitaph
in a few words: an unselfish man. His death has been a sore grief
to me. I loved him, admired him and respected him. I had perfect
confidence in him as a [C]hristian man, and this confidence has not
been changed by his unfortunate end."[40]

It is obvious that his English parishioners equally loved, admired,
and respected their priest and that they shared the confidence of
their bishop in Mr. Julian "as a [C]hristian man." At their vehement
insistence, the clergyman was buried in Holy Trinity churchyard.[41]
His widow, who survived her husband for forty-four years, was

40. Weed, *Episcopal Address* (Florida), 1893, p. 5.
41. Headstone, Holy Trinity churchyard, Fruitland Park.

buried at his side in December, 1936.[42] Mr. Julian's death was not only tragic in itself, but tragic in its effect on his three congregations as well. The convocation journals show that the services of a regular clergyman were not obtained in the Leesburg-Chetwynd-Montclair field for some three years after his death.

The colony of Narcoosee also fostered an English community church. Narcoosee was founded in 1884 by the British firm of Fell and Davidson, which bought some 12,000 acres east of Lake Tohepekaliga about seven miles from the present city of St. Cloud. The greater part of the land was laid off in lots of two to ten acres for citrus and sugar culture, but the 2,000 acres reserved for a village were surveyed and divided into town lots. The firm also purchased 2,500 acres of marshland which was to be reclaimed by drainage. A promotional campaign was conducted in England, and a large number of immigrants came to settle in the vicinity. Some of the new arrivals were disheartened by the wildness of the country and returned to England, but others remained to work and create the prosperous settlement of Narcoosee. By the end of 1888, there were approximately two hundred settlers in the area. A correspondent from the *Florida Times-Union* described the town as having a school, "a church in planning," a blacksmith shop, a railroad station, a post office, a carpenter's shop, the real estate offices of Fell and Davidson, an attorney's office, and a clubhouse for the English residents. The writer declared that the community as yet had no druggist or doctor, but that they were not required since "the country is too healthy" to need their services.[43]

The man largely responsible for the prosperity of the settlement was Lt. Col. William Edwin Cadman, a flamboyant Englishman. Colonel Cadman, late of the Princess of Wales's Own Yorkshire Regiment, arrived in Narcoosee with his wife and four children in 1888 and bought a large grove and house called "The Bungalow." The energetic Cadman was brought to Narcoosee as the manager of Fell-Davidson and after a short time became a partner in the company as well as the natural leader of the colony. He was instrumental in getting the Sugar Belt Railroad extended to Narcoosee so that the produce of the settlers could be more easily shipped to

42. *Leesburg Commercial*, December 25, 1936.
43. Jacksonville *Florida Times-Union*, July 21, 1889.

northern markets. He also was one of the principal founders of the Episcopal congregation in Narcoosee.[44]

At the invitation of Colonel Cadman, Archdeacon J. H. Weddell of Thonotosassa visited Narcoosee sometime in late 1888, held a service in the schoolhouse, and took steps to organize a mission. On January 21, 1890, Bishop Weed visited the settlement, celebrated Holy Communion in the schoolhouse, and preached to the members of the colored community.[45] It is presumed that the congregation formally became a mission of the diocese during this visitation when it was organized under the patronage of St. Peter. Immediate steps were taken by the congregation to raise money for the construction of a church. In his report for the following year, Archdeacon Weddell stated that "funds are in hand, nearly enough to proceed with the building of a good church." He also described Narcoosee as "essentially an English colony, where English customs prevail and prayers for the Queen and Royal Family are said with those for our own civil authority."[46]

St. Peter's Church, a wooden Neo-Gothic structure with one of the tallest wooden spires in the state, was begun late in 1891, but lack of funds prevented its completion until some three years later. An epidemic of banking, railroad, and commercial failures in Florida and the rest of the country during late 1892 and early 1893 precipitated the great depression of 1893 and profoundly affected the overexpanded economy of the Kissimmee Valley. Many of the English residents of Narcoosee lost their savings with the collapse of the First National Bank of Orlando, and there is some indication that a portion of the building fund of St. Peter's Church was also lost with the failure of that institution.[47]

The parishioners of St. Peter's, however, were undaunted by the depression and continued to press for funds to complete the church. During 1894 and 1895, a series of theatricals, concerts, and socials was given for the benefit of the building fund. One such affair is described in a Kissimmee paper in great detail: "Last Thursday

44. *Kissimmee News Leader*, July 24, 1889.
45. Weed, *Episcopal Address* (Florida), 1890, p. 13.
46. *Diocesan Journal* (Florida), 1891, p. 23.
47. Parish Records, St. Peter's Church, Narcoosee, Florida, 1894, in Diocesan Office, Winter Park.

evening an entertainment was given at the Runnymede Hotel
[near Narcoosee] for the benefit of St. Peter's Church, Narcoosee.
A large number of ladies and gentlemen came from Kissimmee on
a special train, arriving about eight o'clock at the hotel, where they
found the inhabitants of Narcoosee and Mr. Hamilton Disston and
his party waiting there to welcome them." The program was under
the direction of the Bullock family and included a number of
tableaux, voice and instrumental solos, and humorous recitations.
One of the highlights of the evening was the performance of an
Anglo-Irish tenor, Villiers Stuart, "who sang one of his choice
Irish songs 'Finegan's Wake.' It was so well received that he sang
'The Mother-in-Law,' with a fine Irish Brogue." The mother-in-
law, the editor commented, "must have been a delightful companion both to her friends and enemies [as] 'She cut them up with
vituperations,/And blackguarded all their female relations.' " The
editor hoped "that Colonel Cadman will soon have enough funds
in hand to complete St. Peter's," and stated that he would then be
delighted to "run over and take a look at the church."[48]

By the time of Bishop Gray's visitation in November 1895, the
building, although not completed inside, was in use for divine service. During the winter of 1896 and 1897, Godfrey W. Radclyffe
Cadman, the son of Colonel and Mrs. Cadman, spent the long
winter vacation from his studies at the college of The University of
the South with relatives in England and raised $80.35 toward the
completion of the interior of the building. This sum, combined
with the Easter offering in April 1897, was enough to finish the
inside of the church and free the building from debt. The following year Bishop Gray consecrated the church "before a full congregation made up of members of the Episcopal church from Orlando,
Kissimmee, and Narcoosee." After the service, the proud parishioners and their guests retired to "The Bungalow" for a festive
garden party. "Refreshments were served and croquet was played
during the reception." Narcoosee had her church at last.[49]

The trials of the British colony at Acton, a few miles from the

48. Jacksonville *Florida Times-Union*, July 21, 1889.

49. *Kissimmee News Leader*, December 6, 1895; *Kissimmee Valley Gazette*, April 7 and April 21, 1897 and February 11, 1898.

present city of Lakeland, were more severe than those of its sister settlements. The colony was founded in the spring of 1884 under the auspices of a largely British corporation, the Florida Mortgage and Investment Company, Limited. The guiding spirit in this syndicate was the Hon. R. W. Hanbury, a wealthy English businessman and Member of Parliament. The settlement was mainly an agricultural enterprise designed to bring the stockholders a quick profit from the sale of land and produce. It is clear, however, that Hanbury was also bent on scientifically experimenting with company crops: truck, citrus, tropical fruits, and sugar. Most of the farms were situated in the low lands between Lakes Bonney and Parker, where the soil was extremely fertile, although the area was given to occasional flooding.

It was natural that the settlers of Acton should want the services of the Church, but like most of the other colonists they did not have sufficient local funds to begin a building program. Piers E. Warburton, the company's resident manager, attempted to alleviate this situation on one of his periodic trips to Great Britian to make business reports to the proprietors. He carried on a fund-raising campaign for the colony by conducting a series of lectures on Florida for which admission was charged. The proceeds were "to create a fund for the erection of a suitable house of worship in Acton, Florida, U.S.A." Considerable interest was aroused by his lectures and a substantial sum was accumulated. Even the Princess of Wales, later Queen Alexandra, became interested in the project and donated some handsome altar brass and hangings.[50]

The little church, called All Saints', was probably completed late in 1887.[51] It was built of wood in the Neo-Gothic style and placed above the village on a high bluff overlooking Lake Parker. The services of a lay reader were utilized for the regular Prayer Book offices, and occasionally the Rev. J. H. Weddell of Holy Trinity Church, Thonotassassa, archdeacon of the central Florida mis-

50. Herbert J. Drane, *History of All Saints' Church, Lakeland* (n.p., 1919), pp. 2–3; also see Jacksonville *Florida Times-Union,* January 17, 1886.
51. Weed, *Episcopal Address* (Florida), 1890, p. 4. This is the first time that the church is mentioned as being completed, although an Acton congregation is mentioned in *Diocesan Journal* (Florida), 1887.

sions, visited the settlement to celebrate Holy Communion. One winter, the church obtained the ministrations of the Rev. Charles F. Garratt, vicar of the Parish of Little Tew in Oxfordshire, while he was visiting his son, an early immigrant to Acton. The congregations at All Saints' were large despite the church's uncomfortable accommodations. A contemporary described the setting for the services: "The furniture of the nave consisted of one dozen cane-seated chairs and perhaps two or three rough benches. . . . The chancel furniture was of the crudest kind, being made at a neighboring saw mill." The music for the services left something to be desired as well. It was provided by "a wheezy little organ" presided over by an ancient Englishman.[52] The altar brass and hangings of the Princess of Wales must have seemed quite out of place in this pioneer atmosphere.

All Saints' Church was never consecrated in Acton, since the settlement fell apart when the Hanbury agricultural ventures failed during 1888 and 1889. This disaster was probably caused by a combination of bad planning, bad weather, and high water, but whatever the causes Acton was a deserted village "without a living soul to call it home" by the fall of 1889. The inhabitants had either left the country or moved to adjoining and more fortunate communities. Vandals broke into the church, smashed some of the windows, stole the altar brass, and made off with the altar hangings.[53] At the Diocesan Council of 1890 permission was granted to the Rev. H. H. Weddell to have the abandoned church moved to Lakeland, where it was later consecrated by Bishop Weed under its original name of All Saints' Church.[54]

An extensive advertising campaign waged in Great Britain by Hamilton Disston and his associates during 1884 brought a large number of British immigrants into the Pinellas peninsula the following year. Most of these settlers became truck farmers and citrus growers. Some, however, bought town lots in the seaside resort of Disston City and speculated in real estate or business. The center

52. Drane, pp. 4–5.
53. Ibid.
54. *Diocesan Journal* (Florida), 1890, p. 21.

of the English community was Pinellas, a village that has long since been a part of the present city of St. Petersburg.[55]

In April 1887, a group of English and American settlers met at the home of Robert Stanton, an English layman in Pinellas, and organized a mission under the patronage of St. Bartholomew. The congregation was put under the care of a visiting English priest, the Rev. Gilbert Holt White of the Diocese of London. Plans were made to raise funds for the building of a church.[56] Some of the young Englishmen contributed their portion to the fund by staging an entertainment consisting of two comical playlets, "Turn Him Out" and "Old Phil's Birthday." Many of the American settlers of Puritan background were scandalized that a theatrical entertainment should be held for the benefit of a church, but scandalized or not, they thronged to see it. So many attended that a repeat performance had to be given the next night, and as a result a large sum was raised.[57] Families and friends of the immigrants in England also helped the new mission by sending sizable contributions to the building fund.[58] St. Bartholomew's Church was completed late in 1887. It was the first church built in the lower portion of the peninsula. The cemetery, which was laid out in the churchyard, gave the little wooden church a particularly English appearance.[59] When Bishop Weed made his first visitation to St. Bartholomew's, in February 1888, there were seven families and forty single persons listed in the parish register.[60] A promising start had been made.

The first Episcopal church in the town of St. Petersburg, built by the congregation of St. Bartholomew's and served for several years by the priest-in-charge of the parent church, was also attended by a number of English settlers. The chapel, called the Church of the Holy Spirit, was a small frame building completed in 1889. It stood on the corner of Eleventh Street and Second Avenue. In

55. Karl H. Grismer, *The Story of St. Petersburg*, pp. 52–53.
56. William L. Straub, *History of Pinellas County*, p. 130.
57. Grismer, p. 57.
58. Straub, p. 130.
59. Ibid.
60. Weed, *Episcopal Address* (Florida), 1888, p. 17 and statistical appendix.

December 1893, the chapel was moved to a better location on Second Avenue and Fourth Street, North, where it achieved the status of an independent mission and changed its name to St. Peter's Church. After the new church was built the Rt. Rev. William C. Gray did much to encourage the two congregations to unite. They did so after the Great Freeze of 1895, and the Church of St. Bartholomew was closed. It was not reopened until the beginning of the Florida Boom.[61]

In addition to the almost totally English congregations of Conway, Fruitland Park, Acton, Narcoosee, and Pinellas, there were churches in Fort Meade, Lake Buddy near Dade City, and Montclair near Leesburg that probably had a majority of English parishioners. There were also numerous churches like St. Luke's, Orlando, and those in Kissimmee, Apopka, Dunedin, Zellwood, and Maitland whose congregations were half English and half American. The churches in Lakeland, Leesburg, Sanford, Ocala, Daytona, and St. Petersburg had strong English minorities, and nearly every parish and mission in the missionary jurisdiction had at least one or two British families who were active in the worship of the Church.

The debt of the Episcopal Church in South Florida to these Britannic pioneers is incalculable. They occupied positions of leadership and contributed financially at the diocesan as well as the local level. English Churchwomen joined their American counterparts in the activities of the missionary guilds which supported the general mission fund of the struggling young diocese, and much of the delicate needlework that went into altar linens and hangings was made by skilled English hands. Important, too, was the fact that much of the cash that went into the construction of the numerous little Neo-Gothic churches of the period was contributed by generous Englishmen in the solid pound sterling.

One of the most enduring contributions to the mission program

61. Straub, p. 131; *Convocation Journal,* 1894, p. 39; *Journal of the Annual Convention of the Church in the Diocese of South Florida,* 1925, p. 3. This publication is cited hereafter as *Diocesan Journal.* Similar publications in other dioceses are cited as *Diocesan Journal,* with name of diocese, and year.

in Florida came from the ministrations of visiting English clergy-men. These men of the cloth, while guests of friends and relatives in Florida, helped to organize and staff missions in the settlements and areas that they visited. Fortunately for the Church, these visits were often prolonged. The Rev. John C. W. Tasker (Diocese of London) and the Rev. Spencer Fellows (Diocese of Norwich) helped found and serve the church at Fruitland Park; the Rev. Charles Garratt (Diocese of Oxford) acted as priest-in-charge of All Saints', Acton, for several months; the Rev. W. A. Noyle (Diocese of Winchester) served numerous missions on the Gulf coast and also acted for several years as Bishop Weed's archdeacon for that area; and the Rev. Gilbert Hope White (Diocese of London) helped to organize St. Bartholomew's in Pinellas where he officiated for several years. The Rev. Charles W. Arnold, a retired priest of the Church of England, gave Conway its first regular services when he settled there in 1885, and a year later resumed the work of an active clergyman in the jurisdiction, serving churches in Orlando, Daytona, Ormond, New Smyrna, and Port Orange until he retired again after twenty years in the mission field. Newspapers of the period show that many other English clergymen officiated from time to time in South Florida. They too rendered needed help by hold-ing services wherever they happened to be visiting.

Another valuable contribution to the Church came from younger English immigrants who received the call to the priesthood after they had settled in Florida. A few names stand out in the journals of the era. For example, Godfrey Cadman, son of Colonel and Mrs. William E. Cadman of Narcoosee, became a postulant for holy orders in 1894 after entering The University of the South.[62] He later served missions in the central area of the diocese. John Fearn-ley, a Cambridge M.A. who settled in central Florida, also read theology at Sewanee. He served churches in the Sanford area dur-ing 1892.[63] Another immigrant, J. Neville Thompson, who lived with his family at Lake Buddy, entered the ministry and served missions in Dade City and Brooksville, and along the adjacent Gulf

62. Gray, *Episcopal Address* (Southern Florida), 1895, p. 50.
63. *Sanford Journal*, January 11, 1892; Weed, *Episcopal Address* (Flor-ida), 1892, p. 11.

coast.[64] Francis Cecil Baylis, a young orange-grower in Conway, read theology under Bishop Gray and was ordained deacon in June 1893, at St. Luke's Church, Orlando. He served churches in Titusville, Courtenay, and Cocoa, and was later transferred to the Kissimmee-Narcoosee field. When he was priested two years later, he served Holy Trinity, West Palm Beach.[65] After some years of mission work, he returned to England, but deeded his orange grove in Conway to the Jurisdiction of South Florida for the advancement of the mission program. Conway gave yet another son to the Church. The Rev. Herbert Cary-Elwes, whose parents, Colonel and Mrs. George Dudley Cary-Elwes, helped found Holy Trinity Church in Conway, entered the ministry and served for a number of years in Melbourne–Eau Gallie before transferring to North Carolina.[66] These young men, and others whose national identity cannot be determined, became veritable circuit riders and helped staff numerous missions in the jurisdiction at a time when the bishop was desperately short of clergy.

Generally speaking, there was little ill feeling between English and American Churchmen on either the diocesan or local levels. Occasionally, however, small rubs did occur. For example, the congregation of Holy Trinity Church in Chetwynd refused to give up the use of their English hymnals. This refusal came in the face of Bishop Gray's insistence that the American version be put into use immediately. The vestry justified the congregation's action on the grounds that funds were not available to purchase the American edition, and the bishop did not press the matter further.[67] Another bone of ecclesiastical contention was the refusal of some of the American clergy to say prayers for the Queen and the Royal Family along with those for the President of the United States. Iza Duffus Hardy, who visited near Maitland, describes with humor the typical Britannic reaction to this slight. "The latest batch of arrivals, dutifully attending the little Episcopal Church on Sunday,

64. Gray, *Episcopal Address* (Southern Florida), 1894, p. 50.

65. Ibid.; also see *Convocation Journal*, 1895, p. 5; *Palm Branch*, Trinity Season 1895.

66. *Convocation Journal*, 1914, p. 6.

67. Vestry Minutes, Holy Trinity Church, Fruitland Park, June 1896.

came home with feelings unreasonably aggrieved, because for the first time in their lives they had heard the blessings of Heaven invoked upon the head of 'the President of the United States' instead of 'the Queen and all the Royal Family.' " This breach of tradition grated on the ears of the new immigrants who complained that "It did not seem natural!"[68] Despite these infrequent assertions of British nationalism, the British and American communities labored together diligently to promote the work of the Church. Through their cooperative efforts the Episcopal Church in South Florida developed one of the most effective missionary organizations in the pioneer state.

68. Hardy, *Oranges and Alligators*, pp. 18–19.

IV

Disasters

THE MISSIONARY DISTRICT OF SOUTHERN FLORIDA WAS BORN in the midst of the great financial panic of 1893. By the fall of 1894, however, the epidemic of bank and business failures was over, and the people of the peninsula looked forward to profits from the bountiful citrus crop ripening in their groves that would soon be ready for harvest. The prospects of the coming season were particularly good since many of the younger groves, planted in the mid-eighties, would for the first time bear enough fruit to make a sizable profit. The newspapers of the state promised a crop in excess of five million boxes with a market in which the prices would hold.

Unfortunately the high hopes of the patient, hardworking settlers were shattered by the weather. Early in the Christmas season of 1894, the northern states were engulfed in a wave of extremely cold weather. The temperature began to fall rapidly in South Carolina and Georgia as the cold wave moved south. On the evening of December 27 the thermometer dropped to fourteen degrees in some places in north Florida; the city of Tampa had the thickest ice it had ever known; and freezing weather extended as far south as Okeechobee. The fruit crop was destroyed throughout central Florida. Since freezing or near-freezing weather continued during the

53

following day and night, many of the younger trees were either killed or severely damaged.[1]

Undaunted by the bitter weather, Bishop Gray made his official visitation on the Feast of the Holy Innocents to Holy Trinity Church in Conway where he confirmed five candidates and preached to a large congregation apparently as undaunted as he, although as he noted in his diary, "there is no way of heating the Church and some of the congregation suffered." After the service, the bishop reported, "in spite of the cold, the good ladies . . . had a sale at the residence of Mr. Cary-Elwes of articles they had been preparing during the year past for the benefit of the Mission Work of the Church." The sale was a success,[2] although on that occasion no doubt many a would-be-stiff upper lip was trembling from the unusual cold. The prayers that must have been offered at Holy Trinity for more seasonable weather were not immediately answered, for cold continued to grip central Florida for another two days. As warm weather returned, the orange groves of the state were flooded by a sea of fallen and rotting fruit. The owners realized no financial return on their unpicked crops, but they could at least be thankful that the bulk of the older trees had escaped destruction.

Following the Christmas freeze there were five weeks of unseasonably warm weather. It was as if spring had come to Florida in the middle of winter. The defoliated orange trees, being evergreens, were inclined to leaf out sooner than under ordinary circumstances, and with the warm spell the sap rose and they sprouted tender leaves. There was a universal feeling that the worst had passed. This feeling, however, was unwarranted, for in early February another freeze struck the state.[3] The recovering trees, their trunks and branches filled with sap, were killed to the ground. In Ocala, an important citrus center, the thermometer fell twenty-five degrees in two hours on February 7, and freezing weather covered the state as far south as Jupiter. At Titusville the mercury dropped from seventy-six to nineteen from the afternoon of the seventh to the morning of the eighth and stood below freezing for two days. In

1. Jacksonville *Florida Times-Union,* January 1, 1895.
2. Gray, *Episcopal Address* (Southern Florida), 1895, p. 61.
3. Rerick, 2: 268.

Orlando the temperature reached a low of eighteen, covering all the lakes with a thin layer of ice, and in the shade the ice remained throughout the next day.[4]

The second freeze was an occurrence without precedent in the history of the state, and its results were tragic beyond description. Years of both capital and labor investment were swept away on that freezing February night. A contemporary Florida historian described the aftermath of the calamity and its effect on the larger grove owners who, "housed in the greatest luxury, awoke to find themselves paupers and the battle of life to be fought again. The orange grower was paralyzed and, for once, stupefied. He asked himself if it were not some dreadful nightmare from which he should awake in the morning." A short time, however, sufficed to show the reality of the situation. Estimates indicated that grove property worth $75 million was destroyed by the freeze. Thus one of the most promising industries in the South was dealt a staggering blow.[5]

The disaster affected every segment of Florida society, including the Church. So many Churchmen were ruined financially that many churches had difficulty paying their clergy and maintaining regular services. One immediate result of the freeze was the cancellation of the campaign of the bishop and the endowment committee to raise $50,000 for the endowment of the episcopate. Ironically, the committee was making its final hopeful plans in Orlando on the very afternoon of the evening the disaster struck.[6] Any thought of an endowed episcopate obviously had to be given up for many years, and it is safe to assume that one of the major factors preventing the missionary jurisdiction from becoming a self-supporting diocese until 1922 was the economic distress which plagued the area for two decades after the Great Freeze of '95.

Another unfortunate result of the freeze which profoundly affected the life of the Church in southern Florida was the mass exodus of British settlers. The younger fruit growers with no reserve capital were financially crippled by the disaster. R. A. Arnold of Conway, son of the Rev. Charles W. Arnold, stated that the younger mem-

4. Jacksonville *Florida Times-Union,* February 8 and 9, 1895.
5. Rerick, 2: 268–69.
6. Gray, *Episcopal Address* (Southern Florida), 1896, p. 55.

bers of the colony were so dumb-struck as the mercury continued to drop that they began to play sports during the day and cards during the night. When it was ascertained that all of their orange trees had been killed to the ground during the three days of the freeze, half of the younger settlers "left precipitately." Arnold estimated that some two hundred left the Conway-Orlando area, abandoning their groves, houses, and furniture. In some houses the owners departed in such haste that the dishes were left unwashed on the dining tables. One young citrus farmer sold a $40,000 investment for the price of a steamer ticket back home.[7] In the Leesburg–Fruitland Park area the freeze was even more devastating than in Orange County, and a mass exodus occurred there as well. Mrs. Granville Chetwynd-Stapylton wrote relatives in England that by June 1, 1895, a bank and sixty-eight stores had failed as a result of the freeze. The following year the entire Stapylton family moved from the grove at Chetwynd to Leesburg where Mr. Stapylton became associated with the only surviving bank in the county.[8]

Archdeacon J. H. Weddell in his report to Bishop Gray stated that the largely English settlement at Lake Buddy, "where there is a small church, is practically broken up," and that other communities with numerous English immigrants, such as Narcoosee, Kissimmee, Ocoee, and Oakland, had their congregations sadly depleted by removals.[9] The removals continued at a slower rate for several years after the great exodus of 1895, although in some cases parochial reports show that the removals increased rather than decreased in the years following the freeze. For instance, St. Luke's, Orlando, listed thirteen removals in 1897, and sixteen in 1899.[10]

The exodus of Britishers was undoubtedly accelerated by their concern over an unfortunate international crisis: the dispute between Great Britain and Venezuela involving the Venezuelan–British Guiana boundary. In July 1895, President Cleveland's secretary of state, Richard Olney, involved the United States in the controversy by sending a strongly worded note to Whitehall demanding that

7. Blackman, p. 128.
8. Letter dated June 1, 1895, Stapylton Papers.
9. *Convocation Journal*, 1896, p. 33.
10. Ibid., 1898 and 1900, *Parochial Abstracts*.

Great Britain submit the dispute to American arbitration on the somewhat fallacious grounds that British designs against Venezuela were a violation of the Monroe Doctrine. The British prime minister, Lord Salisbury, acting also as foreign secretary, haughtily ignored the note for several months, and when he finally replied on November 26, argued that the Monroe Doctrine did not apply to the controversy and that the United States had no "practical concern" with the matter. In mid-December, President Cleveland, usually reasonable in his conduct of diplomatic affairs, exhibited decided jingoistic propensities, by issuing an ultimatum to the British government restating his arbitration demands. The martial spirit was fanned by the Cleveland administration and an irresponsible press. The two great English-speaking nations drifted toward war.[11]

The prolonged crisis brought the hard-hit British settlers in Florida to a point of almost complete despair. Many were still British subjects, and no small number of the younger settlers still retained reserve commissions in British military units. The possibility of a war between the country of their birth and the country of their adoption was heartrending, and no doubt caused many of those settlers who were considering a return to England to hasten their plans for leaving. Bishop Gray sadly recorded in his diary the departure of an active Church family from the state in the midst of the crisis: "With much regret, met the Beste family leaving Avon Park on their way back to England."[12] This sight, with others like it, was more than the bearded old patriarch could bear. As the government pushed the country towards war, the bishop pleaded for peace. Speaking before the Convocation in January 1896, Bishop Gray declared: "I am unwilling to close this address without alluding to the threatening clouds of war that now hang upon the horizon of our beloved country.

"It is marvelous how the madness of politicians can work the country up to a political frenzy, such as threatens to involve the great English-speaking people—one in speech, one in business inter-

---

11. James Ford Rhodes, *A History of the United States* (New York: Macmillan Co., 1920), pp. 443–49.

12. Gray, *Episcopal Address* (Southern Florida), 1896, p. 75.

ests, one in all the best and holiest aspirations of our race—in an unholy and fratricidal war.

"Must we, as a people, sit supinely still, while millions of shocked and disapproving men, women, and children are plunged into ruin and destruction?

"I trust that we will accept our duty . . . and that this Convocation will take such action, as will throw what influence we may possess upon the side of 'peace and good will to men.' "[13]

Hundreds of Protestant clergymen throughout the country chorused the bishop's plea and considerable pressure was brought against the bellicose attitude of the administration. War was averted when Lord Salisbury, under the threat of German intervention in favor of the Boers in South Africa, consented to submit the dispute to arbitration in January 1896. Some of the British claims were honored by the American board, and the controversy was peaceably settled in November of that year.[14] Even though the dispute was settled peaceably, threat of war had driven some immigrants, who would have been valuable additions to Florida communities, to return home or to settle in territories within the Empire.

The Great Freeze and the loss of many settlers profoundly affected the churches in predominantly English communities. St. Bartholomew's in Pinellas closed its doors almost immediately, and the few remaining Britishers united with the congregation of St. Peter's Church in St. Petersburg. The building fell into disuse and decay, but the overgrown churchyard continued to be used as a local cemetery. The property was never deconsecrated or sold, and by 1919 there were enough Episcopalians in the old Pinellas area to reopen the church for regular services. St. Bartholomew's has been in continuous use since that time.[15]

St. Peter's, Narcoosee, did not fare so well as its contemporary in Pinellas. After the first departures, unfortunately, the decline in numbers continued, although at a slower rate, and it became a financial burden on those remaining to support the stipend of a clergyman. After the death of Colonel William Cadman in August

13. Ibid., p. 76.
14. Rhodes, pp. 451–52.
15. Straub, p. 131.

1910,[16] the mission, deprived of its leading layman, began to floun-
der rapidly. By 1913 the congregation had become so sparse that it
did not bother to elect wardens, vestry, or delegates to the diocesan
convocation,[17] and by 1921 St. Peter's had disappeared from the
rolls as an organized mission.[18] With the advent of the automobile
the remaining Episcopalians began to attend St. Luke's Church in
nearby St. Cloud, and in 1930, with the blessing of Cadman's
widow, it was decided to remove the building of St. Peter's at
Narcoosee to St. Cloud and unite the two missions under the name
of the Church of St. Luke and St. Peter. The church was moved,
freed from debt, and finally reconsecrated on November 25, 1935,
by Bishop Wing.[19] Thus the last vestiges of Anglicanism ceased to
exist in the once thriving English colony of Narcoosee.

The church in Conway suffered a similar decline. Some time
after the freeze the Cary-Elwes family moved to Orlando, depriving
the mission of an important force holding it together. In 1919 there
were only eleven communicants reported on the rolls and only nine
services were held in the church.[20] By 1921 the communicants had
dwindled to seven.[21] Several years later the congregation ceased to
function even as an unorganized mission, and during the depression
the trustees of the diocese attempted to sell the property, which was
deconsecrated by Bishop Wing. The reversionary clause in the deed
delayed the process for some time, but a sale of the property was
finally made, to the Conway Methodist Church, in 1938.[22] Subsequently, an Eastern Orthodox congregation moved the building
to a site near Maitland where it is in use as a church once again.

Holy Trinity Church, Chetwynd, on the outskirts of Fruitland
Park, declined sharply in the decades following the freeze, but a

16. Washington, D.C., *National Tribune*, August 25, 1910.

17. *Convocation Journal*, 1914, p. 93.

18. *The Living Church Annual and Church Almanac, 1921* (Milwaukee:
Morehouse Publishing Company, 1921), p. 379.

19. "Program of the Consecration of the Church of St. Luke and St.
Peter, St. Cloud," Bishop Wing's *Scrapbook*, 2.

20. *Convocation Journal*, 1920, p. 62.

21. *Living Church Annual*, 1921, p. 379.

22. *Report of the Actuary to the Trustees of the Diocese of South Florida,* October 4, 1932, and March 18, 1958, Diocesan Office, Winter Park.

number of the settlers who stubbornly hung on to their groves in those dreary years kept their church open as well. In 1916 Bishop Mann visited the vestry and requested that the church be moved from its site in Chetwynd to a lot in Fruitland Park. After a heated debate the request was refused.[23] Holy Trinity Church, Chetwynd, is the only English church still standing where it was built and the only congregation that has maintained the regular services of the Church since its inception. In 1969–70 St. Bartholomew's, St. Petersburg, was dismantled and moved from its original site to a new location on Thirty-fourth Street, South; the cemetery, however, is still at the old site.

American growers and businessmen were, of course, hit as hard by the freeze as the British immigrants. Archdeacon John H. Weddell, whose archdeanery covered the Gulf coast and the central area, reported to the Convocation of 1896: "We feel the result of last winter's disaster. The population has become, more than ever, migratory. The losses of the people and material resources have told upon the work in most all the missions in small towns and villages having a country constituency. The effect is seen not only in the reduced number of the membership that has survived—some having gone to the larger centres of business, and some having left the State to better their condition. It is gratifying, however, to note an occasional exception."[24] Bishop Gray reported that "distress notes reach me from every quarter," and that the groves as far south as Avon Park were cut back to the ground.[25] Many of the groves in the Ocala-Leesburg area were ruined beyond redemption, and the small citrus communities north of Orlando never recovered their prosperity. The convocation journals in the years following the freeze also report a sharp decline in church activity in the tiny grove communities of Thonotosassa, Montclair, Orange Lake, Zellwood, Ocoee, Yallaha, Orange City, Lake Mary, Glen Ethel, and Cassia. The numerical and financial resources of the Church in these places were so depleted by the catastrophe that the remaining parishioners

23. Vestry Minutes, Holy Trinity Church, Fruitland Park, May 6, 1916.
24. *Convocation Journal*, 1896, pp. 32–33.
25. Gray, *Episcopal Address* (Southern Florida), 1896, pp. 55, 63.

could not keep the missions opened. At least ten missions were forced to close their doors as a direct result of the freeze.

The churches in Polk County also suffered from the prolonged economic depression. The congregations were still good, but the bishop lamented the "sad conditions" of the towns. He noted that many people had moved away and that more were planning to go. Bartow and Fort Meade were the most depressed towns in the county. On August 29, 1898, Bishop Gray wrote of his visit to Fort Meade: "Conditions here sadder than at Bartow. My heart bleeds for the poor people. Nearly all the inhabitants in this place are disheartened, and anxious to get away to some more prosperous place."[26]

The upper east coast was particularly hard hit by the disaster. The orange industry around Daytona never again recovered its vitality, and the groves in the low hammocks adjoining Port Orange and New Smyrna were almost annihilated. The thriving town of Titusville, at the head of the Indian River, received a crippling blow from the freeze, and was almost completely destroyed by the series of calamities that followed. Archdeacon Benjamin F. Brown gave a gloomy picture of the place: "Our Work at Titusville this year has been one of great depression, and peculiar discouragement. The freezes of two years since bore especially hard on Titusville. This was followed by the discontinuance of the line of steamers on the river, occasioning the removal of a number of families. Then came the disastrous fire of January last impoverishing some of our best people and causing the removal of a number of families. Following that came the Miami boom [the railroad boom of 1896], in all we have lost nearly half of our communicants from St. Gabriel's Church." The archdeacon grieved at the removals in the Cocoa area as well.[27]

The financial stability of the infant diocese was destroyed by the freezes, and the diocesan treasurer, Frederic H. Rand, noted a sharp decline in church revenue.[28]

26. Ibid., 1899, p. 75.
27. *Convocation Journal*, 1897, p. 42.
28. Ibid., 1895, p. 15; 1896, p. 14; 1897, p. 20.

Year	Total Receipts
1894	$13,826.76
1895	$12,420.95
1896	$10,333.64
1897	$ 9,902.77

Another alarming trend during the depression that followed the freeze was the increase in the amount owed on the missionary assessment by parishes and missions.[29] It was from this source that the bishop operated the bulk of the diocesan missions:

Year	Missionary Assessment Unpaid
1894	$1,163.65
1895	$1,489.72
1896	$1,639.15
1897	$1,837.63

Not until the opening years of the twentieth century did the revenues of the diocese begin to show a decisive upward swing.

Floridians had often in the past been called upon to endure the cosmic treacheries of killing frost, hurricane winds, and wilting drouth. The bulk of the settlers, now as then, remained in the state, and with a stubbornness born of despair, set to work restoring their groves or experimenting with other livelihoods. The revival of the citrus industry was pressed with determination. By 1900 the restored groves produced a yield of almost a million boxes, and the economy of the peninsula began to improve. It should be borne in mind, however, that this figure was still four million boxes below the yield anticipated in 1894.[30] Florida, except in the Biscayne area, did not really emerge from the financial doldrums until the boom years that followed the end of the First World War.

29. Ibid.
30. Rerick, 2: 268.

V

The Seminole Mission

WHEN THE UNITED STATES ACQUIRED FLORIDA FROM Spain in 1821, the American government was forced to come to grips with the vexing Seminole problem. Since the Indians occupied the most promising agricultural lands, the area between the Apalachicola and the Suwannee rivers, the government found it necessary to move them to a reservation composed of less desirable lands so that the northwestern area could be surveyed and settled by white pioneers.

After two years of negotiations in which both bribery and intimidation were used, an agreement known as the Treaty of Moultrie Creek was reached in September 1823. The Indians, with few exceptions, consented to move into a reservation that included most of the interior of the peninsula south of the Withlacoochee River. The government, for its part, agreed to assume the cost of moving the tribe to its new lands, to make an annual payment of money for twenty years, and to protect the Seminoles and their lands from molestation by white settlers for the same period.

When Andrew Jackson came to power in 1829, the United States government under his leadership decided to move all the southern Indians to lands west of the Mississippi. The Seminole elders reminded the government of the stipulations of the Treaty of Moultrie

Creek, but showed, despite some reluctance, a willingness to negotiate. They finally agreed to the government's removal plan by signing the Treaty of Payne's Landing in 1832. The younger Seminoles, however, refused to accept the treaty. After several years of unsuccessful negotiations, the tribe took to the warpath to defend its lands, and the costly Seminole War of 1835 to 1842 ensued. After seven years of intermittent fighting, the bulk of the Indian population was rounded up and shipped to the Arkansas territory. However, a remnant of some three hundred under the leadership of Billy Bowlegs hid out in the fastness of the southwestern Everglades and defied government efforts to remove them. These Indians lived unmolested for a dozen years in the general area of the Caloosahatchee River behind Fort Myers, despite the uneasiness of the small groups of white settlers in the area.

In December 1855, an irresponsible army surveying party caused another Indian conflict by destroying Billy Bowlegs's cornfield just "to see old Billy cut up." The obliging chief took to the warpath, and panic seized the southern frontier. There were, however, no extensive military operations. Government troops, state militia, and frontiersmen, spurred on by the promise of a reward of $500 per brave, $250 per squaw, and $100 per child, quickly rounded up the majority of the Seminoles, including Billy, and shipped them west by sea. A part of the original remnant, however, eluded capture and retreated farther into the fastness of the Everglades.

When the Diocese of Florida was partitioned in 1892, the memorial to the General Convention requesting the division estimated, quite erroneously, that the number of Indians living in the Everglades was about 2,500. The memorial hoped that the National Church would provide the new missionary jurisdiction with the means to evangelize this long-neglected race.[1] Bishop Gray, during the first year of his episcopate, began to turn his attention to various ways of reaching the Seminoles, whom he more realistically estimated as numbering between five and six hundred souls.

In 1893 a female philanthropic organization called the Women's

1. *General Convention Journal: House of Deputies,* 1892, p. 264. In an article in the *Florida Times-Union,* February 25, 1899, the U.S. Indian Agent, Dr. Brecht, estimated the number of Seminoles at 600.

National Indian Association turned over to the bishop a tract of land in the Everglades known as the "Allen Place" for the work of the Church among the Seminoles. The property, consisting of three hundred twenty acres of land and a small house, was located some forty miles southeast of Fort Myers, railroad terminus of the southwestern coast.[2] When Bishop Gray went to inspect the property he had to hire an ox-drawn wagon to make the forty-mile trip inland from the railroad terminus on a rough trail that was under water most of the way. Deciding to utilize the property for an Indian mission, Bishop Gray named it "Immokalee," the Indian word for home.[3] Soon a small building, Christ Church, was erected, and in the spring of 1895 it was given to the charge of the Rev. Henry Gibbs. Christ Church was forty miles beyond the nearest place of Christian worship, yet barely on the fringe of Indian territory. The mission attracted only occasional Indians to its services, so another mission station which the bishop named "Everglade Cross," often called "Glade Cross," was opened forty miles farther into the interior. He gave a glowing and hopeful account of its founding: "Using a fine palmetto tree, prominently located, for the standard, we placed across it, for the arms of the cross, a large cypress beam. Our little company gathered around this 'Everglade Cross' and sang 'Rock of Ages,' then we all said the Apostles' Creed, after which kneeling down upon the ground, I offered up fervent prayers for the work, for the Indians, for the Missionaries, for all the scattered inhabitants of the region, and for the work of Christ's Church throughout the world—and so set apart and consecrated this spot, whose name recognizes the locality, the Everglades, and the centre, ground, and hope of the effort, the Cross."[4]

The bishop rallied the whole missionary jurisdiction around the

---

2. *Palm Branch* (Supplement), August 1899. During the depression the trustees of the diocese lost 319 of the 320 acres for failure to pay taxes. One acre was carried on the Collier County Tax Roll as the "Episcopal Cemetery." *Collier County Tax Roll, Episcopal Cemetery*, on deposit, Diocesan House, Winter Park.

3. Ibid.

4. Harriett Randolph Parkhill, "Our Work Among the Seminoles," manuscript, Diocesan Library, Winter Park, p. 6.

efforts of the Church in the Everglades. The Women's Auxiliary helped to provide the Gibbses with a stipend and supplies, a pair of mules and a wagon were donated to the mission, and the Junior Auxiliary gave a pair of ponies and a buggy to aid the effort.[5]

Soon the Rev. Henry Gibbs and his wife were dividing their time between Immokalee and Everglade Cross, where a small lodge was constructed for the use of the Indians and a two-room cottage was built for the use of the missionaries. The mission was located about three miles from the most important Indian trading post in the area, Bill Brown's Store.

The Seminoles, although they occasionally visited the rude chapels at Immokalee and Everglade Cross, were largely indifferent to the religious traditions of the white man. There were no baptisms or confirmations in the first years of this mission work,[6] but the missionaries and the bishop were prepared for a long wait. In November 1897, the first confirmation in the area was held but, alas, the confirmand was not a Seminole. It was Rose Brown, daughter of the trader who had for years been intimately associated with the Seminoles around the Everglade Cross.[7]

In a letter to the *Palm Branch* the Rev. Mr. Gibbs described his lonely, often discouraging work among the Indians: "The isolation here is great, sometimes painful, as it often happens that we do not see even one person during the whole week. The Indian comes and goes, never staying very long in one place, and always moving. We have made numerous trips to Indian camps, but in the majority of cases the shacks were empty, the occupants being miles away in the 'Everglades' or 'Big Cypress' hunting. Last Christmas we saw no one. We made a search of several miles, but failed to see any one. At other times we came in contact with quite a number at Everglade Cross and at their camps.

5. *Bishop's Diary*, 1898, pp. 58–59. (The official diary of the bishops of Southern Florida, published with the *Palm Branch*, the *Convocation Journal*, and, after 1922, the *Diocesan Journal*. Unless otherwise indicated, diary entries are from the *Convocation Journal*, 1893–1922, or the *Diocesan Journal*, 1923–68, with year and page cited.) *Convocation Journal*, 1900, pp. 19–20.

6. *Convocation Journal*, 1898, *passim*.

7. *Bishop's Diary*, 1898, p. 60.

"They are not all interested in the Word, and this for many reasons: To them we cannot speak as intelligently as we would, nor they to us. Their language is difficult, and they are extremely suspicious of the white man acquiring it. But their opposition to the work now is not nearly so great as formerly. At one time they looked upon our house as a kind of trap for them; now they take almost full possession of it when they come. They seem to think I know, or ought to know, all things. And they are generous, too, according to their light, but their light seems often cloudy.

"One poor fellow came for liniment for his wife. He then remembered that he also was sick, and before he went away he told me that his little boy was sick. Truly, it was a helpless family, so I made up medicine for all, and I out-doctored myself, since the medicine was so good that he came several times for a new supply. . . . The last time he came, he came to pay with a pumpkin! It was hardly the price of the medicine, but I suppose it was 'his best,' and the best could do no more."[8]

The Gibbses found that the Seminoles were such wanderers that it was impossible to conduct school or vocational classes for them, and that the best way to draw them to the services of the Church was medicine. In 1905, the bishop interested an English immigrant, Dr. William J. Godden, in becoming a medical missionary to the Seminoles—a move as brilliant as it was humane. Giving up his friends and congenial employment in St. Petersburg, Godden joined the Rev. Mr. and Mrs. Gibbs in the Everglades, arriving just in time to treat a fierce epidemic of measles, with attendant pneumonia. He housed the ill Indians in his dwelling and labored with them during the entire period of sickness, cooking their meals, nursing them, and giving them medicine. Out of the twenty-seven cases that Dr. Godden treated there were only two deaths, both of them the result of the carelessness of the patients themselves.[9] It was no wonder that at his next visitation Bishop Gray was given the warmest reception that he had ever received.[10]

8. *Palm Branch*, October 1900.
9. *Convocation Journal*, 1906, pp. 36–37; Parkhill, "Our Work Among the Seminoles," p. 12.
10. *Bishop's Diary*, 1906, p. 37.

After giving over seven years of their lives to work among the Seminoles, the Rev. Mr. and Mrs. Gibbs went to another mission field, leaving Dr. Godden to carry on alone and with no congenial contacts except those he made on the hard monthly trip to Fort Myers for supplies. With the financial help of Bishop Gray, Dr. Godden erected a small hospital at Everglade Cross, a building which proved to be helpful and useful to the physician in his dealings with the Indians.[11]

In February 1908, the store owned by Bill Brown was purchased by the Church to prevent it from falling into the hands of whiskey vendors. The store was even more strategically located than the Cross, since it was at the head of canoe navigation, the resting place for the Indians in their hunting campaigns. The bishop placed Dr. Godden in charge of the enterprise, which sold provisions, clothing, guns, and ammunition to the Indians and purchased their animal hides and furs. In July 1909, a new building was erected by Dr. Godden as a store and dwelling and the old store was fitted up as a chapel and hostel for the visiting Indians. When the chancel end, with altar and organ, was not in use, it was veiled by a heavy duck curtain, which also served as a screen for stereopticon pictures in lectures to the Seminoles. The carpentry work and the painting of the chapel were done by Dr. Godden and the Rev. Irenaeus Trout, the priest-in-charge of St. Luke's Church, Fort Myers, who now made regular trips to Immokalee and the Glade Cross mission. The Rev. Mr. Trout, who often traveled with his young son, not only celebrated the Eucharist, but also relieved Dr. Godden of the terrible burden of loneliness that his calling demanded.[12]

Despite the efforts of the mission team, before 1908 there had been no conversions among the Seminoles, even though the missionaries had won the good will of the nation. The distrust and suspicion felt by the Indians had previously been so great that they had been forbidden by tribal edict to receive instruction in the white man's ways or religion. In June 1908, however, at the "Shot-ca-

11. Paul A. Leonard, "The Growth of the Episcopal Church in South Florida, 1892–1932" (Master's thesis, University of Florida, 1950), p. 76.
12. Parkhill, "Our Work Among the Seminoles," pp. 12–13.

taw" or Green Corn Dance, the annual council of the tribe, this great obstacle, which had hampered missionary work for years, was removed. The Indians were now permitted to hear the gospel and receive baptism if they so desired. News of the dispensation brought fresh hope to the missionaries, and justifiably so. Within a few months the long labor of love began to bring forth first fruit: No-tul-ca-hat-sie, a subchief of the Tiger clan, received the sacrament of baptism from the hands of the Rev. Irenaeus Trout. Several months later, a prominent tribal elder, E-faw-lo-harjo, otherwise known as Charlie Osceola, was baptized on profession of faith, and later a few other Indians followed. There was, however, no mass conversion.[13]

The Rev. Mr. Trout explained some of his doctrinal problems to Bishop Gray in a letter: "I find the creed, the Lord's prayer and eight of the commandments fairly easy for them [the Indians] to understand, but the second ['Thou shalt not make to thyself any graven image'] and the fourth ['Remember that thou keep holy the Sabbath-day'] they do not seem to grasp. The idea seems to be that one day is like another, and never having had totems or graven things of any sort they cannot see why these should be forbidden as they never had any idea of using such things." Another problem for the Indians was the doctrine of the Real Presence in the Eucharist. Mr. Trout wrote: "This morning we had a celebration at sunrise, three communed (Dr. Godden, my son, and myself) and the Indians stood in the back of the chapel with folded arms, looking on. After the service I explained to them what we were doing, but they could not make out how Jesus could be there and not be seen."[14]

It is said that Bishop Gray was the first white man to be admitted to the Green Corn Dance, a sacred feast of the Seminole nation as well as the annual council. He left a vivid description of this experience in his diary:

"I had arranged my visit purposefully so as to strike the 'little moon' in June, which is the time of the annual gathering of the Seminoles known as the 'green corn dance.' With all the assistance

13. Ibid., p. 13.
14. Ibid., pp. 15, 17.

I could command I found it impossible to ascertain accurately the very days or the exact location chosen for this festival. We knew, however, the little moon meant the first days of the new moon, and the 'Old Doctor's' [the chief's] camp was somewhere in the very fastness of the Big Cypress Swamp. We also knew that neither horses nor mules could ever get through the boggy passages of the various cypress heads and so had to provide ourselves with a cart and a yoke of oxen. With a guide who knew the country well, we started from Everglade Cross at 4 o'clock in the morning. The day proved to be full of incidents. At the very start the oxen drew the iron pin from the cart's tongue, which shot into the air, and the Bishop, with a large part of the load, provisions, etc., was landed some distance in the rear, among the rocks and bushes. . . .

"Before the middle of the afternoon the trail led us to a deserted camp composed of at least a score of 'shacks' in a remarkably good state of preservation. We knew, however, that we were now on the right trail, for this was the camp formerly occupied by Old Doctor. We had about three miles further yet to go, and were fortunate enough to strike the right trail. After passing another cypress barrier, we drew near to the very suitable spot selected for the encampment, about the middle of the afternoon."

The two guides went forward as an embassy, while the prelate remained with the cart. Old Doctor received the embassy and sent word that the bishop and his party were welcome to watch the dancing that night. The bishop described what he saw.

"In the most prominent part of the well-wooded circle was Old Doctor's camp, with fifteen or twenty tents, and a large number of men, women, and children, showing quite a variety of costumes and color, which the dark-green palmettoes in the back-ground threw forward in bold relief. Several hundred yards distant and towards the east were the Miami Indians, who had come a greater distance than any of those present. A third camp, toward the northeast, contained a number both from the Everglades and Big Cypress. It was a picturesque scene, and we, sitting upon the ground, under our crowns of palms, enjoyed it to the full.

"After supper in the various camps the signal was given, and all repaired to the dance circle. A fire of lightwood was blazing in the center around which the dancers moved on the bare ground, in a perfect circle. The males had a rendezvous on one side, and on the opposite side the females had their place of assembling, far enough back to be invisible. At a signal from a kind of whistle, or rude musical instrument, the men and youths, decked out in new hunting shirts of various colors, and some in white, all with picturesque turbans, plumes and streamers, moved first into the circle, the leader giving forth a strain, the others answering in a corresponding refrain. The women fell in later, and from the opposite side. They looked very solemn and moved along behind the men with short, mincing steps, the yuck-chop-a-lund-kies, which are invisible, but are fastened on their limbs, keeping time with the step. These gopher shells, filled, as they are, with a kind of hard round seed, can scarcely be held in the hand without giving forth a rattling sound; and yet, as soon as the dance is over, the females step out of the ring on their side and not a sound is heard as they glide away to their quarters. In only two of the dances did the men even touch the women, and then it was only to swing them around as they clasped the hand. In all the movements, which were modest and graceful, I did not see, on the part of male or female, any movement inconsistent with the strictest modesty.

"Soon after eleven o'clock the closing dance was called for, and immediately after the whole space around the fire-light was cleared as by magic."

The bishop and his party spread their blankets and were soon asleep, content with the knowledge that they were probably the first white men to see the Green Corn Dance. Bishop Gray was certainly the first to describe it in writing.[15]

The next morning Bishop Gray had a brief interview with Old Doctor and was the first to inform him of the action of the Florida state legislature to set aside nearly a million acres of the Everglades for the Seminoles. The reservation included the land on which the Indians were then camping and thirty-six townships which reached the lower Gulf at Chuckaliskee, or Chokoloskee. The old chief seemed gratified, and was pleased to learn that Captain F. A.

15. *Bishop's Diary*, 1900, pp. 53-56.

Hendry, the Fort Myers legislator, was the sponsor of the bill.[16] This bill, however, was never implemented, and almost seventeen years passed before the state took appropriate action on the Seminole land problem.[17] Undaunted by this setback, the bishop continued throughout his episcopate to press the legislature to grant land to the Indians.

Since Bishop Gray's concern and sympathy for the Seminoles was steadfast and enduring, he was no doubt much criticized for pushing the Indian mission program when both white and black missions were in dire need of funds. Many of the clergy and laity felt that the returns of the Seminole harvest were so slight that they did not justify the time, labor, and financial resources that yearly were plowed into the Everglades project. The bishop, however, defended the Seminole mission eloquently and valiantly in the *Convocation Journal*:

"Strong as are the appeals which come to me from my white and black people, none move me quite so deeply as those from the Seminole Indians. Our great American Church has not been roused to more than a faint consideration of the members of this tribe, occupying as they do their own ground, and yet not daring to claim a foot of it any where; outcasts of society, but for all this, still remaining in feeling and in fact the full-blooded aristocrats of Florida. When I stand before them as the Church's representative, an overwhelming sense of obligation sweeps over me. What have I?— What have *we* to give to this defrauded people? May I beg for the Seminoles . . . a tribe deformed, exposed to every evil influence and yet for all this, struggling to hold itself proudly apart."[18]

In order to acquaint Episcopalians with the Indians and the work of the Church among them, Bishop Gray invited Chief Tom Tiger to visit him at the Bishopstead in Orlando. Chief Tom arrived with war paint, feathers, and blanket. The room assigned to him in the house seemed strange and confining and often the rest-

16. Ibid., p. 56.

17. Kathryn Abbey Hanna, *Florida: Land of Change* (Chapel Hill: University of North Carolina Press, 1941), p. 219; *Convocation Journal*, 1903, p. 44.

18. Leonard, p. 84.

less Indian would steal out in the silent hours of the night, don his blanket, and pace up and down the streets near the Bishopstead. When he tired he would sit under the great oak tree in front of the house. Unforunately, there was little communication between Indian and white.[19]

On another occasion, Billy Tigertail Tiger, son of Chief Tom Tiger, accepted an invitation to visit the bishop, with results that were even more colorful and equally useless. The young Indian arrived in the city wearing a calico shirt, moccasins, and a turban with a silver buckle. He brought his hostess a present from his mother, a beautiful squaw dress made of brightly colored calicoes trimmed with an abundance of ruffles and furbelows. Billy not only went to St. Luke's Church but attended a number of social functions as well. An Orlando pioneer recalled Billy's attendance at an ice cream social given for the benefit of St. Luke's at the house of a Mrs. Sperry. The young girls of the church were hawking ice cream and cake vigorously when Billy entered in full dress. He was warmly welcomed by his hostess and the two sat down on a sofa. One of the young ladies offered him refreshments, but he took only the ice cream, refusing the cake. He put a spoonful in his mouth and gave a hard bite. A look of amazement spread over his face. The young brave felt his mouth and found no ice cream there. Then he looked inside his shirt, and finding nothing there, stooped over to look under the sofa. In bewilderment, he felt his throat, but the lump of cream had vanished.

There were by this time visible smiles and audible laughter about him. Billy knew from tribal accounts that white people were not always to be trusted, so hurling the dish to the floor, he started for the door. Mr. Sperry tried to pacify the angry man by giving him an ornate matchbox that opened and shut with a loud click. The gift did placate the Indian, and after a while he consented to try another dish of ice cream. The results were the same as before. This time Billy could not be pacified. Flushed with anger he strode quickly to the door and into the street muttering "Holi-wagus,"

19. William R. O'Neal, *Memoirs of the Pioneer* (privately printed for the Orlando *Sentinel Star* by the Florida Press, Inc., 1932), p. 199.

which the Seminole authorities in Orlando interpreted to mean
"Hell!"

Later in the week, Chief Tom arrived in Orlando to join his son
at the Bishopstead. Bishop Gray took the two Indians to see their
first movie. When the old chief saw a runaway horse come tearing
across the screen, he started up with a sudden leap down the aisle
of the theater yelling, "Me ketch um, me ketch um." The audience
apparently felt the impromptu extra was worth more than the
whole picture.[20]

A story was told that a friend of Bishop Gray's asked one of the
Indian elders what the Seminoles thought of the bishop. The old
Seminole pondered, then replied, "Bishop he good man—preachy,
preachy—all time, Injun huntee, huntee all time; Bishop let Injun
lone—Injun let Bishop lone."[21] The Seminole's reaction to the
bishop was understandable. The story was probably true, in the
spirit if not in the letter. It did not make the Church's work among
the Indians sound too promising. This and similar contemporary
tales naturally brought the whole Seminole project under considerable criticism, but they never discouraged Bishop Gray. The old
prelate answered his critics in the same way he answered his vestry
when it disapproved of an unproductive Negro mission he founded
while he was a parish priest in Tennessee: "Gentlemen, my march-
ing orders from the great Captain are 'Preach the Gospel to every
creature.' It is my business to obey and leave the results with
God."[22]

As the years passed, the Indians became quite fond of the devoted
Dr. Godden. He was their physician, their storekeeper, and later
their clergyman. This dedicated layman began reading theology
under the bishop and was ordained to the diaconate in October,
1912. He returned to the Everglades to add pastoral duties to his
already heavy schedule.[23]

As civilization pushed farther south into the peninsula, the wild
game in the Everglades showed signs of becoming increasingly

20. Fries, p. 30.
21. Ibid., p. 79.
22. Gray, *Episcopal Address* (Southern Florida), 1908, p. 29.
23. *Convocation Journal*, 1913, pp. 80–81.

scarce. The bishop and Dr. Godden realized that the Church must teach the Indians to become self-supporting by agricultural pursuits. Soon the mission established a farm where the Seminoles could be taught better methods of raising both crops and livestock. The farm was never a success, however, because the Church lacked funds to hire a trained agricultural agent as teacher. But the project did interest the United States government in the plight of the Indians.[24]

Meanwhile Dr. Godden began to make some progress with the Seminoles. They came more often to the services at the chapel and dropped in at the store to hear him play the little organ or to see him show pictures from his projector. The ritual of the Eucharist, however, continued to baffle them. Dr. Godden received a severe shock at the apparent ineffectualness of his teaching methods when he discovered that some of his charges believed that Bishop Gray, with his long white beard, was the third member of the Trinity.[25] Nevertheless, a number of the nation received baptism, and occasionally Bishop Gray confirmed a smaller number on his visitations.

The Seminole endeavor suffered two serious setbacks during the eventful year of 1914. One was the retirement of the aging Bishop Gray in January; the other was the death of Dr. Godden in September. Bishop Gray's retirement had been anticipated for some time, but Dr. Godden's death was a complete surprise. On September 29, Dr. Godden's teamster and helper found him lying dead in his room. Although the cause of death was unknown, it was assumed that he had died of a heart attack, alone and untended. The teamster made a rude coffin from some of the store shelves, lined it with cloth, and took Dr. Godden's body in his cart some forty miles to the little church in Immokalee. A few friends gathered while the priest from St. Luke's, Fort Myers, read the burial office. The body was temporarily interred in the yard of Christ Church, but later some of Dr. Godden's friends in St. Petersburg obtained permission to move the body there, since the doctor

24. Parkhill, "Our Work Among the Seminoles," pp. 19–20; *Convocation Journal*, 1913, p. 37.

25. Leonard, p. 86.

had taken a prominent part in church affairs in that city before going to the Seminoles.[26]

Bishop Gray's newly instituted successor, the Rt. Rev. Cameron Mann, paid an appreciative tribute to the life and labor of William Godden: "A great man has fallen among us, a saint and a hero braver than those who die in the heat of earthly battlefields, for he stood faithfully at his far-off, lonely outpost of his Lord's army, not for a few hours, to be relieved by another sentry, but for weeks, months, years, enduring the awful isolation, the hardships, physical and mental, the discouragement of hope deferred, and inadequate means to the desired end, never wavering because the King of Kings had placed him there."[27]

After the death of Dr. Godden, the Very Rev. Lucien Spencer, Dean of St. Luke's Cathedral, Orlando, resigned his deanship to become the United States Commissioner to the Seminoles. Although Dean Spencer continued to function as a priest of the Church on Sundays, it was in his role as Indian Commissioner that he brought increased financial aid and more efficient management to the Seminole program. Under his leadership the agricultural program envisioned by Bishop Gray and Dr. Godden eventually became a reality. Spencer used Dania as his home base for Indian work in later years. He died there of a heart attack on April 21, 1930, after assisting a federal census-taker to enumerate the Seminole nation.[28]

26. *Palm Branch*, October 1914.
27. Ibid.
28. *Diocesan Journal*, 1930, p. 40; *Palm Branch*, May 1930.

VI

The Biscayne Area

WHEN WILLIAM CRANE GRAY ASSUMED HIS EPISCOPAL duties as Bishop of the Missionary Jurisdiction of Southern Florida in January 1893, there were no Anglican congregations between Lake Worth and Key West. The lower Atlantic coast of the peninsula, a vast stretch of some 225 miles, was thinly populated, difficult to reach, and of little economic promise. Nevertheless, the new bishop considered the area and its inhabitants worthy of the attention of the Church. Within two weeks of his arrival in Florida, Bishop Gray was in Key West consulting the rector of St. Paul's, the Rev. Gilbert Higgs, D.D., about the prospects of mission work in the Biscayne area. On April 29 he journeyed to the region to investigate its possibilities firsthand.[1]

The bishop was abetted by an energetic pioneer widow, Mrs. Julia D. Tuttle, formerly of Cleveland, Ohio, who, through inheritance and purchase owned a large portion of what is now downtown Miami.[2] Bishop Gray wrote appreciatively of her role as his trailblazer: "I became at once the guest of Mrs. Julia D. Tuttle at

1. Gray, *Episcopal Address* (Southern Florida), 1894, pp. 37–38, 47.
2. E. L. Pennington, *The Beginning of the Episcopal Church in the Miami Area* (Hartford, Connecticut: Church Missions Publishing Co., 1941), p. 1.

Miami, and certainly my thanks are due to her for the careful and painstaking way in which she had prepared for my visit, making it known far and wide, and arranging for the different services I was to hold, where to hold them, and placing her private launch at my disposal."[3]

Mrs. Tuttle had indeed prepared a busy schedule for her visitor. On April 30, the day after his arrival, Bishop Gray preached at the schoolhouse in Lemon City where he conducted a baptism, a confirmation, and a celebration of the Holy Communion. That night he journeyed thirteen miles down the bay to the settlement of Coconut Grove, where he read Evening Prayer and preached to an attentive congregation. The bishop was enthusiastic. "The prospect is certainly good for the Church in this whole region, provided the ground be occupied at once," he wrote. Bishop Gray proceeded to "occupy" the region, if only for a week. He revisited and preached among the people in Miami, Lemon City, and Coconut Grove, and prepared a small number for baptism and confirmation.[4] Before he left for Key West on May 8, the seeds of the Church's first congregation on the shores of Biscayne Bay were sown, and Bishop Gray was determined that they be kept well watered.

In November 1893, the bishop made his visitation to Bethesda-by-the-Sea on Lake Worth. While there he decided to return again to the Biscayne area to encourage the little band of frontier Churchmen. He arrived in a dilapidated stage from Lantana, after traveling along the rough boggy edge of the Everglades on "the most trying and expensive journey" he had undertaken in his entire jurisdiction. He was the only passenger on the stage, but even in this desolate country he was called upon to minister to an isolated family. The stage stopped a few miles from Lemon City at a small house which also served as a post office. When he stepped inside the bishop saw a number of children and inquired of their parents, "Have these children been baptized?" Both answered in the negative, but stated they were anxious to have the ceremony performed and wondered if the bishop would perform it immediately. As the driver was impatient to keep his schedule, the bishop promised to

3. Gray, *Episcopal Address* (Southern Florida), 1894, p. 46.
4. Ibid., pp. 46–47.

prevail on him to start early enough on his return trip to allow time for the bishop to baptize the younger members of the family. On his return, Bishop Gray found the children and the parents waiting in the post office. He secured two men to act as sponsors with the parents, put on his vestments, and baptized six youngsters.[5]

The bishop's second visit to the bay proved most rewarding. The lots were donated for the erection of a church in Lemon City and the bishop appointed a committee to raise subscriptions for the project. Two parties offered lots for a church in Coconut Grove also, but as the bishop was not satisfied with either location, he held out for a more desirable property. With Mrs. Tuttle's launch again at his disposal, Bishop Gray conducted services at Coconut Grove, at Lemon City, and in the Tuttle residence, which had formerly served as the officers' quarters of the Fort Dallas garrison during the period of Seminole unrest. It was obvious that the Biscayne area would develop rapidly as soon as the proposed extension of the Florida East Coast Railroad was completed, and both Bishop Gray and his hostess thought that a clergyman should be placed in the region as soon as enough money for his stipend was available. In the meantime, the Rev. Dr. Higgs of Key West, "Archdeacon of Monroe, Lee, and Dade to Lake Worth," would follow up the bishop's trips by occasional visits to minister to the scattered Churchmen of the area.[6]

On a visit in January 1894, Doctor Higgs was taken in tow by Mrs. Tuttle in Miami and by the formidable Miss Flora McFarlane, a London spinster who had settled in Coconut Grove in 1886. Miss McFarlane was described affectionately by a contemporary as "Coconut Grove's first school teacher and the first woman in Dade County to homestead, the first to plan and found a club, the Housekeeper's Club." She was also the first to work for the Episcopal Church.[7] She made sure that Doctor Higgs worked as hard as she during his visit to Coconut Grove. The doctor's report of his activi-

5. Ibid., pp. 64–65.
6. Pennington, *The Beginning of the Episcopal Church in the Miami Area*, pp. 2–3.
7. Helen Muir, *An Outline History; St. Stephen's Episcopal Church, Coconut Grove, Florida* (Miami: n.p., 1959), p. 1.

ties speaks eloquently of Miss McFarlane's zeal: "On Jan. 29, in company with Miss Flora McFarlane, a most energetic and faithful communicant, I made four visits in the morning. In the afternoon I made eleven visits. Was called out twice that night to read prayers to a sick woman." His labors in Miami with Mrs. Tuttle were equally arduous. In one day he made fourteen calls in addition to making a trip to Lemon City. After a week of such heavy but satisfying schedules, the exhausted cleric left Miami for Key West, only to be "detained all day" on the rocks offshore where his sloop went aground at low tide. Three days later, he again took up his duties in St. Paul's Parish.[8]

Both Doctor Higgs and Bishop Gray visited the Biscayne area in 1895. The bishop's report of his journey not only describes his labors but also gives an indication of how uncertain travel was during the pioneer era. He took a sailing vessel from Key West to Biscayne Bay on February 6 at 9:00 A.M.: "The wind was dead ahead, and the sea very rough. At night we had by tacking gone 60 miles of distance, to make 20 miles towards our destination." The bishop did not reach Miami until noon, February 8.[9]

Bishop Gray was compelled to make similarly time-consuming journeys to the bay area until the Florida East Coast Railroad was extended to Miami from West Palm Beach in 1896. The advent of the railroad did as much as the great freezes of the previous year to throw the shore of Biscayne Bay into a frenzy of population growth and economic development. Ruined citrus growers from central Florida rushed to the area to experiment with tropical fruits, and hundreds of speculators and settlers hurried southward to share in the profits that came in the wake of the railroad boom. Before Flagler let the contract for the railroad extension in the summer of 1895 there were but three homes in what is Miami proper today: "the Tuttle house [at Fort Dallas] and the Brickell home, on the point south of the Miami River, and F. S. Morse's house, just south of the Brickell home. . . . There was very little cleared land—everything a perfect wilderness outside the little clearing around the

8. *Convocation Journal*, 1895, p. 24.
9. *Bishop's Diary*, 1896, pp. 57-58.

homes."[10] Within a year Mrs. Tuttle had opened up Avenue D, now Miami Avenue, which ran from the Miami River north to 14th Street, and several shacks, pool halls, and tents began to spring up along its sides. Mrs. Tuttle also began the construction of the Miami Hotel located slightly east of Avenue D, while the Flagler interests began to erect the palatial Royal Palm Hotel, which had its own railroad spur to accommodate its future guests.[11]

John Sewell, sent by Henry Flagler to represent his interests in Miami and to lay out the town, gives a delightful account of one of the bishop's early visits to Miami. Not long after Sewell arrived in town he received a note from Miss Fannie Tuttle, daughter of the enterprising Julia, which showed that the daughter was as interested in the Church as the mother: "She wanted me to go with her in her launch to Lemon City to hear some Episcopal bishop preach and she was going to bring the bishop back with her and he would preach in the Congregational tent that afternoon. She stated in the note that, if I could not go, she would like to borrow my light rowboat, called the *May*, as she feared the water was so low in the bay that her launch could not get to the dock at Lemon City. I wrote her in reply I was sorry that I could not go, but she was welcome to the *May*, and that I would hear the bishop that afternoon in the tent. About 3:30 that afternoon I strolled over to the tent. I found the bishop sitting on the preacher's stand, Mrs. Plass was at the organ, and Miss Tuttle and the bishop's secretary were sitting in the choir seats—only the four in the tent. The bishop rose and said that 'we have a preacher, an organist and a choir, and one for a congregation and that we had better begin the service.' I rose and asked him if he was going to preach and he answered in the affirmative. I told him just to wait a few minutes and I would get him a congregation, for there was no use of his wasting a sermon on me. He said that he was afraid to let me go for fear I would not come back. Miss Tuttle assured him that I would come back and he agreed to wait.

"First thing that I did was to go over to Avenue D where there

10. John Sewell, *Memoirs and History of Miami, Florida* (Miami: Franklin Press, Inc., 1933), p. 6.

11. Ibid., pp. 10–11.

was a pool room with a crowd of men playing pool. I told the men that ran the pool room to close up the pool room right then and for the whole bunch to go across the street to the gospel tent, as there was a preacher over there who wanted to preach and had no congregation and that I was not going to have a preacher come to Miami and go away and say that he could not get a congregation to preach to. So they closed the pool room and the men began to file out and go over to the tent. I went to the cold drink stands and gave them the same spiel. So they closed up shop and went to church. Then I went to our quarters in the Miami Hotel, where a great many of us were kind of camping then, and went up and down the halls giving the same spiel. . . . Some of the men that were asleep on their cots didn't take to the idea of getting up and going to church. Those of that class I turned their cots over and spilled them out on the floor and the shock waked them enough to know that I meant business. So they quietly dressed themselves and went to church. . . . Altogether I sent between twenty-five and forty out of the hotel. Then I went around to the tents and shacks looking for a congregation, and sent all that I found to the tent."

When Mr. Sewell returned to the tent he found Bishop Gray enthusiastically leading his somewhat lethargic but large congregation in song and preparing to preach to them. The response from the more established members of the community must have been heartening, for soon after his visit the bishop decided to place a priest in the Biscayne area.[12]

The Biscayne assignment went to the Rev. Henry Dunlop, a presbyter who had spent his ministry in the Diocese of Georgia. The Rev. Mr. Dunlop arrived in June 1896 to begin work in Miami and the outlying settlements. His Miami ministry, however, was of short duration, for he died at his post December 5, 1896, of an unspecified illness. The building of the first Episcopal church in Miami, named in honor of the Blessed Trinity, was begun during Mr. Dunlop's tenure, on land given by Mrs. Julia Tuttle.[13]

Into the void caused by the untimely death of Miami's first priest moved three members of the Order of the Holy Cross, led by the

12. Ibid., pp. 112–15.

13. *Convocation Journal*, 1897, p. 12: *Bishop's Diary*, 1897, p. 69.

quiet but determined Father Superior of the order, the Rev. James Otis Sargent Huntington. This Boston-born Harvardian and his colleagues, who agreed to labor for six months in the area until a parochial clergyman could be found to replace them, brought new life and vitality to the mission field. Taking up residence in a houseboat docked five minutes from the unfinished church, they traveled to the nearby settlements by sail, by buggy, by bicycle, and on foot. From an article written by Father Huntington in *The Holy Cross Magazine*, November 1897, it is evident that he loved both the challenge and the location of his new assignment, and that he appreciated the enormous effect that his labors might have on the booming area. He described Miami as a town of "recent growth. ... Two years ago there were only two houses here; now there are about four thousand people and smaller settlements up and down the coast. The town is well laid out, the main street, really a noble avenue. There is a great hotel, the Royal Palm, with accommodations for nearly a thousand guests." Trinity Church was "a plain little wooden structure and needs almost everything in the way of appointment and adornment. Even the windows are not in yet but that is of slight deficiency in this climate. ... There is a splendid field for the church here, the people seem very ready to listen and learn. We have begun to visit them, and hope to build up many souls into the mystical Body of our Blessed Lord. There are a good many negroes from the West Indies and the Bahamas, brought up in the English Church ... and these, too, we hope to reach."[14]

The monks made a concerted effort to reach the Bahamian Negroes, and the success of their efforts was remarkable. In the December issue of the order's magazine, Father Huntington wrote: "These Bahamians were rejoiced to have us come to them; they have had no opportunity of attending Church or making their Communions since they came. Most of them are young men and women; there are a few families. They are intelligent and thoroughly at home in the Church." The order rented a hall in the Negro settlement, which men of the congregation whitewashed. Benches were added later. The fathers secured funds for a wooden

14. Pennington, *The Beginning of the Episcopal Church in the Miami Area,* p. 11.

altar for the hall, and soon there were seventy to eighty regular worshippers. The new congregation placed itself under the patronage of St. Agnes and continued to grow.[15] When Bishop Gray made his next visitation to the Miami area, he confirmed a class of twenty-four candidates from the enthusiastic congregation,[16] a remarkable yield for a labor of such short duration. A year later, the church was moved to a new location on lots which were to be deeded to the mission by Henry M. Flagler "when the church is erected."[17] By 1901 the new church was completed, and the Rev. G. I. Smith, a Negro clergyman, was placed in charge. This energetic cleric not only strengthened the fabric of his own congregation, but very quickly founded another mission for Negroes in Coconut Grove. His efforts there eventually led to the organization of Christ Church.[18]

Meanwhile Trinity Church continued to grow. By 1900 there were 107 baptized members in the congregation; five years later the number had grown to 258.[19] In January 1905, Trinity became the first mission to be admitted by the Convocation as a self-supporting parish since the organization of the Missionary Jurisdiction in 1893.[20] The original frame structure naturally was enlarged several times as Trinity's congregation grew, but by 1912 the community and the parish had grown so much and the number of winter visitors had so increased that the old church had to be torn down. The congregation began to erect a larger concrete building, the first ecclesiastical edifice of masonry construction in the city. The church was finally finished in 1916, but even at its completion there were indications that the new structure would soon be too small.[21]

At the turn of the century, the scattered but unorganized mission congregations around Miami, which had been begun by Bishop Gray in the early 1890s and to which Father Huntington and the

15. Ibid., p. 13.

16. *Bishop's Diary*, 1899, p. 55.

17. Ibid., 1900, p. 41.

18. Pennington, *The Beginning of the Episcopal Church in the Miami Area*, p. 21.

19. *Convocation Journals*, 1901 and 1905, *Parochial Abstracts*.

20. Ibid., 1905, p. 4.

21. Irving Hiller, "Trinity Church, Miami, Florida" (appended to Vestry Notes, Trinity Church, Miami).

Holy Cross fathers had ministered, were crying for attention and care. The rector of Trinity Church could no longer meet the physical demands of ministering to them while caring for his own flock. A mission priest was desperately needed. Bishop Gray called the Rev. Dwight Frederic Cameron to this post in 1903. The Swiss-born cleric, educated at Cornell University and The University of the South, assumed his duties after three years of mission work and study in the Diocese of Tennessee.[22] He held regular services in the schools and meeting houses of Coconut Grove, Cutler, Little River, and Buena Vista, and occasional services in Dania. Only Little River possessed a church building, a tiny frame structure which eventually took the patronage of St. Andrew. It was blown off its foundations during the hurricane of 1904 and rebuilt at great sacrifice to the small congregation.[23] In 1905 the Rev. Mr. Cameron resigned his post to become priest-in-charge of Holy Trinity Mission in West Palm Beach. Early in 1906, the Rev. George Bernard Clarke, formerly of the Diocese of Vermont, took charge of the Miami mission field.[24]

In spite of bad health, Clarke proved himself to be an energetic and resourceful missionary. He was entirely dedicated to his labors and was successful in obtaining funds from interested friends in the North for his struggling missions. During Clarke's ministry in the Biscayne area a Lutheran donated a lot for an Episcopal mission in Dania, and after several years enough money was on hand to erect St. John's Church. The Rev. Mr. Clarke also added to his circuit the new communities of Hallandale and Fort Lauderdale in the north, and Redland, Naranja, and Homestead in the south. He continued as well to hold services for the older mission congregations at Coconut Grove, Little River, and Buena Vista.[25]

Not long after his arrival in his new field, Mr. Clarke began to

22. *Stowe's Clerical Directory of the American Church*, 1917 (Minneapolis: edited and published by the Rev. Andrew David Stowe, 1917), p. 68. This publication is cited hereafter as *Stowe*, with date.

23. Hiller.

24. *Convocation Journal*, 1907, p. 3.

25. Pennington, *The Beginning of the Episcopal Church in the Miami Area*, p. 27.

solicit funds for the erection of a church in Buena Vista, where he resided. Largely through the help of wealthy Northern friends, including members of the Vanderbilt, Cluett, and Phillips families, he was able to purchase a lot and begin a place of worship. While the church was being built this dedicated mission priest, oblivious to the comforts of life, lived in the vestry room of the building and did his cooking on an open fire outdoors. Mrs. Gertrude Westgaard Reid, an original member of the mission, humorously recalled, "He had a standing invitation to eat with us in rainy weather." After a year of intermittent labor, the church was complete enough in April 1907 for its first service to be held. The congregation named the building The Church of the Holy Cross in honor of Father James Huntington, the unwavering Superior of the Order of the Holy Cross, who gave the Church people of Buena Vista their first regular Anglican services. Eventually, but not by design, Holy Cross Church superseded St. Andrew's mission in nearby Little River. After several years of struggle and sacrifice, the mission was regretfully abandoned, and some of its members attached themselves to the Buena Vista church.[26]

There were new signs of vitality among the Episcopal settlers in Coconut Grove. In April 1909, with the encouragement of the Rev. Mr. Clarke, the indomitable Miss Flora McFarlane organized the Episcopal ladies of the Grove into a guild for the purpose of raising money to build a church. The enthusiasm of the women attracted the attention of Bishop Gray and in 1910 he formally organized a mission under the patronage of St. Stephen. The Rev. Charles Percival Jackson, a physician who had later entered the ministry, was assigned as first priest-in-charge of St. Stephen's. With great vigor Dr. Jackson pressed for the building of a church. In the meantime, however, services were held in the Housekeeper's Club. The women spared no energies in raising money for the new building. They made pot holders, dressed dolls, baked pies, cakes, and cookies, and held benefit entertainments at the residences of winter visitors. On the Feast of St. Barnabas, June 11, 1912, the cornerstone of the building, Spanish mission in design, was laid in

26. Ibid., pp. 26–28.

the presence of a happy priest and congregation. It was ready for use the following Christmas. The Miami *Metropolis* described the church on that occasion: "The pretty little building was transformed into a bower of flowers and Yuletide greens. Christmas music and the beautiful service that marks the day in the Episcopal Church was greatly enjoyed by the worshippers. On the following evening a Christmas tree for the children made another happy occasion."[27] St. Stephen's was solemnly consecrated by Bishop Gray on Sexagesima Sunday, January 26, 1912. Six years later it became a parish.[28]

The progress of the Church in Coconut Grove was evidenced also in the activities of the Negro congregation. The old frame building of Christ Church was gradually being replaced by a stone structure, and the student body of the parochial institute, St. Alban's School, continued to grow.[29]

The advance of the Church in Coconut Grove would have rejoiced the heart of the energetic Mr. Clarke, but he was not present to see these early dreams fulfilled. He died in July 1912, having built Holy Cross Church, the Dania mission which survives in St. John's Church, Hollywood, and the now dormant church in Redland. The small church at Naranja was also begun under his direction, although it was not completed until after his death. Clarke indeed "did good work" and the Church in the Miami area owes him an immense debt.[30]

The advent of the Florida East Coast Railroad brought the town of West Palm Beach into being on the western shores of Lake Worth, and with it a new Episcopal mission. Holy Trinity Church, like St. Stephen's, Coconut Grove, began through the activities of a women's guild. The guild in West Palm Beach was organized in 1896. Prior to that year occasional services were held in the town by the Rev. Joseph Mulford, priest-in-charge of Bethesda-by-the-Sea, but usually Episcopalians had to row over to Palm Beach for Sunday services. In 1897 the first regular Church services were

27. Muir, p. 2.
28. *Bishop's Diary*, 1913, p. 94; *Convocation Journal*, 1919, p. 15.
29. *Convocation Journal*, 1913, p. 49.
30. Ibid.

held in an old building used as a library. They were conducted by an English-born lay reader, Louis Fitz-James Hindry, who served as principal of the local school. Through his efforts, a small frame church was erected in 1900 on two lots, one of which was donated by Henry M. Flagler. The following year, Bishop Gray sent the Rev. J. J. Vaulx, formerly of the Diocese of North Carolina, to take charge of the mission. In February 1903, a rectory was built on the east church lot, and the following year the church was enlarged by the addition of a chancel and a vestry room.[31] The enlargement was necessary because of the splendid growth of the mission: from 1900 to 1905 the congregation grew from seventeen communicants to forty, and during the winter season the number of worshippers was augmented by numerous visitors.[32] When Holy Trinity was admitted as a parish in the Convocation of 1908, it boasted fifty-four communicants and a growing Sunday school.[33]

The Negro population of the area grew along with the white. It was increased by a large immigration of Bahamians and Jamaicans who came to booming southern Florida to work in construction projects and as domestics. Since many of these new arrivals had been raised in the English Church, it was imperative that they be provided with places of worship. In 1911, Bishop Gray assigned the Rev. J. C. G. Wood to the Lake Worth area, and two new Negro congregations were organized: St. Patrick's in West Palm Beach and St. Matthew's in Delray.[34] By 1914 Negro congregations had been organized in Boynton and Fort Lauderdale, and Mr. Wood had started parochial primary schools in both West Palm Beach and Delray. It appears from Bishop Gray's report that the new schools were aided through monthly donations from his discretionary fund.[35] Two new white congregations were also organized in 1914: St. Paul's, Delray, and All Saints', Fort Lauderdale.[36]

31. J. J. Vaulx, "A History of Holy Trinity Church" (in the Parish Register, Holy Trinity Church, West Palm Beach).

32. *Convocation Journal*, 1901 and 1906, *Parochial Abstracts*.

33. Ibid., 1909.

34. *Convocation Journal*, 1912, p. 19.

35. William Crane Gray, "Status of Work Among Negroes" (attached to *Convocation Journal*, 1914).

36. *Convocation Journal*, 1914, p. 7; also, *Parochial Abstracts*.

Before Bishop Gray assumed his episcopal duties in 1893 there was only one Episcopal church in that long stretch of land now constituting Palm Beach, Broward, and Dade counties. When the bishop resigned his duties in 1914 there were four parishes and twelve missions within the area. The Church had made a valiant if not always successful attempt to keep pace with the rapid development and astounding growth on the southeast coast.

VII

The Gray Episcopate

WILLIAM CRANE GRAY UNDOUBTEDLY BEGAN HIS EPISCO-pate with many hopes and plans for the Missionary Jurisdiction of Southern Florida. Foremost in his mind, perhaps, was the conversion of the Seminole remnant, but there were other needs which occupied his thoughts as well. One was the establishment of a Church hospital and home for the aged; another was the founding of a pair of diocesan schools for boys and girls; and the third was the creation of a proper episcopal seat, a cathedral church, which was to be the center of worship and ecclesiastical government in the Missionary Jurisdiction of Southern Florida. During the twenty years of his episcopate, Bishop Gray was to see the fruition of each of his plans, to a greater or lesser extent.

Perhaps the first was the most ambitious and most charitable of the bishop's projects. During the Convocation of 1894 in Key West, a resolution was presented by the Rev. Charles M. Gray, brother of the bishop, "That the Bishop be requested to appoint a permanent Committee in reference to the establishment of a Church Hospital, with full power to act in consultation with the Bishop." On the passage of the resolution, Bishop Gray obligingly appointed his three archdeacons, the Ven. John H. Weddell, the Ven. Gilbert Higgs, D.D., and the Ven. Benjamin F. Brown, and two laymen,

Howard W. Greetham and Leslie Pell-Clarke, to serve on the committee.[1] Plans for starting a church hospital were given to the Convocation of 1895 with the recommendation that the property secured
by Howard W. Greetham in Orlando, a gift of Leslie Pell-Clarke,
be used for the purpose, and that the institution be incorporated.
The Convocation gave its approval, and the institution was chartered under the name of "The Church Home and Hospital" on
April 24, 1895. The incorporators, who represented a wide geographic distribution, were Bishop Gray, the Rev. John J. Andrew
of St. Luke's, Orlando, the Ven. Benjamin F. Brown of St. Gabriel's,
Titusville, the Ven. John H. Weddell of Trinity, Thonotosassa, William C. Comstock of Winter Park, the Hon. Louis C. Massey and
Howard W. Greetham of Orlando, Frederic H. Rand of Longwood,
and Dudley G. Cary-Elwes of Conway. The bishop was named
president of the corporation and Mr. Greetham secretary and treasurer.[2] The incorporators, or trustees, adopted a typically Victorian
seal engraved with "Good Samaritan" in the center and the admonition "Thou shalt love thy neighbor as thyself" emblazoned around
its edges.[3] The Church Home and Hospital, the only charitable
institution of its kind in the southern portion of the state, bravely
opened its doors at Orlando the year of the Great Freeze.

The hospital began in two small cottages with meagre equipment
and a tiny operational budget. Individual subscriptions from all
over the jurisdiction totaled a mere $609.04, to which was added
a $250 donation from Bishop Gray. Since the amount received from
each sick boarder was only fifty cents per day (if he could pay at
all), a general appeal had to be made to the Church people of South
Florida to keep the hospital open. The bishop appointed mid-Lent
Sunday as "Hospital Sunday," a day on which the parishes and
missions of the jurisdiction were asked to donate their loose collections to the struggling hospital. The response, considering the recent
calamity of the Great Freeze, was not ungenerous: $141.33 was
sent to the treasurer from the appeal.[4] This additional amount did

1. *Convocation Journal*, 1894, p. 32.
2. Ibid., 1896, pp. 19–20.
3. *Bishop's Diary*, 1896, pp. 66–67.
4. *Convocation Journal*, 1896, pp. 19–20.

not meet the expenses of the institution, however, and the applications of new patients had to be rejected during the closing months of 1895. It was chiefly the determination of the bishop and the efforts of the physicians of Orlando that kept the hospital in operation its first year despite the lack of funds.

The following year, 1896, saw a seventy-five per cent increase in the number of patients in the hospital and a proportionate increase in gifts. Three more lots were added to the hospital property by purchase. The board of trustees considered the advisability of building a "Home for Consumptives" on the new lots, and a committee was appointed to canvass the cities of New York, Boston, Philadelphia, Baltimore, and Washington in an effort to secure $20,000, the sum deemed necessary for embarking on the venture. The committee's success, however, was small, as the country was still in the depths of the depression caused by the panic of 1893. Only $470.00 was raised by their efforts, but the trustees felt that a wider interest had been created on behalf of the work of the hospital.[5] Since sufficient funds were never subscribed for a Consumptives' Home, consumptive patients were kept in a special ward built for that purpose with the funds raised in the Northern cities.

By 1899 the number of permanent patients in the hospital rose to twenty-eight and the healthy but elderly inmates in the home numbered four. Another cottage had to be added to the plant and the nursing staff had to be increased. The expenses of the hospital increased also despite the fact that some of the patients now paid for room, board, and care.[6] The number of charity cases, however, always exceeded the number of paying patients.

Soon the Church Home and Hospital became a South Florida institution. Since it was the only hospital in the jurisdiction for several years, it drew to it patients from various cities and from every walk of life. Gradually the simple cottages were replaced by more comfortable buildings, and by 1905 a considerable medical plant had evolved.[7] Miss Corinne Robinson, a devoted Churchworker and hospital enthusiast, described the institution in its hey-

5. Ibid., 1897, pp. 40–41.
6. Ibid., 1899, pp. 15–17.
7. *Palm Branch*, November 1903, August 1905.

day: "The main hospital building had its operating room, its wards and private rooms, while other buildings included a home for elderly women, a nurses' home, a building for colored patients, separate laundry, dining room and kitchen, a chapel and the chaplain's cottage." The buildings were connected by covered walks. According to Miss Robinson, the Very Rev. L. A. Spencer, while Dean of St. Luke's Cathedral, greatly aided the development of the hospital "through giving unstintedly of his talent and personal labor in designing these buildings and in personally superintending their erection." The hospital had its own clergyman. For many years the spiritual welfare of the patients was under the care of the attentive chaplain, the Rev. Alfred A. Rickert, whose "saintly character and devoted ministrations" were "of untold blessings to patients and workers."[8]

Since no distinction was made on the basis of race or creed in considering the application of patients, the institution aroused the interest of Churchmen and non-Churchmen alike. Newspapers from time to time made elaborate appeals to South Floridians for the benefit of the institution. An undated editorial in the *Lakeland Sun* appealed to its readers to support the drive for the construction of the central building. The editorial showed the catholicity of the hospital's ministry: "The Church Home and Hospital is under the patronage of the Episcopal Church, but knows no sect or creed. Its humanity is as broad and deep as the world; its sweet and tender charity and sympathy is extended to saint and sinner alike until it envelopes all mankind. This institution," the editor opined, "deserves to grow and grow,"[9] and for several years, with the help of rich and poor, Churchmen and non-Churchmen, it did.

One of the most diversified sources of support for the hospital was the "Daily Bread Fund," which received gifts of every description from all over the state and nation. The variety of these gifts was great, as a glance at the *Palm Branch* for the years 1901–3 demonstrates. Money, canned goods, vegetables, fruit, candy, baked goods, and linen were the usual donations, but on one occasion a

8. Corinne Robinson, "The Church Home and Hospital," manuscript, Diocesan Library, Winter Park, pp. 2–3.
9. See Leonard, p. 90.

milk cow was loaned for several months. A cage of chickens was given at another time, and one Christmas turkeys were bestowed. One benefactor sent a gramophone and records all the way from Philadelphia for the use of the patients, and another patron on Sanibel Island sent a crate of tomatoes every month to the kitchen. Subscriptions, however, were the largest and most lucrative source of revenue, and these came from well-established Churchmen in the jurisdiction and from philanthropic winter visitors. The more prosperous English settlers who survived the freezes and had additional income from British investments were particularly generous. Cadman of Narcoossee, Arnold and Cary-Elwes of Conway, Lord and Haden of Orlando, and Stapylton, Budd, and Bosanquet of Fruitland Park were bulwarks to the frail financial structure of the institution.

The variety of the hospital donors was exceeded only by the diversity of the patients themselves. A typical admissions list in the fall of 1908 included a clergyman from South Carolina "stricken with paralysis," a crippled child, a cadet from West Point with a leg injury which later resulted in amputation, a stranger hurt at the Orlando racecourse, and an "army captain with advanced heart disease, complicated with asthma."[10] There were many indigent English patients and frequent Negro admissions as well.

Treatment at the hospital was not always successful, and the hospital reports in the *Convocation Journals* frequently carried death notices. In September 1905, the journal noted that, "for nearly a week the daily attendance of a priest was required for the dying. There are three deaths to record, two of whom were ladies who were almost at death's door when they were brought to the hospital. The third was the blessed release of Capt. J. E. Stratford, retired officer of the English army, who has for the past two years drawn out a living death of great suffering. He was buried from the Cathedral on the afternoon of Sept. 6, the Bishop officiating." The late Capt. Stratford had acquired a devoted friend during his long confinement. As his body lay in the hospital chapel, "it was touching to see the single little bunch of simple wild flowers, placed upon

10. *Palm Branch*, April 1908.

the coffin by the loving hands of the little cripple girl who is an inmate of the Hospital."[11]

In the later years of Bishop Gray's episcopate, increasing difficulties confronted the hospital authorities. The welcome expansion of the building and grounds brought added institutional expenses which were always difficult to meet, especially since the number of paying patients had decreased. With the rapid growth of Orlando private sanitoriums were erected which attracted the patients who could pay for services, leaving mostly charity cases to be cared for by the Church Home and Hospital.[12]

A year after Bishop Gray's retirement, the trustees of the Church Home and Hospital decided to change the name of the institution to St. Luke's Hospital.[13] The new name was chosen to signify the beginning of a new regime. The former title was found to be somewhat misleading and consequently financially damaging, since most people considered the "Church Home and Hospital" a place for charity cases only. The trustees hoped that the new title would attract patients who could pay their expenses and thereby take some of the financial burden of charity cases off the shoulders of the overtaxed institution.[14]

The reorganization of the hospital did not solve its fiscal difficulties, however, and the work of the institution progressed under constant monetary strain until the new bishop, the Rt. Rev. Cameron Mann, was forced to close its doors for lack of funds in 1916. The hospital, between 1910 and 1916, had been sinking deeper and deeper into debt, and Bishop Mann did not see how the frail financial structure of the jurisdiction could continue its support. The bishop and the trustees expressed the hope that St. Luke's Hospital would resume operations as soon as a sufficient endowment could be raised, but the hope was never entirely fulfilled.[15] The church-sponsored hospital that opened in DeLand several years later proved an ephemeral affair. Despite its financial frailty during the twenty-

11. Ibid., October 1905.
12. Ibid.
13. *Convocation Journal*, 1916, p. 19.
14. *Palm Branch*, May 1915.
15. *Convocation Journal*, 1916, p. 19.

one years of its existence, the Church Home and Hospital provided the central Florida area with a much-needed social service at a time when state relief programs were unknown. It was the only institution in the Orlando area where the destitute sick could obtain Christian care and medical attention.[16]

Bishop Gray's second objective—the establishment of two separate diocesan schools for girls and boys—was not realized until the Church Home and Hospital had been in operation for some five years. Both schools were opened in 1900 after substantial plots of real estate had been given to the bishop for diocesan use.

The benevolent Leslie Pell-Clarke of Cooperstown, New York, and Orlando, Florida, deeded the house and grounds of his winter residence to the Jurisdiction of Southern Florida for use as an episcopal residence. Bishop Gray and his family quickly moved into the commodious Victorian house, located on the site of the present Orange County Courthouse, and the bishop began to formulate plans for turning the old Bishopstead into a diocesan school for girls. The plans were well laid, for the first school term began in October with Miss Barbara Mason, formerly of the Castle School of Tarrytown, New York, as headmistress. There were eighteen girls enrolled, and, of that number, five were boarding students. In tribute to the benefactor whose gift of his winter home had made the school possible, Bishop Gray named the new institution "Pell-Clarke Hall."[17] Mr. Pell-Clarke's additional gift of five hundred dollars on opening day was an encouraging sign of his interest in the school.[18] Later, as the school expanded to include other buildings, its name was changed to the "Cathedral School for Girls," while the name "Pell-Clarke Hall" was retained for the original hall.

The school was described in the *Palm Branch* as a "pleasant home, surrounded by large grounds, against the background of an orange grove, and overlooking Lake Eola" on the outskirts of Orlando. Its faculty was drawn from Groton, Bryn Mawr, Wellesley, and the Royal University of Dublin, and promised to give the stu-

16. "The Church Home and Hospital," *Orange County Historical Quarterly* (March 1967), p. 4.

17. *Convocation Journal*, 1901, pp. 49, 60, 63.

18. *Palm Branch*, November 1900.

dents through Christian training, as well as to maintain the highest intellectual and social standards. The diocesan paper enthusiastically supported the new institution: "How well it would be for Florida mothers to send their daughters here, before sending them off to college in distant states. Here they are so near as to be easily reached in case of sickness, and it is equally easy for them to get home for holidays. In the two years of the school's life its boarders have been exceptionally healthy, the delicate girls improving visibly." The school year extended from October 1 to June 1. Charges for board and tuition including French and Latin were two hundred dollars. Music, Spanish, and German were extra.[19]

Although the school was in constant financial difficulty, it grew steadily in enrollment, faculty, and facilities. The majority of the pupils were invariably day students, but the boarding contingent, drawn mainly from Florida towns and winter visitors, made up from a quarter to a third of the enrollment. To take care of the increase in numbers, "Bishop Gray Hall" was built in 1905. The new building was a gift of George B. Cluett, a winter resident of Palm Beach, who stipulated that it be named for the bishop. The following year, Mr. Cluett united with other friends of the school to erect "Parkhill Hall," named for Harriet Randolph Parkhill, a founder of the Women's Auxiliary, the *Palm Branch,* and the Cathedral School. Miss Parkhill, who took orders as a deaconess, assumed the principalship several years after the school's founding and gave years of dedicated service to the institution during its formative stage.[20]

In 1907, Bishop Gray appointed as Rector of the Cathedral School the Rev. J. J. Bowker, an alumnus of St. Augustine's College, Canterbury, England. Under Mr. Bowker's direction the school continued to grow.[21] In 1909, he reported: "We have added new departments such as Scientific Physical Culture, provided additional rooms, enlarged the faculty, inserted steam heat and arranged the entire educational course on an elective basis with teachers of much experience in charge of each branch of study. Today we open the

19. Ibid., August 1902.
20. Corinne Robinson, "The Cathedral School—A Diocesan Institution," manuscript, Diocesan Library, Winter Park, p. 1.
21. *Palm Branch,* July 1907.

second part of the second year under my supervision with nineteen in the boarding department and twenty-six in the day school—a total of forty-five."[22]

A class building was given in 1910 at a cost of $10,000 by that steadfast patron of the school, George B. Cluett. After his death, Bishop Gray named the building "Cluett Hall" in his honor. The Cluett family continued to take an interest in the institution. In 1911, a gift of $1,000 was made by the widow and daughter to the meagre endowment of the expanding school.[23] Notable improvements were made in the older buildings from time to time through the personal appeals of Bishop Gray and his successor, the Rt. Rev. Cameron Mann. An additional lot and house were added to the grounds some years later when the O'Neal residence was purchased.[24]

By the eve of World War I, the Cathedral School had grown to ninety-two students. There was never a design to expand the institution into a female college. It was simply a school for girls and "young ladies," beginning with the primary department for small children and continuing through the "intermediate and academic" grades to the twelfth year. Its aims were to prepare the girls for college and to give a broad general education to those who did not intend to take a college degree. The fees were never very high, but through constant appeals to interested friends Bishop Gray was able to keep the school self-supporting during the closing years of his episcopate.[25]

Bishop Gray's plans for a boys' boarding and day school also materialized in 1900. The male institution, known as the Southern Florida School for Boys, opened its doors October 1 in Sanford at the residence of the Rev. William H. Bates. This project was decidedly more modest than its female counterpart in Orlando. There were but six students, none of whom were boarders, "the boys coming on wheels from Sanford and its vicinity," and there was but one classroom, and one master. It was hoped that "Onoro," a larger

22. *Convocation Journal*, 1909, p. 28.
23. Ibid., 1911, p. 20.
24. Robinson, "The Cathedral School," p. 1.
25. *Convocation Journal*, 1914, p. 22.

house outside the town , might be procured to accommodate a greater number of boys,[26] but for the first two years the school was operated at the Bates home. By the opening of the 1902 term, the school had been moved to a site outside Sanford "situated in the pine woods among the beautiful lakes of clear living water." The name of the school was changed with its location from the "Southern Florida School for Boys" to the "Bishop Whipple School for Boys" in memory of the Rt. Rev. Henry B. Whipple, Bishop of Minnesota, for many years a winter resident of nearby Maitland. The master, the Rev. Mr. Bates, who had been both a pupil and a teacher at St. Paul's School in Concord, New Hampshire, hoped to draw boys from the North as well as from Florida. The *Palm Branch* declared that "parents may entrust their boys to him with perfect confidence that they will be well cared for physically and mentally and spiritually, while being trained in true manliness and prepared for college or for business pursuits."[27]

The boys' school, however, did not grow as quickly as its sister institution on the shores of Lake Eola. In the first place, its location in the smaller and poorer town of Sanford prevented the school from drawing an adequate number of day students to support an expanding curriculum; in the second, the school did not enjoy the patronage of the Cluetts in Palm Beach or the contributions of the English communities in the state who insisted that the Cathedral School be maintained for the education of their daughters. (Their sons were usually sent to England or to established American boarding schools.) In the seventh year of its operation the Bishop Whipple School for Boys burned to the ground, and the following fall the school was unable to resume operation for lack of funds. Efforts by Bishop Gray and the headmaster to procure funds evidently failed, as no further mention of the institution or its headmaster occurs in the publications of the missionary jurisdiction after 1908.[28] No attempt to establish another boarding school for boys was made after the disastrous fire of 1907, and for years the Cathedral School for

26. *Palm Branch*, November 1900.
27. Ibid., August 1902.
28. *Bishop's Diary*, 1908, p. 69.

Girls was the only Episcopal institution in the state which maintained a boarding division.

Bishop Gray exhibited a profound concern not only for the Seminole mission and for charitable and educational projects, but also for the work of the Church among the Negroes. When the Missionary Jurisdiction of Southern Florida was created in 1892, there were but three Negro congregations in the entire area: St. Peter's, a numerically strong but financially weak Anglo-Catholic parish in Key West; St. Alban's, a tiny congregation in the same city meeting in a rented shack; and St. James's, a struggling but dynamic mission in the Negro section of Tampa.[29]

When Bishop Gray began his work in the jurisdiction in 1893, he found that St. Peter's, Key West, was carried on the rolls of the convocation as a parish church, but that in reality the congregation was not a self-supporting unit. The church, rebuilt after a hurricane, had a debt resting on it and was still unfinished. The rector, the Rev. Samuel Kerr, lived in a rented house which cost the congregation over two hundred dollars per annum. The drain of this rent from the parish coffers made it impossible for the congregation to pay off the church debt, complete the church building, and provide a rectory for the clergyman. With the help of Dr. Higgs at St. Paul's, funds were raised to help pay the debt, and Bishop Gray provided a rectory by buying a comfortable house and lot near the church with money from his discretionary fund. Despite the help given it from the outside, St. Peter's did not become self-supporting until the Rev. E. Thomas Demby arrived to take over the parish in 1903. This lively priest increased the number of active communicants from around two hundred fifty to six hundred, enlarged the church, and put the financial affairs of the parish on a sound footing. Under Father Demby's leadership, St. Peter's again became the premier Negro church of the jurisdiction.[30]

The other Negro church in Key West, St. Alban's, was a very small mission without even a lot to call its own. The congregation worshipped in a rented shack several miles from St. Peter's on the

29. *Convocation Journal*, 1893, pp. 3–4.
30. Gray, *Episcopal Address* (Southern Florida), 1908, pp. 30–31.

edge of a pool of stagnant water. About 1895, Bishop Gray purchased two "admirable lots" for the mission near the old fort, but neither the bishop nor the congregation could raise enough money to build a church.[31] After a persistent struggle, however, the congregation was finally able to erect a small frame church in 1904, thanks largely to the efforts of Montraville E. Spatches, a Negro lay reader and school teacher who later became a postulant for holy orders.[32] Bishop Gray was so impressed with the work of the Rev. Mr. Spatches, who in addition to his labors at the church opened a parochial school in a shack near the church, that he decided to make a special appeal for a school building and rectory for the recently ordained clergyman. The bishop went North for the funds: "I was in Calvary Church, Germantown, Pennsylvania, with good Dr. Perry, who allowed me to appeal for my work. I poured out my soul in anxiety for a combined building, school and rectory on my St. Alban's lot, back of the church. We had not more than finished the recessional in the vestry room when one of the choirmen, with his vestments still on him, came to me and said 'Bishop, I will build that school and rectory.' " With this donation the building was built, and within a year of its completion the Rev. Mr. Spatches and his wife were teaching one hundred eighty-two pupils in the school as well as tending a growing flock in the mission.[33]

Spatches was a valued and much-respected clergyman. Born and reared in Key West, he may have been one of the first infants baptized in St. Peter's Church in that city. He probably received the basics of an education at the sporadically operated parochial school of St. Peter's and was able to pursue his studies at Fisk University in Nashville, Tennessee, where he graduated in 1898. He later took courses at Hoffman Hall, an Episcopal theological training institution in the same city. When he returned to Key West, Mr. Spatches continued to read Greek under "a fine Greek scholar and well-informed churchman." He was ordained deacon in 1904 and priest in 1905, by Bishop Gray. The work of the Rev. Mr. Spatches as both priest and teacher won him the admiration of Negro and white

31. Ibid., p. 31.
32. *Bishop's Diary*, 1904, p. 45.
33. Gray, *Episcopal Address* (Southern Florida), 1908, p. 31.

alike. When the United States government began the process of annexing the site of St. Alban's because of its location near the fort, Spatches resigned his charge and accepted an appointment to St. Mark's Church, Macon, Georgia. During the closing years of his ministry, he served as priest-in-charge of St. Philip's Church, Jacksonville.[34]

St. James's, Tampa, like its sister churches in Key West, was without a rectory when Bishop Gray acceded to the episcopate. The Rev. Matthew McDuffie, priest-in-charge, was able with the help of the bishop to secure a lot adjoining the church for this purpose. Leading a battalion of carpenters and laborers from his flock, McDuffie built not only a home for himself and his family but a parochial school as well. The congregation continued to grow under Mr. McDuffie and under his successor, the Rev. John F. Porter. Although Mr. Porter also founded El Salvador, a mission in West Tampa which served a congregation of Spanish-speaking Negroes in that section, the bulk of both men's efforts was spent among their own people in the growing neighborhood around the church. However, the congregation never reached the point of becoming a self-supporting parish as much of the energy of the mission was dissipated in maintaining and enlarging the parochial school.[35]

In the spring of 1896 the Rev. Matthew McDuffie began working among the Negroes of Orlando, where Bishop Gray had constructed a small but neat church under the patronage of St. John the Baptist. Within a year the bishop assigned a newly ordained white deacon in riper years to the mission, and it soon boasted a baptized membership of some thirty-six persons with a small parochial school next door.[36]

Through the efforts of the bishop's brother, the Rev. Charles N. Gray of Grace Church, Ocala, a Negro mission, St. James's, was started in that town. By 1898, a Negro clergyman, the Rev. A. E. Jensen, was working full time in Ocala, and there was a small

34. Ibid.; also see *Stowe*, 1917, p. 270.
35. *Convocation Journal*, 1899, p. 7; also Gray, *Episcopal Address* (Southern Florida), 1908, p. 31.
36. *Bishop's Diary*, 1897, p. 68; see also *Convocation Journal*, 1897, *Parochial Reports*.

school operating in conjunction with the church. The prospects in Ocala were even brighter than those in Orlando. Within a year of its organization, St. James's possessed sixty baptized members and twenty-nine communicants.[37] The missions in Orlando and Ocala, however, did not fulfill their early promise but rather remained relatively small numerically. Both were located in inland towns and therefore did not have the large number of British West Indian immigrants, imbued with the Anglican tradition, to draw from as did their sister missions along the east coast.

The Negro missions in the Biscayne Bay area founded under the auspices of the Holy Cross Fathers continued to thrive, and their parochial academies supplied their communities with the rudiments of an education in an area where public schooling for Negroes was hopelessly inadequate. These churches, along with those in the Lake Worth area, were composed mainly of Bahamians, called "Nassaus" by their American brethren, and of other British West Indian immigrants. The flow of this immigration from the depresssed islands enriched the membership of the Episcopal Church in the southern portion of the peninsula for decades.

It is difficult to obtain a full picture of the typical Negro layman of the period. If he was American, he was probably a remnant, or a descendant of a remnant, of the house servants who attached themselves to the religion of their owners during the antebellum period. While the vast majority of their colored brethren wandered off into evangelical African sects following emancipation, some of this class clung tenaciously to the old faith and reared their children in its teachings. As the races began to segregate in the decades after Reconstruction, these Churchmen formed themselves into Negro congregations, often with white help, and built separate parochial units. The British West Indian, on the other hand, had often been Anglican for generations. He demanded the services of the Anglican communion as part of his Christian heritage, and was often surprised and hurt to find that he was not as welcome in the white parishes along the lower east coast as he was in their West Indian counterparts. He could not accept the primitive religious

37. *Bishop's Diary*, 1899, pp. 76, 80.

practices of the African sects and, rather than do so, he organized congregations of his own and appealed to the white clergy for services. These services were gladly given, and before long entire congregations of West Indians began to dot the southern coast of the peninsula. These churches remained almost exclusively West Indian, making little attempt to proselyte American Negroes. As a result, they are still known today by the bulk of the Negro population as "Nassau churches" rather than as Episcopal churches.

Of the several Negro clergymen who served in the jurisdiction under Bishop Gray, the Rev. Matthew McDuffie of St. James's, Tampa, particularly stands out for his dedicated labors. Mr. McDuffie was born in Statesburg, South Carolina, probably just before or during the Civil War.[38] Since the slave-holding aristocracy in the area around Statesburg was predominantly Episcopalian, it is safe to conjecture that young McDuffie was "born" in the Church and more than likely attended services at the Church of the Holy Cross. Holy Cross churchyard contains the grave of the first Bishop of Florida, the Rt. Rev. Francis Huger Rutledge, who in his long ministry was a devoted laborer among the slaves of his native state and in Florida. The possibility that Bishop Rutledge influenced the early life of the future priest is a matter for intriguing speculation. Somehow during his youth, taught by his white masters or by the teachers of the Freedmen's School, McDuffie got a basic education which prepared him for his studies at St. Stephen's College at Annandale-on-Hudson, New York. After graduation he returned to South Carolina, where he taught in a parochial school for a number of years. Some time later, he removed to the Diocese of Florida, read theology under Bishop Weed, and was ordained deacon by him in St. Philip's Church, Jacksonville, May 25, 1892. He began his ministry with the charge of St. Alban's Mission, Key West, where he held services in a rented shack as well as in the Marine Hospital and the Monroe County jail. In August 1892, he was assigned the charge of St. James's Church in Tampa where he spent the rest of his ministry. Because of his experience as a teacher, he was soon able to open St. James's School, the only Negro parochial

38. No date of birth is given for McDuffie in *Stowe*.

institution in existence in the jurisdiction when Bishop Gray assumed authority. He was ordained to the priesthood on September 25, 1893, in St. James's, by Bishop Gray.[39] McDuffie was effective not only as a teacher, but also as a priest. When he took charge of the Tampa mission there were but thirteen persons listed as communicants of his cure;[40] within five years he built his communicant list to one hundred ninety-seven.[41] McDuffie, more than any of the clergy working among his race, was successful in blending the divergent British and American Negro elements of his charge into a unified parish organization.

McDuffie's labors among the Negroes of Tampa won him the admiration of the whites as well as the blacks. On one occasion a much-respected Negro was passing two white businessmen on the streets of Tampa, when one of the whites remarked: "There goes the best Negro I ever knew—except one, Matthew McDuffie," a sincerely complimentary statement for the time although today it sounds condescending. A group of his fellow clergymen described McDuffie in these words: "As a man and Priest of the Church he was a rare type of excellence and moral worth. Educationally he was fully armed for his high office, and to this preparation he added those qualities of humility, gentleness and patience, which adorn the doctrine of God our Savior."[42]

In the sixth year of his ministry, the Rev. Mr. McDuffie contracted a fatal illness, probably tuberculosis. Bishop Gray visited his sickbed whenever he was in Tampa. On his last visit the bishop was distressed to see the faithful priest so near death. "Poor McDuffie," he wrote in his diary, "has had seven hemorrhages within a week, and his physician thinks he cannot get up again. I stayed long at his bedside talking to him, found him resigned to God's will, had prayers with him and gave him my blessing." When the rector of St. Andrew's, Tampa, wired Bishop Gray of McDuffie's death several days later, the bishop took the first train to Tampa to preside at the cleric's funeral rites where, contrary to the usual custom,

39. *Convocation Journal*, 1899, p. 7.
40. *Diocesan Journal*, 1891, *Parochial Abstracts.*
41. *Convocation Journal*, 1897, *Parochial Reports.*
42. *Convocation Journal*, 1899, p. 39.

he delivered a funeral address to a crowded congregation of both
Negroes and whites.[43]

The average Negro clergyman was not paid as well as his white
brethren, but it is remarkable that in this era there was no greater
difference between the salaries of the two groups. The stipends of
white mission clergymen were invariably about one hundred dollars
a year more than those of Negro clergymen. The priest-in-charge
of St. James's, Tampa, for instance, received four hundred dollars
per annum, while the priest-in-charge of St. Agnes's, Miami, received
five hundred dollars. The truth is that at the turn of the century
neither the Negro nor the white clergy enjoyed the financial stability that they enjoy today. Negro teachers employed in parochial
institutions generally received a monthly salary of about thirty dollars for an academic year that lasted only six months.[44]

From a consideration of the work of the Negro clergy among their
people during the episcopate of William Crane Gray, it is clear that
both they and the bishop considered their roles as educators almost
as important as their roles as priests. The schools opened in Orlando, Ocala, Miami, Coconut Grove, Key West, and Tampa, and
later in West Palm Beach and Delray, indicated that the Church
deemed education the chief means by which the Negro could overcome racial prejudice and become a useful, accepted member of
American society.

Bishop Gray's third prominent interest during his episcopate was
the foundation of a cathedral church. Since Orlando was the most
important city in the central part of the new jurisdiction, the residence of the bishop, and the site of such diocesan institutions as
the Pell-Clarke School for Girls and the Church Home and Hospital, it was only natural to declare the parish church of the town,
St. Luke's, the official seat of ecclesiastical government and worship. The cathedral movement had been gathering momentum for
a number of years when the idea came to fruition at the Convocation of 1902, which met in St. Andrew's Church, Tampa.

At the request of the convocation, the bishop appointed a committee to report on a plan to make Orlando the see city, to make

43. *Bishop's Diary*, 1899, p. 70.
44. Gray, "Status of Work Among Negroes."

St. Luke's Parish the seat of the "cathedra" or bishop's throne, and to introduce the "cathedral system" into the local church. Prior to this request, the vestry of St. Luke's Church had asked the bishop to take permanent charge of the parish and its government. The committee (composed of two clergymen, Archdeacon John H. Weddell of the West Coast deanery and the Rev. William W. DeHart of St. Andrew's, Tampa, and one layman, the Hon. Louis C. Massey of St. Luke's, Orlando, chancellor of the jurisdiction) reported favorably on the scheme and recommended a number of legal steps to put it properly in motion. Besides placing the Orlando parish under the charge of the bishop, the committee recommended that a civil corporation be formed to govern the ecclesiastical and fiscal affairs of the cathedral and its dependencies.[45]

A charter was drawn up which declared that the governing powers of the new institution were vested in the hands of a cathedral chapter with the bishop at its head. The chapter would be composed of the bishop, a dean elected by the chapter, and eleven members (two clergymen and two laymen to be elected by the convocation; one member, either clerical or lay, to be appointed by the bishop; and six laymen to be elected by the qualified parishioners of the cathedral congregation).[46] According to the charter, the cathedral chapter would take charge and have control of the church and rectory (deanery) of St. Luke's, the colored mission of St. John the Baptist and its parochial school, the Pell-Clarke School for Girls in Orlando, the Southern Florida School for Boys near Sanford, the Church Home and Hospital in Orlando, and the administration of the Clergy Relief Fund. The cathedral staff, which was to be considerably enlarged, would serve the numerous mission churches in the Orlando area under the direction of the bishop.[47]

45. *Convocation Journal*, 1902, pp. 10, 15.

46. The eleven charter members of the cathedral chapter were: the Rev. William H. DeHart, Tampa; the Rev. (Deacon) H. W. Greetham, Orlando; M. E. Gillett, Tampa; the Hon. George M. Robbins, Titusville; the Hon. Louis C. Massey, and Messrs. T. P. Warlow, Algernon Haden, A. W. C. Smyth, W. W. Dade, Charles Lord, and T. P. Robinson, Orlando.

47. Parish Register, vol. 1, St. Luke's Church, Orlando, Florida.

When the charter of the Cathedral Church of St. Luke in Orlando was signed into law on March 17, 1902, by the Hon. Minor S. Jones of Titusville, Judge of the Seventh Judicial Circuit, that church and its chapter became the richest and most powerful institution in the missionary jurisdiction.[48] The following properties and evaluations passed under its surveillance:

St. Luke's Cathedral	$ 5,000
Deanery	1,200
Bishopstead	12,000
Pell-Clarke School	10,000
Church Home and Hospital	5,000
Fair Grounds deeded to Church Home and Hospital	8,000
St. John the Baptist Church and School	900
Southern Florida School for Boys	2,500
Four acres in Orlando (gift)	200
Total	$44,800

To most non-Churchmen the designation of tiny St. Luke's Church with its unimpressive board-and-batten architecture and two hundred "sittings" as the cathedral of the jurisdiction seemed almost farcically pretentious. No doubt many Churchmen felt the same way. The bishop spoke out to justify his new creation to them: "My idea of the Cathedral system is not necessarily a large, fine Church building (though I trust that would come in due time), but the centre of manifold work and energy, reaching out in every direction—schools, hospitals, a staff of missionary clergy, daily Morning and Evening Prayer and contant Communions in the Cathedral Church, a vested choir of men and boys and a high standard of services which might be a model for the churches throughout the Jurisdiction to approve and aim at."[49] With these concepts in mind, the cathedral chapter elected the Rev. Lucien Allen Spencer, priest-in-charge of Christ Church, Bradenton, as the first dean of St. Luke's. He assumed his new duties on Low Sunday, 1902.[50]

The Missionary Jurisdiction of Southern Florida was strongly in-

48. *Convocation Journal*, 1903, p. 59.
49. Gray, *Episcopal Address* (Southern Florida), 1902, p. 42.
50. *Convocation Journal*, 1903, p. 69.

fluenced by Bishop Gray's plans and work, but it was also affected by the more secular occurrences of his episcopate. The effects of the panic of 1893 and the catastrophic freezes of 1894–95 have already been discussed, as has the great Anglo-American diplomatic crisis of 1895. There were two other happenings, however, which involved the future of both Church and state: the outbreak of the Spanish-American War, and the completion, in spite of three hurricanes, of the Flagler rail system to Key West.

There had been strained relations between Spain and her Cuban subjects since the middle of the nineteenth century. Cuban unrest led to the Revolution of 1868 and the repressive measures the Spanish authorities used to quell it. Following the abortive revolt thousands of Cubans fled the island to Florida and settled in the port towns of Key West, Tampa, and Jacksonville. Florida's cigar industry resulted directly from the immigration. The plight of the refugees aroused the sympathy of Floridians; and the Episcopal clergy under the leadership of Bishop Gray's predecessors, the Rt. Rev. John Freeman Young and the Rt. Rev. Edwin G. Weed, made a valiant effort to reach the immigrants in both Key West and Tampa. When the Cubans again revolted in 1895, public sentiment in Florida, and indeed in some of the rest of the United States, demanded American intervention to secure Cuban independence. The Florida coast bristled with filibustering activities as ships slipped out of ports on illicit voyages smuggling arms and supplies to the Cuban rebels. Exaggerated stories of Spanish atrocities fanned anti-Spanish sentiment to a roaring blaze. Only an excuse was needed to bring about American intervention. It was provided in February 1898, when the U.S.S. *Maine* was sunk in Havana harbor by an undetermined cause, killing two hundred sixty officers and men.

Bishop Gray, who had just returned to Orlando from a visitation to Punta Gorda, recorded the famous event in his diary on February 16: "Learned of the dreadful calamity at Havana, the blowing up of the *Maine*. Our whole nation struck dumb. Wonderful self-control on the part of those in authority. A most thorough and complete investigation to be made. May God make plain the duty of our country."[51] One of the first duties was to bury the dead

51. *Bishop's Diary*, 1899, p. 58.

from the disaster, and the Church in Florida was called upon to provide its services. Many of the bodies recovered from the explosion were sent to Key West, where the Rev. Gilbert Higgs, rector of St. Paul's Church, conducted some of the funeral rites.[52]

When war broke out in April 1898, Florida's coastal towns fancied themselves the object of Spanish attack. Fortifications were begun or reactivated near Jacksonville, St. Augustine, Fernandina, and the peninsula towns of Miami and Tampa (Egmont Key). To protect Florida from the Spanish fleet a naval squadron was stationed at Key West, where it remained until it was transferred into the Cuban blockade. During the summer of 1898 military camps were established at Tampa and Miami, the former becoming the main concentration point for embarkation to Cuba.

Episcopal clergymen were active in all the centers of military and naval operation. Because of its proximity to Cuba, Key West was a particularly important naval, supply, and medical base, and the clergy of the island were kept busy ministering to the sick and wounded in the hospitals. The report of the Rev. Gilbert Higgs to the Convocation of 1899 gives an idea of the local clergy's duties:

> Held pre-burial service over the remains of Ensign Worth Bagley.
> Buried the remains of some of the seamen killed on the "Maine."
> Buried the remains of all the seamen killed on the "Winslow," Torpedo Boat.
> Buried the remains of one seaman killed on the Battle Ship "Iowa."
> Buried the remains of two soldiers killed by the explosion of a gun at Fort Taylor, Key West.
> Administered Holy Communion to Seaman Sherman Walker, of Torpedo Boat, "Cushing."
> Read prayers on deck of Torpedo Boat, "Winslow," with Com. Bernadou.
> Visited Miss Clara Barton on steamer "City of Texas," and had a conversation with her with reference to aiding the poor and needy Cubans here.

52. *Convocation Journal*, 1899, p. 37.

Visited Hospitals, Convent Hospital, Marine Post, College Hospital, and "Coronado." Sixty-eight visits.[53]

The Rev. William DeHart of St. Andrew's Church, Tampa, ministered to the camps and hospitals of that area and, working closely with an Episcopal army chaplain, the Rev. J. Woods Elliott, assisted in preparing a number of soldiers for confirmation. Bishop Gray was a frequent visitor to the army camps near Tampa and held services whenever he could. He described one such occasion in his diary: "July 13. Had a very interesting service in the camp of the 5th Regiment Maryland Volunteers at night. The lanterns hanging in the live oak trees shining through the hanging moss upon the large congregation standing around me on the ground presented a striking scene. . . . I preached and confirmed five soldier boys." A few months later the war ended abruptly, and the soldiers returned to their own homes.

Bishop Gray, like many Americans, saw the Spanish-American War as part of a divine plan to overthrow the Latin aristocracy and the Roman Catholic Church throughout the world. In his convocation address of 1899 in Holy Trinity Church, Melbourne, he lashed out against the Roman Pontiff, Leo XIII, calling him "the poor old 'Prisoner of the Vatican'—the so-called Vicar of Christ," and pointed out centuries of papal shortcomings. "Those once in full authority over a majority of Christendom have failed," he declared. "God is removing authority from them *because* they have proved unworthy of it. The Papacy as a system has failed to permeate, with the true leaven, the nations which it dominated, and therefore, *it* and *they* must give place to others, that it may be demonstrated whether or not *they* will in all humility and Christlikeness prove more worthy of the responsibility and honor devolved upon them." The bishop believed that the Anglo-Saxon race and the Anglican Church should step into the political and spiritual void caused by the collapse of the Latin world and the Latin Church and lead the people "into the way of truth . . . in the bond of peace and in righteousness of life."[54]

The successful conclusion of the Spanish-American War gave

53. Ibid., pp. 36–37.
54. Gray, *Episcopal Address* (Southern Florida), 1899, pp. 47, 49.

America hegemony in the Caribbean; and to buttress that dominance the United States government decided to build the Panama Canal. The astute Henry Flagler, aware of this development, determined to move the terminus of the Florida East Coast Railroad south of Miami closer to the Caribbean. Late in 1904 he designated Key West as the Caribbean terminus and began to extend the railroad through the southern glades and over the Florida Keys. This construction opened the Homestead area to settlement and in 1906 a mission, St. John's Church, was organized in the village.[55]

The presence of a large number of naval and military personnel in Key West during and after the war, plus a marked increase in the civilian population caused by the railroad extension, brought new life to the Churchmen of the island. The old parishes, St. Paul's and St. Peter's, continued to grow, and two new churches were begun to take care of the rapid increase in population—Holy Innocents Church in 1901 for whites, and St. Alban's in 1903 for Negroes.[56] When the railroad extension was finally completed in the spring of 1913 the communicant list of these four churches totaled almost a thousand. An imposing new stone church was being planned to replace the frame structure of St. Paul's, which had been destroyed by the hurricane of 1909.[57] The completion of the railroad and the advent of World War I brought Key West and its churches two decades of prosperity.

55. *Convocation Journal*, 1907, *Parochial Reports*.
56. *Bishop's Diary*, 1901, p. 39; *Diocesan Journal*, 1904, *Parochial Reports*.
57. *Diocesan Journal*, 1914, *Parochial Reports*; Vestry Minutes, St. Paul's, Key West.

VIII

William Crane Gray
Missionary Bishop

WILLIAM CRANE GRAY WAS BORN IN LAMBERTVILLE, NEW Jersey, on September 6, 1835, into a prominent clerical family. His father, the Rev. Joseph Gray, was an Episcopal clergyman and a physician. His mother, Hannah Price Crane, had a clergyman brother and was from a family steeped in the traditions of the Church. Young William's great-uncle was the Rt. Rev. John Croes, first Bishop of New Jersey, a descendant of Joseph Fray, an Irish immigrant who settled in Pennsylvania in the latter part of the seventeenth century. William's great-great-grandfather on his mother's side, the Rev. Mr. Price, a clergyman of the Church of England, was the forebear of many ministers of the American Church.[1]

When the future bishop was a lad of ten, his father moved with his family from New Jersey to Tennessee, where the Rev. Dr. Gray began missionary and parochial work under the Rt. Rev. James Hervey Otey, D.D., the dynamic first Bishop of Tennessee. William's secondary education was completed in his adopted state, and in about 1850 he was sent to Gambier, a tiny village in central Ohio, where he enrolled in Kenyon College. Shortly before his son matriculated

---

1. *National Cyclopaedia of American Biography*, 13: 502.

at Kenyon, Dr. Gray became rector of Trinity Church in Clarksville, Tennessee.[2]

Sometime after William entered Kenyon, he began a diary, which he kept intermittently throughout his long life. From a perusal of the first volume of the diary, it is evident that even before he embarked on his college career the young student intended to study for the ministry. He took theological courses at Bexley Hall, the seminary at Kenyon, along with his academic subjects in the college. Being well-grounded in Latin before he matriculated, William pursued an undergraduate program typical of the period: Greek grammar and literature, Latin literature, classical history, mathematics, Hebrew, and German. In the seminary he prepared himself for his calling with courses in Old Testament history and literature, advanced Hebrew, New Testament Greek, the Synoptic Gospels, the Pauline Epistles, and other New Testament literature. He had some work in Patristics and enjoyed his courses in Church history and doctrine, finding the Reformation period especially appealing. His studies in this period were attacked from a Protestant point of view and prejudiced his attitude toward Roman Catholicism during his entire ministry. Somewhat removed from classics and theology, astronomy was another subject he found interesting. As a senior William spent many evening hours in the quiet countryside around Gambier observing the movements of the heavenly bodies, an occupation which no doubt gave him much pleasure later in life when he roamed the wilds of the Florida peninsula making his episcopal visitations.[3]

While a senior at Kenyon, William Gray got his first taste of mission work in the area around Gambier and elsewhere in Knox County. He preached and read Morning and Evening Prayer on Sundays in such rural communities as Millweed, Danville, Brandon and Centerville, often walking to and from his assignments. He was conscientious in his pastoral work and diligent in preparing

2. *Palm Branch*, July 1897.

3. William Crane Gray, "The Journal of William Crane Gray, 1858–1860," vol. 1, *passim*. This is the first of four unpublished volumes in possession of Bishop Gray's grandson, the Very Rev. Francis Campbell Gray, former dean of the Cathedral Church of St. Luke, Orlando, Florida. Hereafter cited as "Gray's Journal" with the volume and date of entry.

his sermons, although he frequently had difficulty in organizing his thoughts and writing them down. From his diary entries, it is obvious that the young seminarian was strongly evangelical in his Churchmanship, an approach confirmed by the ecclesiastical atmosphere of Bexley Hall. From time to time William confessed doubts concerning his own "sanctification" and a mortification at what he called his "arrogance" and "hardness of heart." The diary entry for October 21, 1858, written in his florid Victorian style, gives a typical expression of his state of mind. "How cold and backsliding have I been, Oh blessed Lord. May I not live nearer to thee, wilt thou not help me, and every day may I not have directly the assistance of thy Holy Spirit. . . . Give me humility, true humility," he implored. William not only had doubts about his spiritual welfare, but he periodically complained about his physical condition as well. He had a discomforting "nuralgia [*sic*] in my teeth," and was forced to make several trips to Mount Vernon, the county seat, to have his teeth filled.

There were two outstanding non-academic events in Gray's Kenyon career. One was a journey to Toronto, Ontario, during winter recess, as the guest of a college friend. This trip also included a visit to Niagara Falls, and William's description of the sight showed that he fully appreciated its majesty: "That great volume of water comes rolling over that awful precipice, with the noise of thunder, and falls into the abyss below from which continually ascends a thick cloud of mist that rises like a great column of smoke, far above the Falls." The other event was a tragic one. William's father died in Clarksville of tuberculosis, leaving him the sole support of his widowed mother, three sisters, and two younger brothers.[4]

Although Gray completed all the requirements for a bachelor's degree, he did not graduate formally but received his degree *in absentia*. This unexpected occurrence was noted in the diary: "Received two letters, one from my Mother . . . and one from Bishop Otey of much importance since it summons me away before Commencement [to assume a post in the mission field]." The young seminarian left Kenyon on June 15, 1859. On June 26, while his

4. "Gray's Journal," 1, January 18, 1859.

class was preparing for graduation, William was ordained to the diaconate by Bishop Otey in Christ Church Parish in Nashville. The new deacon was immediately assigned to the mission field in west Tennessee and took up his residence in a boarding house in Trenton.[5] From there he served small congregations in Dyersburg, Humbolt, Union City, Dresden, and Brownsville. There was no Episcopal church in any of the communities under his care, so the enterprising clergyman was forced to conduct services in court-houses, masonic halls, and local schools. He unfortunately encoun-tered a great deal of prejudice and apathy toward the Church and often felt that his ministry was doomed to failure. After almost a year of extremely hard work in Trenton, the young deacon harvested only five for confirmation, and an embarrassing incident occurred at the service which reduced the number even further. "He [Bishop Otey] preached again this afternoon and confirmed three persons, two of my candidates failing to come forward, which latter thing gave me much distress, much more as they had determined up to the very day to take their baptismal vows upon themselves." The harvest was as meagre in Brownsville as in Trenton—only four were confirmed there.[6]

On May 17, 1860, in St. Peter's Church in Columbia, Tennessee, the energetic deacon listened to a powerful sermon by Bishop Otey on the priesthood, after which he knelt before that aging prelate to "receive the Holy Ghost for the Office and Work of a Priest in the Church of God." Two months after his ordination, the new priest received his first call to a parish, St. James's Church in Bolivar, Tennessee. Despite his reluctance to leave the mission field, he ac-cepted the call several months later and took up residence in Boli-var.[7]

William Crane Gray began his ministry in a stormy and eventful period of American history. His journals, however, show no strong interest in either the political or the social problems which con-fronted the people in both North and South. His views on the moral-ity of slavery are unstated, the problem of "Bleeding Kansas" is

5. Ibid., May 18 and June 16, 1859; *National Cyclopaedia,* 13: 502.
6. "Gray's Journal," 1, March 11 and 16, 1860.
7. Ibid., May 17 and October 11, 1860.

ignored, and neither the electrifying effects of John Brown's Raid in October 1859 nor the storm created by his execution are mentioned in the bulky first volume.

The first indication that Gray realized there was a crisis in the American union came with his mention of the fateful presidential election of 1860, and even here his statement is quite brief. He lists the four candidates and their parties without partiality. His absence from Bolivar on election day prevented him from casting his ballot, but there are indications in the journal that he favored the candidacy of the moderate Constitutional Unionist, John Bell of Tennessee.[8] When the election of Abraham Lincoln triggered the secession of South Carolina, there is no indication that he approved of the disruption of the union. He may even have shared the sentiments of his diocesan, the peppery old Bishop Otey, who branded the secession of South Carolina a "criminal action." That Gray viewed secession with at least a dubious eye is evident in his entry of December 5, 1860: "Political news today is still more dark and gloomy than before. I fear there is a dark future in store for our distracted country. The Southern States seem determined to secede under any and all circumstances. May God help us in our extremity." Although Gray followed Bishop Otey's request that his clergy "let their moderation be known to all men" and that they "study to be quiet and to mind their own business,"[9] when Tennessee seceded in June of 1861, Gray, like thousands of other moderates, became a loyal Confederate and was soon enthusiastically supporting the Southern cause.

His enthusiasm led him to enlist as a chaplain in the Fourth Regiment of Tennessee Volunteers in the summer of 1861, but ill health forced him to return to his parochial duties in Bolivar before the end of the year.[10] Gray occupied a rented house with his widowed mother, his sister Emma, and his two younger brothers, Charles and Ridley, all of whom had joined him after he had assumed his charge at St. James's Church. The domestic duties of the family

8. Ibid., November 5, 1860.
9. James W. Silver, *Confederate Morale and Church Propaganda* (Tuscaloosa, Alabama: Confederate Publishing Co., Inc., 1957), p. 21.
10. Leonard, p. 13.

were considerably lightened by the presence of the family servant, Diana, who accompanied Mrs. Gray from Clarksville.[11] Two married sisters lived elsewhere.

Because many of his parishioners took refuge in other states and many of the men of his congregation were serving the Confederate forces, there was a drastic reduction in the annual stipend of the rector. To augment the financial loss, Gray was forced to open a boys' school in Bolivar where he taught "classes in Latin, Greek, Algebra, and Geometry."[12] When the town was occupied by Federal troops, he continued both his teaching and his priestly duties until August 13, 1862, when he was arrested along with sixteen others for refusing to take the oath of allegiance to the United States government. The Southern patriots were confined to the crowded Federal Military Prison in Alton, Illinois, a mental hospital converted into a prison for the duration of the war.[13] After a trying confinement of nearly three months, Gray was transferred to the Gratiot Street Military Prison in St. Louis, Missouri. After a further detention of two weeks, he was paroled without taking the oath and permitted to return to Bolivar and his family.[14] His imprisonment had made an indelible and bitter impression on his mind, although his homecoming was a joyous one.

William Gray resumed his duties at St. James's Church and reopened his school on his return. He was continually harassed by Federal military authorities for refusing to take the oath and to pray for the President of the United States during divine service. On December 27, 1862, the Federal commander in Bolivar closed the church and converted the building into a barracks for occupation troops. Gray was again threatened with arrest and his family with deportation. Three days later, the hounded clergyman with two other Confederate hold-outs took the oath to avoid arrest. After this distasteful event, the harassment eased and sometime later the church was restored to the rector.[15]

11. "Gray's Journal," 2, March 6, 1861.
12. Ibid., January 20, 1862.
13. Ibid., 3, August 30 and 31, 1862.
14. Ibid., October 19, 1862.
15. Ibid., December 27, 28, and 29, 1862.

Life was not all unpleasant for the parson of Bolivar during the war, for on his return from St. Louis he conducted a vigorous courtship which resulted in his marriage to Margaret Locke Trent on May 20, 1863. "Maggie" was the daughter of William H. Trent of La Grange, Fayette County, Tennessee.[16] The newlyweds were given passes through the Federal lines and permitted to honeymoon in Canada. A part of the trip included the traditional visit to Niagara Falls. The couple returned to Bolivar in late June after Federal forces temporarily evacuated the town in the wake of a Confederate offensive.[17]

When peace finally came to the beleaguered South in the spring of 1865, Mr. Gray threw himself wholeheartedly into the task of rebuilding his warworn parish. During the repressive Reconstruction years, he was able to build a new church, a new rectory, and a parochial academy for girls. Gray also began an ardent missionary endeavor to reach the Negro freedmen of the vicinity. His labors in this direction resulted in the erection of St. Philip's Mission, the first Negro church to be constructed in the South after the Civil War. The postwar years at Bolivar were saddened by the death of Maggie, but in 1877 the future bishop married a second time. His new bride was Fannie Campbell Bowers, daughter of the Rev. William V. Bowers of Philadelphia. From these two marriages five children were born, three sons and two daughters.[18]

In 1880, after a tenure of twenty years at Bolivar, the Rev. William Gray received a call to be rector of the Church of the Advent in Nashville, the former parish of his diocesan, the Rt. Rev. Charles Todd Quintard, who moved from that position to become the second Bishop of Tennessee in 1865. During his twelve years as rector of the Nashville church, Gray exhibited the same energy and concern for his people that he had shown in Bolivar. He succeeded in removing a large debt of long standing and in completing the unfinished church, which was consecrated during his rectorate. Gray also held a number of important diocesan offices and served as a clerical delegate from Tennessee to the General Convention on sev-

16. Ibid., May 14 and 20, 1863.
17. Ibid., June 5 and July 3, 1863.
18. *Palm Branch*, July 1897.

eral occasions.[19] The years at the Church of the Advent also marked a decided change in the Churchmanship of the rector.

That William Gray was an enthusiastic Evangelical during his college and seminary days at Gambier cannot be doubted. His diaries amply illustrate that fact. If the diaries are accurate, and there is no reason to assume that they are not, Gray was so concerned with the "preaching of the Word" after his ordination to the priesthood that he neglected to celebrate his first Holy Communion until after he had been priested a month.[20] During the cruel years of the war, however, he slowly began to appreciate the sacramental aspects of the Book of Common Prayer and the number of his eucharistic celebrations gradually increased. Gray's interest in sacramentalism was encouraged by his old friend, Charles Quintard, who early in his ministry had fallen under the spell of the English Tractarians or Oxford Reformers. When Quintard became diocesan in 1865, his intellectual and spiritual leadership caused the Churchmanship of the diocese to move in a moderately Catholic direction.[21] When Gray assumed his duties as rector of the Church of the Advent in Nashville, he found a congregation already profoundly influenced by Quintard's views and decidedly more sacramental in its approach than the parishioners he had left in Bolivar. By the time Gray was elected to the episcopate, he had blended his early Evangelical background with the newer outlook of the moderate Anglo-Catholic school. It was this blend of Churchmanship that Bishop Gray was to bring to his newly created jurisdiction.

Bishop Gray was hardly a ritualist and he would no doubt be puzzled or even horrified if he could see the "Romish" ceremonials of some of the clergy in recent years. He was, however, a "High" Churchman intellectually, a pronounced sacramentarian and sacerdotalist. A reading of the episcopal diaries leaves no doubt about this. The Eucharist to him was the central act of Christian worship, and the Morning and Evening Offices were by no means a sub-

19. Ibid.; *General Convention Journal: House of Deputies*, 1892, p. 173.

20. "Gray's Journal," 1, May 17 and June 16, 1860.

21. Charles Todd Quintard, *Doctor Quintard, Chaplain C. S. A. and Second Bishop of Tennessee* (Sewanee, Tenn.: The University Press, 1905), p. 7.

stitute for the Sunday celebration. In the visitations around the jurisdiction, Bishop Gray generally used the Morning Office as a preparation for the Eucharist. When he spoke of a "full service" he meant a combination of Morning Prayer, sermon, confirmation, and the Eucharist. It is obvious that the endurance of the Victorian clergy and congregations was considerably greater than that of their counterparts today.

To Gray baptism was not what the Latitudinarians called a theory or notion; it was a gift and a power. Baptized children, in his view, were to be educated, not with the idea of becoming Christians, but because they already were Christians. Therefore, he regarded confirmation not merely as an act of renewing one's baptismal vows, something that man does for God; but as the bestowal of the gifts of the Holy Spirit, something that God does for man. Confirmation, then, was in its highest sense the ordination of the laity. With these views, it was not surprising that he was constantly admonishing his clergy to give their earnest attention to the preparation of candidates. His veneration for the liturgy of the Book of Common Prayer was great, also, and he did not encourage any deviation from its use. To Bishop Gray the Prayer Book was adequate, felicitous, and final—the great bond of unity that tied the Anglican Communion together.

Bishop Gray's reverence for the institution of marriage was high indeed, and consequently his opinion on the question of divorce was conservative. Marriage to him was a union that could be dissolved only by death, even when one party of the union was guilty of adultery. On the question of remarriage of an "innocent party" in such a divorce case, his opinions were reactionary even for his times, although he agreed to govern his judgment in accordance with a modified marriage canon. "That while I do not, myself, believe that even the 'innocent party' in the case of a divorce for the cause mentioned in Holy Scripture, should be accorded the right to be married to another, so long as the guilty party shall be alive, still as long as the Canon remains as it is, the innocent party is accorded the right to remarry." A careful reading of the convocation journals will show that Bishop Gray did permit a number of "innocent parties" to be remarried in the Church even though he himself was opposed to the trend.[22]

William Gray was determined to be a good shepherd to his sheep. Although South Florida was still largely a frontier area when he became its first bishop, he administered the affairs of the vast jurisdiction and performed his episcopal duties single-handedly, sometimes visiting congregations twice a year. He was forced to traverse a peninsula that is currently tied together by railroads, four-lane highways, hard-surfaced secondary roads, and air transportation, by the most primitive methods of travel—foot, horseback, buggy, rowboat, and river steamer. Whenever possible he used the constantly growing railroad system, and as the railroads slowly spread through the area year after year, the burden of his visitations was considerably eased. On one occasion during his first years as bishop he had been compelled to sail to Havana, Cuba, to get from Key West to Tampa,[23] and so the completion of the overseas railroad in 1912 was particularly welcome.

Since to Bishop Gray an episcopal appointment was a sacred trust, he would go to great lengths to keep his ecclesiastical engagements. For example, he left Orlando for All Saints' Church, Lakeland, in the midst of what turned out to be the October hurricane of 1893. A "fearful gale" had raged all the previous night. "The next morning it was still raging with unabated violence, but it was necessary for me to go on to my next appointment. As I went to the depot the rain was being driven absolutely in a horizontal direction and I was thoroughly drenched. As my train, southbound, approached, the wind dashed a box car in front of the engine and it was shivered to splinters. As soon as the train was extricated from the wreck I went aboard and found myself the only passenger. Before we reached Kissimmee, a large tree, dragged up by the roots, fell in our pathway as we flew along, but a good Providence so ordered it that it fell slanting in the same direction in which we were moving, and so while we dashed through its top we escaped unhurt." A little later, the train slowed up, which caused the conductor to come running through the coach (obviously forgetting the

22. Gray, *Episcopal Address* (Southern Florida), 1900, p. 71; 1895, p. 51.
23. *Bishop's Diary*, 1894, p. 39.

episcopal presence) exclaiming in terror, "My God! I wonder is that another tree top!" After the epic journey, Archdeacon Weddell met the bishop at the depot in Lakeland, and although the fury of the gale had somewhat abated, the wind was still high. Evening Prayer was conducted at the appointed time. Bishop Gray recorded nonchalantly: "We had a wonderfully good attendance that night. I preached and confirmed one person."[24]

Sometimes the bishop was forced to sleep in the open because of communication problems. This happened on one occasion when he visited the English colony at Hobe Sound: "Reached the dock the night previous at 11 o'clock. It was quite cold and the wind was blowing very hard. My letter had miscarried, and no one was at the dock to meet me. It was very dark and I did not know the country, so I was compelled to take my valise for a pillow, lie down on the dock and spend the night."[25] His early interest in astronomy perhaps helped the bishop while away some of the hours that cold evening.

Sailing was usually a slow and undependable mode of travel, yet it was often the only means of reaching a destination. In the spring of 1896 Bishop Gray and his traveling companion were sailing from Courtenay on Merritt Island to Titusville when they ran into difficulty: "Left Courtenay in a sail boat, with head winds. It soon became evident that we could not reach Titusville in time for the train, so put in towards shore, ran aground and had to wade ashore. Walked to station in time to flag the train, and so made connection at Titusville via Enterprise and reached Orlando at 5 P.M."[26]

If hurricanes and head winds did not deter the bishop, neither did the cold. During the bitter week of the December freeze in 1894, the railroad schedule was interrupted by the freakish weather, but this did not stop the bishop. He hired a wagon and drove from Orlando to Narcoossee with Archdeacon Weddell and arrived in time for the 11:00 A.M. service at St. Peter's: "I took all the service as the Archdeacon's vestments were lost on the way, as we plunged through freezing water or jolted over palmetto roots. Baptized three

24. Ibid., pp. 57–58.
25. Ibid., 1895, p. 38.
26. Ibid., 1897, pp. 61–62.

babies in the morning in spite of the bitter cold. Held service and preached again at night." The next day Archdeacon Weddell recovered his vestments and the half-frozen clerics held another service at St. John's Church in Kissimmee.[27]

When Bishop Gray began his travels in Florida in 1893 he quickly took notice of the vicious little insects that were to plague his journeys for the twenty-one years he was missionary bishop—the mosquitoes. His reports in the convocation journals show that he developed a high respect for these sanguineous, diminutive monsters, especially those insects that inhabited the Indian River area and the islands south of Tampa Bay. The mosquitoes of Fort Pierce were particularly pious for they attended Evening Prayer in "clouds" while Bishop Gray and Archdeacon Brown were attempting to organize St. Andrew's mission. The insects were even worse in Eden and Jensen: "I must say that the mosquitoes at these two places were something fearful. At the hotel the clerk comes out with a palmetto whip to clear the insects off the guest before hurrying him within the screened door. I went to bed with my face blotched and swollen by the multitude of bites."[28]

Despite the difficulties of travel, Bishop Gray's primary interest was always the mission field, and to him that field embraced all who came within the boundaries of his jurisdiction—whites, blacks, Indians, tourists, British immigrants, and Cuban refugees. Since he regarded himself as the chief missionary of the Church in Florida, he pressed the building of new missions with all the resources in his power. He often traveled into the hinterland or down the thinly settled coast ahead of his missionaries so that he could best ascertain where to place them.

His passion and energy for mission work were tremendous, and he supervised every detail of it. The presence of an isolated Church family in the vicinity in which he was traveling was enough to make him go miles out of the way to visit them. Once, while coming up the Banana River on a launch, he heard of a Church family at Artesia, so he walked three miles to their dwelling to encourage them in the faith. On the same trip he made a long detour to bap-

27. Ibid., 1895, p. 61.
28. Ibid., 1894, p. 62.

tize a sick man on Merritt Island who was unable to come to Grace Church.[29] The bishop's ardor for the Church and its people knew no bounds and seemed to increase rather than diminish with age.

Bishop Gray's activities were constantly hampered by a lack of funds, and he continually had to appeal to his flock and to the General Mission Board in New York for the means to maintain and accelerate his program. "This is emphatically a mission field," he declared at a convocation. "Everything that helps missions helps the work here. Your canonical offerings to Domestic and Foreign Missions [of the National Church] helps the General Board towards making for us a larger appropriation. Your co-operation with the Women's Auxiliary is of the very greatest help, and you scarcely realize how I find myself leaning upon that reliable and increasing source of strength." When some of his congregations dragged their feet in meeting their missionary assessments he upbraided them. The assessments were laid by the convocation and the bishop warned that they were as "binding [an] obligation as that of the Clergyman's salary." Moreover, he declared that "the work of the Church is crippled and hindered if these dues are not met, and, besides, the neglect causes undue pressure and anxiety in other directions."[30]

It was remarkable that Bishop Gray was able to keep so gigantic a program going when his own jurisdiction was in the midst of a crippling depression for almost his entire episcopate. Not only did Bishop Gray constantly expand the mission field, but with shockingly meagre resources he maintained the Church Home and Hospital, two diocesan schools for girls and boys, and the Seminole mission as well. His approach to financing these multiple projects was hardly businesslike, as his expenses were seldom budgeted. When money ran out he simply asked his people for more, and they usually came through. "I know well the trying times of depression in which we live, but I am sure that the more we struggle to do our duty to God and carry on His work, the more all our worldly interests will be blessed and prospered."[31] Perhaps the struggle of the bishop to do his duty inspired his people to do theirs.

29. Ibid., 1900, p. 43.
30. Gray, *Episcopal Address* (Southern Florida), 1894, p. 69.
31. Ibid., 1895, p. 63.

Bishop Gray was much traveled. He not only covered the Florida peninsula on his annual visitations; his position as Bishop of Southern Florida also required that he journey to the General Convention of the American Church every three years. The General Conventions were always held in the larger cities of the United States and they seldom met in the South, so that by attending them Bishop Gray got a refreshing change of scenery and people and also acquired a national outlook on the ecclesiastical problems of the day. Every ten years his travels took on an international flavor when he, along with his fellow American prelates, attended the Lambeth Conference in London. After these Pan-Anglican conferences, the Florida bishop emerged more spiritually fortified as an Anglican and more ardently Anglophilic as an American. Bishop Gray's first Lambeth Conference (actually the fourth of the decennial meetings, held in 1897) was one of the high points of his life.

Accompanied by Mrs. Gray, the bishop embarked from New York on May 28 and arrived in Glasgow on June 8 after a twelve-day voyage in which they both "proved to be good sailors." The couple spent nearly two weeks in Scotland visiting such places as the Firth of Clyde, Rothsay Bay, the Kyles of Bute, Edinburgh, Melrose, Abbotsford, and the island of Iona, which, because of its association with the early Celtic Church, was of particular interest to the bishop. Then after a slow journey southward, the Grays arrived in London in time to attend some of the events of Queen Victoria's Diamond Jubilee celebration. The festivities honoring the sixtieth year of the queen's reign climaxed in a colorful royal procession through the city followed by a solemn service of thanksgiving in St. Paul's Cathedral, both of which Bishop Gray proudly witnessed. He caught and recorded some of the electrifying spirit that was abroad in London during that historic patriotic festival: "I need not to say more than that being with the Bishops upon the front steps of St. Paul's Cathedral, I had the best possible position from which to observe the wonderful, voluntary outpouring of loyalty and affection to her Majesty . . . from all Quarters of the globe. It was a spectacle especially gratifying to Her Majesty, and doubtless made an addition of many years to her life. A very noticeable and gratifying characteristic of the Jubilee festivities was that it took the form not of an arrogant and boastful claim of superiority over other nations, but of humble and devout thanksgiving to Almighty God for all the mercies and blessings vouchsafed by Him, during the sixty years of Queen Victoria's gracious reign."[32]

The bishop was as pleased with the Lambeth deliberations as he was with the Jubilee and quite delighted by the comprehensiveness and tolerance in the Church: "I deem it the very greatest achievement of the Conference that nearly 200 Bishops from all parts of the world, representing widely different surroundings and interests were able to come together, and for a whole month consider the most important practical questions of our day and time . . . and yet send out reports on all these questions, and also an Encyclical Letter with perfect unanimity. No minority report was presented, no dissenting voice was lifted against the Epistle sent out to the whole world. Only God can make men to be of one mind. Surely He presided during our deliberations." Bishop Gray emerged from the conference more convinced than ever that the Anglican Communion, having received overtures from both the Orthodox and the Presbyterian Churches, was eventually to become "the centre and rally point" for Christian unity.[33]

A memorable occasion during the Lambeth Conference was the reception accorded the delegates by the queen at Windsor Castle. At this reception the good bishop was permitted to meet, if only for a moment, one of the great idols of his life, the Queen-Empress herself. Her Majesty did not mingle long with episcopal guests, however, and when the reception was over she prepared to take her usual afternoon drive. In the meantime the bishops "were placed in rows, on either side of the driveway in the park, through which the Queen passed in her carriage bowing on each side as she went, the Bishops bowing low in return."[34] One wonders if a scene like this gave Gilbert the inspiration for his lines in *The Gondoliers,* "And bishops in their shovel hats/Were plentiful as tabby cats."

If this reception was one of the great moments of Bishop Gray's

32. *Bishop's Diary*, 1898, p. 53.
33. Ibid., pp. 55–56.
34. Fannie C. Gray, "Letter from England," *Palm Branch,* January 1898.

life, it certainly was not one of Queen Victoria's. To the monarch it was a dull and "exhausting" affair. The queen's opinion of the reception was told to Princess Marie Louise by Lady Lytton, who accompanied Her Majesty on the drive. The princess recorded the story years later with charming humor in her memoirs.

As the queen and her lady-in-waiting began their drive "there was a rather prolonged silence at first, and then the Queen said, 'A very ugly party.' " Lady Lytton admitted that the affair was a bit drab. "Of course," the princess comments, "black shovel hats, black gaiters, black silk aprons, and the whole rather gloomy tailoring of these worthy divines was in striking contrast to the gorgeous and colourful Indian and Eastern guests she [the queen] had been entertaining [during the Jubilee]. Then," the princess goes on, "after a further pause, the Queen continued to express her opinion as regards the party she had described as 'very ugly.'

" 'I do not like bishops!' she pronounced."

Lady Lytton nearly fell out of the carriage in horror at the outspoken remark about the revered leaders of the Church. However, in good courtier fashion, she quickly recovered. " 'Oh, but your dear Majesty likes some bishops—for instance the Bishop of Winchester (Randall Davidson, later Archbishop of Canterbury) and the Bishop of Ripon (Boyd Carpenter).'

" 'Yes,' said her gracious Majesty, 'I like the man but not the Bishop!' " and that ended the conversation.[35] It is fortunate that Bishop Gray did not learn of this incident or of his idol's pronounced Presbyterian proclivities.

Before and after the Lambeth Conference Bishop and Mrs. Gray were lavishly entertained by English families who had relatives in Florida, and this heart-warming hospitality was deeply appreciated by the couple. When the conference ended, they crossed the English Channel and enjoyed a leisurely trip up the Rhine, followed by an extended trip to Italy. After almost five months of travel, the Grays returned to Orlando where a relaxed bishop again began the grueling task of administering his jurisdiction.[36]

35. Her Highness Princess Marie Louise, *My Memories of Six Reigns* (London: Evans Brothers, Limited, 1957), p. 146.

36. *Bishop's Diary,* 1898, pp. 56-58.

Much information is available about William Gray the prelate, but what of William Gray the man? What of his private life, his taste in literature, his moments of relaxation? These are questions that can be partially answered by a close reading of his earlier diaries and of the episcopal journals. Bishop Gray was devoted to his family, but unfortunately the demands of his office did not permit him to spend a great deal of time with them. He was particularly fond of his son Campbell, the only child of his second marriage, who as a teenager frequently accompanied his father on visitations about the peninsula. Young Gray's choice of career after graduating from Sewanee greatly pleased his father. Campbell entered General Theological Seminary to study for the ministry in 1903 and after completing his studies he was accorded the rare privilege of being ordained both deacon and priest by his father. Campbell served the mission field in Southern Florida a number of years before transferring to the Diocese of Fond du Lac. In 1925, some six years after his father's death, he was elected Bishop of Northern Indiana.[37] From family accounts there was always a close and touching relationship between the two clergymen.

Bishop Gray also showed great affection for his sister, Miss Emma Gray, a vivacious lady who made her home with the episcopal couple at the Bishopstead. Like Mrs. Gray, Miss Emma was active in the diocesan Women's Auxiliary and in St. Luke's Guild, and she shared the warmth and esteem that the clergy and laity accorded the Grays. Miss Corinne Robinson, a communicant of St. Luke's, Orlando, described the three with these words: "Devoted to young people, 'the Bishopstead Trio' attracted friends of all ages, their home a favorite gathering place where always a cordial welcome awaited." Bishop Gray purchased a horse and buggy as their only means of making local calls; and faithful old "Robin" took Mrs. Gray and Miss Emma on numerous errands of kindness—wherever they knew of sickness or trouble.

The first Bishopstead had a splendid view of Lake Eola, and its large grounds were a constant delight to Bishop Gray, who enjoyed working in the yard whenever he had time between visitations. His

37. *Stowe*, 1926, p. 138; see also *The Episcopal Church Annual* (New York: Morehouse Barlow Company, 1965), p. 292.

especial joy was a huge live oak tree which stood in the parkway directly in front of the house, spreading its great branches with welcome shade over a large area. Some years later a severe storm broke off half of the great tree, tearing its branches from the trunk and leaving the remainder in an unsafe condition. The tree had to be cut down, and the bishop felt its loss keenly. The Grays lived in this house until 1900, when the bishop deeded the property for the use of the Cathedral School and moved into the commodious Pell-Clarke house nearby.[38]

In his rare moments of relaxation, Bishop Gray often occupied himself with reading. From his college days he had been passionately fond of ancient history and particularly of the works of the eighteenth century French historian Charles Rollin. Entries in his diaries show that the bishop waded through most of Rollin's thirteen tomes on the histories of the Egyptians, the Carthaginians, the Assyrians, the Babylonians, the Medes, the Persians, the Macedonians, and the Greeks. Presumably this gigantic task was accomplished in the English translations of James Bell and not in the original French, but the diaries do not make this clear. For lighter reading Bishop Gray frequently dipped into the novels of Scott, Dickens, and Thackeray. The bishop's favorite outdoor recreations were fishing, sailing, and swimming, and he indulged in these sports when he visted the east and west coasts of the jurisdiction. As he advanced in age, however, Bishop Gray was forced to curtail both his reading and his outdoor recreations because of the demands that his office placed on his time and strength.

The rapid growth of the peninsula began to tax the bishop's physical and mental capacities to the limit during his later years. As an administrator he had to work as many as sixteen hours a day sending and answering letters, raising funds, and supervising the great projects of the jurisdiction. There began to be complaints that little things escaped his notice.[39] In the nineteenth year of his episcopate, he spoke realistically of his limitations before the Convo-

38. Robinson, "Cathedral School," p. 7.
39. Ibid., p. 12; see also Elizabeth Rand, "Memories of the Church in the Early Days in Florida," manuscript, Diocesan Library, Winter Park, pp. 8–9; Leonard, pp. 107–8.

cation of 1911: "Increasing opportunities and various needs call for more and more attention, while as I grow older, I feel my powers for grappling with so much and many new calls, are scarcely equal to the demands."[40] A year later in the Cathedral of St. Luke, Bishop Gray spoke again of his age and his increasing responsibilities. The remarks concerned the financial anxieties caused by the indebtedness on his beloved Cathedral School and the Church Home and Hospital. There was also the monetary plight of the jurisdiction's program among the Negroes and the Indians. The bishop seemed no longer able to cope with such knotty problems.[41] It became apparent to both the bishop and his people that he must soon retire.

During the Convocation of 1913 in Key West Bishop Gray announced his intention to present his resignation to the House of Bishops at the General Convention the following October. His announcement overshadowed all else at the meeting. Although it came as no surprise, it was received with keen regret on the one hand, if with thankful relief on the other. No one could have heard the seventy-eight-year-old prelate's bittersweet words without some touch of emotion: "I have now for a whole year been thinking it all over, studying it in all its bearings carefully and prayerfully, and have at last reached the conclusion that for the welfare of the Church and the proper continuity of the work for Christ and for those for whom He died, it is my duty to step down and out, that a younger and stronger man, in his prime and with all the force and vigor and ability demanded by the situation, may correct the mistakes that have been made, meet the increasing number of openings demanding prompt attention, and by God's blessing lead on to the coronation of this branch of Christ's Holy Catholic Church in Southern Florida."[42] An attempt was made by the convocation to alter the old patriarch's decision, but it was to no avail. The resignation was received and accepted by the House of Bishops in New York on October 14, 1913. At the same meeting, the prelates

40. *Convocation Journal*, 1911, p. 64.
41. Ibid., 1912, p. 33.
42. Ibid., 1913, pp. 34, 41.

chose Bishop Gray's successor. They translated the Rt. Rev. Cameron Mann, D.D., Missionary Bishop of North Dakota, to the jurisdiction of Southern Florida.[43]

In the cathedral in Orlando, January 14, 1914, Bishop Gray made his last episcopal address. After twenty-one years as a prelate and fifty-four years as a priest, the bearded old man could point to a number of satisfying accomplishments. Though seventy-eight, he had traveled the whole of his jurisdiction to confirm 415 candidates during the previous year. He had watched the number of his parishes grow from five to thirteen and he had seen the number of missions, organized and unorganized, increase phenomenally from fifty-one to eighty-eight. The clergy had increased in number from twenty to thirty-four.[44]

Within a few weeks of his retirement, Bishop Gray, his wife, and his sister, Miss Emma, moved from Orlando to Nashville, Tennessee, the place of the bishop's last parish before his elevation to the episcopate. For some months in 1914 he was called upon to give episcopal help in the vacant see of New Jersey. His ministrations there included a service at the church in Lambertville, his birthplace. Later that year he returned to Nashville where he was able to perform episcopal ministrations at the request of Bishop Thomas Gailor, the diocesan of Tennessee. On May 11, 1915, Bishop Gray lost his wife, Fannie. Following her death he spent the majority of his remaining years at the home of his son, Dr. Joseph A. Gray of Nashville, although he made yearly visits to Florida and continued to show great interest in the work of the Church in his former jurisdiction.

Bishop Gray died of a heart attack at the home of his son in Nashville on November 14, 1919. On the day of his death he seemed in good health and was active about the house during the morning. About 2:00 P.M. he walked unaided to his room, lay down, and died almost at once. On the Sunday before his death, he had sent a touching message to his many friends in South Florida who were urging that he make his yearly visit. "Tell them all," he said, "to

43. Ibid., 1914, p. 39.
44. Ibid., p. 12.

get together every Sunday at the Holy Eucharist and I will meet them at the Altar."[45]

If the churches of the Anglican Communion are a continuous blend of the Catholic and Evangelical traditions, William Crane Gray was a living example of that blend in its most vigorous expression. The two traditions did not seem to contradict each other in his mind. Both were ways to bring men to Christ, and he championed them with equal fervor and equal love. Although not a ritualist, he diligently kept the feasts and fasts of the Book of Common Prayer, celebrating the Eucharist on all days of obligation. The cope and mitre would have been foreign to his nature, yet he was careful to wear a stole over his chimere and rochet when performing any sacramental function.

Churchmen in South Florida who remember his sermons nearly all agree that he was not a great preacher, but at the same time they recall that he spoke with dedication and concern. The bishop was a typical Victorian in the pulpit, given to flowery phrases and guided in many instances by his emotions. He preached and sang with great gusto and loved such militant hymns as "Onward, Christian soldiers," "Stand up, stand up, for Jesus," and "The Church's one foundation." His favorite pulpit themes were "The Faith once delivered to the Saints," "The harvest truly is plenteous, but the laborers are few," and (particularly in relation to the Seminoles) "Go ye therefore, and teach all nations." As his age increased, Bishop Gray became obsessed with the various European crises and saw in them an impending clash of arms that would signal the end of the world. Toward the end of his episcopate he was often given to preaching lengthily on such themes as "The signs of the times," and "The Second Coming."

In his secret heart the bishop was an "unreconstructed Confederate," a great admirer of the Southern way of life, and it is said that he did not return to the Union until he was seized by the great patriotic fervor that engulfed the nation with its entry into the Spanish-American War. In his international outlook he was decidedly pro-British. He believed in the eventual triumph of Anglicanism

45. *Palm Branch*, April 1920.

and was strongly prejudiced against other churches, Roman or Protestant. Yet he was almost universally loved. One layman wrote, "All who came in touch with Bishop Gray and his work, realized his zeal, devotion, and consecration to it. . . . A strong clasp of the hand and a friendly smile made him the friend of the rich, the poor, and the Indian."[46]

Following Bishop Gray's death, the Very Rev. James G. Glass, Dean of St. Luke's Cathedral, voiced for his congregation and the whole jurisdiction his appreciation of the quality of the bishop's life and labor. "It has been my privilege, on account of the condition of my life, to know many Bishops and Priests of God's Church, and I think I have never known any one of them more deeply and profoundly consecrated to the service of God and His Kingdom, than was Bishop Gray. Essentially reverent and devout, profoundly humble-minded in the presence of God, supremely self-sacrificing in his burning zeal for the cause of Christ, and deeply imbued with the missionary spirit of his Master, no effort, however great—no work, however laborious—no tax or strain, however severe, stopped, or halted, or checked him in the absolute consecration of himself and all that he had, and all that he was, in the service of God. In this District of Southern Florida, where for twenty-one years he labored unremittingly, in season and out of season; in cold and heat; in fair and foul weather; amidst the brightness and the glory and beauty of its lakes and rivers and coasts, or amid the gloom and shadows of its swamps, moss-draped and solemn, he laid his foundation broad and deep for the future building of God's house, and the nurture of His children."[47] The foundation that Bishop Gray laid was indeed broad and deep, and the prelates who followed the bearded patriarch have found it a firm basis on which to continue his work.

46. W. R. O'Neal, "The Protestant Episcopal Church," manuscript, Diocesan Library, Winter Park. Interview with the Very Rev. Francis Campbell Gray, grandson, July 1967.

47. *Palm Branch,* November 1919.

IX

A New Diocese

T HE GENERAL CONVENTION OF THE PROTESTANT EPISCOPAL
Church met in the massive, unfinished nave of the Cathedral
of St. John the Divine in New York City, October 1913. At that
meeting, the House of Bishops accepted with reluctance the resignation of William Crane Gray and came to grips with the task of
choosing a suitable successor. Rather than elect a new man to the
vacant see as Bishop Gray and his Southern brothers preferred, the
House, after due deliberation, decided to transfer an experienced
missionary to Southern Florida from another jurisdiction. The
choice of the House of Bishops was the Rt. Rev. Cameron Mann,
D.D., Bishop of the Missionary District of North Dakota. On October 17 Bishop Mann was translated from North Dakota to the Missionary District of Southern Florida.[1]

In January, Bishop Mann arrived in Orlando to take charge of
his new jurisdiction at the Convocation of 1914. He had had some
twelve years' experience as a missionary bishop and twenty-five as
a parish priest. He was also a student of some attainment in the
area of Tudor-Stuart literature as well as an amateur critic and
poet.[2] The new bishop brought to his largely rural see a scholar-

1. *General Convention Journal: House of Bishops*, 1913, p. 82.
2. *Stowe*, 1917, p. 198.

liness rarely found in the American episcopate, and with it the sensitivity and perceptiveness that are usually the products of a classical education.

During the convocation, Bishop Mann wisely chose to stay in the background while his venerable predecessor tied up the loose details of twenty-one years as Bishop of Southern Florida and bade the clergy and laity of the jurisdiction a fatherly farewell. Toward the end of his last episcopal address Bishop Gray showed that he had overcome the sectional prejudice that had at first made him apprehensive about his successor: "I am increasingly gratified, satisfied and thankful to God for the strong, vigorous and well-equipped successor, physically, mentally and spiritually, to whom I now fully and completely turn over all authority which I have had."[3]   A week before the formal transfer of authority, the old bishop and his family moved out of the Bishopstead and the new bishop with his wife and a freight-car-load of furniture and books moved in.[4] Another ecclesiastical rule had begun.

The first convocation over which Bishop Mann presided was held in one of the younger parishes of the jurisdiction, Trinity Church, Miami, in January 1915. From the pulpit of this dynamic church Bishop Mann signaled the changes of the new regime, but he first paid appropriate tribute to the old prelate whom he had succeeded: "The dominant figure of last year's convocation was the venerable man who for twenty-one years had been going over this huge district planting and nourishing missions in its centers of population and ministering with solicitous searchings to its scattered families. It was fit that he should make, as he did, the convocation address, with its retrospect and its yearning vision of Christian Unity. There is no need that I should dilate, least of all to the churchfolk of Southern Florida, upon the service and accomplishments of William Crane Gray. Truly, there is written for him all over the work of the Church in this district the famous old eulogy, 'Si monumentum requiris, circumspice.' "[5] The new bishop also thanked his people for the warmth with which he had been received in Southern Flor-

3. Gray, *Episcopal Address* (Southern Florida), 1914, p. 45.

4. *Bishop's Diary*, 1914, p. 89.

5. Cameron Mann, *Episcopal Address* (Southern Florida), 1915, p. 40.

ida. He acknowledged the "large and cordial welcome" he had received from the clergy and laity of the district, and the assurance that "the people here are anxious to further the work for which I was appointed overseer."[6] Then he got down to the changes he intended to make in episcopal polity and in the work of the Church in South Florida.

Bishop Mann divided this work into four categories, giving a realistic appraisal of the projects in each of the four. First, he said, was the establishment and support of the missions and parishes for white people; second, the establishment and support of missions and parishes for colored people; third, the labor of the Indian mission; and fourth, what he called "Institutional Work."

The first category, work among the whites, was the "immensely larger one," and the bishop declared that its needs were essentially the same as those all over the rest of the United States. He intended to attempt to satisfy those needs in the vigorous manner of his predecessor. The second category, work among the Negroes, Bishop Mann saw as a special labor. "Not merely is Florida a Southern State with a big Negro population, but it differs from the other Southern States in that a considerable part of this population has come from the Bahamas and belongs to the Anglican Church. We are bound," he declared, "to care for these people baptized in our communion." The tone of his address made it clear that this effort was to be pressed as never before.

The third category of work, the Seminole mission, would be deemphasized. The death of the Rev. Dr. Godden the previous year had stopped the work of the mission, and Bishop Mann doubted his ability to procure a replacement. He no doubt felt the funds used in this project could be more profitably utilized in work among the Negroes, and since the United States government was taking over much of the social program of the Church for the Indians through the offices of the Rev. Lucien Spencer, the bishop felt justified in reducing the Church's role. Dean Spencer, Bishop Mann stated, "can be relied upon to promote all humanitarian endeavor, and to render any Christian service which the Indians may desire."[7]

6. Ibid., p. 29.
7. Ibid., p. 34.

Bishop Mann subdivided the last category, the Church's institutional work, into three parts: the Cathedral School for Girls, the Church Home and Hospital, and the schools for Negro children. The Cathedral School, the bishop said, "furnishes a pleasant home and thorough education at a charge almost absurdly small"; the Church Home and Hospital "has done and is doing the most charitable work for the sick poor that is done in this State." Of the Negro schools he said, "there is nothing more helpful to the colored folk than [these] are, in the places where they exist." He added that since the Cathedral School barely made its expenses it needed many gifts to improve its facilities; that the Church Home and Hospital could not continue operating in the red but would have to be closed unless "it soon receives speedy and substantial aid"; and that the Negro schools existed almost entirely through an appropriation from the General Board of Missions of the National Church and a small tuition fee. It was clear from his address that Bishop Mann considered the Church Home and Hospital the greatest drain on the meagre resources of his jurisdiction. The private hospitals in the Orlando area had deprived the institution of its paying patients. Without this source of revenue, and with little help from the public although it was largely operated as a public institution, the hospital found it impossible to carry on its charitable activities.[8] After running it for another year with a deficit and with no outside financial aid, Bishop Mann closed the doors of the hospital in June 1916.[9] The real property and other assets of the hospital were preserved by the trustees for future medical projects.

In his first address Bishop Mann also tackled the vexing problem of unpaid missionary apportionments which had accrued during the episcopate of his predecessor in the parishes and missions of the jurisdiction. Since the missionary endeavors of the jurisdiction and of the National Church depended largely on the prompt payment of local apportionments, the bishop was determined to see that the obligations were met. The "indifference and laxity" about payments must cease, he declared; instead, he hoped that all the congregations would feel honor-bound to meet their missionary

8. Ibid., pp. 34–35.
9. *Palm Branch*, February 1924.

obligations. He wisely asked the convocation to give every church "a general amnesty" which would wipe out accrued obligations and permit each parish and mission to enter upon the coming year with "a clean slate." This boon was to be granted only "with the distinct understanding and irrevocable decision" that all future assessments were to be paid in full if the local churches wished to continue in good standing and have the services of the bishop. Bishop Mann placed the chief blame for this financial indifference and laxity on his brother clergy. "Rarely, if ever," he informed the convocation, "have I known a congregation which did not pay its assessments, if its priest was determined that it should." But the laity did not escape the episcopal tongue-lashing. "The amounts asked of you," he scolded, "are so pitifully small that you should crimson with shame if they have to be asked twice."[10]

The bishop also mentioned another matter, "and a great one," that of making the Missionary District of Southern Florida into an independent diocese. "This ought to be done very soon," he declared. "We are big enough, and we should be zealous enough. . . . We must create a diocesan endowment fund, whose income will relieve the Board of Missions from its present support of the Bishop. And this means at least $50,000.00; it should mean $100,000.00, so as to meet other current expenses." Bishop Mann later appointed a board of trustees from the clergy and laity of the jurisdiction to receive, invest, and increase the monies of an independent diocesan endowment fund. He also set aside Quinquagesima Sunday as a day on which an offering was to be taken in every church for the endowment fund.[11] The bishop and the trustees unfortunately had to start from scratch since the meagre endowment raised by Bishop Gray had long since been expended on such projects as the Church Home and Hospital and the Cathedral School. Under the new regime, however, it was obvious that none of the resources of the fund were to be touched for any purpose until the goal of self-support had been attained.

The bishop appropriately devoted the remainder of his address to the Great War in Europe. While deploring "the bloody happen-

10. Mann, *Episcopal Address* (Southern Florida), 1915, pp. 35–36.
11. Ibid.

ings" in Flanders, France, Poland, and Galicia, he urged his flock to engage in an even greater war, a war "for the truest salvation" of mankind, the war of the Church Militant. He pleaded with his people to put "the cause of Christ's Gospel so vividly before their minds and hearts that they will gladly make the sacrifices—ordinarily not very big—and perform the duties—ordinarily not very hard—" which the Church demands of its soldiers. The new bishop left no doubt that he expected the soldiers of his jurisdiction to do their duty in the greater war, little suspecting that the country would be drawn into the lesser war within a few years.[12]

Most Floridians were appalled by the tragedy of the war in Europe, and yet the jurisdiction shared with the rest of the United States the economic benefits of that conflict. The demands for food no longer obtainable from Europe brought increasingly higher prices for Florida's citrus crops and for the agricultural products of the rich Lake Okeechobee area. The war also affected the state's tourist trade favorably, causing the very rich who formerly wintered on the Italian or French Riviera to spend their winters at Palm Beach or in other areas of the lower east coast. Palm Beach in particular prospered, gaining a cosmopolitan flavor with its larger and richer clientele, but the whole peninsula became a better-known tourist resort and an appealing area for judicious agricultural investments. New workers, settlers, and tourists came to Florida in unprecedented numbers. It was only natural that the Church should share in the prosperity of the region.

The sudden influx of population bolstered the strength of the Church in numerous parishes and missions throughout the jurisdiction. During the five years from 1913 to 1918 the Church kept pace with the growing population. For instance, the communicant strength of Trinity Church in Miami increased approximately thirty per cent, while the roll of nearby St. Stephen's, Coconut Grove, increased some forty-eight per cent. Key West's growth, stemming from the rapid expansion of the naval facilities on the island, caused old St. Paul's Parish to add one hundred ninety-three communicants to the congregation, representing an increase of over forty-six per

12. Ibid., pp. 36–37.

cent. In the manufacturing port of Tampa the downtown parish of St. Andrew increased some thirty-five per cent, while the new suburban parish of St. John increased a startling seventy-four per cent. The most phenomenal growth in the jurisdiction, however, occurred at Holy Trinity Church in West Palm Beach. During the war years eighty-seven communicants were added to the parish register, representing an increase of over one hundred eleven per cent. Although the statistics of the seasonal parish of Bethesda-by-the-Sea across Lake Worth reflected little change in communicant strength, the revenues of the church increased by slightly over seventy per cent, indicating that the remarkable growth of the winter colony benefitted the church financially. Far to the north, in the predominantly agricultural town of Sanford, the Church of the Holy Cross exhibited a substantial growth of twenty-five per cent in its communicants.[13]

St. Andrew's Church, Lake Worth, was typical of the missions founded during the early war years of Bishop Mann's episcopate. The story of the organization of the mission was told in the *Living Church*. That periodical described the town of Lake Worth, which formally came into being in April 1912, as "an absolutely new town, seven miles south of West Palm Beach, having a population of from eight hundred to one thousand people." The mission was founded less than two years later when "four of its residents, three women and one man, all Church people, walked to West Palm Beach to attend evening service at Holy Trinity Church." After the service the group walked back, a distance of fourteen miles in all. The rector of the church, the Rev. Gilbert A. Ottman, met them after Evening Prayer and, learning how far they had come, determined that if there were such loyal Church people in Lake Worth they should have the services of the Church there. He went to the settlement, gathered the Episcopalians, and organized St. Andrew's Mission. He regularly held two services a month in the "Club Hall" until a little frame building was built, the first building erected by any religious body in Lake Worth. The church, the pews, the altar, and the choir vestments were largely homemade. When the church

13. *Convocation Journal*, 1914, *Parochial Abstracts*; ibid., 1919, pp. 66–71.

was finished in October 1914, there were about twenty-five communicants, and there was the "promise of rapid increase."[14]

The work among the Negroes of the east coast had moved steadily along since its inception by the Holy Cross fathers, and by the beginning of the war in Europe St. Agnes's Church in Miami had become one of the strongest churches, numerically, in the entire jurisdiction. At the close of 1914, there were 784 baptized persons listed in its congregation, and with the help of the national mission board, funds were regularly provided to continue the growth and development of the mission.[15]

As the world war increased in ferocity, many cynics and free-thinkers in the United States pointed to the conflict as a demonstration of the ineffectiveness of Christianity in the modern era. The clergy of the nation could not ignore the war or the critics of the Christian tradition. Bishop Mann, always attuned to contemporary intellectual currents, rallied his clergy and became a lucid defender of the relevancy of Christianity during this time of change and chance. "I do not wonder," he said in a sermon in 1916, "that unbelievers point to the war in Europe as evidence of the failure of Christianity. Still I would remind you that the correct translation of the Angels' Christmas Song is not 'Peace on earth, good will toward men,' but 'Peace on earth to men of good will.' It was never positively promised that the Gospel would abolish wars. And the peace which Jesus did declare should come to his disciples is a peace which the world cannot give and cannot take away. The War in Europe has not affected that."[16]

German submarine activities along the Atlantic coast caused naval installations to grow rapidly. The naval base at Key West was no exception. Bishop Mann described that bustling base during an episcopal visit to the naval yard: "There is great activity, and the place swarmed with 'Jackies.' I saw half a dozen torpedo vessels, and as many submarines, besides various other craft. The tall wireless towers were imposing, especially so when one learns they get

14. *Palm Branch*, November 1914.
15. *Convocation Journal*, 1915, *Parochial Abstracts*.
16. Miami *Herald*, January 12, 1915.

messages from Honolulu."[17] The tiny town of Sarasota also bristled with naval activity. There a highly efficient unit of the United States Naval Reserve was organized months prior to the American entry into the war. Well officered and uniformed, the unit was activated in April 1917, just as the United States entered the hostilities. One of the local ceremonies which preceded the unit's activation was its attendance at Divine Service in the Church of the Redeemer.

The *Palm Branch* reported numerous patriotic services throughout the jurisdiction after the United States entered the war. As the war continued, each issue of the magazine described more flag-blessings, patriotic addresses, and corporate worship services for the various local military units. Florida churches and church guilds threw themselves wholeheartedly behind the Red Cross, Belgian Relief, Liberty Bond, and Naval League drives. As a matter of fact, the Churchmen of the jurisdiction showed such patriotic zeal in supporting these drives that Bishop Mann had to caution them that he hoped their financial ardor for these causes would "not interfere in the support" of diocesan mission projects.[18]

The high schools and colleges of the state were almost totally depleted of male students of enlistment age. When Bishop Mann gave the graduation address at the high school in Arcadia on April 29, 1917, he found that out of a class of twenty-four students, twelve boys and twelve girls, only four of the boys were on hand to receive their diplomas. The other eight had previously enlisted in the United States Navy.[19] In the Church-owned University of the South, it was reported that all of the senior class who could physically qualify had enlisted in the armed forces just before commencement.[20]

The bishop, in addition to his taxing ecclesiastical duties, assumed state leadership in the Food Conservation Program of the United States Food Administration. So effective was he in promoting the aims of the program that he was commended for his services by

17. *Palm Branch*, May 1916.
18. Ibid.
19. *Bishop's Diary, Palm Branch*, May 1917.
20. *Palm Branch*, June 1917.

future president Herbert Hoover in the summer of 1917.[21] The female portion of the bishop's household was also active in patriotic and humanitarian endeavors. Mrs. Mann was a leader in the local work of the Red Cross and Belgian Relief, and one of the bishop's daughters, Miss Dorothea Mann, R.N., joined the Red Cross for overseas duty as a nurse in the spring of 1917.[22]

Of the thirty-three active clergymen in the diocese, two enlisted as army chaplains at the beginning of hostilities: the Rev. Lucien A. Spencer, former cathedral dean and currently U.S. Indian agent and Church missionary to the Seminoles, and the Rev. Henry A. Brown, Rector of St. Andrew's Church, Tampa. Charles Gray, a nephew of the former bishop and the accomplished organist of St. Peter's Church, St. Petersburg, also enlisted in the navy.[23] Chaplain Spencer was assigned to Camp Wheeler at Macon, Georgia, and Chaplain Brown to Fort McPherson, Georgia. Brown obtained the rank of Lt. Colonel, went to France with his unit, and after serving for over a year past the duration of the conflict, died following a surgical operation before his discharge from the army. There are indications that both clergymen took a special interest in servicemen from South Florida. For instance, in July 1918 Chaplain Spencer of the 124th Infantry, Camp Wheeler, reported to Bishop Mann the first death among South Florida Church boys. "He [Private Ralph E. Cooper of Mount Dora] was a particularly fine boy and had a splendid record. His hand became infected while he was at the rifle range and he went to the Base Hospital to have it treated. While there he contracted pneumonia which resulted in death. His mother was with him some time before his death and I saw them on my daily visits to the hospital. I gave him the Holy Communion a few minutes before death claimed him. He was buried at Mt. Dora, his home town."[24]

Towards the close of the war, the entire state was shaken by the great influenza epidemic of 1918. The epidemic reached its height in October of that year and continued with almost unabated fury

21. Ibid., July 1917.
22. Ibid., May 1917.
23. Ibid., May 1919.
24. Ibid., July 1918.

into November. State and county health units closed numerous schools and colleges, and in addition strongly discouraged public meetings and attendance at public worship. The Episcopal Church was at a particular disadvantage during the influenza scare because of its mode of eucharistic worship. Attendance at divine service declined sharply in nearly all churches, and in some places churches were closed. The revenue of some parishes and missions dropped to dangerously low levels. The regular celebrations of the Holy Communion sustained the greatest drop in attendance. There were so many objections (by Church people and non-Church people alike) to the use of the common chalice that Bishop Mann, who had himself caught the disease, addressed the problem. He protested against what he called "the irreligious and unscientific hygienic fads . . . which displayed themselves throughout the jurisdiction." The bishop declared that "a church is about the safest place wherein to avoid people with contagious diseases," simply because an afflicted person would consider it a duty not to attend church and spread the disease. As to those who objected to the use of the common chalice, he stated that the high alcoholic content of the wine plus the metallic composition of the chalice would destroy most chances of an infection. He demonstrated, at least to his own satisfaction, "that no physician has ever traced the origin of anybody's disease to the communion cup," and that "all scientists nowadays acknowledge the immense influence of mind over body, and consequently must allow that the peace and joy of soul, created and supported by holy worship and sacramental grace, are as real prophylactics against contagious diseases as are potions and pills."[25] Apparently neither the bishop nor the clergy of the jurisdiction seriously considered the alternative of delivering communion in one kind. There is no record of such a proposal in either the *Convocation Journal* or the *Palm Branch* during the period that the flu was raging.

The Church institution hardest hit by the epidemic was the Cathedral School for Girls in Orlando. School opened in October with "an able and experienced faculty" and a larger enrollment of boarding pupils than in any previous year, while the attendance

25. Mann, *Episcopal Address* (Southern Florida), 1919, pp. 41–42; see also *Palm Branch*, November and December 1918.

of day pupils, even after the disease had broken out, was above the average. Within a few days, however, the prevalence of influenza in the vicinity of Orlando caused the State Board of Health to close all schools and churches in the area. For several weeks day students were excluded from classes, though the boarding students continued to attend. Then, just as the ban was lifted and the regular schedule resumed, there was an outbreak of the disease among the boarding group, which of course closed the school again, while the epidemic raged through the inmates. At one time there were twenty-eight cases simultaneously under treatment, but fortunately there were no deaths. Needless to say, the Cathedral School operated for the rest of the academic year considerably behind schedule.[26]

When the armistice was declared on November 11, 1918, the lingering remnants of the influenza epidemic prevented any great public services of thanksgiving in most of the parishes and missions of the jurisdiction. Instead the thanksgivings for peace were returned more soberly and perhaps more naturally during the season of Christmas. Bishop Mann expressed their spirit in his quiet, perceptive way in his Christmas message to his people for 1918. " 'On earth peace,'—who of us will listen to these familiar words, when the Second Lesson is read next Christmas morning, without a fresh glow and thrill? . . . Those who sneered or wept last Christmas, when they heard the repetition of the angelic words, can hearken now without cynical doubt or mournful question." The bishop then naturally turned his thoughts to the dead. "Christmastide is the season above all others when we are keenly mindful of our beloved dead. It was they who made so large a share of the joyance of those festivities wherein they shall never take part again. . . . It may be the gray head of our father or mother, it may be the golden curls of our baby, it may be the strong man or the gracious woman, —but in most homes some person is missing, and there is 'a spray of cypress twining in the holly wreath'. . . . This year, in many households, the one who will not join in song and game is the soldier boy who at the very unfolding of his manhood passed away from this world's scene. The loss of such youth, beauty, courage and loyalty

26. *Convocation Journal*, 1919, p. 28.

is, indeed, very great; and grief over the loss must be very great."
But "the consolations," the bishop reminded his people, "are very
great also." They were to be found in the birth of the Babe of
Bethlehem.[27]

In the controversy which followed the peace conference, over
American entry in the League of Nations, the clergy of the jurisdiction generally supported American participation. In the heat of the
debate during the summer of 1919, the *Palm Branch* boldly en-
dorsed the League. "Unquestionably," went the editorial, "it is an
experiment that must be made; it has its dangers, but the dangers
must be braved. . . . It is humiliating and exasperating," the *Palm
Branch* declared, "to have 'party politics' bemuddle the consideration of this question. And the politicians who seek to make the
President's mistakes in the handling of this matter a cause for reject-
ing the proposed League are very short-sighted. They will hurt
themselves much more than they will hurt him. . . . The League of
Nations," the editorial ended, "however novel it may seem, is imper-
atively demanded by the present world conditions. A French wit
has said 'it is impossible and indispensable.' But a nobler and truer
saying is that 'It is a venture of faith.' And 'the just shall live by
faith,'—the just Nation as well as the just man."[28]

Another venture in faith, but a venture closer to home, was the
increased tempo in the work among the Negroes of the jurisdiction.
During the early years of his episcopate Bishop Mann made numerous appeals to white Episcopalians for the support of Negro work.
The appeals were made on both a practical and a spiritual basis.
His address before the Convocation of 1916 was typical and reflected
the attitude of the era toward Negroes. In it the bishop said: "We
all know that the colored population is in this region to stay. It is
a serious element and factor of the community. We must desire,
even for our protection, that they should be educated mentally and
morally. We Episcopalians believe that our system is the best for
the colored folk, as curbing excessive emotionalism and insisting
upon conduct. We must exhibit that belief by doing what we can to
promote that system. Here surely is an instance where 'faith with-

27. *Palm Branch*, December 1918.
28. Ibid., January and July 1919.

out work is dead.' "[29] In spite of his efforts Bishop Mann was unable to unite white Churchmen behind Negro work; therefore, the bulk of the funds. expended on this project continued to come from the National Church. After the war the newly organized missions in such towns as Delray and Fort Lauderdale continued to grow slowly, while unorganized missions in Daytona, Deerfield, Hallandale, Homestead, and West Tampa barely held their own. The main concentration of Negro work was, as it had always been, in the older and stronger missions in Key West, Coconut Grove, Miami, West Palm Beach, and Tampa. Work in these older missions did not always go smoothly, and the largest mission, St. Agnes's in Miami, received more than its share of trouble.

Following a clerical scandal in 1917, Bishop Mann placed a white Bahamian, the Rev. Philip S. Irwin, in charge of St. Agnes's Church. This English-educated clergyman, with his twenty years' experience in the Bahamian mission field, was well qualified to serve in the predominantly Bahamian Miami church. He was soon made Archdeacon for Negro Work in the jurisdiction.[30] The newly appointed archdeacon began his work with eagerness. He was not only a good pastor to his flock, but he also took a dedicated interest in supervising the missions committed to his charge. He exhibited a quiet determination to raise both the educational and the living standards of the Negroes in the Miami area. As time went on, the social work of the clergyman aroused increasing opposition among the poorer and more bigoted white elements of the city. A man as outspoken as he could not fail to make enemies. The easiest, the most plausible, and perhaps the most deadly way for his opposition to attack him was to say that he was an advocate of complete "racial equality," an accusation which the archdeacon often denied. He was, however, a vehement advocate of equality before the law and equality of opportunity. More and more, Archdeacon Irwin came to be regarded as a dangerous zealot by the unenlightened element in the city.[31]

29. *Convocation Journal*, 1916, p. 42.
30. Ibid., 1918, p. 7; *Stowe*, 1917, p. 161.
31. *Palm Branch*, August 1921.

The 1920s like the 1960s were times of fanaticism and violence, and both came prominently into focus in the Irwin case. In the summer of 1921, the archdeacon was attacked and tortured by a gang of thugs, presumably in the pay of higher-ups, who warned him to get out of town or more of the same treatment would follow. The testy clergyman would not be bullied, but immediately brought his attackers before the grand jury. Bishop Mann hastened to the city to appear with his priest before that body. The grand jury, however, refused to indict anyone for the assault on Archdeacon Irwin, "neither the cowards who attacked him, nor the cowards higher up who presumably planned the attack."[32] Furthermore there were strong hints from the legal officers of the city that they could not guarantee the safety of the clergyman if he remained at his post. Shortly after the hearing, the archdeacon resigned his cure and accepted a position on the staff of the Philadelphia City Mission.[33] Bishop Mann, frustrated and disillusioned, lashed out against the legal authorities of Miami for their handling of the case. "For, consider what happened," he indignantly told the next Convocation. "A bunch of men decided that they would capture and torture a man, whose supposed opinions they disliked; and that they would compel him to abandon the home where he was dwelling and go to some other state. And they did. There was no arrest by an officer; there was no trial by jury; there was no sentence by a judge. These men dispensed with the whole apparatus of civilization, and acted as a band of savages."[34]

The attack on Archdeacon Irwin sent a shiver of fear up the spine of the Miami Negro community, but this incident was only one of many that occurred with alarming frequency throughout Florida and the nation during the violent decade that followed the passage of the Volstead Act. Bishop Mann was one of the few clergymen in the state who spoke out against the lawless current of the times. "The duty of the Church is plain," he said. "She must confront the American people and tell them that if they mean to be Christians they have got to obey the laws of the land, without picking and

32. *Bishop's Diary, Palm Branch,* August 1921.
33. *Palm Branch,* January 1922.
34. Mann, *Episcopal Address* (Southern Florida), 1922, p. 45.

choosing, without evasion and sophistry."[35] It was some time before the parochial life of St. Agnes's Church resumed its normal pace, although the general work of the Church among Negroes progressed in spite of the archdeacon's departure. As the decade of the twenties drew to a close, there were fourteen colored congregations in existence in the diocese, many of them in a flourishing condition. To serve these fourteen missions there were six Negro priests working under the supervision of the new bishop coadjutor, John Wing.[36] There was even talk of the advisability of obtaining the services of a Negro suffragan as the number of colored congregations increased.[37]

The years that followed the war were as prosperous for the state as the war years. As early as 1919 Bishop Mann again began to press the jurisdiction to establish its independence and assume its place as a self-supporting diocese of the National Church. The poverty of the prewar years was no longer an excuse for inaction in raising a sufficient endowment for the episcopate. When Bishop Mann returned from the General Convention in Detroit he faced the problem with renewed vigor. That session of the convention had been a humbling experience for the prelate from Southern Florida. "As I looked around the hall in Detroit, where the House of Deputies assembled last October, and saw jurisdictions, not having two-thirds of our clergy and communicants, represented by full diocesan delegations, while Southern Florida was represented by one clergyman and one layman who had no vote on any important question, I felt—well, how would you feel?"[38] Bishop Mann was adamant that his missionary jurisdiction would apply for diocesan status at the next General Convention.

The bishop's proposal was implemented by the action of the Convocation of Southern Florida which met at St. Mary's Church, Daytona Beach, in January 1920. The Very Rev. James Glass, D.D., Dean of St. Luke's, Orlando, offered the following resolution which was adopted by the delegates: "That the convocation of the

35. Ibid.
36. *Diocesan Journal*, 1930, p. 30.
37. *Palm Branch*, February 1926.
38. *Convocation Journal*, 1920, p. 37.

missionary district of Southern Florida hereby declares that its first and most important duty is to set in motion the necessary machinery and organization for constituting itself an autonomous diocese and for petitioning the General Convention of 1922 for admission as such."[39] Bishop Mann at once set out to raise the $50,000 necessary under canon law for episcopal endowment and an additional $50,000 for increasing diocesan expenses. It was not long before the jurisdiction echoed with the bishop's battle cry: "It should be done, it can be done, it must be done, it will be done!"

The endowment was raised through the cooperative efforts of the bishop, the clergy, and the laity of the jurisdiction. Congregations donated special offerings to the cause; women's organizations held socials, fairs, bazaars, and suppers for the benefit of the fund; and laymen from every walk of life contributed in varying amounts to the success of the drive. In January 1919, the endowment fund stood at only $7,500; by January 1921, the $50,000 necessary to make the jurisdiction a full self-supporting diocese was secured, and nearly $17,000 of the second $50,000 was on hand.[40] Bishop Mann continued his persistent and effective canvass to raise the remaining $33,000 during the coming year.

The bulk of the endowment came in large gifts from the laity in the jurisdiction. The Vails in Palm Beach, the Morses and Comstocks in Winter Park, the Knights, Lowrys, and Gilletts of Tampa, and O'Neals, Warlows, and Masseys in Orlando were among the many substantial givers to the campaign. Large gifts also arrived from outside the jurisdiction, mainly from former parishioners of Bishop Mann's in Kansas City, Missouri. A $10,000 contribution was received from the Harold Brown Fund. The vast majority of givers, however, made more moderate contributions. Churchmen in Brevard County were typical of this group. Louis A. Brady and Thomas G. Knight of Titusville, Otto Grosse of Merritt Island, Thurston Ballard and Dr. S. J. Mixter of Eau Gallie, and the Bond sisters of Georgianna contributed sums which ranged from $15 to $125, while Archdeacon Cresson and the Rev. Herbert Cary-Elwes made individual gifts of $50 and $100. In addition,

39. Ibid., p. 42.
40. *Palm Branch*, January 1919; *Convocation Journal*, 1921, p. 40.

some revenues were also secured from the sale of certain church lands in Cutler, Glade Cross, Key West, Ocoee, and Port Tampa. A summary of the sources of the diocesan endowment fund follows:

Gifts from outside Florida	$ 8,955.00
Individual gifts from jurisdiction	46,129.15
Church women's organizations	3,186.31
Offerings from parishes and missions	6,140.82
Sales of land	8,263.68
Miscellaneous (H. Brown Fund, interest on holdings)	30,440.83

When the contributions were totaled at the end of the drive, the assets of the fund had reached $103,115.79.[41] The time of independence was almost at hand.

The thirtieth and last Annual Convocation of the Missionary District of Southern Florida, which convened in Trinity Church, Miami, in April 1922, heard a jubilant Bishop Mann announce that the $100,000 Endowment Fund for the Episcopate was complete and that the jurisdiction was therefore financially stable enough to apply to the coming General Convention for diocesan status. The veteran chancellor, the Hon. Louis C. Massey, who had been present at the formation of the missionary jurisdiction in Sanford in 1893, rose to suggest that a committee of three be appointed by the chair to ascertain what steps should be taken to originate proceedings for the erection of a diocese in Southern Florida. Bishop Mann speedily appointed Chancellor Massey and two clerics: the Rev. L. A. Wye of Holy Trinity Church, West Palm Beach, and the Rev. Robert McKay of St. Mary's Church, Daytona.

Mr. Massey reported comprehensively for the committee that the missionary jurisdiction now met almost all the requirements of diocesan status for the General Convention, showing that a sufficient endowment had been raised and that the jurisdiction contained many more parishes and missions than the general canons required. There were, however, some minor technicalities which had to be met by the convocation, namely, that it choose a name for the new diocese, and that Article II, section 1, of the Constitution of the

41 *Diocesan Journal*, 1923, pp. 69–75; Mann, *Episcopal Address* (Southern Florida), 1922, p. 44.

Protestant Episcopal Church be fulfilled. This requirement provided that when a new diocese was formed out of a missionary jurisdiction, the missionary bishop in charge should become the bishop of the diocese if he so elected. The committee also suggested the convocation fulfill the requirement of electing one clerical and one lay deputy to represent the missionary district at the opening of the General Convention and that four clerical and four lay deputies be elected to represent the new diocese after it was admitted to full union with the General Convention.[42]

The convocation nimbly and enthusiastically dealt with these unfulfilled canonical requirements. The dean, the Very Rev. James G. Glass, was elected clerical deputy to represent the missionary district at the General Convention, and Mark P. Cornwall of Daytona was chosen for the laity. Three additional clergymen were elected to represent the new diocese later: the Rev. Messrs. William C. Richardson of the House of Prayer, Tampa; Robert T. Phillips of Trinity Church, Miami; and Lester A. Wye of Holy Trinity, West Palm Beach. The additional lay deputies elected were the efficient treasurer of the jurisdiction, Frederic H. Rand of Longwood, Myron E. Gillett of Tampa, and John W. Claussen of Miami. The Convocation also selected the name "the Diocese of South Florida" rather than "the Diocese of Southern Florida," and when Bishop Mann elected to become its first bishop, the Convocation received his decision with an unanimous rising vote. An elated Bishop Mann dramatized the historic significance of the occasion at the close of his address: "This is the final convocation of our Missionary District. The chief report made here was that which declared that the endowment fund has been raised. The chief business done here was to prepare our request for admission into full diocesan rank and power. When we adjourn it will be to meet in our next assembly as the First Convention of the Diocese of South Florida."[43]

When the delegates from Southern Florida reached Portland, Oregon, the scene of the General Convention of the Protestant Episcopal Church, in September 1922, the Very Rev. Dr. Glass

42. *Convocation Journal*, 1922, pp. 23–25.
43. Ibid., pp. 30–31, 38, 39.

presented the memorial requesting diocesan status to the House of
Deputies. The memorial, which ably stated Southern Florida's case,
was referred to the Committee on New Dioceses for consideration.
On September 9, the committee returned a favorable report on the
request and on the same day both houses of the convention passed
motions accepting South Florida as a diocese. On September 11,
amidst great applause, all eight delegates from South Florida took
their places in the House of Deputies. Thus South Florida formally
became the seventieth diocese of the American Church.[44]

Diocesan status gave South Florida a greater degree of independence. Her local policies were no longer controlled by the national
House of Bishops. She could elect her own prelate and his auxilia-
ries, and her delegates now had a full voice in the General Convention of the Episcopal Church. But diocesan rank also gave South
Floridians something quite intangible—a sense of pride in achievement. For thirty years, as a missionary district, the area had been
the ward of the National Church. It was now ready to stand on its
own and help carry the burden of the domestic and foreign mission
program of the General Convention.

The Cathedral Church of St. Luke was the scene of the primary
convention of the Diocese of South Florida which convened in
Orlando on January 16, 1923. A bit of sadness mingled with the joy
of the occasion as the aged Frederic H. Rand of Longwood, who
had served the Missionary District of Southern Florida as Treasurer
since its inception in 1893, resigned his office. After thirty years of
devoted and often trying service, Mr. Rand reported the diocese
completely out of debt and in sound financial condition. After his
resignation had been gratefully accepted, Bishop Mann, with the
approval of the convention, appointed John W. Claussen, a Miami
insurance broker and financier, to the post. The Hon. Louis C.
Massey of Orlando continued to act as Chancellor of the new diocese, but much of the legal and administrative burden of the office
was shared by his younger law partner and business associate, T.
Picton Warlow of Orlando. Mr. Warlow had served as Vice-Chancellor of the missionary jurisdiction since 1909.

44. *Palm Branch,* September–October 1922; *Diocesan Journal,* 1923,
p. 40.

Bishop Mann's opening remarks expressed the feelings of most of the delegates on this joyous occasion. "What Bishop Gray hoped for when he came to Orlando thirty years ago, and toiled for during the twenty years of his episcopate—what I hoped for when I came here nine years ago—what all the faithful priests and loyal people of the Missionary District of Southern Florida looked forward to and labored for—has come to pass. We assemble today in glad recognition that our special subdivision of the National Church is now a normal unit with all diocesan rights and privileges." Typically, however, the bishop did not dwell on the past and the joy of the moment. "While we thus triumph and congratulate," he said, "we must remember that new privileges imply new duties and that new power imposes new tasks; our new diocese is, in truth, mainly a summons to larger visions, larger ventures, larger labors, larger givings, and larger sacrifices."[45] Bishop Mann could not know how sorely these larger visions, labors, and sacrifices would be needed in the coming decade, a decade marked paradoxically by the prosperity of the boom and the poverty of the bust.

45. *Diocesan Journal*, 1923, p. 30.

X

The Florida Boom

THE MOST REMARKABLE EVENT OF CAMERON MANN'S EPISCO-
pate was the great Florida land boom. The boom, generally
designated as the period from 1922 to 1926, was an outgrowth of
the prosperous war years. Numerous causes led to this frenzied era
of economic development and speculation. It should be remembered
that during the war the usual exodus of wealthy Americans to the
south of France and northern Italy was prevented by the fighting
and that much of the exodus was diverted instead to southern Florida. The Palm Beach and Biscayne areas prospered greatly as a result of this seasonal immigration, and when the conflict ended the
immigration continued to increase rather than to decline. The postwar years also witnessed an extraordinary increase in automobile
sales and a remarkable extension of highway mileage all over the
United States. Florida was tied into the highway network of the nation and became more accessible than ever to winter tourists and
permanent settlers. Thus the hotels and housing facilities, already
overtaxed by war immigration, were found to be completely inadequate to meet the postwar demands. This situation naturally contributed to the beginning of a building boom which was followed
by a natural rise in real estate speculation. Numerous capitalists who

156

had accumulated a considerable reserve of wartime profits observed the increased economic activity in southern Florida, and quickly realized that the area would be a profitable depository for their investments. It was these investors, men like W. J. Connors in Palm Beach County, and Carl G. Fisher, John S. Collins, George E. Merrick, and Edward E. Dammers in Dade County, who caught the imagination of the American people and touched off what one chronicler of the period called "the wildest and largest 'rush' in the whole of American history."[1]

The vortex of the Florida whirlpool was Miami and the outlying area of Dade County. In the downtown area of the city, hotels, apartments, and business buildings were constructed at an unbelievable pace, while in the residential surroundings housing developments and subdivisions began to extend in every direction. Planned cities like Coral Gables and Boca Raton sprang up in the pine scrub. As the construction and speculative mania increased in tempo it seemed as if everything in Miami was "for sale." Land prices were unbelievable. Downtown real estate at one time commanded a higher price per square foot than land in the most expensive districts of New York City.[2] The Florida historian, Kathryn Abbey Hanna, recorded that land values over the rest of the peninsula were almost as high. According to one report, an eighty-acre tract in the vicinity of Sarasota, appraised at $4,000 in 1923, was sold the following year for $240,000, while another tract in St. Petersburg went up in price from $40,000 to $250,000 in slightly over six months.[3] Land changed hands with amazing rapidity, sometimes as often as ten or twelve times in a few months and nearly always at a profit. These sales increased the craze for speculation, and unfortunately the banks of the state became involved in extending credit to the speculators who had nothing more than pipe dreams for collateral. The boom drew thousands of settlers, businessmen, developers, laborers, and speculators from all over the

1. T. H. Weigall, *Boom in Florida* (London: John Lane, Bodley Head Limited, 1931), p. 2.
2. Ibid., p. 8.
3. Kathryn Abbey Hanna, *Florida: Land of Change*, p. 390.

United States. In the fall of 1925 the whole wild business reached its height—madness *in excelsis*.

Nearly every Episcopal parish and mission in South Florida was affected by the influx of people and by the acceleration of economic development. These churches shared in the growth and prosperity of the peninsula. The churches in the city of Miami, like the community in which they were set, experienced the greatest growth and as a result embarked on the largest construction programs. This was especially true of Trinity Church, Miami's only downtown parish.

Trinity Church, the second building to bear that name, was the first stone church to be erected in the city. It was completed in 1916. Soon after it was occupied by the parishioners, however, the church was deemed too small to take care of its regular congregation and the increased number of winter visitors. The parish was faced with all the problems of a downtown church. Situated in the heart of the commercial section, it had no parking facilities for the ever growing number of automobiles. The congestion and noise of its surroundings made the conducting of services difficult. Then, too, the church had ceased to be in the geographic center of its congregation, which in recent years had been moving farther and farther out into residential areas. Consequently, the vestry of the parish decided in 1922 to sell the downtown property and construct a new church nearer the center of the largest Episcopalian population in the Miramar section of the city. The vestry also made plans for extending the reach and activities of the church by purchasing what it was hoped would be the first in a series of land parcels in other sections of the city for the site of future chapels, a plan that may have been modeled on the chapel system of Trinity Parish in the city of New York. The vestry executed its plans in the spring of 1923 when it sold the downtown property for $275,000 and subsequently purchased two church sites for $80,000, one on Bayshore Drive at North East 16th Street for the parish church and the other at South West 13th Avenue and Second Street for a chapel, which was built later under the name of the Chapel of the Holy Comforter.

Designed by one of the most promising Florida architects, H. Hastings Mundy, in a modified Renaissance-Mediterranean style and resplendent with mosaics and a rose window, new Trinity Church was to endure as one of the great monuments of boom architecture. Planned at an estimate of some $400,000 in 1923, the church eventually cost the vestry over $70,000 more, because of the rising costs of building materials and labor. Unfortunately the additional $70,000 did not include the sum needed to complete the interior, which meant that much of the sculpture, mosaic, and glass work was left unfinished when the congregation moved into the new church in 1925.[4] The nearly completed sanctuary, however, with its altar of veinless Carrara inlaid with a delicate mosaic of the *Agnus Dei* surmounted by a baldachine of variegated Botticini marbles with a soaring, richly carved pediment which framed a colorful mosaic of jade and cerulean blue, gave promise of the beauty of the finished church. The rear of the sanctuary was enclosed by a balustrade of Botticini inlaid with paneling of pink and gray marbles. Above the panelings an enclosure of hand-wrought grillwork extended to the ceiling. The white marble rail with its finely fashioned iron gates also enhanced the beauty of the sanctuary.[5] Both altar and sanctuary were memorials to Julia Frances Rand, given by her children. The rose window at the west end of the nave was given as a memorial to that pioneer of both parish and city, Julia Tuttle. The erection of the new church left the property heavily mortgaged to a Missouri banking house anxious to invest its capital in Florida real estate, the Commercial Bank and Trust Company of St. Louis.

The expense of the new church, a new rectory, and the Chapel of the Holy Comforter left the congregation of Trinity Parish with a debt of over $200,000 when it occupied the Bayshore property in 1925, but the immensity of the debt was not uncommon for the era and the parishioners were not unduly concerned. The congregation was riding the crest of the wave of boom prosperity and had increased in numbers almost one hundred per cent in four short years. The numerous winter visitors, formerly turned away, could be comfortably accommodated in the new church and surely would willingly help to alleviate the burden of the debt during their sojourn. Most important, the parish held bayfront property valued

4. *Diocesan Journal*, 1923, p. 40.
5. *Palm Branch*, June 1927.

at $150,000, which covered almost three-quarters of the debt. The congregation, like the other inhabitants of the area, looked to the future with optimism. After all, they possessed a building that promised to be one of the most beautiful churches in the South when its decor was completed.[6]

Elsewhere in the Biscayne area, other Episcopal churches were experiencing growing pains. St. Stephen's in Coconut Grove was no exception. The building, erected in Spanish mission architecture in 1912, was inadequate almost before it was completed. The growth in the congregation and in the number of winter visitors during the war years forced the vestry to expand and beautify the little church in 1919, when it was enlarged, reroofed, and repainted. When these changes were completed the *Miami Metropolis* devoted several columns to describing the remodeled edifice. "A cloister runs from the west end of the church to the picturesque wall which shuts out the noise of the street and makes it a sanctuary indeed. Pews placed in the cloisters enable the church to take care of any overflow attendance and the little church is always crowded. . . . The restful atmosphere of the little church, its beautiful grounds and rectory, form a picturesque whole about which the community life of Coconut Grove revolves."[7]

The church and the community entered what a local historian called their "golden period" as the decade of the 1920s began. Winter residents were building their bayshore villas, the older residents were prospering from lucrative land sales, and the Grove was beginning to fill up with a well-traveled group of retired army and navy officers who preferred the village to Palm Beach with its more formal and more expensive pace. Families such as the Mathesons, the Munroes, the McCormicks, the Justisons, the Doyles, the Jeffreys, the Blodgetts, and the Meads were active in both church and community life. Perhaps the most colorful Grove couple during this period was Major Reginald Owen, a British army officer who had served in the Royal Engineers during the late campaign in Egypt and Palestine, and his wife, the former Ruth Bryan, daughter of

6. *Convocation Journal*, 1922, and *Diocesan Journal*, 1924, *Parochial Abstracts*.

7. Muir, p. 6.

the "Great Commoner" William Jennings Bryan, three-time candidate for the presidency of the United States.[8]

Ruth Bryan Owen's name appears in the parish records on numerous occasions. On one she was the author of a Christmas play called "The Star of Bethlehem," which she wrote for the children of the Sunday school; on another, she gave a talk on "The Entry of General Allenby and His Crusaders Into Jerusalem" at a tea for the benefit of the women's guild. Both the ladies of the Grove and the Miami *Herald* were intrigued by her outlandish attire for that affair. "Mrs. Owen," the *Herald* stated incredulously, "wore a black gown with a white hat covered with white ostrich. Against her breast shone the Gallipoli Star, one of the decorations given her husband by the commanding officer of the last detachment of the Turkish Army when it surrendered." Mrs. Owen's flair for dress, her magnetic personality, and her genuine social concern soon made her a leader in ecclesiastical and community activities. She was president of St. Stephen's Guild three times and during one of her terms sponsored a garden party at El Jardin that brought some $6,000 into the guild's coffers, the largest amount ever realized from a long tradition of such ventures. In her civic activities she later became president of the Miami Women's Club, a speech instructor at the new University of Miami, and eventually a Florida delegate in the United States House of Representatives. Her public career was crowned by her appointment as Minister to Denmark by the late President Franklin D. Roosevelt.[9]

By 1926 the boom had brought such an influx of new people into Coconut Grove and Coral Gables that St. Stephen's Church could not cope with them. The vestry, after some differences of opinion, decided to sell the old property and build a new church in Coral Gables. The *Diocesan Journal* reported that the property was sold for some $80,000 in late 1925, and that a city block had been given the parish in the city of Coral Gables for a new church, parish house, and rectory. The new church, according to the architect's sketch in the Miami *Herald*, was of an impressive Spanish design with a Moorish flavor. It would cost in the neighborhood of

8. Ibid.
9. Ibid., pp. 6–7.

$165,000 to build. The collapse of the boom, however, prevented the fruition of these plans and the church remained on its original site.[10]

In the Buena Vista section, Holy Cross Church was forced to extend the west end of the church by an addition which accommodated some sixty people, but even so the building was still inadequate. Eventually the vestry made arrangements for a new site and a more commodious building. Late in 1923 an initial payment was made on the property.[11] This congregation, perhaps more than any other, shared its boom prosperity with the missions of the diocese and with the program of the National Church as a whole. During the boom years the parish consistently overpledged on its missionary apportionment. In 1925, for example, the parish overpaid its share by one hundred fifty per cent, an act of unparalleled generosity in South Florida.[12]

The Negro missions in Miami were also profoundly affected by boom growth. At St. Agnes's Church the priest-in-charge reported that an average of fifteen children per month were baptized during 1924,[13] and by the end of the following year the communicant strength of the church had grown to 997. It was not surprising that the foundations of a new church were laid early in the boom to accommodate such phenomenal growth.[14] In Coconut Grove, the congregation at Christ Church grew to 334 communicants. It, too, was forced to enlarge its church building, and by the end of 1925 almost $5,000 had been raised to cover the addition. Late in that year, however, construction was suspended because of "the extraordinarily high cost of materials,"[15] but the following year saw the enlarged church completed enough for use. St. Peter's Church in Key West, the oldest Negro congregation in the diocese, also reported the construction of a new church.[16]

10. *Diocesan Journal*, 1926, p. 101; Muir, p. 7.

11. *Diocesan Journal*, 1924, p. 80.

12. *Bishop's Diary*, 1926, p. 69.

13. *Palm Branch*, January 1925.

14. *Diocesan Journal*, 1926, *Parochial Abstracts*; Mann, *Episcopal Address* (South Florida), 1924, p. 49.

15. *Diocesan Journal*, 1925, p. 75; 1926, p. 109 and *Parochial Abstracts*.

16. *Palm Branch*, January 1924.

To the north of Miami the city of West Palm Beach and its environs were experiencing the effects of the boom almost as vibrantly as Dade County. The atmosphere and pace, however, were more staid. The Palm Beach area was crowded with buyers and sellers of land, its roads were often clogged with high-powered cars, and its hotels were filled with visitors and speculators, but its tone was different, its activities quieter. An English speculator living in Miami observed this difference. "I always noticed this same thing —that, although that community [the Palm Beaches] was enjoying all the fruits of the boom, and although even as in Miami great fortunes were being made there within a few days, there was never anything of that frenzied 'boosting' and general delirium that is the civic characteristic of the more southern city." The Englishman complimented the resort of Palm Beach by adding that "of all the places I ever saw in Florida, it was the most self-controlled and the least blatant."[17] The expansion of Holy Trinity Church 'in West Palm Beach was also more controlled than that of its counterpart in the city of Miami, but the results were as far-reaching.

Holy Trinity Church, during a period of splendid growth, purchased a new site south of the business section on Lake Worth. The property was part of the J. R. Anthony Estate, and the frame church was moved from downtown to its new setting in June 1917. The Anthony house, which had been left on the property, became the new rectory. When the Florida boom began in 1922, West Palm Beach, after Miami, was the community most affected by its bustle. So fast did the city and the parish grow that the frame church became hopelessly inadequate. Under the leadership of the rector, the Rev. Lionel A. Wye, and his vestry, plans were drawn for a new church edifice with the capacity to house a growing congregation of local residents as well as an ever increasing number of winter tourists. The new church, like so much of the architecture of the period, was "American-Spanish" in design. It was of pleasing proportions and possessed an attractive bell tower and an exquisite baptistry with a canopied marble font. The nave of the church was capable of seating a congregation of seven hundred, and the chancel

17. Weigall, p. 26.

seated a choir of fifty. The sanctuary, with its altar of Italian marble
and mosaics, dominated the interior of the church, and a magnificent
Skinner organ gave promise of enhancing the beauty of the liturgy.
The cost of the new church, in addition to the fee charged for having
the rectory and old church (which was to be used as a parish house)
moved to nearby sites, exceeded $125,000. Most of the construction,
like that of Trinity Church in Miami, was financed by the Commercial Bank and Trust Company of St. Louis. The first service
was held in the new church on February 24, 1924.[18] Although the
congregation of Holy Trinity Church was heavily in debt, it was
extremely optimistic. There was room for optimism. The parish had
grown from 159 confirmed persons in 1921 to 320 at the close of
1923,[19] and there were no signs that the growth was diminishing.

Across Lake Worth in the winter colony of Palm Beach, the congregation of Bethesda-by-the-Sea also felt the boom. The rector of
the church, the Rev. James Townsend Russell, D.D., an honorary
canon at the National Cathedral of St. Peter and St. Paul in Washington, D.C., began a drive for a new building in 1924. The Rev.
Canon Russell envisioned the edifice in the "Spanish Gothic" style:

A little Spanish Church
set in a grove
of coconut palms
a hundred yards
from the sea . . .

The new church was incongruously intended to serve as a memorial
to the landing of Juan Ponce de Leon, the discoverer of Florida,
and to the "qualities" of the Spanish people "which, for a brief
century, lifted them to the summit of the world."[20] It perhaps did

18. Historical Sketch, Parish Records, Holy Trinity Parish, West Palm
Beach.
19. *Convocation Journal*, 1921, p. 57; *Diocesan Journal*, 1924, *Parochial
Abstracts*.
20. Kathryn E. Hall, "History of the Episcopal Church of Bethesda-by-
the-Sea," *Chronicles, The Church of Bethesda-by-the-Sea, 1889–1964* (West
Palm Beach, Florida: Distinctive Printing, Inc., 1964), pp. 62–63.

not occur to the idealistic mind of the parson that whatever these "qualities" may have been, toleration was not included among them, and that for almost half a century, the Spanish king, His Most Catholic Majesty, Philip II, had attempted by every means in his power to uproot the Anglican Church and all its pernicious doctrines. The spirit and conception of the good canon's incredible dream were embodied in a booklet, *The Spanish Memorial*, which he published in 1924, describing the proposed new church. The booklet, despite its historical incongruities, was immensely successful in raising money to make the dream a reality. The cornerstone of the church, which bears witness to Canon Russell's romantic scheme for a Spanish memorial, was laid March 15, 1925. The dates on the stone read "A.D. 1513–1925," but the connection between the date of Ponce de Leon's landing and the start of construction of the church is left to the imagination of the viewer.

The new church, the third building to be occupied by the congregation, was located at the corner of County Road and Barton Avenue facing the lake. Designed by the architectural firm of Hiss and Weeks of New York, it emerged as possibly the most Britannic "Spanish Gothic" church ever built! Constructed of stones which were dressed on the premises, it is contemporary with Palm Beach's finest and most elaborate buildings: the new Breakers Hotel, the Bath and Tennis Club, and St. Edward's Roman Catholic Church. When it was completed, at a cost of some $650,000,[21] Bethesda-by-the-Sea was the most expensive and probably the most beautiful Episcopal church to be constructed in the Diocese of South Florida during the boom period. Taken as a whole, the church and the later parish house, garth, and cloisters have carefully adhered to the Gothic theme, and even the adjoining Cluett Memorial Gardens blend into the Gothic design. The restrained and simple beauty of the original exterior, interior, windows, sculpture, and decor of the church has only been enhanced by later additions. The congregation occupied the new church in November 1927.

The expanding Bahamian congregation of St. Patrick's in West Palm Beach enlarged its church building in Spanish style early in

21. Ibid., pp. 64–65.

the boom. With the help of Palm Beach winter visitors, the mortgage was rapidly retired and by 1924 plans were in the making for a new parish house.[22] The boom years also witnessed the organization of Negro missions in other southeast coastal towns: St. Matthew's, Delray; St. Mary's, Deerfield; St. Christopher's, Fort Lauderdale; St. Cyprian's, Homestead; and St. Ann's, Hallandale.

Just south of West Palm Beach in the newer community of Lake Worth, St. Andrew's Church attempted to keep pace with boom growth by enlarging and improving its church building. In the southernmost mainland city, Homestead, the story was similar, but the stable agricultural enterprises in the vicinity made the growth less ephemeral. Many improvements were made on the property of St. John's Church and the mission petitioned for parish status during the Diocesan Convention of 1926.[23] All Saints' Church in Fort Lauderdale considered a new building to accommodate the influx of people, but continued to share the ministrations of its priest with St. John's Church, Dania, where that tiny congregation was swelled by Episcopalians from the boom town of Hollywood. St. Paul's, Delray Beach, was, like the town it served, largely a creature of the Florida boom, and during those years it was able to build a small church whose congregation was also served by the priest-in-charge of All Saints', Fort Lauderdale.[24]

Farther north, Melbourne experienced more building and growth than the other towns in Brevard County. Hotels, clubs, and houses mushroomed on the beach and in the palmetto and oak scrub west of the river. Holy Trinity Church, which at the turn of the century had been moved from its original site on Crane Creek to the center of the village, found itself more financially fit to deal with the boom growth than either of its sister churches in Cocoa or Titusville. The congregation sold a tract of some sixty-five acres on Crane Creek, given by the benevolent Mrs. Lucy Boardman of New Haven in the 1880s, and used the proceeds ($12,000) to build a new parish house and enlarge and stucco the church. A square belfry and electric organ were also added. The cost of the new parish

22. Mann, *Episcopal Address* (South Florida), 1924, p. 52.
23. *Diocesan Journal*, 1926, pp. 22, 33.
24. Ibid., p. 117.

house was about $10,000, of the additions to the church, about
$2,000; so the vestry emerged from the expansion program rela-
tively free from debt.[25] In Cocoa, St. Mark's Church enjoyed a
similar but perhaps more tasteful enlargement and remodeling.
Large transepts were added and the entire building was stuccoed.
St. Mark's, however, was to suffer for a number of years from the
lack of an adequate parish house.[26] In Titusville, the less spectacular growth of the town did not force an enlargement of the well-
proportioned board-and-batten church, which until the more recent
boom remained one of the best examples of its architectural type
in Florida.

South of Fort Pierce, in the growing settlement of Stuart, a
church with parish status was organized under the patronage of St.
Lucia. Although the congregation used the facilities of All Saints'
Church, Jensen-Waveland, several miles down the coast, plans
were made to build in the near future a church in the Spanish mission style, at a cost of $55,000.[27] St. Andrew's Church in Fort
Pierce also reported much growth and assisted in establishing a
Negro mission in the city. Following the collapse of boom construction in the Miami–Palm Beach area, additional Bahamians had
migrated to Fort Pierce to work in citrus and other farming. By
November 1927 these Churchmen were formally organized as a
diocesan mission under the patronage of St. Simon the Cyrenian.
With the guidance of the rector and vestry of St. Andrew's Church
a class of fourteen candidates was presented for confirmation.[28]

Central Florida, like the southeast coast, was profoundly affected
by the growth engendered by the boom. As early as the summer of
1921, the cathedral chapter in Orlando decided that the already
enlarged frame church was too small, and discussed a motion to
build a new cathedral. The chapter communicated its general ideas

25. Ibid., pp. 38 and 78–79; see also Amey R. Hoag, *Thy Lighted Lamp:
A History of Holy Trinity Church, Melbourne, Florida* (Eau Gallie: Undersea Press, 1958), pp. 33 and 84–85. According to the Hoag estimate, 93
acres were involved in the original Boardman gift.

26. *Palm Branch,* September–October and November 1925.

27. *Diocesan Journal,* 1926, p. 105.

28. *Palm Branch,* December 1927.

to a "specialist" for advice and an estimate,[29] and after several years of negotiation with builders and architects, engaged the celebrated eastern firm of Frohman, Robb, and Little to draw plans for a new church. In the meantime the chapter contracted to have the old cathedral moved to the south side of its property so that building could begin when the architectural plans were accepted. The price for moving and settling the old building was $400. The Frohman, Robb, and Little plans for an elaborate Spanish Gothic church were submitted and accepted by the chapter on February 25, 1925, but because of a lack of funds it was decided to build only the nave of the proposed building. A number of bids were submitted by local and regional contractors ranging from $109,000 to $123,000 exclusive of plumbing, lighting, and heating. These bids evidently horrified the chapter, which rejected them and ordered the architects to submit a simplified version of the nave with a seating capacity of six hundred. The cost of this portion of the cathedral was not to exceed $75,000. The simplified plans were submitted in the spring, but none of the new bids was less than $90,000. After a period of agonizing delay the chapter finally accepted the bid of A. B. Struble, who was awarded the contract for $90,200. The chapter borrowed $70,000 at eight per cent interest from the State Bank of Orlando against a subscription of that amount, and the new church was begun.[30] When this price is compared with the bids submitted for similar churches on the lower east coast during this period, it appears that the cathedral chapter did not come out badly. The cornerstone of the cathedral was laid on Easter Monday, 1925.[31]

On Easter Even a year later the parishioners of St. Luke's "witnessed the partial fulfillment of a dream long cherished" when the nave of the cathedral was dedicated by Bishop Mann with the assistance of Dean C. Stanley Long. One of the most beautiful features of the structure was the great stone portal at the entrance of the church (given as a memorial by the Payne family) and the rose

29. Chapter Minutes, Parish Records, St. Luke's Cathedral, July 6, 1921, pp. 180–81.

30. Ibid., pp. 191, 233, 247, 255, 265.

31. *Palm Branch*, May 1925.

window above it.[32] This noble entrance has dignified the church
for over two generations, and it, more than any other adornment,
has enabled the viewer to imagine the beauty of the completed
structure. Since 1926 no attempt has been made to complete the
cathedral, although the bulk of the stained glass has been placed in
the nave. Without its soaring Spanish tower, its transepts, its great
choir and sanctuary, and its decorative Gothic pinnacles, the building presents a box-like, unfinished appearance. The Cathedral
Church of St. Luke is the only ecclesiastical structure in the diocese
designed in the manner of a great European cathedral, so it is particularly unfortunate that financial difficulties incurred at the time
of the bust prevented the fulfillment of the "grand design."

During the boom years the city of Sanford and the venerable
Church of the Holy Cross were making steady if less spectacular
progress than neighboring Orlando. This progress, however, was
interrupted on November 27, 1923, by a catastrophe. A fire which
started before daylight in a bowling alley behind the parish house,
supposedly from a forgotten cigarette, spread rapidly through the
parish house and into the church and rectory. The Sanford Fire
Department was powerless to stop the blaze, for lack of water pressure. The high-spired Upjohn frame church, built in 1873 and rebuilt after the storm of 1880, was totally consumed in the flames
along with the parish house and rectory. The destruction of the
church was not only an architectural loss but a historic one as well,
since within its walls the primary convocation of Southern Florida
had organized itself in February 1893. The loss of the parish house
was also keenly felt. Not only was the parish deprived of its social
center and church school facilities, but the town lost a well-equipped
community recreation center. Most of the church furniture and
vestments were saved, with much of the rectory furniture on the
first floor, but all of the rector's clothing and other personal belongings on the second floor were lost, including a personal library
valued at over $15,000. The genial rector, the Rev. Arthur S. Peck,
and his eighty-two-year-old mother themselves only narrowly escaped injury. The insurance on the buildings covered only $20,000

32. Ibid., April 1926.

of the estimated damage of almost $60,000, leaving the congregation to make up the difference.[33]

The community of Sanford reacted to the desperate plight of Holy Cross Church in a touching and truly Christian way. Long before the terms came into wide use, the citizens of the town demonstrated "social involvement," "Christian concern," and "ecumenism." The Knights of Columbus held a special meeting on the day of the fire to send a resolution of sympathy and to offer the congregation the use of their meeting hall, and other denominations also offered the parish the use of their buildings. When the vestry of Holy Cross began a drive for funds for a new church, the glee club of Baptist Stetson University gave a benefit concert for the drive, and checks were received from the Methodist "Daughters of Wesley," the pastor of All Souls' Roman Catholic Church, and the Congregational minister, whose church Father Peck's parishioners were using temporarily.[34] The new church was built in the prevailing Spanish mission style at a cost of about $41,000 with its furnishings. It was first used on Easter Day, 1925. Some time later the new parish house was completed in the same Spanish mission design. It contained a stage and an auditorium seating 250 persons, together with classrooms for the church school and an office for the rector. The cost of the parochial building was approximately $30,000.[35]

All Saints' Mission in Winter Park also kept pace with a growing community. Under the leadership of its new priest-in-charge, the Rev. James Bishop Thomas, Ph.D., the strength of the congregation increased to such an extent that in 1924 the mission was admitted by the bishop and the Standing Committee of the diocese as a self-supporting parish. A new parish house was built as a memorial to Mrs. Charles R. Switzer, and the church was enlarged by the addition of a chancel. Mrs. C. H. Morse gave the parish a new rectory, and the church was enriched by the gift of an organ in memory of Nannie V. Hayes. In addition to being rector of All Saints', the Rev. Dr. Thomas served to great effect as professor of philos-

33. Ibid., December 1923.
34. Ibid.; see also January 1924.
35. Ibid., October 1927.

ophy at nearby Rollins College.[36] In nearby Eustis, St. Thomas's Church, like the church in Winter Park, was enlarged and remodeled in a curious combination of Tudor and Spanish architecture. The frame church of St. Barnabas in DeLand experienced similar alterations.[37]

Farther south in the progressive citrus community of Winter Haven, the comparatively new mission of St. Matthew was maturing rapidly. Organized in 1912, for a number of years the mission shared the ministrations of the Rev. James H. Davet with Holy Trinity Church in Bartow. In 1917, however, the congregation completed a church. At the time of construction there were only 21 communicants in the mission. Four years later the number had more than doubled, and in 1924 there were 85 confirmed persons attached to the congregation.[38] What had been St. Matthew's Mission became St. Paul's Parish when the vestry requested a change of name and parish status in November 1924. The new parish moved and enlarged the church, purchased land for a rectory which it soon constructed, guaranteed a clerical stipend of $2,000, and called the Rev. James H. Davet to be its first rector.[39] The enlarged church was later brick-veneered in Gothic style at a cost of approximately $50,000, and a considerable number of pledges were made for memorial windows.[40]

In Bartow, the county seat of Polk County, the congregation of Holy Trinity outgrew its building during the late 1920s and was forced to enlarge and remodel the old frame church. The exterior was entirely refinished in the Old English style of half timber and stucco, and a parish house in much the same style was appended to the church.[41] East of Bartow in the booming town of Lake Wales, another Episcopal congregation was formed when in July 1925

36. *All Saints' Church: The History of the Parish* (Winter Park, Fla.: Orange Press, 1947), pp. 12–13.

37. *Palm Branch*, June 1923.

38. *Convocation Journal*, 1918, p. 70; 1922, p. 76; *Diocesan Journal*, 1924, *Appendix*.

39. *Palm Branch*, January and December 1925.

40. *Diocesan Journal*, 1927, p. 103.

41. Ibid., June 1929.

some twenty-six communicants from the vicinity met and organized the mission of the Good Shepherd. Within a year the number had grown to forty and a church had been erected.[42]

Lakeland, which had grown from a tiny village into the metropolis of Polk County in a matter of a few decades, experienced an even more accelerated growth during the boom years. The parish, which expanded from 142 communicants in 1922 to 267 five years later,[43] found that the old frame church which had been moved from the abandoned English colony of Acton was hopelessly inadequate. Under the direction of its rector, the Rev. G. Irving Hiller, the vestry of All Saints' Parish undertook a building program that would accommodate the growth of its congregation. In 1923 a new church was begun. The building, like so many of its contemporaries, was "Spanish Mission" in architecture and hollow tile in construction. It possessed a massive but puzzling bell tower without bells, and a side chapel which housed much of the original furniture and appointments from Acton Church. The congregation used the basement of the church for a parish house and church school. The new church, which cost in excess of $38,000, could seat about 500 persons. Looking to the future the vestry of All Saints obtained a lot in the southern section of the city for the purpose of building a chapel or mission, since the continued growth of the city would soon make another Episcopal congregation a necessity.[44]

In Ocala, the most northern city of the diocese, Grace Church found it necessary to enlarge its facilities during the boom years. To accomplish this expansion the vestry persuaded the trustees of the diocese to sell the property of the dormant Negro mission of St. James for $3,500. Half the proceeds of the sale were given to Grace Church and the other half to St. Peter's, the Negro congregation in Key West which was also in the process of building a new church.[45] During this period the foundations of St. Agnes's, Sebring, and Trinity Church, Mount Dora, were laid. The mission

42. Ibid., August 1925; 1927, *Appendix.*
43. *Convocation Journal,* 1922, p. 56; *Diocesan Journal,* 1927, *Appendix.*
44. *Palm Branch,* January 1924; *Diocesan Journal,* 1926, p. 32.
45. *Diocesan Journal,* 1925, p. 25.

in Mount Dora, however, was unable to weather the collapse of the boom and so lapsed into a state of dormancy.[46]

The growth of the Church on the west coast of the peninsula was even more spectacular than that in central Florida. Building new churches was a characteristic activity of almost every parish in the city of Tampa. At St. Andrew's, the mother parish of the city, the stone church less than two decades old was already inadequate. After considerable disagreement, the vestry voted to sell the downtown site and build a new edifice in the residential area around Plant Avenue. In 1925 the Standing Committee of the diocese gave the vestry permission to complete the sale and to increase the mortgage on its other holdings to the amount of $100,000.[47] Not long after, construction was begun on the parish house at the new site. Contemporary with the expansion of St. Andrew's Church was an ambitious building program in the suburban parish of St. John's. There a commodious church was begun in the Neo-Gothic style. It was to cost $60,000, but before ground was broken the congregation had some $24,000 on hand to deal with initial costs. The vestry also had a promise of $5,000 for an organ on the completion of the church.[48] In another section of the city, Tampa Heights, the congregation of the House of Prayer completed a stone Gothic church in 1923, just before the bustle of the boom reached the city, and within two years a new rectory was purchased.[49] The Negro mission in Tampa also was enjoying a new church. Just before the boom a brick church was constructed for St. James's, and in 1923 the mission obtained a suitable rectory. The dynamic priest-in-charge, the Rev. John E. Culmer, capably brought his people through these hectic years of expansion by obtaining a considerable portion of the necessary funds for construction from the diocese and from other sources outside the parish.[50]

Across Tampa Bay in St. Petersburg, St. Bartholomew's Church, which was closed following the English exodus after the Great

46. Ibid., 1923, p. 27.
47. Ibid., 1926, pp. 21–22.
48. Ibid., 1925, p. 38.
49. *Palm Branch*, March 1923.
50. Mann, *Episcopal Address* (South Florida), 1924, p. 52.

Freeze, was reopened at the end of the war as a mission. By 1925 the growing congregation was able to secure the services of a resident clergyman and to build a rectory.[51] The mission continued to prosper during the boom years and for a while it appeared that the congregation would become a self-supporting parish. However, the downtown church, St. Peter's, experienced the greater growth. During the boom years the communicant strength of this parish increased from 234 to 367.[52] In the tourist season the church was crowded to utmost capacity. To cope with the problem of growth and space the vestry was forced to begin an ambitious building program. Unlike parishes of comparable size, however, St. Peter's decided to enlarge the existing church rather than begin anew. The parish provided a budget of $100,000 for additions to the old building in the late spring of 1925. When the alterations were completed the church seated a congregation of about 1,000 persons. Bishop Mann remarked after a visitation to the enlarged church that St. Peter's was doubled in "size and stateliness."[53] Although St. Peter's is one of the largest churches in the diocese, it cannot be classified as one of the greater buildings of the period as it lacks the architectural unity of its contemporary churches in the Mediterranean or Gothic styles. It does, however, have a warmth that comes from not being rigidly stylized, and this warmth along with the concern of its congregation and clerical staff has continued to draw over the years the largest winter congregation in the state of Florida.

To the north of St. Petersburg, the boom infused new life into the Gulf coast city of Clearwater and the Church of the Ascension. In 1920 the little church was a struggling mission with only forty baptized members, but as the boom brought other inhabitants to the town the mission was able to garner more than its share of newcomers. Two years later Ascension Church became a parish, and by 1926 its baptized members numbered some 281 persons.[54] The rapid expansion of the congregation and an increasing number of

51. *Diocesan Journal*, 1926, p. 53.
52. Ibid., 1921, p. 55; 1926, *Parochial Abstracts*.
53. *Palm Branch*, June 1925; *Diocesan Journal*, 1926, p. 53.
54. *Convocation Journal*, 1920, p. 51; 1922, p. 54; *Diocesan Journal*, 1927, *Parochial Abstracts*.

seasonal worshippers called for more space than the little wooden church could possibly provide. During 1925 the vestry conducted a building drive and that same year a new church, a "white stone Gothic" building, was constructed. A parish house was also built on an adjacent lot. These buildings cost over $60,000 while the property on which they were situated was valued at $20,000, yet when the year closed the congregation owed only $3,250 on the plant.[55]

Just south of Tampa Bay in the bustling town of Bradenton, Christ Church, which became a parish church as early as 1907, shared with other Gulf coast congregations the growth of the boom. This parish solidly supported the diocesan missionary program, the episcopal endowment fund, and the Cathedral School, and made regular contributions to The University of the South.[56] South of Bradenton the old Scottish settlement of Sarasota seemed to have a promising future. Bishop Mann, after his spring visitation in 1923, made the following observation and prediction: "The town is growing rapidly, and, with its beautiful location, is certain to be one of the leading places in South Florida in a few years." The Bishop confirmed a class of eight and preached to a congregation of over sixty "even after the winter people had gone."[57] During the boom years the Church of the Redeemer was enlarged to accommodate a congregation of 400, a two-manual organ was installed, and a "modern" rectory was secured for the priest-in-charge. According to a report in the *Palm Branch* in January 1925 the mission declared itself ready for parish status, but no formal petition was presented to the Diocesan Convention or the Standing Committee that year, and the collapse of the boom delayed the mission from assuming a self-supporting role for a number of years thereafter.

Few churches in the diocese, if any, made more progress during the boom than the southernmost mission on the Gulf, St. Luke's, Fort Myers. Before the boom the church had only a score of worshippers, who met in a small wooden structure "inconveniently located," and its clergyman shared his ministrations with a number of other nearby missions. The growth of St. Luke's kept pace with

55. Ibid., 1926, p. 101.
56. *Convocation Journal*, 1907, p. 4; *Diocesan Journal*, 1923, p. 77.
57. *Palm Branch*, June 1923.

the town, however, and in 1924 the mission became a parish. Property was purchased in a strategic part of the city and a new parish house of hollow tile with a massive beamed roof was constructed on the site. A new rectory of similar material and in the same Spanish style was built adjoining the parish house. An impressive church of mission architecture was to complete the complex, but the parish house served as a temporary place of worship until plans for the construction of the church could be completed and financed. It contained a main hall seating some 300 persons and a stage that was suitable as a temporary chancel. The new parish house and rectory cost over $40,000, the bulk of which was paid soon after the completion of the building.[58]

The Diocese of South Florida made a very advantageous land transaction in central Florida during the boom years. The commissioners of Orange County were desirous of buying the site of the Bishopstead in Orlando for the purpose of building a new courthouse. The chancellor of the diocese, the Hon. Louis C. Massey, pointed out that since the Bishopstead was old, maintenance was becoming exceedingly expensive while the land was quite valuable as business property. With the blessings of the bishop and the Standing Committee, he arranged the sale of the property to the county commissioners. The sale price was $250,000 payable with a $1,000 binder on the execution of the agreement, $24,000 on April 1, 1925, and the balance in annual payments of $25,000 each with interest at the rate of six per cent per annum. The county commissioners permitted Bishop Mann to occupy the premises until January 1, 1926. Several months after the sale Bishop Mann selected two lots on Lake Virginia in Winter Park as the new site of an episcopal residence. The Endowment Fund Corporation bought the lots on the bishop's recommendation at a price of $22,000, a purchase easily made by the corporation since its assets at that time stood in the neighborhood of $375,000. The members of the corporation were given to understand that the episcopal residence would be built on the eastern half of the property so that the western half could be sold at a later date if necessary. Shortly after the settlement

58. Ibid., March 1924; April 1923.

of this land transaction the aging Louis Massey resigned the chancellorship. He had served the missionary district and diocese thirty-two years. He was succeeded by the Hon. Floyd L. Knight of Miami.[59] Thomas Picton Warlow, Judge Massey's law partner, continued to serve as vice-chancellor.

Construction of the new Bishopstead began almost as soon as the lots in Winter Park were purchased. The house, built in the style of a Spanish villa, was completed at a cost slightly in excess of $50,000. Bishop Mann described the house in this way: "I merely say that it is ample, convenient, durable, beautiful, of the best materials and workmanship, and practically fireproof. It has, what its predecessor lacked, a small chapel. Also, it has a proper safe for the storage of Diocesan records." A number of relics were incorporated from the old house, and of these the bishop was most pleased to have the sturdy old wrought iron fence "which Bishop Gray regarded with honest pride."

Bishop Mann was well aware that the cost of the new residence was considered somewhat extravagant by a number of his clergy and laity. With them he was quite honest: "I will frankly say that I wish the property might have cost less. But I say with equal frankness that I think what has been done was the proper thing. You will all, I am sure, acquit me of self-seeking motives to sway me." He went on to explain that "both my feeling and my judgment are that the Diocese should have this commodious and dignified Bishop's House. Especially, since the people have not been asked to contribute one cent toward its erection,—the whole cost being only a quarter of what the Bishopstead in Orlando was sold for." He also pointed out that if the diocese should ever wish to dispose of the property, it could be done at "a large pecuniary profit." On the night of December 14, 1925, Bishop and Mrs. Mann moved into the new residence.[60]

The institutions of the Diocese of South Florida as well as its parishes and missions were affected by the growth of the state during the boom years. The Cathedral School for girls fared well. The

59. *Diocesan Journal*, 1925, pp. 27–31.
60. *Bishop's Diary*, 1926, p. 56; *Palm Branch*, January 1926.

buildings were kept in sound repair, a capable and enthusiastic headmistress was employed, and a competent faculty, which ranged from fifteen to eighteen members, considerably raised the standard of scholarship. The school also enjoyed the addition of a fully equipped science department, the gift of over 500 volumes to its library, and a number of modern shower baths in Cluett Hall. The boom years saw a steady increase in the number of students in the school, both day and boarding.[61] In January 1926 the enrollment reached its peak with 167 scholars. Of this number, a third were in the high school, a third in the intermediate grades, and a third in the primary department. Of the forty-five boarding students thirty-six were from Florida, with St. Petersburg and Winter Park leading the representation with five pupils each, and Miami–Coconut Grove and Tampa following closely with four and three students respectively. Eight other states and one foreign country, Cuba, also sent boarders to the institution. The religious affiliation of the student body was also interesting: sixty-five were Episcopalians, thirty-two Methodists, twenty-two Presbyterians, eleven Christian Scientists, nine Baptists, six Christians, two Roman Catholics, two Lutherans, two Congregationalists, and two Jews. A number of girls listed affiliations with smaller denominations and seven belonged to no church whatsoever.[62]

Despite its heavy enrollment the Cathedral School did suffer a physical setback in December 1925. At that time the city of Orlando extended Pine Street directly through the school grounds, separating the primary department and the music rooms from the remainder of the school and ruining the tennis and basketball courts. This action was accomplished by the city commission through condemnation proceedings, which awarded the school the inadequate price of $7,000. A frustrated headmistress reported to the Diocesan Convention of 1926 that "every classroom is in use all of the time during school hours and every foot of the playground during recreation hours."[63] The shortage of classroom space was greatly relieved by

61. Mann, *Episcopal Address* (South Florida), 1923, p. 33; *Diocesan Journal*, 1923, p. 66.
62. *Diocesan Journal*, 1926, pp. 29–30.
63. Ibid.; *Palm Branch*, June 1925.

a gift of $30,000 to the school for the construction of another academic building. The new building, first used in 1929, proved to be the most handsome and useful hall on the campus. Built in a Spanish design, it was named Bishops' Hall in honor of the school's founder, William Crane Gray, and the current diocesan, the Rt. Rev. Cameron Mann. In addition, the endowment fund of the school was increased to almost $9,000 and a number of scholarships, full and partial, were established. These scholarships were used in the main for the benefit of deserving daughters of the clergy, but occasionally a scholarship was given to the daughter of a layman.[64]

The other diocesan institution, St. Luke's Hospital, had but an ephemeral career in the postwar years. The hospital, which closed its doors in Orlando in 1916 for lack of funds, reopened them in DeLand in 1920 after a merger with DeLand Memorial Hospital. The merged institution was called St. Luke's Memorial Hospital, but the union of the ecclesiastical with the secular did not prove to be a happy one. The merger was dissolved in 1923 when the DeLand institution became publicly supported.[65] St. Luke's salvaged its endowment from the merger, and this fund later served as a nucleus for the establishment of a diocesan home for older people.

The University of the South, partially owned by the Diocese of South Florida, increased its physical plant during the prosperous 1920s. A number of stone dormitories, Hoffman Hall (1921), Elliott Hall (1922), Cannon Hall (1925), and Johnson Hall (1926), were built.[66] The preparatory school, Sewanee Military Academy, rejoiced in the construction of a new gymnasium and swimming pool. During this period the enrollment in the college was roughly 350 students, and that of St. Luke's Hall, the seminary, was about 50. In addition to contributing approximately $1,000 per annum to the university, the Diocese of South Florida also participated with some success in the $2 million endowment drive for the institution.[67]

64. *Diocesan Journal*, 1926, pp. 29–30; *Palm Branch*, March 1924, June 1925, and May 1929.
65. *Palm Branch*, February 1924.
66. *Bulletin of The University of the South, Annual Catalogue 1966–67* (Sewanee, Tennessee: The University Press, 1966), p. 16.
67. *Palm Branch*, April 1925.

A charitable enterprise of the National Church, the Seamen's Church Institute of Tampa, was also partially supported by the diocese. The institute proved so popular with seafaring folk that it was forced to move into larger quarters at the close of 1924. This charity did such service for the community that the city of Tampa made substantive contributions to its maintenance. A partial summary of one year's activities follows.

Number of persons received	587
Number of night lodgings	4,890
Number of free lodgings	2,976
Positions secured in ships	454
Positions secured on shore	37

The superintendent of the institute, the Rev. F. Barnby Leach, reported that he also made thirty visits to hospitals and twenty-seven times visited seamen confined to the local jails.[68]

With the rapid growth of the diocese the administrative and pastoral duties of the diocesan grew proportionately, and it was becoming apparent that additional episcopal assistance was imperative. The necessity was driven home to all concerned Churchmen by the age and declining health of Bishop Mann. He was approaching the mid-seventies, and the demands of his high office promised to multiply rather than diminish. Cognizant of these facts, the Diocesan Convention of 1924 requested that Bishop Mann appoint a committee to study the feasibility of additional episcopal supervision. That committee returned a report the following year that the majority of its members favored the election of a bishop coadjutor if the diocesan so desired. Bishop Mann stated to the Convention of 1925 that he expected to request such an election in the near future.[69]

After two months of study and deliberation, the aging prelate called a special convention of the diocese to be held on May 6 in the Cathedral Church of St. Luke in Orlando. On the appointed day thirty-four clergymen and seventy-four lay delegates converged

68. Ibid., January 1925; March 1929.
69. *Diocesan Journal*, 1925, p. 31.

on the see city to elect a bishop coadjutor. The convention opened with celebration of the Holy Communion with the bishop as the celebrant. He was assisted by the cathedral dean, the Very Rev. Stanley C. Long; the archdeacon of the diocese, the Ven. James G. Glass; and the rector of Trinity Church, Miami, the Rev. Robert T. Phillips. Of the three priests assisting at the Holy Mysteries two were nominated for the coadjutorship several hours later. Following the Eucharist the bishop addressed the assembled delegates on the purpose of the special convention. "After careful thought, and after consultation with many of you, I concluded that at my present age, and with the tremendous development going on in Southern Florida, there is need of a Bishop Coadjutor for the proper episcopal supervision of this Diocese. . . . Accordingly, I have summoned you to consider and act upon my request for a Coadjutor; and, in case the request is granted, to proceed to the election of a Bishop Coadjutor for the Diocese of South Florida."[70]

The request was immediately granted, and the preliminaries to the election were quickly performed. They included the reading of reports stating that the diocesan endowment fund could bear the burden of an additional episcopal stipend, which was set at $5,000 per annum with a house rent allowance not to exceed $2,000. The coadjutor was to receive an additional $1,000 for traveling and secretarial expenses. Permission was granted by the convention for visiting clergymen to have seats during the session, and the chair recognized the unexplained presence of the Rt. Rev. Charles Minnigerode Beckwith, Bishop of Alabama. On motion, nominations for the office of bishop coadjutor were ordered. The following nominations were made: the Rev. Wiltshire W. Williams, rector of St. Peter's Church, St. Petersburg; the Rev. Harry L. Taylor, Ph.D., rector of St. Barnabas's Church, DeLand; the Rev. John Durham Wing, D.D., rector of St. Paul's Church, Chattanooga, Tennessee; the Rev. Cleland K. Benedict, D.D., rector of Christ Church, Glendale, Ohio; the Ven. James G. Glass, Archdeacon of South Florida; the Very Rev. C. Stanley Long, Dean of St. Luke's Cathedral, Or-

70. *Journal of the Special Convention of the Diocese of South Florida,* 1925, p. 3.

lando; the Rev. G. Irvine Hiller, rector of All Saints' Church, Lakeland; the Rt. Rev. Theodore Payne Thurston, D.D., Missionary Bishop of Oklahoma; and the Rev. Croswell McBee, D.D., rector of St. David's Church, Radnor, Pennsylvania. After the first ballot it was clear that the coadjutor-elect would be one of three— Dr. Wing of Chattanooga, Bishop Thurston of Oklahoma, or the Rev. Mr. Hiller of Lakeland.

Dr. Wing had a number of advantages over the other nominees. In the first place he was well known as a preacher, having taken a prominent part in the missionary campaign of the National Church on the Gulf coast during the previous year; and in the second, he was nominated by two respected laymen who attested to his powers in the pulpit, H. S. Hampton and Sumter L. Lowry, Sr., both of St. John's Parish, Tampa. Dr. Wing's chief clerical supporter was the Rev. F. W. B. Dorset of Holy Trinity Church, Melbourne, who properly stressed his candidate's pastoral abilities. Dr. Wing's age was also an advantage; he was forty-two at the time of his nomination. He was also Southern (Atlanta-born) and a Prayer Book Catholic in his Churchmanship. Bishop Thurston, on the other hand, had powerful supporters as well. Both the clerical and lay delegates from St. Luke's Church, Fort Myers, made nominating speeches in his behalf as did Archdeacon Glass and the chancellor of the diocese, Mr. Massey. But the bishop was approaching sixty and was a Northerner to boot. There was also opposition to his translation. The youth of the Rev. Mr. Hiller prevented many delegates from giving his name serious consideration. Seven successive ballots were cast before Dr. Wing received a clear majority: nineteen out of thirty-four clerical ballots and fifty-two out of seventy-four lay votes. On the motion of Bishop Thurston's leading supporter, the Rev. Frank A. Shore of Fort Myers, the election was made unanimous.[71] Dr. Wing accepted his election and was duly consecrated a "Bishop in the Church of God on the Feast of St. Michael and All Angels, Tuesday, the 29th of September, 1925."[72]

Bishop Wing not only took over the supervision of the white and

71. Ibid., pp. 11–12.

72. John Durham Wing, *The Bishop Coadjutor's Address*, appended to the *Diocesan Journal*, 1926, p. 62.

Negro missions of the diocese, but also became concerned about the work of the Church among the college students of the state. The prosperous boom years had greatly increased the enrollment of the two state institutions. On February 10, 1926, at Bishop Wing's instigation, a conference was held at Gainesville with representatives of the Diocese of Florida to consider plans for a program among the students. The conference was fruitful. The Dioceses of Florida and South Florida each agreed to give $1,500 annually to support a resident chaplain at the University of Florida at Gainesville and $750 to support a worker at Florida State College for Women in Tallahassee.[73] This initial conference laid the foundations for what eventually became the Chapel of the Incarnation on the Gainesville campus and the Chapel of the Resurrection on the campus of what is now Florida State University.

The overall growth of the church in South Florida was remarkable during the years of the boom. The statistics of the diocese show an amazing increase in the number of communicants and in the number of self-supporting parishes. In 1920 there were 5,271 communicants within the Missionary District of Southern Florida. Five years later the number had mushroomed to 8,323, an increase of over fifty-seven per cent. The increase in the number of parishes was also extraordinary: in 1920 there were fifteen parishes listed on the roll of the Diocesan Convention, and five years later there were twenty-five.[74] But what was more impressive, the Missionary Jurisdiction of Southern Florida had achieved diocesan rank and had elected a young and vigorous coadjutor. In financial matters, by wise management and investment, the episcopal endowment had more than tripled. These accomplishments, considerable as they were, lost much of their lustre in the period that followed the boom.

73. *Palm Branch*, March 1926.
74. *Convocation Journal*, 1920, p. 65; *Diocesan Journal*, 1926, *Parochial Abstracts*.

XI

The Bust and Depression

W HEN JOHN DURHAM WING WAS CONSECRATED BISHOP
coadjutor in the fall of 1925, the boom was at its height.
The speculative frenzy had reached unbelievable proportions. Properties were changing hands so rapidly that it was difficult for the
county record keepers and local abstract companies to keep up with
the changes of title. Of course there were few cash purchases. Most
of the land transactions were made by loan or installment buying,
a method which often involved the banks of Florida in the delirium
of speculation. The municipalities of the state sold securities to
provide streets, sidewalks, water, and sewerage facilities as housing
projects and subdivisions mushroomed within and without their
boundaries. Cautious voices were raised against the hysteria, but
as long as the profits came rolling in these voices went unheeded.
Each large land purchase seemed to quiet the doubters and assure
the speculators that "the big money" was confident the boom would
continue. Bishop Mann was one of the few Doubting Thomases. On
a tour through Fort Lauderdale in the spring of 1925, the bishop
could hardly believe what had taken place since his last visitation.
"I looked and marvelled," he wrote in his diary. "When will it stop?
'Never,' was the prompt reply of all the people. But I can not assent.
There must be some pause for the taking of breath."[1]

1. *Bishop's Diary, Palm Branch*, April 1925.

184

The Rt. Rev. William Crane Gray
First Bishop, 1892–1914

The Rt. Rev. Cameron Mann
Second Bishop, 1914–32

The Rt. Rev. John Durham Wing
Third Bishop, 1932–50

The Rt. Rev. Henry Irving Louttit
Fourth Bishop, 1951–69

The Rt. Rev. Martin J. Bram
Suffragan Bishop, 1951–56

The Rt. Rev. William Francis Moses
Suffragan Bishop, 1956–61

The Rt. Rev. James L. Duncan
Suffragan Bishop, 1961–69

The Rt. Rev. William L. Hargrave
Suffragan Bishop, 1961–69

Granville Chetwynd-Stapylton, who founded Chetwynd (now Fruitland Park) and Holy Trinity Church, Chetwynd.

The barn used as a church at Chetwynd.

Interior of the converted barn.

Holy Trinity Church, Chetwynd, built in 1888.

Back row (from left): the Rev. B. F. Brown, the Rev. A. A. Rickert, and Dean L. A. Spencer. *Center:* the Rt. Rev. William Crane Gray. *Front row left:* the Rev. (Deacon) H. W. Greetham. Remaining members of the group have not been identified.

St. Mark's, Cocoa. Priest-in-charge, the Rev. Charles H. Bascom.

Glade Cross Mission, Everglades.

Cathedral School May Day Dance, 1938.

Conference of Church workers at St. Patrick's, West Palm Beach, Michaelmas, 1940. Vicar, the Rev. J. DaCosta Harewood.

On the steps of St. Luke's Cathedral, Orlando, February 7, 1936. *Standing*: the Rev. F. Barnby Leach (1), Superintendent of the Seamen's Church Institute, Tampa; the Rev. Henry I. Louttit (10), West Palm Beach; the Rev. E. L. Pennington (9), Ocala; Miss A. Tulane (8). *Sitting (back row)*: the Rev. William L. Hargrave (2), Cocoa; Dean Melville E. Johnson (7), Orlando; Miss A. Tulane (6). (The Misses Tulane, of St. Peter's, St. Petersburg, headed Camp St. Mary for Girls and were counsellors and instructors at other camps of the diocese.) *Front row*: Mr. Lynn S. Nichols (3), West Palm Beach, member of the Diocesan Executive Board; the Rev. John B. Walthour (4), St. Andrew's, Tampa; the Rev. J. M. Taylor (5), Fort Pierce.

Confirmation class presented by the Rev. John E. Culmer in St. Agnes's Church, Miami, 1940.

All Saints' Church, Winter Park.

The Church of the Good Shepherd, Maitland, built in 1880 through the generosity of Bishop Whipple of Minnesota.

The Church of the Good Shepherd, Dunedin.

St. Gabriel's Church, Titusville.

St. James's Church, Leesburg.

Church of St. Luke and St. Peter, Saint Cloud. The building (then St. Peter's, completed 1898) originally stood at Narcoosee. It was moved and rebuilt in 1930.

Holy Cross Church, Sanford, rebuilt after the hurricane of 1880. An Upjohn church.

Trinity Church, Miami. Building completed in 1925.

West portal of St. Luke's Cathedral, Orlando.

St. Andrew's Church, Lake Worth, destroyed in 1928 by hurricane.

St. Mark's Church, Venice, 1940.

Christ Memorial Chapel, Hobe Sound, 1939.

There were signs in the winter of 1925–26 that this "pause for the taking of breath" had come. In the late summer of 1925 a crisis in transportation slowed the pace of building development. The railroads of the state were so overtaxed transporting construction materials that the Railroad Commission had to put regulations into effect which set an order of priorities on incoming goods such as food. Coastal shipping lines were even more overburdened. In December of the same year, thirty-one vessels loaded with food and construction materials waited to enter Miami harbor while some sixty other ships already in port waited to be unloaded.[2] Dock laborers worked in shifts around the clock to keep the goods moving, but they could not untie the shipping snare. The lull caused by the transportation crisis provided a moment for thought. Speculation by this time had reached a peak too high for safety. The fact began to sink into the heads of buyers that there was no adequate earning potential to justify the price of land sales, and some fraudulent promoters were already being hauled into the courts. Suspicion turned into panic, and almost all real estate transactions ceased. As installments came due, purchasers refused to honor them, deeming it unwise to send good money after bad. The price of land plummeted along with the value of local stocks and securities. Many of the banks which had become involved in unstable land and business speculation failed, ruining thousands of individuals and businesses. But the worst was still to come. The *coup de grace* for the Florida land boom was administered by Nature herself.

In September 1926 a hurricane of unbelievable ferocity struck Biscayne Bay and blew across Lake Okeechobee to the Gulf of Mexico leaving severe damage in its wake. Losses were estimated in the millions. Nearly all the churches in the diocese were profoundly affected by the collapse of the land boom or by the catastrophic hurricane of 1926. Many were affected by both, particularly in the Miami area. The clergy of the area sent vivid reports of the catastrophe to Bishop Mann. The Rev. Charles R. Palmer of Holy Cross Church in the Buena Vista section wrote: "The hurricane was a strange thing. It literally took up the waters of the ocean and poured

2. Hanna, *Florida: Land of Change*, p. 391.

them down on us in unbelievable quantities and tore up the earth until our upstairs rooms were thick with sand. Everything has rusted, —the springs of the beds, the knobs on the doors, the coat hangers, etc. In fact, everything metal. All cloth materials are mouldy and covered with mildew. It will take us months to get back to normal again." The clergyman reported that no one in his parish was killed and that only two were injured, but that about "ten or twelve families lost their homes completely." In downtown Miami, sturdy Trinity Church suffered considerable damage to roof and window, and water injury. The losses there were estimated to be between $30,000 and $40,000, and at Holy Comforter Chapel the loss was approximately $10,000.

St. John's Church, which had recently moved from Dania to Hollywood, was nearly demolished. The priest-in-charge, the Rev. Easton E. Madeira, described the results of the disaster. "The day after the storm Mrs. Madeira and I went up to see if we could salvage anything from the wreck, and I am astonished at the things we did manage to get out. I secured the Altar Cross, the Processional Cross (both bent considerably but able to be repaired), one candlestick, and one Altar Vase, the Lectern Bible, Altar Book, Altar Hymnal, the Communion Set and several cottas. The Communion Set was rescued from where it was held down under the fallen roof, wedged in between a mass of timbers, by my prying up the mass with scantlings, while Mrs. Madeira crawled under it and worked the box loose. I was well scared during the operation lest my lever should slip and she should be crushed underneath." The Madeiras, who stayed in the rectory during the storm, were profoundly shaken by their experience. "I cannot begin to describe to you the horror of that night and morning, as we sat here whipped by wind and drenching rain, with the water of the ocean creeping up around us, watching roofs flying over us, watching my garage go, and expecting any minute to feel our house crash down upon our heads. It simply cannot be described. But thank God, we came out without a scratch."[3]

Churches in other places also suffered considerably. The roof was

3. *Palm Branch*, October 1926.

blown off St. Cuthbert's Church in Boynton, and at Delray, both St. Paul's and St. Matthew's were blown from their foundations. The damage at St. Matthew's was particularly heartbreaking since the Negro congregation had recently completed the new church at some sacrifice. St. Mary's Church in Deerfield was also blown from its foundations, and St. Ann's, Hallandale, was wrecked. At Fort Lauderdale, All Saints' Church suffered little damage, but the rectory was severely injured. St. Christopher's, the Negro church, was totally destroyed. The church and rectory at Coconut Grove received only slight damage, but the storm raised havoc amongst the trees and shrubs on the grounds. The Negro congregation at Coconut Grove was the hardest hit on the east coast. The old church building was completely destroyed and St. Alban's School was seriously damaged. St. Agnes's Church in Miami proper was also badly hit. There the damages to parochial property were reported at $12,000.[4]

On the west coast, churches in Fort Myers and Sarasota suffered only slight damage, but at Punta Gorda, the tiny Church of the Good Shepherd was not so fortunate. The Rev. Henry E. Payne reported, "The Church building is a total wreck, —tower fallen across the street, building blown off its foundation and very badly buckled. The Rectory roof," he added, "is in bad condition, but there is one dry room upstairs. We are shut off from the world and have no way of telling whether others have been afflicted." Early estimates of damage caused by the storm to Church property in the diocese were set at over $75,000, but this figure does not include the injury done to Christ Church, Coconut Grove. Of the damaged properties, only that of Trinity Church, Miami, was completely covered by insurance.

When they heard the news of the catastrophe Episcopalians from all over the country rallied to help the distressed congregations. By the end of January over $10,000 had been sent to Bishop Mann to reconstruct the property damaged by the storm.[5] These funds were distributed over the diocese and did much to help the many congre-

4. John Durham Wing, *Bishop Coadjutor's Diary, Palm Branch*, September 1926.

5. *Palm Branch*, October 1926, February 1927.

gations already saddled with a boom debt to repair their churches, rectories, and parish houses.

Just as South Floridians were recovering from the disastrous results of the collapse of the boom and the massive assault of Nature, a second hurricane, more costly in its toll of human life, hit the peninsula. The storm of 1928 entered the state near West Palm Beach, blew across the Lake Okeechobee region, and almost destroyed the towns of Belle Glade and Pahokee. Twenty-four hundred persons were estimated to have lost their lives in this disaster. The damage to property was estimated in the millions. Bishop Wing, who was visiting Chattanooga at the time of the hurricane, rushed home to assess the damage. He made an inspection trip down the coast beginning at Melbourne. His diary entries for September 27 and 28 describe the journey.

> September 27. Drove to Micco and found St. Mary's Church in bad condition. Roof gone, windows broken, interior dreadfully damaged. Went on to Fort Pierce. St. Andrew's Church and rectory damaged considerably and parish house demolished. St. Simon the Cyrenian I found to be leaning badly to one side. Spent night in Fort Pierce.

> September 28. Left Fort Pierce at 9 A.M. for Walton. St. Paul's Church had most of its tile blown off, most of its windows blown in, and its furnishings ruined by water. . . . Drove on to West Palm Beach. Found Holy Trinity Church and rectory damaged by water, and parish house demolished. St. Patrick's Church totally destroyed; parish house and rectory badly damaged. . . . Proceeded to Lake Worth where I found St. Andrew's Church in ruins.

The next day amidst the ruins of St. Andrew's Church, Bishop Wing confirmed one person before continuing down the coast.

> Drove to Boynton, where I found St. Cuthbert's Church demolished. On to Delray Beach, where both St. Paul's and St. Matthew's were totally destroyed. Proceeded to Deerfield to find St. Mary's there also wrecked. Went on to Miami.[6]

6. *Bishop Coadjutor's Diary, Palm Branch,* October 1928.

When Bishop Wing returned to Orlando he at least had the con-
solation of announcing to his people in the *Palm Branch* that no
Episcopalian had perished in the calamity. However, within a short
time he received a letter from a clergyman in Tarpon Springs con-
tradicting his statement: "Mrs. Edna Bright Hughes, wife of John
W. Hughes, formerly of this parish, was drowned. Miami-Lock (I
think) was the name of the place. Her little son, Paul Dennisto
Hughes, born August 12, 1924; baptized April 26, 1925, died with
her."[7]

As the estimates of damage from the various parishes and missions
of the diocese were tabulated, it was discovered that the less sub-
stantially built Negro missions had sustained the greatest losses. The
damages estimated for five Negro missions were set at slightly over
$50,000, while the damages incurred by the seven white congrega-
tions were estimated at approximately $34,000, making the total
damage from the catastrophe an unbelievable $84,200.

The *Living Church* came to the aid of the beleaguered diocese by
announcing the needs of South Florida through its news and editorial columns and volunteering to serve as agent to receive and forward funds for the relief of the diocese. The General Convention
sympathetically requested that the offering for Sunday, November
18, in all churches throughout the United States be devoted to the
relief of fellow Churchmen in Florida and Puerto Rico. As a result the distressed missions and parishes of South Florida received
$84,200 from the National Church, the exact amount of estimated
damages. The two most badly hit churches in West Palm Beach received the largest share of this amount. St. Patrick's was given
$40,000 to rebuild its plant, and Holy Trinity $17,000 to recon-
struct its parish house.[8] In addition to this grant, the National
Council appropriated out of undesignated legacies the sum of
$25,000 for the rebuilding of Negro missions which had been de-
stroyed during the storm of 1926: $10,000 was given to Christ
Church, Coconut Grove, and $15,000 to St. Agnes's Church,
Miami.[9] With its grant the congregation of Christ Church com-

7. *Palm Branch*, November 1928.
8. Ibid., February 1929.
9. Wing, *Bishop Coadjutor's Address*, 1929, pp. 53–54.

pleted a new church in time for the Christmas season the following year. The building was solemnly consecrated on May 25, 1930. St. Agnes's Church was not finished until several years later.[10]

Ironically, as the Churchmen of the peninsula were rising to their feet after the second hurricane they were struck down again by the crash of the New York stock market in the fall of 1929. In less than a month the securities listed on the exchange fell twenty-six billion dollars, a loss of over forty per cent of their face value. Although the rapid deterioration of the market was checked in the coming months, a slow decline continued for several years, and in the summer of 1932 the face value of securities reached an all-time low. Hard-hit Florida reeled from this blow. There was no more talk of booms or recovery. Instead, towns, counties, banks, and even churches found themselves heavily in debt. The depression was on.

To add to the economic plight of the state, the Mediterranean fruit fly was discovered in an orange grove near Orlando in 1929. It was soon realized that the infestation was widespread, and that hundreds of groves were infected by the insect. State and federal authorities placed a citrus embargo on the peninsula, and temporarily employed several thousand men in destroying infected trees. The fruit fly epidemic caused the loss of almost all the citrus crop for 1929–30, as well as a subsequent decline in citrus production for a number of years. Although the embargo was lifted in November 1930 the damage inflicted on Florida's growers accelerated the already alarming rate of bank and business failures throughout the state.[11] There is no doubt that the tiny invaders from the Mediterranean reduced even more the decreased revenues of the churches of the diocese.

Even before the stock market crash, the effects of the boom's collapse showed in the inability of the churches of the diocese to meet their diocesan assessments and missionary apportionments for 1928. Pledges were made to the assessment that year for $9,058, yet of that amount only $7,380 was paid. The churches' failure to meet the

10. Ibid., 1930, pp. 37–38; see also "Consecration of Christ Church, Coconut Grove, May 25th, 1930," Bishop Wing's *Scrapbook*, vol. 2.

11. Charlton W. Tebeau, *A History of Florida* (Coral Gables, Florida: University of Miami Press, 1971), p. 395.

diocesan missionary apportionment was even more pronounced; of the $36,217 pledged only $20,647.93 was sent to the diocesan treasurer.[12] Although the diocesan convention for the following year optimistically set the budget at $46,800, the churches refused to pledge more than $26,875, so it became the sad duty of the executive board of the diocese to cut appropriations: $14,000 was trimmed from the quota asked of the diocese by the National Church, $3,000 from the diocesan missionary program, and $3,300 from the diocesan allotments in the fields of religious education, young people's work, and Christian social service. As a result of these cuts, no new missions were opened, no new congregations were organized, and no new clergy were added to mission circuits. Some missionary clergy were even forced to take reductions in their already meagre stipends. When the year 1929 ended, only $15,788.17 of the approximately $27,000 pledged had been sent to the diocesan treasurer.[13] The following year the situation worsened, as can be seen from these extracts from the payments on diocesan assessments and missionary apportionments for 1930:[14]

Church	Assess-ments	Paid	Apportion-ments	Paid
Clearwater, Ascension	$145.00	000.00	406.00	406.00
Daytona, St. Mary's	538.00	000.00	1,506.00	106.42
Miami, Trinity	712.00	330.00	1,994.00	1,258.00
Miami, St. Stephen's	469.00	469.00	1,313.00	85.00
St. Petersburg, St. Peter's	538.00	538.00	1,506.00	1,106.00
Tampa, St. John's	295.00	000.00	826.00	505.06
Palm Beach, Holy Trinity	562.00	150.00	1,574.00	280.28

The diocesan treasurer was constantly embarrassed by the failure of local church treasurers to make regular payments on their assessments and missionary apportionments. So sporadic did the payments become that the Standing Committee recommended that the Convention refuse to seat delegates from parishes and missions who had not paid at least their assessments. When the year 1929 ended the

12. *Palm Branch*, February 1929.
13. Ibid., February 1930.
14. Ibid., February 1931.

diocesan treasurer discovered that twenty-eight churches had failed to pay their assessments in full, while some sixty-three churches out of eighty-six in the diocese had not paid their share of the apportionment. Three east coast churches, Trinity, Miami, Holy Trinity, West Palm Beach, and St. John's, Hollywood, were in such financial straits that they could not even pay the pension premiums of their clergy.[15]

In some areas of the state, towns were decimated by the boom's collapse, which of course affected local churches. The Rev. G. W. R. Cadman, priest-in-charge of St. Mark's, Haines City, reported to the Diocesan Convention in 1930 that "every member of this congregation has left Haines City on account of the business depression. The Church is closed." He also reported that the church had a balance of only $38.00 in the bank, but even this small sum was lost when the bank failed. In Dunedin, on the west coast, the collapse of the boom scattered the congregation of the Church of the Good Shepherd, forcing the priest-in-charge to close the church. It was reported in the *Diocesan Journal* that most of the remaining Episcopalians in the town attended the local Presbyterian church.

On the east coast the parochial reports of Holy Trinity Church, Melbourne, illustrated how hard that area was hit by the collapse of the land boom and the subsequent plummeting of the stock market. Dr. Frederick W. B. Dorset stated that fifty-five communicants had left the town to seek employment elsewhere, but added that he hoped they would "return as soon as they can make a living here." In Bartow, the congregation of Holy Trinity Church, which had only recently remodeled its church building in "the English Tudor style," found it was months in arrears on the salary of its clergyman. Their priest, the Rev. Frank M. Brunton, agreed to cancel $377.50 of this indebtedness to help the church through the financial crisis. In addition to this humiliation, the vestry was forced to borrow $500 from outside sources to meet the interest payment on the church property.[16] In Palm Beach County, the Church was so crippled by the depression that the Rev. Arthur D. Caslor, priest-

15. *Diocesan Journal*, 1930, pp. 15, 47–51; 1931, p. 24; *Palm Branch*, January 1931.

16. *Diocesan Journal*, 1930, pp. 75–79.

in-charge of St. Andrew's, Lake Worth, not only maintained regular services in his own church but on occasion also had the oversight of Holy Trinity and St. Patrick's as well.[17] The number of
removals from the diocese, caused by the slump, was reflected in the
confirmation statistics of the various parishes and missions. From
1928 to 1929 the number fell from 781 to 575. There was also a
marked drop in the number of baptisms.[18]

A phenomenon which accentuated the financial crisis in Florida
from 1928 through 1933 was the epidemic of bank failures. Caught
up in the frenzy of real estate speculation, many bankers loaned
large sums to fraudulent promoters without proper collateral. When
the price of real estate fell and purchasers stopped sending installment payments, many banks, holding worthless real estate mortgages,
failed. Numerous congregations had funds on deposit when the
banks of the state began to close their doors. St. Agnes's Church in
Miami lost over two thousand dollars in the financial institutions of
the city, mostly in the Bank of Biscayne, a loss which delayed the
completion of the new church by over a year.[19] The congregation
of Christ Church, Coconut Grove, lost the balance of its new fund
for the new church when the City National Bank failed, but the
pews were paid for by a timely gift from Bishop Wing.[20] One of the
hardest hit of the smaller churches in the diocese was St. James's,
Ormond Beach. This mission lost $3,246.43 in the failure of the
Merchants Bank and Trust Company of Daytona Beach, while the
Church women lost $400 when the Ormond bank failed.[21] Even
the young people were affected by the banking fiasco. In Cocoa,
for instance, the League of St. Mark's Church lost about $25.00
when a bank in that town went under.[22]

Two churches on the lower east coast, St. Stephen's, Coconut
Grove, and St. Patrick's, West Palm Beach, were so debt-ridden
and impoverished by the depression that suits were brought against

17. *Palm Branch*, February 1930.
18. *Diocesan Journal*, 1929 and 1930, *Parochial Reports*.
19. *Palm Branch*, September 1930; *Diocesan Journal,* 1931, p. 100.
20. *Diocesan Journal*, 1931, p. 99.
21. Ibid., 1930, p. 31.
22. *Palm Branch*, December 1928.

their properties by contractors to collect for labor and materials allegedly furnished for improvements and repairs during the boom. St. Agnes's Church, Miami, had similar claims to face.[23] These cases were in litigation for a long period, and construction on the two properties was delayed until settlements had been reached.

The three churches in the diocese which prospered most during the boom and suffered most during the depression were Trinity Church, Miami; Holy Trinity, West Palm Beach; and St. Luke's Cathedral, Orlando. All three had built elaborate new church buildings; all three were heavily mortgaged; and all three mortgages were held by the Commercial Bank & Trust Company of St. Louis, Missouri. Trinity Parish, even after repeated efforts to refinance its obligations, found itself saddled with a debt of over $186,000. Of this amount about $150,000 was owed to the St. Louis bank. For years the situation seemed hopeless, until the rector and vestry of the church worked out an arrangement with the mortgagee whereby the bank took the two Biscayne Bay lots for the value of $75,000 and reduced the amount of the mortgage by that figure.[24] After much negotiation with the same bank, the rector of Holy Trinity, West Palm Beach (the Rev. Henry I. Louttit) and his vestry finally transferred the crippling indebtedness of $125,000 into bonds which the bank agreed to accept at thirty cents on the dollar. In Orlando, the cathedral chapter with the aid of Bishop Mann accepted and eventually paid the amount of the mortgage at the approximate face value of the debt.[25]

No parish of the Gulf coast was hit harder by the depression than St. Andrew's Church, Tampa. Saddled with a debt of over $57,000 and interest payments of approximately $7,000 annually, the parish also lost 169 persons by removal during 1929. As a result the church was so economically maimed that it is to this day a "split" parish; that is, the parish church is downtown at the original site and the

23. *Diocesan Journal*, 1929, p. 28.

24. *Trinity Episcopal Church* (Germantown, Pa.: Arman L. Davis, 1942); also interview with the Rt. Rev. Henry I. Louttit, May 12, 1968.

25. Interview with Bishop Louttit, May 12, 1968.

parish house and Sunday school are on the Plant Avenue property.[26]

One of the diocesan institutions hardest hit during these years was the Cathedral School in Orlando. The collapse of the boom caused a sharp drop in enrollment which created an $8,000 deficit during the 1927–28 term. Although expenses were kept at a minimum, the school found that it could not operate in the black during the depression years. Despite the annual appeals that were made to underwrite the deficits, the school was forced to close its doors for one term, 1932–33. The hard-pressed Diocesan Standing Committee, however, agreed to reopen the school the following year.[27]

One of the ways by which the standing committee and diocesan trustees were able to maintain the mission program of the diocese and such diocesan institutions as the Cathedral School was by selling the properties of dormant missions. In 1930 the trustees authorized Bishop Mann to sell lots in Cassia (Lake County), Miami, El Vallee de Tampa, Mulberry, and Sanibel Island.[28] But the chief bulwark against the depression was the diocesan endowment. Even at the depth of the depression, the Diocesan Endowment Fund was evaluated at over $310,000, which provided the diocese with an income of over $17,000. The program of the Church was also strengthened by the use of the income from the St. Luke's Hospital endowment. This source provided an additional amount of approximately $5,000 which was used largely to supplement missionary stipends.[29] The St. Luke's Hospital endowment was not used to support a home for the elderly until the depression was well over.

Nearly every parish and mission in the diocese was plagued by the problems of the depression: removals, mortgage payments, and sharp drops in parochial income. However, most attempted to meet their commitments to the diocese and to the National Church al-

26. Ibid.; also *Diocesan Journal*, 1930, p. 73.

27. *Diocesan Journal*, 1929, p. 44; *Palm Branch*, February and April, 1934.

28. *Diocesan Journal*, 1931, p. 53. The acreage bought in 1907 by Bishop Gray on Sanibel was not sold until the 1950s.

29. Ibid., pp. 59, 63.

though they did not always succeed. The way in which St. Andrew's Church, Tampa, met its parochial and diocesan obligations during these years was typical of many churches in South Florida.

During 1930, a particularly difficult year, St. Andrew's Parish was assigned the largest missionary apportionment of any parish in the diocese—$2,582. The church was also struggling with a debt of over $57,000, with interest and principal payments that had to be met, and met with resources no better and no worse than those of most of the congregations of South Florida. Despite an awareness of the financial problems of the diocese, St. Andrew's had not been able to pay its diocesan assessment of $922 and found that it still owed a balance of $511 on its missionary apportionment as of December 1, 1930. Yet, when the Diocesan Convention met at Bethesda-by-the-Sea in Palm Beach in January 1931 the energetic rector of the parish, the Rev. Willis G. Clark, was able to report that St. Andrew's had paid in full its diocesan assessment and missionary apportionment for 1930.

From the middle of December to the middle of January the rector and vestry of St. Andrew's had made a concerted attempt to acquaint the parishioners with the missionary program of the diocese. The Rev. Mr. Clark asked that his vestry guarantee the amount of the assessment as a matter of honor. The vestry agreed, and resolved not to borrow the money ($922) but first to raise what they could among themselves and then get other men in the parish to do the same. A committee was appointed by the rector which solicited the men of the parish, and by Christmas the whole amount of the assessment was raised. The way was now clear for work on the balance of the missionary apportionment ($511), although some in the parish wanted to let that balance go. It did not seem possible to them that another cent could be found for work outside the debt-ridden parish.

At this point the rector again sprang into action. He called a meeting of both the men's and women's organizations of St. Andrew's Church. At the meeting he told them once more of the Church's program, both diocesan and general, and of how their missionary apportionment was the measure of their Christian responsibility. The Rev. Mr. Clark also reminded them of their fine record in past years and stated how much it would distress him personally to have his parish, for the first time in his ministry, fail to pay in full its missionary obligations. As a result of his talk everyone went to work again and within a few weeks the balance was raised. This accomplishment was a great source of satisfaction to the parishioners of St. Andrew's Church and an example for the parishioners of other parishes to follow during the hard times ahead.[30]

In St. Luke's Cathedral, the chapter generally managed to pay all of its diocesan assessment and most of the missionary apportionment, but Bishop Mann himself was often found "canvassing for the next payment of interest on the Cathedral debt."[31] The women's organizations of the various churches of the diocese also helped defray the parochial expenses. In the Cathedral the women had benefits such as bridge parties, silver teas, Hallowe'en carnivals, suppers, and rummage sales to help relieve the building debt.[32] The young people of the diocese also helped. At St. Gabriel's Church in Titusville, the secretary of the Young People's Service League, Mary Pritchard, reported to the *Palm Branch* that for several months the league had been paying part of the utility bills of the mission in addition to helping to keep the church clean during the lean summer months "when we were unable to have a sexton." She also stated that the members of the Titusville league during Thanksgiving collected a basket of groceries for every needy family in the town.[33] The children of the various Sunday schools also contributed their bit to maintain the program of the Church. During Lent, 1930, the church school mite box offerings totaled the amazing sum of $3,490.34,[34] and despite the hard times, the Sunday school of St. Andrew's Church, Tampa, sent a record mite box offering of $1,044 to missions on Easter Day.[35] All of these amounts were

30. *Palm Branch*, March 1931.

31. *Bishop's Diary, Palm Branch*, October 27, 1931; *Palm Branch*, November 1931.

32. *Palm Branch*, November 1931.

33. Ibid., March 1931.

34. *Diocesan Journal*, 1930, pp. 67–68.

35. Church School Bulletin, May 30, 1930, Parish Records, St. Andrew's, Tampa.

utilized either in the national mission program or by diocesan missions.

The hardest hit communicants in the diocese of South Florida were the Negroes. There was a drop in parochial support among the members of the various black congregations as well as a corresponding rise in unemployment. Had it not been for diocesan support and help from the National Council many of these missions would have folded. Most of the Negro congregations were able, however, to keep the services of the Church going during hard times, and some of the larger churches were able to open programs of Christian social service as well. No church in South Florida was more engulfed in an active program of worship or in a more penetrating offering of social service than St. Agnes's Church in Miami.

In order to relieve the hunger suffered by many members of the Negro community in Miami during the summer of 1931 on account of unemployment, the congregation of St. Agnes's Church opened an "Unemployment Relief Station" during the slack months of August and September. The station was open seven weeks, during which time 160 families, representing 638 persons, were helped by gifts of food. Station workers printed application cards with spaces for pertinent information: name, address, number in family, ages of children, length of time out of work, occupation, needs, remarks, and the name of the member of the congregation by whom the investigation was made. The station provided relief for all deserving applicants without regard to creed. Baptists, Methodists, Roman Catholics, Seventh-Day Adventists, "Sanctifieds," and Episcopalians came for their food baskets every Saturday and nearly all of these baskets contained a dozen items of sustenance. The Seventh-Day Adventists came for their baskets after sundown, Saturday being their Sabbath, but there were always station workers on hand to distribute their dole.

The relief station at St. Agnes's was made possible through the efforts of the Rev. John E. Culmer, vicar, and the cooperation of the Negro grocers, insurance companies, professional men, and other interested individuals. No collections were taken in church. Station workers placed printed signs over baskets in all the larger grocery stores which read, "Help the Needy and Unemployed."

Customers making their purchases were thereby reminded to make an additional purchase which they dropped into the basket. Each week an article appeared in the Negro weekly newspaper urging shoppers to patronize stores where the signs appeared. Names of other Negro businesses, professional men, and individuals who contributed to the cause were also published in the weekly. According to Father Culmer the results of the campaign were "marvelous." Relief to the needy and unemployed was provided, and the grateful recipients spread much favorable comment throughout the Negro section of Miami.[36]

A few years later, the Rev. Father Culmer offered the use of St. Agnes's Parish House as the site for a Works Progress Administration sewing project. The Miami City Commission spent a large sum of money fitting up the building. Sessions were held four days a week, and more than a hundred women were provided with work.[37] These and other activities of Christian charity kept the vicar and communicants of St. Agnes's close to the pulse of the Negro population of Miami long before the term "relevant activities" came into wide use.

Although St. Agnes's Church was heavily engaged in Christian social work, the congregation of the parish did not neglect the duty of worship. The number of services in the church was expanded, but the worship of the church was sadly handicapped by a storm-battered old building too small for the growing congregation. This handicap was removed on Advent Sunday, 1930, when the new church building was put into use for the first time. This edifice, begun in 1923, was built only as funds became available. In the summer of 1926, when the walls had reached the point where they were ready to receive the roof, they were leveled to the ground by the hurricane. The congregation faced this disaster, cleared the debris, and again raised money to build anew. With the help of a large donation from the National Council and under the leadership of Father Culmer, the building was finally completed in 1930.

The first service held in the new building was, of course, the Eucharist, celebrated at 7:30 in the morning. A second celebration

36. *Palm Branch*, December 1931.
37. Ibid., April 1936.

with a sermon by the vicar followed at 10:45, and at 4:00 in the afternoon a sacred concert was given by the choir, at which time ·addresses of congratulation were made by some of the leading citizens of Miami, white and Negro. At 7:30 P.M. solemn evensong was sung at St. Agnes's, at which time the Bishop Coadjutor, the Rt. Rev. John Durham Wing, confirmed a class of eighty-two persons and preached. The *Palm Branch* reported that all the services were crowded to capacity, but that in the evening "in spite of the seating accommodation of 1,500 people, so great was the crowd seeking admission that it became necessary to lock the church doors some time before the service began." With so balanced a program of Christian worship and Christian service, it was not difficult to see why the congregation had grown to some 1,500 members, the largest of any Episcopal church in the South. The new building represented an outlay of over $60,000, and soon housed a new pipe organ built by the M. P. Moeller Company.[38]

Another depressed Negro church which brought its building program to a successful conclusion during the depression, largely because of a liberal grant from the National Council, was Christ Church, Coconut Grove. In the spring of 1930, this mission, almost destroyed by the hurricane of 1926 and damaged again by the hurricane of 1928, completed a new parish house and church building which boasted two concrete towers and a substantial concrete exterior. The inside of the church was described as "very simple and churchly, with everything necessary for the Service."[39] The church was consecrated on Rogation Sunday, May 25, 1930, by Bishop Wing, who also confirmed a class of fifty candidates presented by the vicar, the Rev. John S. Simmons. Christ Church provided very few of the urban social services which so engrossed the vicar and congregation of St. Agnes's.

Another great piece of Christian social service work was carried on in the diocese, however, at the Seaman's Church Institute in Tampa. The institute, housed in a remodeled warehouse containing accommodations for approximately fifty sailors, served as a seaman's home between ships. Although the institute was not pri-

38. Ibid., December 1930.
39. *Bishop's Diary, Palm Branch*, May 25, 1930; *Palm Branch*, June 1931.

marily a charitable operation, the unemployment crisis caused by the depression occasioned many destitute sailors to seek shelter within its walls.[40] In 1930 the Seamen's Church Institute gave a total of 9,567 free meals, and during the following year almost a thousand free meals were given to unemployed sailors each month. About eighty per cent of the sailors could not afford to pay for their lodgings, but they were still taken in. The Tampa institution was presided over by the Rev. F. Barnby Leach, who with the help of his wife provided not only food and lodgings for the seamen, but post office, baggage, and banking facilities as well. The Rev. Mr. Leach also served as an employment agent with some of the shipping firms of the port. He was constantly trying to get the citizens of Tampa and Churchmen in the diocese to extend their help, sympathy, and understanding to these unfortunate mariners. In a typical letter to the editor of the *Tampa Tribune,* Mr. Leach pled for them. "These men are not bums," he declared. "They are men who are a part of the life of Tampa's port, just as much as are ships and cargoes. Not a man of them but came in on a job. They are strangers, it is true, from other ports, even from other nations, but their home is on the seas. Men from Tampa are being cared for by Seamen's Church institutes in other ports. Tampa, looking to the continual welfare of its commercial life, owes a real obligation to these men. What is more, they are a splendid type, these sailors of today. I would not hesitate to invite any young people's guild to meet with them in a social gathering, and Mrs. Leach would tell you the same thing."[41]

The work of the Seamen's Church Institute was maintained by the Diocese of South Florida and by the National Council. From thirty to fifty per cent of the budget in Tampa, however, was supported by the Tampa Community Chest.

In the early 1920s, to cope with depression-spawned problems such as unemployment, poor labor relations, and the difficulties of migrant workers, and with remedial measures such as health services and welfare programs, the Diocesan Convention had set up a standing committee called the Department of Christian Social Serv-

40. *Tampa Tribune,* April 30, 1931.
41. Quoted from *Tampa Tribune* in *Palm Branch,* December 1931.

ice, which became an important arm of the diocesan social service program. Since 1922 the chairman of this committee had been the redoubtable F. Barnby Leach, that same priest who was spearheading the program of the Seamen's Institute in Tampa. The Rev. Mr. Leach was a remarkable man. Born in Vermont in 1868, he attended the University of Vermont and General Theological Seminary in New York. Ordained to the priesthood in 1899, Mr. Leach spent a number of years in parochial work before becoming the assistant superintendent of the Seamen's Institute in New York. He came to the diocese in 1925, as superintendent of the Seamen's Institute in Tampa, just in time to feel the full brunt of the Florida bust followed by the economic doldrums of a national depression.[42] His often heartbreaking work at the Seamen's Institute during these critical years gave him both the experience and the compassion needed to chair the Department of Christian Social Service. The energetic secretary of the committee was the Rev. Randolph Fairfax Blackford, rector of St. James's Church, Leesburg, a man particularly interested in the rural aspects of social service. A product of Episcopal High School in Alexandria and of the University of Virginia, Mr. Blackford graduated from the Virginia Theological School in 1915. He came to the diocese in 1928 as rector of Leesburg[43] and was appalled at the suffering that ensued in Lake County among both white and black laborers when the boom collapsed and the depression engulfed the state.

Under the leadership of these two concerned clerics the Department of Christian Social Service endeavored to cooperate with all agencies interested in promoting sound social welfare programs: private, local, state, and federal. The members of the department also spread information on social legislation and asked the clergy and laity of the diocese to support state and federal bills dealing with workmen's compensation, child labor restrictions, social security, and school lunch programs.[44]

An interesting way in which the Church and the federal government cooperated in the cause of social betterment occurred in

42. *Stowe,* 1941, pp. 165–66.
43. Ibid., 1953, p. 32.
44. *Diocesan Journal,* 1936, p. 31.

Miami. Near the end of 1937 the trustees of the Diocese of South Florida released to Christ Church, Coconut Grove, a part of the funds held by them for that congregation, the sum of five hundred dollars, in order that St. Alban's Industrial School might be reconditioned to house the Works Progress Administration's homemaking project for the benefit of the Negro people of the community. In this enterprise the Church provided the building, equipment, and materials needed, while the W.P.A. appointed, supervised, and paid the teaching staff. Instruction was offered in domestic service, gardening, cooking, hand laundering, and canning. The training afforded by the project met an urgent local need and placed a number of persons in employment in the Miami area. The Rev. T. T. Pollard, Vicar of Christ Church, was an important instrument in setting up the school.[45]

The Rev. Messrs. Leach and Blackford, through the diocesan department, urged the clergy and laity of the various churches to set up parish committees to deal with the social problems of the depression on a local level. In addition to the splendid work already being done by Father Culmer and the parochial committee of St. Agnes's in Miami, there were other local efforts. In one unspecified town, probably Leesburg, an attempt was made by a parish committee to alleviate both unemployment and the food shortage. A cannery for surplus fruits and vegetables was opened and managed by an Episcopal clergyman under the auspices of the local welfare association.[46] In another city the Women's Auxiliary made supplies for the county hospital; a branch of the same auxiliary assumed the care of a needy family; and the Young People's Service League of the parish also adopted a family consisting of a mother and five children. The members of the league also accompanied the rector of the parish on his weekly visits to the county hospital and jail.

Grace Church in Ocala was particularly given to good works. The women of the parish distributed baskets of food weekly to needy families and also carried flowers to the poor who were ill. The members of the Young People's Service League made numerous

45. *Palm Branch*, May 1938.
46. *Diocesan Journal*, 1934, p. 65.

visits to the inmates of the Girls' Reform School, talking to the girls, playing games with them, and supplying them with reading material. Another parish assisted in housing and feeding unemployed transients and fed underprivileged children in the local schools as well as rendering most of the services noted above.[47] In Tampa, during Christmas, 1935, the Scout troop of St. Andrew's Parish indefatigably delivered hundreds of Christmas baskets (collected by the Citizens' Christmas Committee) to all the depressed areas of the city. In addition the troop collected and distributed toys and gifts of clothing to underprivileged children of the bay area.[48]

To say that the young people of today have more social conscience than the young did in the 1930s would be an argument difficult to support, for many were very active in social service during the thirties. The Young People's Service League at Christ Church, Bradenton, provides a typical example. One of their projects during 1936 was to assume the care of an impoverished woman who was seriously ill. The league provided a cot for her use when taking health-giving sunbaths and took her fruit, vegetables, eggs, soup, and other nourishing food during her long convalescence. League members also paid weekly visits to the county hospital and prison. The rector of Christ Church, the Rev. Frank M. Brunton, like most of the clergy of the diocese who engaged in programs of social service, impressed upon the league and other church organizations the opportunity of bringing the spirit of Christianity into social work by cooperating with the community welfare agencies.[49] He also often stressed the connection between social service and Christian observance, as he did in Lent, 1936, when he encouraged the young people to endeavor "to attend at least one service each Sunday and as many as possible of the special weekday services."[50] The Rev. Barnby Leach of the Seamen's Institute believed that "every churchman who is a member of any community welfare

47. Ibid., 1937, pp. 75–76; see also *The Belfry of Grace Church*, Ocala, Florida, May 19, 1935.
48. *Tampa Tribune*, December 23, 1935.
49. *Palm Branch*, May 1936.
50. Ibid.

agency should be a connecting link between that Agency and the Church."[51]

The members of the Department of Christian Social Service followed the plans of the national government concerning social legislation closely. President Franklin D. Roosevelt, when he assumed office in 1933, attempted to revitalize the economy by encouraging industry and labor to work together rather than against each other so that the welfare of the nation could be better served. The leaders of business and labor agreed, often uneasily, to cooperate with this end in mind. Under the dynamic General Hugh Johnson, the National Recovery Administration (N.R.A.) attempted to cement the alliance. An elaborate series of self-imposed codes was drawn up by almost every major industry. Although these codes differed widely, they had many characteristics in common. They invariably forbade child labor; minimum wages were set at between thirty and forty cents per hour; and working hours were limited to between thirty-five and forty-eight hours per week. Business also recognized the right of labor to bargain collectively. Most of the codes forbade false advertising and commercial bribery, as well as the selling of goods below the code price. The industries and businesses which cooperated with the N.R.A. displayed the famous "Blue Eagle" of recovery and the motto "We do our part."

Most of the clergy and many of the laity of the diocese supported the president's program as expressed through the policies of the National Recovery Administration. They acted on and headed social service committees in the counties and cities of South Florida, and urged Episcopalians "to look for the N.R.A. Blue Eagle" especially when buying garments. This was done "in order that the sweat shops of our land may be given their deathblow." The Department of Christian Social Service and local committees also approved heartily of the activities of the Civilian Conservation Corps in Florida. "Our clergy have volunteered services in the camps of the diocese and have been of other service to the boys away from home," a report read. The diocese contributed one priest, the Rev. Heber Weller of St. Agnes's Church in Sebring, as a regular

51. *Diocesan Journal*, 1937, p. 76.

chaplain for a six-months tour of duty with the C.C.C. camps. The bishop and clergy of South Florida were also exceedingly active in promoting state and national legislation for the benefit of the unemployed and the aged during the economic crisis.[52]

In the middle 1930s the pall of hard times began to lift in Florida. Although the diocese was hit hard by the depression, the Church in the peninsula held its own. Only two missions had to suspend operations for lack of funds, although many had to curtail their activities; no clergyman was thrown into the ranks of the unemployed, although many experienced reductions in pay; and no established work in the diocese was discontinued, although much was cut back. No new work was begun during these hard years, but when they ended the Church had survived and retained her vitality.

52. Ibid., 1934, pp. 65–67.

XII

Cameron Mann
Prelate and Poet

C AMERON MANN WAS BORN IN NEW YORK CITY, APRIL 3, 1851, the son of the Rev. Duncan Cameron Mann and the former Caroline Brother Schuyler. He grew up in Watkins, New York, a village of some two thousand persons on the south end of Seneca Lake in the heart of the beautiful and romantic Iroquois country. There he lived in the small rural parish of St. James's Church, of which his father was rector. Although the village was small, it was the center of some commercial activity and a shipping point for many of the farm and dairy products raised in the region. Watkins was also the seat of Schuyler County, and it is quite possible that the county received its name from some of the antecedents of Cameron's mother. The village was a popular summer resort since the numerous nearby mineral springs were used in bath treatments for rheumatism, gout, heart, kidney, and liver diseases. Partly within the village limits lay Watkins Glen, a narrow winding gorge about two miles long with walls and precipices ranging from one to three hundred feet. Through the glen ran a small stream which formed many falls, cascades, and forest pools as it wound its way to Seneca Lake. It was in this idyllic setting that the future bishop spent his boyhood, hiking in the hills, swimming in the streams, ranging the shore of the lake, and collecting botanical specimens in the forests.

His boyhood gave him a Wordsworthian appreciation of nature that was to last for the rest of his life.[1]

Young Cameron received his early education in his native state, enriched by the society and influence of his father and mother, and the numerous visitors who flocked to the mineral springs and scenic views near Watkins each summer. As time passed, several brothers and sisters enlarged the family group in the rectory. Duncan Mann's long cure at St. James's was that of a typical country clergyman in Western New York. Although his career was hardly spectacular, he must have exerted a strong influence on his sons, for two of them, Cameron and his younger brother Alexander, went into the ministry of the Church and both later became bishops. The Rt. Rev. Arthur Cleveland Coxe, Bishop of Western New York, described the elder Mann as a clergyman "eminently useful not only in parochial work, but in the general business of the diocese."[2] The Rev. Mr. Mann was also bookish enough to encourage bookishness in his son, for Cameron matriculated at Hobart College at an early age and was awarded his bachelor's degree in the spring of 1870 when he was barely nineteen. The following year he enrolled in General Theological Seminary in New York City and received the B.D. degree three years later. In 1874 he was given the M.A. from his alma mater, Hobart. He was ordained to the diaconate the year he finished at General and immediately went into missionary work under Bishop Coxe at St. Luke's Church, Branchport, and St. John's Church, West Dresden, in Yates County. These small rural churches, which numbered but forty-eight and thirty-six communicants respectively, were served by the deacon for over a year. In 1875 Cameron Mann left the Diocese of Western New York to become curate of St. Peter's Church, Albany.[3]

In less than a year Mann was back in Watkins filling the vacancy at St. James's caused by the death of his father. The young deacon

1. Edgar L. Pennington, "Cameron Mann, Bishop and Doctor," *The Angelus*, a publication of Grace and Holy Trinity Church, Kansas City, Missouri, February 1932.

2. Arthur Cleveland Coxe, *Episcopal Address, Diocesan Journal* (Western New York), 1876, pp. 56–57.

3. *Diocesan Journal* (Western New York), 1874, pp. 9, 157.

was made rector of St. James's late in 1875 and a few months later, on the feast of St. Matthias, Bishop Coxe advanced him to the priesthood. The new priest threw himself into the work of his calling. Within a year he presented a class of eighteen candidates for confirmation. That same year he baptized twenty-one adults and twenty-four infants.[4] The rector took a deep interest in the children of his parish, and when he left St. James's in 1881 to become rector of Grace Church, Kansas City, Missouri, there were thirty boys and fifty girls enrolled in the Sunday School.[5]

When the New Yorker assumed his duties at Grace Church he was thirty years of age and still single. He had 215 communicants under his charge who could be described as "generally indifferent." Within a year the energetic priest had changed matters considerably. He presented a large confirmation class to his bishop and secured a wife.[6] On June 14, 1882, he married Mary LeCain of a prominent Cincinnati family and brought her to live in the rectory of Grace Church. Four children were born to the couple: two daughters, Justine and Dorothea, and two sons, Duncan Cameron and LeCain. Justine and Dorothea grew up in the noise and bustle of Kansas City and moved with their parents to the quiet prairie town of Fargo, North Dakota. Neither of the boys, however, survived childhood. The sadness of one son's death and the bereavement felt by all parents who have lost young children is expressed compassionately in a tender poem of Bishop Mann's published years later.

A CHILD'S DEATH

A tiny blade of grass has withered on the prairie;
   A water drop breathed back from ocean to the skies;
And now the total landscape widens dim and dreary,
   And on the water surface no bright bubble lies.

From myriads uncounted a single face is missing,—
   A sturdy, brave-eyed boy, with tossing golden hair,—

4. Ibid., 1876, p. 131.
5. Ibid., 1881, pp. 71, 140.
6. *Diocesan Journal* (Missouri), *Parochial Reports.*

> And so all else seems hopeless,—thinking, toiling, kissing,—
> What made this earth so precious is no longer there.[7]

The boys were buried in the Mann family plot on the hillside in Watkins Glen. Mary Mann, after the death of her sons, turned her full attention to raising her daughters and to the women's work of the Church on both the parochial and the diocesan level.

Cameron Mann worked hard in Kansas City. He was a good pastor and a thought-provoking preacher. With his strong will, scholarly mind, and quiet but strangely vigorous personality, he soon became a leader among the clergy of the Diocese of Missouri. When that diocese was divided in 1889, he was elected to the Standing Committee of the new Diocese of West Missouri and within a short time was serving as its president. His congregation grew from a feeble two hundred into one of the "commanding parishes" of West Missouri, a growth that forced the rector and his vestry to draft plans for a new church and parish house. The new facilities, of massive Neo-Gothic design, possessed much warmth and beauty, and the buildings aroused no little architectural comment. New Grace Church was consecrated on May 15, 1898. It was later described by the Rt. Rev. Edward R. Atwill, Bishop of West Missouri, as a monument to Cameron Mann's "financial and executive ability no less than to the generosity of a devoted people."[8] In addition to caring for a growing congregation, building a new church and parish house, and serving on an increasing number of diocesan and civic committees, the rector of Grace Church found time for writing, reading, and reflection. He passionately devoured the works of the English poet George Herbert and read widely in both ecclesiastical and secular history. Metaphysics always had a strong appeal for him, hence the affection for Herbert. The English Romantic poets, particularly Coleridge, Wordsworth, and Byron, were also highly esteemed by the cleric, as was the Victorian poet Tennyson. During his years at Grace Church he wrote

7. Cameron Mann, *The Longing of Circe and Other Poems* (New York: privately printed, 1922), p. 54.

8. Edward Robert Atwill, *Episcopal Address, Diocesan Journal* (West Missouri), 1902, p. 27.

and published two books: the controversial collection *October Sermons: Five Discourses on Future Punishment* (1888), and the highly spiritual Good Friday meditation, *Comments at the Cross* (1893).[9] During his rectorate Cameron Mann was honored by the Diocese of Missouri in 1886 and 1889 and by the Diocese of West Missouri in 1892, 1895, 1898, and 1901 by being elected a member of the House of Deputies of the General Convention of the Protestant Episcopal Church. In 1888 his alma mater conferred on him the honorary degree Sacrae Theologiae Doctori.

When the General Convention of the Church met in San Francisco in the fall of 1901, one of the many questions that had to be considered was the filling of the vacant bishopric of the Missionary District of North Dakota. The vacancy was caused when the Missionary Bishop, the Rt. Rev. Samuel Cook Edsall, D.D., accepted his election to the See of Minnesota. The House of Bishops nominated the Rev. Charles Campbell Pierce, a presbyter of the Diocese of Washington, as Missionary Bishop, but the House of Deputies rejected the nomination, probably because of Pierce's lack of parochial experience. Apparently Mr. Pierce, a former Baptist minister, had spent the greater part of his priesthood in the Episcopal Church as an army chaplain and was at the time of his nomination the chaplain at the garrison at Fort Myer, Virginia. On reconsidering the vacancy in North Dakota, the bishops nominated "the Rev. Cameron Mann, D.D., a Presbyter from the Diocese of West Missouri." This nomination brought a quick ratification from the House of Deputies, and Cameron Mann returned to his people in Kansas City as Bishop-Elect of North Dakota.[10]

On December 4, 1901, as the *Veni, Creator Spiritus* was sung over him, this devoted priest with a plenteous shock of greying hair knelt in the chancel of the massive Neo-Gothic church that he had helped build in Kansas City. Cameron Mann received the "Holy Ghost for the Office and Work of a Bishop in the Church of God" from his consecrators, the Right Reverend Fathers in God, Bishops

9. *Lloyd's Clerical Directory, 1898: A Treasury of Information for the Clergy and Laity of the Protestant Episcopal Church* (Chicago: edited and published by Frederic E. J. Lloyd, 1898), p. 266.

10. *General Convention Journal*, 1901, pp. 124, 148, 153, 262, 276–77.

Tuttle of Missouri, Talbot of Bethlehem, and Atwill of West Missouri. There were four other bishops present at the service. Mann became the third bishop of the Missionary District of North Dakota and the two hundred and first bishop of the American succession. He was fifty years old. On January 5, 1902, the new bishop was formally received in Gethsemane Cathedral, Fargo, where, he reported, "I entered upon my duties by celebrating the Holy Eucharist."[11]

North Dakota was primarily an agricultural state. Its chief crops were wheat and flax, with wheat the most important money crop. According to the U.S. Census of 1900, the entire population numbered but 319,146, and of this number, 113,091 were foreign born. Norwegians, Russians, Germans, and Swedes, along with a good smattering of English Canadians, made up the bulk of the group. The population spectrum was further complicated by the presence of some eight thousand American Indians. No town in the state exceeded a population of ten thousand inhabitants. Fargo, the largest town, was also the see city. About one third of the state was Roman Catholic, one third was Lutheran, and one third was affiliated with a large number of other Protestant denominations. There were slightly more than 1,700 communicants of the Episcopal Church in the whole missionary district. When Mann became bishop, Gethsemane Cathedral had two hundred thirty communicants on its rolls and was by far the largest church in the jurisdiction. Two of the other larger congregations were the Indian missions on the Sioux reservation. There were no Episcopal schools, hospitals, or colleges in the state. The Church population was scattered widely into some sixty-seven parishes and missions. The strongholds of the Church, if such they could be called, were mainly in the towns and in the areas that contained concentrations of English Canadians.[12]

Cameron Mann was of necessity missionary-minded in a largely rural and polyglot state. A glance at the *Convocation Journals* of the Missionary District of North Dakota will show how hard the

11. Mann, *Episcopal Address, Diocesan Journal* (Missionary District of North Dakota), 1902, p. 19.

12. *Living Church Annual and Church Almanac,* 1903 (Milwaukee: The Young Churchman, 1903), p. 227.

bishop worked. During his episcopate there, he opened twenty-five new missions and enlarged the work of the Church among the Indians. But after eleven years of labor the number of communicants in North Dakota had grown by only two hundred seventy-six.[13]

Years later the Dean of Gethsemane Cathedral and the bishop's close friend, the Very Rev. Hugh Latimer Burleson, recalled Mann's work and travels in North Dakota and gave an illustration of his sense of humor: "The journeys were long, and the little groups of Churchfolk almost inaccessible. He spent many a night curled up on the seat of a day-coach, and occasionally attempted to sleep on a trunk in the baggage-room of some lonely station amid the snows of the prairie, while waiting for a belated train. I remember meeting him one morning, looking rather weary as he emerged from a two-car train. 'Well,' said I, 'Where have you been this time —to the jumping off place?' With a glint of humor flashing through his fatigue, he replied: 'No, it was the place where you land after you jump off.' "[14]

It could have been that Bishop Mann welcomed his translation from North Dakota to Southern Florida when the General Convention met in New York in 1913. If the bishop felt relief in acquiring a new field of labor, he did not show it, and his people were sorry to see him leave. His successor, the Rt. Rev. John P. Tyler, spoke appreciatively of his predecessor for the Churchmen of North Dakota: "During the many years of his labors among us, we all grew to love Bishop Mann . . . [for] his ripe scholarship, and royal loyalty to the clergy, his staunch insistence upon the strictest interpretation of and obedience to the Church's doctrines and practices, his constant and arduous travels in and about his field of labor."[15] Even after he moved to Florida, Bishop Mann followed the work of the Church in North Dakota for many years with keen interest. His years in North Dakota stamped that state

13. Ibid., 1913, pp. 270–71.

14. Hugh Latimer Burleson, D.D., "Memorial Sermon to the Late Bishop Mann," appended to the *Diocesan Journal*, 1932, p. 62; hereafter cited as "Memorial Sermon."

15. John P. Tyler, *Episcopal Address, Convocation Journal* (North Dakota), 1914, pp. 22–23.

indelibly on his mind—the loneliness of the plains, the immense expanse of wild flowers, the vast "green floor of the prairie," and the vast "blue dome of the sky."[16]

It was during his episcopate in North Dakota that Mann journeyed to England for the Lambeth Conference of 1907. His quiet humor and erudition made him a popular figure among the American prelates attending the great ecclesiastical convocation. At its close, Bishop Mann, always an Anglophile, wrote the following verses expressing his sense of obligation to the English and their heritage.

A PARTING WORD
After the Lambeth Conference

"Kings, Lords, and Commons,"—so you style
The free Republic of this Isle,—
One from the democratic West,
Of late your kindly-treated guest,
Would say his word of gratefulness,
And debts of centuries confess.
A host of us can claim no trace
Of bloodship with your English race;
But stronger than all ties of blood
Is spiritual fatherhood.
You gave our speech, religion, law;
You first our great ideals saw;
Your Bible, Shakespeare, Parliament,
Shape life upon our continent.
So for the old and rich bequest
Our gratitude abides professed;
And for all recent courtesy,
Accept this simple word from me.[17]

These lines were published in *The Spectator*. They received such wide and favorable comment that the poem was reprinted in numerous British and American periodicals. The verses had both graciousness and poetic merit. They were simply done, but showed

16. Mann, "North Dakota," *The Longing of Circe*, p. 15.
17. *Spectator*, August 1, 1908, p. 164.

the reader something of Cameron Mann: a glimpse of his kindliness, his courtliness, and his sense of history.

When Bishop Mann came to his new jurisdiction, he must have been aware that he had been translated from North Dakota against the wishes of Bishop Gray. The retiring prelate felt strongly that the bishops and deputies of the Province of Sewanee should have had the opportunity to vote for nominees "who live in our region," probably because he felt they understood the problems of the area better than the bishops and deputies from other regions of the country.[18] Bishop Gray also had a strong prejudice against Northerners. The new prelate, however, soon won the good will and affection of Bishop Gray. When the old man relinquished his episcopal authority to Bishop Mann at the Convocation of 1914, he tenderly turned to his successor before the whole convocation and said: "And to you, beloved brother, my esteemed successor, I turn over all power and authority which I have had for more than a score of years, and do most earnestly invoke God's abundant blessing upon you and all your work for Christ and the Church, 'til we come again in the unity of the faith and of the knowledge of the Son of God. . . . Farewell."[19] Despite their different backgrounds, the two men had come to understand and respect each other.

The new bishop brought his special qualities of warmth, humor, scholarship, elusiveness, and sweetness to his see in Florida. His fondness for flowers evidenced itself even before he moved into his new Orlando residence. On arriving in a cold January, he wrote in his diary, "It is not the flower season yet, but many plants are in bloom—especially the poinsettias. I never saw such large and vivid splashes of their scarlet before." He could not resist his new yard: "Office work all morning. . . . In the afternoon I wielded axe and saw, trimming up some trees and shrubs, and really enjoyed it. I make discoveries of new botanical treasures each day. Our begonia vine is glorious with orange trumpets, a jessamine has white stars, and an elder is just beginning its lacelike fringe."[20] The bishop's passion for botany was so strong that it would take him miles to

18. *Bishop's Diary, Palm Branch,* December 1913.
19. *Convocation Journal,* 1914, pp. 45–46.
20. *Bishop's Diary, Palm Branch,* February 1914.

see a flowering shrub or an exotic wild flower. In the summer of 1917 he recorded: "In the afternoon I motored to a fine woods and bog near Kissimmee, where I found a superb Scarlet Hibiscus and a White Spider Lily and the Clematis Vivina,—making red, white, and blue."[21] Many of the wild flowers that he found on his botanizing trips were successfully transplanted in the yard of the Bishopstead.

Cameron Mann's diary shows what an avid reader he was. Entries such as "I spent the evening with Wordsworth" (or "with Herbert") occur again and again. He enjoyed reading novels, and the range of his taste ran from Dickens to Galsworthy to the short stories of O. Henry. During and after the war he devoured current books on world affairs and could write excitedly about them. He was drawn to biography and autobiography as well. In the summer of 1919 he wrote: "Began the reading of *The Education of Henry Adams,* a unique and fascinating work." A few of his comments on the book illustrate the bishop's power, perception, and sensitivity as a critic of literature and of life. "It is the work of one who had pretty much all the advantages; it seems written with perfect honesty; it is kindly in temper; it abounds in clever epigrams and has some passages of sombre eloquence; it throws light on many of the big men and events of over half a century; there is not a dull page between its covers. And its title is suggestive,—*The Education of Henry Adams,*—he was born into this world, was shown its sights, was battered by its forces, was conversant with its men and women, and it taught him,—what? That he knew nothing, nothing, that is, of what is ultimate and durable. It is not pessimism of any gross strain that he utters; it is an irony, sadder than any such pessimism, as proceeding from a gentle and modest soul. And the cause of all this was that he had no religious faith; he was not a Christian, not even a Deist. Unless it were subconsciously; for one cannot help thinking that in the dark background Adams surmised some stirring of the Divine; his love of nature, of clouds and trees and blossoms, of mountains and sea, must have had some Wordsworthian feeling in it. But he says distinctly that he grew up without religion; that the religious instinct had vanished and never returned, though in

21. Ibid., August 1917.

later life he made attempts to recover it. And his description of the Unitarianism, which was the ecclesiastical atmosphere of his boyhood, goes far to explain this; it was not a faith to teach a child." The bishop commented enthusiastically that this autobiography interested him "more than any other book I have gone through in a long time."[22]

The bishop's remarks on reading John Forster's *Life of Charles Dickens* show that he had a love both for Dickens and for the wonderful characters that he created. In an amusing extract Mann wrote, "It is delightful to learn what a good Christian, and, in all essentials, good Anglican Christian he was. A propos of this latter, there is given a remark made by his father, richly humorous though not so intended. He, who, by the way, was in several traits the original of Mr. Micawber, had listened to some dissenter who was boasting of the superior piety of the dissenters in general, and of his own family in particular, and their greater acceptableness to God. At last Mr. Dickens remarked, 'The Supreme Being must be an entirely different individual from what I have every reason to believe Him to be, if He would care in the least for the society of your relations.' "[23]

The reports of Bishop Mann's occasional trips to New York show how well he followed the theater, the exhibitions, and even the cinema showings of that great metropolis. He enjoyed "sweetest Shakespeare" and "learned Jonson," particularly the racy and sometimes raucous *Volpone*. The bishop was so moved by the Albrecht Dürer Exhibition at the Metropolitan Museum of Art that he was compelled to write two poems, perhaps his best, to express the depths of his feelings on seeing the woodcuts—"Knight, Death, and Devil" and "Knight and Lady."[24] His observations about the new art of motion picture making were often as critical of the audience as of the picture. "In the afternoon I went to a 'Movie-Talkie' presentation of Sutton Vane's play *Outward Bound*. It was excellently acted all the way through and has a high moral . . . consequently the attendance was small." A favorite haunt of Bishop

22. Ibid., August 1919.
23. Ibid., September 1917.
24. Mann, *The Longing of Circe*, pp. 5–7.

Mann's during his New York visits was the Museum of Natural History. He would slip away from wife, family, and friends, and amble for hours through its corridors. Another pleasure the prelate enjoyed was a walk to Washington Square, where he was fond of listening to Italians sing the folk songs of their native land. On one of these trips to the great city the bishop, as usual, made observations in his diary about his fellow railroad passengers, many of whom were returning servicemen from World War I. "We woke up to find that a freight train ahead of ours had gone off the track, causing another delay. But the weather had cooled off, so that we were comfortable. We had a bunch of soldier and sailor boys on board, and our train was stalled near a large field of watermelons, so I saw the military operation called 'looting'."[25]

It is clear from anecdotes the bishop enjoyed repeating that he responded warmly to children and particularly appreciated their spontaneity. During an episcopal visitation to a South Florida parish he made a talk to the children of the Sunday school. Noticing, as he invariably did, many beautiful flowers on the altar and thinking perhaps that some women's guild had labored to place them there, he asked, "I wonder if you can tell me who put those lilies there?" Instantly a small girl shrilled from under a bright bonnet, "Mama did!" On another occasion when he was being taken to a home to be entertained for a Sunday meal after a service, the boy of the family exclaimed, "You're going to have a good dinner, Bishop— chocolate ice cream!"[26]

On numerous occasions Bishop Mann went into the lairs of the very rich with hat in hand to raise money for diocesan projects. His forays always included a trip to the Breakers in Palm Beach and the Ormond in Ormond Beach. Even during these expeditions he showed a sense of humor. At the Ormond Hotel on one such visit he viewed the guests in the lobby and recorded his feelings in his diary. "The amount of wealth represented at this hotel was almost appalling. I felt like Coleridge's 'Ancient Mariner' who saw 'Water, water everywhere, Nor any drop to drink.' "[27]

25. *Bishop's Diary, Palm Branch*, January 1931, September 1919.
26. *Palm Branch*, June 1917.
27. *Bishop's Diary, Palm Branch*, April 1916.

Preaching was, and is, one of the chief duties of a bishop. Nearly all contemporaries of Cameron Mann agree that he was a polished preacher. His sermons were direct, scholarly, well put together, but low-keyed. Most of his addresses, particularly in the later years of his episcopate, were read from a manuscript. Some of his less so-phisticated flock would perhaps have preferred that the bishop preach extemporaneously, but he rarely if ever did this. Bishop Mann drew large crowds during his early years in South Florida. A reporter from the *Palm Beach Post* commented on a sermon that the bishop delivered in Holy Trinity Church during a visitation: "Bishop Mann preached a sermon on the sin of ingratitude, taking as his text the passage referring to the healing of the ten lepers of whom only one returned to give thanks to the Saviour, which, he said, was the classic illustration of ingratitude. In words plain, but eloquent and forceful, Bishop Mann described the unenviable plight of the sufferer from black leprosy, a pariah, an outcast from his kind; he portrayed the growing delight of each of the ten men thus afflicted as he noticed on his journey to 'show himself to the priest' that the loathsome disease was leaving him, and his culminating joy upon realizing that all signs of it had totally disappeared. . . . The preacher delved deep into the minds of the ungrateful nine in order to reveal the excuses they made to themselves for their ingrati-tude. The behaviour of the tenth victim—'and he a Samaritan'— was dwelt upon in vivid contrast. Under the Bishop's skillful treat-ment the lepers became very real everyday persons, whose processes of mind were familiar to all his hearers. The lesson drawn from their conduct was driven home to the minds of the congregation with a trenchant simplicity that postulated an intelligence that could not miss its meaning and with no superfluous verbiage."[28]

The Rev. Charles Hamilton Bascom, retired vicar of St. Gabriel's, Titusville, remembered that Bishop Mann's sermons were nearly always good and on occasion "fine and powerful." This cleric re-calls that Bishop Mann's sermon in Westminster Abbey during a Lambeth Conference was much admired by his hearers. The only published sermons that survive the bishop other than his episcopal addresses are the series he preached on future punishment at Grace

28. West Palm Beach *Palm Beach Post*, February 17, 1915.

Church in Kansas City, Missouri, in October 1887. The preacher treated his subject in five sermons: The General Subject, The Theory of Final Restoration, The Theory of Eternal Probation, The Theory of Everlasting Misery, and The Theory of Final Destruction. These sermons are an unabashed defense of the orthodox Christian view of punishment. "I may be accused of rashness in dealing at all with this mysterious and awful doctrine," Bishop Mann wrote, but he made no apology for the topic. "I can only reply that it must be dealt with; that to keep silence is to speak, and, in my case, to speak what I do not believe."[29] The bishop dealt with his subject by using scholarly sources which he put into the everyday language of his hearers. He was a convincing champion of orthodoxy and a polished and succinct defender of Christian doctrine against the attacks of what he called "modernism."

The other published works of Bishop Mann are *The Longing of Circe and Other Poems* and *A Concordance to the English Poems of George Herbert*. By modern standards, his volume of poems is Victorian in outlook and technique, contrived in rhyme, sometimes clumsy in meter, and repetitious in detail. The poetry does, however, contain some fine phrasing and evidence of a bright and original mind. Some of the poems appeared in the *Atlantic Monthly*, the *Century*, *Life*, and the London *Spectator*, as well as in a number of lesser periodicals and newspapers. The bishop did not preface his volume of poems, so there is no *apologia* for them. He was seventy-one years old when the little volume made its appearance in 1922. The edition was limited to four hundred copies and privately printed. One poem, "A Modern Decalogue," illustrates the disapproval with which the elderly prelate viewed the social mores of his age, as well as the irony with which he combatted them.

I

Have but one God; and let him be
A God acceptable to thee.

29. Cameron Mann, *October Sermons: Five Discourses on Future Punishment* (New York: Thomas Whittaker, 1888), p. 3.

II

Unto no graven image bow;
We print all wealth on paper now.

III

Blaspheme no holy thing by word;
Enough that it is deftly slurred.

IV

Desist one day each week from work,—
And all the rest, if you can, shirk.

V

Let parents not in poorhouse sit;
Newspapers will get hold of it.

VI

Destroy no man with sword or gun;
He can be otherwise undone.

VII

Keep to thine own wife; but, of course,
Thou mayest have others, by divorce.

VIII

By no means snatch; how very crude,
When 'tis so easy to delude.

IX

Speak out no lie. Insinuate;
Much safer, and of greater weight.

X

Naught covet! Well,—here I opine
We must reduce our laws to nine.[30]

The distinguished critic and poet, Allen Tate, singled out the
following poem as Bishop Mann's best, illustrating his scope and
sophistication:

A GENTLE BLUEBEARD

Yes, Dear, this is your house; do as you please;
    Keep, change, cast out,—whatever suits you best.
Walk through room after room,—here are the keys.
    But stop! That key does not go with the rest.

30. Mann, *The Longing of Circe*, pp. 25-26.

Is there no door it opens? Yes; but then
    There's nothing worth while stored up there! 'Tis just
The merest closet, a small dingy den,
    With scattered rubbish thickly clothed in dust;—
A photograph now faded into naught,
    A rose in pieces, on discoloured leaves
The lines wherein long since somebody sought
    To tell a story no one now believes.
When did I get those letters? Years ago,
    When I was still a sentimental boy,—
And you, a baby, taught your dolls to sew,
    And gravely mimicked housewifely employ.
May you go in and clear the room? Ah no!
    Let it stay as it is; it does no harm.
You see, I'm used to having it just so;
    Although unentered, it retains a charm.
You need not be disturbed. A skeleton
    Abides in every home; you would search far
Before you found the closet holding one
    With bones so slight and fleshless as these are.
No tragedy is hinted at by them;
    They do not call for either frown or sigh;
They ask you not to pardon or condemn;
    They rustle this, "There was a time,—gone by."[31]

Bishop Mann's *A Concordance to the English Poems of George Herbert* was primarily a labor of love, the fruition of an affair with the poet that began while Cameron Mann was an undergraduate at Hobart. The compiler stated that while he could not add to the substance of English literature by creating a classic, he could furnish a little help to some of its students by compiling a concordance. "Concordances," the bishop explained, "are not merely for the purpose of hunting down half-remembered sayings—though this is a worthy service. They contribute much to the investigation of the history of words, and so to the history of thought. I have gained such assistance from them that I have made myself possessor of every one I could find—from Bartlett's majestic Shakespeare to

31. Ibid., pp. 20–21.

Cook's modest Gray. . . . They retain the same applicability on their hundredth year as they had on their first."[32] Although the bishop's concordance has not reached its hundredth year, its compiler has done much to help future generations appreciate the power, the beauty, and the importance of the poems of George Herbert.

Tucked in a well-used volume of Herbert's poems in the library of the Bishopstead was found a later poem by John Keble:

> Lord, make my heart a place where angels sing!
>   For surely thoughts low-breathed by Thee
> Are angels gliding near on noiseless wing;
>   And where a home they see
> Swept clean, and garnish'd with adoring joy,
>   They enter in and dwell, and teach that heart to swell
> With heavenly Melody, their own untired employ.

By placing Keble's lines with the poems of George Herbert, Bishop Mann revealed a great deal about himself. This simple act showed that he shared the range and depth of faith of both poets as well as the sheer joy that compelled him to express that faith in poetry.

Bishop Mann worried constantly about the problems of peace which Americans faced following World War I, but he worried even more about the pessimism and indifference that followed the end of the Wilson era. In a sermon he preached in St. Luke's Cathedral in January 1921, the bishop looked at the disillusioned world and commented on it in the Wordsworthian tone that he used so often in his sermons, talks, and addresses.

"We are now facing some exceedingly, unwontedly dark and dismal world problems. There has been a pessimistic reaction from the heroic inspirations of the great war; men are engaged in sweeping up the foul rubbish, and are disgusted by it; there is a huge confusion wherethrough we can hardly grope our way. Even the Christians of Europe and America seem dubious of and at variance with each other. The appeal of the Lambeth Conference for unity

32. Cameron Mann, comp., *A Concordance of the English Poems of George Herbert* (Boston: Houghton Mifflin Company, 1927), pp. vii–viii.

has yet few sympathetic responses. It is natural that we should become discouraged.

"It is natural; yes. Then let us turn to the supernatural, of which the natural does, if we will look for it, hold a prophecy. Let me quote some lovely words from Dr. Campbell's *A Spiritual Pilgrimage*, written in view of just such discouragements as I have mentioned. He describes the dreary landscapes of the Fall when all verdure is dying and the outlook is to the torpor of the Winter with no blossoms or birds. Then he says, 'Nevertheless I remember, and the knowledge brings comfort, that a horticulturist once told me to look not to April but to October for the springtime of the year. Under all the death and decay the new life is already preparing its advent. Within those falling petals yonder are the ripened seeds of next years's summer glory. Pinch those diminutive husks, so like mummy cases, that are pushing the fading leaves off the trees, and you will find within, beautifully folded, delicately perfect, the buds that are to be. Nature sleeps, but she is not idle; the miracle of regeneration is going on all the time unhindered, unresting, unexhausted, with the infinitude of God behind it. We wait in hope, —nay, in confidence,—that brightness, wealth and splendor will come again with azure skies and the singing of birds.' "[33]

Bishop Mann was at his best when writing prose, whether for a sermon or for his diary. In prose he mingled his scholarship, his poetic flair, and his active imagination with ease and naturalness. Once before a convocation in South Florida he upbraided his clergy and people on a multitude of topics: international brotherhood, their domestic and foreign missionary obligations, their unpaid parochial assessments and apportionments, and their duty to make South Florida a self-supporting diocese within the framework of the American Church. These obligations were what he called some of the ordinary "commonplace" essentials of the Christian life. He cited the English Franciscan friar Thomas of Eccleston, who once made a public confession that the worries of building monastic houses and chapels for the order had robbed him of the inclination to preach the gospel and had made him less devoted to the ideals of a Christian life.

33. *Palm Branch*, January 1921.

"On this occasion," the bishop said, "I would rather have spoken upon the mysteries of the Christian faith, the beauties of the Christian law, the charm of the Christian worship, the splendors of the Christian hope, than upon the activities and operations where Church and world run in much the same grooves and employ much the same machinery. But the commonplace, dusty, unexciting tasks have to be performed. And if we will only enter upon them in the right spirit they will be transformed. After all, our prosaic, humdrum activities are necessary activities. The Franciscan friars had to have houses, even if the famous preacher must deliver fewer sermons. And the loss of his devotion was not inevitable or irretrievable.

"The 'commonplace, dusty, unexciting' tasks are those for which the majority of us are best fitted; and even those who are more brilliantly endowed are also called upon to march in the ranks and at times to share in the discipline and fighting. When we become discouraged with commonplace tasks, let us recall the simplicity of our Lord's life, the carpenter shop at Nazareth, the humble home at Bethany, the fishermen and the common people with whom He cast His lot. He gloried in daily toil and blessed sweet human relations. And no matter how matchless the beauty of the cathedral, the foundations must be laid and the scaffolding erected in order that it may be perfected and completed."[34]

Throughout his episcopate Bishop Mann was an ardent champion of the Cathedral School. He took a particular interest in both the students and the faculty and was careful to see that only the most highly qualified teachers were chosen for the staff. He studied the design of all the new buildings before their construction and was anxious that all available space be utilized to the fullest for playing fields and gardens. During the Florida boom when the city of Orlando tried to cut a street through the crowded educational facilities, he fought the attempt in the courts. He felt that the street would take valuable space away from the school as well as destroy the physical unity of the plant. In speaking of the condemnation proceedings he wrote sarcastically in his diary, "Of course, the 'best citizens' do not approve. But they have acted as the 'best citizens'

34. *The Living Church*, March 29, 1921.

usually act. That is they have done nothing."[35] The bishop was soliciting funds for the school's endowment in New York City when the Panic of 1929 broke out. In spite of the disaster he noted in his diary with justifiable pride that he was able to raise fifteen hundred dollars.[36]

As a Churchman, Bishop Mann would probably be classed as a Catholic, a Prayer Book Catholic, but hardly a ritualist. He always wore his pectoral cross and delighted in the use of his crozier, which was presented to him by John C. Jessup of Holy Trinity Parish, West Palm Beach.[37] In the main, however, the bishop refused to involve himself in controversies of ritual so long as his clergy adhered to the liturgy of the Book of Common Prayer. The Church was Catholic with or without an elaborate ritual, with or without the adjective "Protestant" in its title. At one point in his life, Bishop Mann did favor changing the name of the Church from "Protestant Episcopal" to "The Church in the United States" because he felt the title "Protestant Episcopal" was too confining.[38]

Bishop Mann's loyalty to and appreciation of the Book of Common Prayer was monumental. He believed that the book was "absolutely unique." "The great Roman Catholic Church has its Missal and Breviary, wonderful, beautiful, inspirational. But neither of them is a Book of *Common* Prayer, to be used by all people, clerical and lay, learned and ignorant. They are in a language foreign to most congregations. And even when translated they are plainly meant to be used *for* rather than with and by the attendants at a Service.

"Much the same observation can be made as to the Greek and Oriental Liturgies.

"Several Protestant Denominations have put forth handbooks of worship. But these at the best are only *a* book of common prayer; —not *the* Book, not authoritative, not meant for and binding upon all members of the Society.

35. *Palm Branch*, June 1925.
36. *Bishop's Diary, Palm Branch*, November 1929.
37. *Palm Branch*, June 1925.
38. Mann, *Episcopal Address, Convocation Journal* (Missionary Jurisdiction of North Dakota), 1913, pp. 7–8.

"Assuredly, the uniqueness of our Book is most impressive and instructive."

The bishop agreed with the nineteenth-century British historian Henry Hart Milman, who did much work in Jewish, Early Christian, and Renaissance history. "The Prayer Book," Milman stated in his eloquent appraisal, "is the best model of pure, fervent, simple devotion as it were, and concentration, of all the orisons which have been uttered in the name of Christ since the first days of the Gospel; that Liturgy which is the great example of pure vernacular English, familiar yet unvulgar; which has an indwelling music, which enthralls and never palls upon the ear with the full living expression of every great Christian truth, yet rarely hardening into stern dogmatism, satisfying every need and awakening and answering every Christian emotion, entering into the heart, and, as it were, welling forth again from the heart, full and general voice of the congregation, yet the peculiar utterance of each single worshipper."[39]

Bishop Mann defended the Prayer Book not only for its beauty but for its utility as well. He firmly believed that its liturgy was the most useful mode of worship in the English language and that it was the great bond of unity in the Anglican Communion. He warned against "that curious mental aberration which leads men to underrate their own possessions,"[40] yet he also thought that the liturgy should be revised from time to time to keep pace with changing times. The Rt. Rev. Hugh Latimer Burleson, Bishop of South Dakota and Assistant to the Presiding Bishop, recalled a revision which Bishop Mann favored: "I can never forget that moment in the House of Bishops when it seemed that the brief petition for the dead inserted in the prayer for Christ's Church—'Grant them continual growth in thy love and service'—might fail of passage. He [Bishop Mann] came to me almost trembling with eagerness and said: 'It must not fail! I want to feel that in the years to come the Church will be saying those words for me.' "

Bishop Burleson recalled another attribute of Cameron Mann— his humility. There were some, said Bishop Burleson, who thought

39. Mann, *Episcopal Address* (South Florida), 1929, pp. 48–49.
40. Ibid.

that Bishop Mann was "almost too great a man" to be a missionary bishop, but this thought never occurred to Bishop Mann "for he was utterly without conceit. He rejoiced, almost like a boy, in a good sermon, or a fine poem, or a new orchid which he had created or discovered, but he loved it for itself, and not because it was his."[41] Hidden among the Diocesan Records is an admonition to a parish priest who was a bit stiff-necked with pride in regard to his priestly prerogatives with his vestry. The admonition was penned in the bishop's own hand and stated with his own gentle humor. "*Et qui se exaltat humiliabitur, et qui se humiliat exaltabitur.*"[42] Much was said of Bishop Mann's learning, his literary taste, and his preaching ability, but he was careful not to exalt himself over his clergy and people. This was his greatest appeal.

The Manns formed a close family circle. The bishop's wife, Mary LeCain, was of French origin on her paternal side. The original spelling of her family name was LeQuesne, but when Mrs. Mann's forebears moved from Nova Scotia to Boston in the early nineteenth century they Anglicized the name.[43] Although they later moved to Cincinnati, Mary inherited much New England brusqueness and frankness from her progenitors. She never quite understood the Southerner, nor did the Southener quite understand her. South Floridians knew that she was a hard Church worker and certainly one of the most generous. But they also knew she was a woman of strong opinions which she did not hesitate to utter. As the wife of the Bishop of South Florida she considered it her duty, perhaps her privilege, to preside over the Women's Church Service League. She sometimes diminished the significance of the bishop's visits by her officiousness. One old-timer remembers her as "bossy," another as "tactless," and an old clergyman recalls that she was "well-meaning, but not weak." There was little doubt that she was the "chief hen of the hen yard" and the "Empress of the Bishopstead." The bishop, especially as he grew older, deferred to her, and if he did not she volunteered her opinions anyway. One crusty veteran priest

41. Burleson, "Memorial Sermon," p. 65.

42. Vulgate. "He that exalteth himself shall be humbled, and he that humbleth himself shall be exalted."

43. *Bishop's Diary, Palm Branch,* September–October 1921.

of the diocese complained that Bishop Mann was given to "uxori-
ousness," while an Orlando layman declared him to be "hen-
pecked." There are slight but gentle hints in the bishop's diary
that this was not quite true. During a trip to New York he wrote
with amused irony and an almost Olympian awareness, "Spent the
morning shopping, under Mrs. Mann's guidance, and getting various articles which I learned from her I was in great need of."[44]

Despite Mrs. Mann's outspokenness the Manns were a devoted
couple. The bishop delighted in the society of his wife and daughters, and particularly enjoyed family festivals and feasts when his
daughters would come back to the Bishopstead after their marriages.
At Christmastime, 1923, Dorothea (Mrs. Clinton Harbison of Lex-
ington, Kentucky) arrived with her husband and child for the
holidays. The bishop recorded gleefully, "The whole family drove
out to the woods to get a Christmas tree." On Christmas Day he
wrote, "In the evening we read aloud Christmas poems and Christmas carols. And so ended a day which, largely because of having a
child at home, was more like the old Merry Christmas than I have
had in a long time."[45] Perhaps on that Christmas evening the
bishop read one of his own poems—"The Christmas Contrasts":

> The countless stars, each one a world, look down;
> A few sheep huddle on the hillside brown.
>
> Angels, archangels, cherubs, seraphs, blaze;
> Some simple shepherds listen in amaze.
>
> A maid fulfils what mighty prophets said;
> Wan, weak, and lying in a cattle-shed.
>
> Almighty Love upon this earth appears;
> But shows Himself through baby smiles and tears.[46]

When his daughters did not come to Winter Park the bishop and
Mrs. Mann entertained friends without families of their own for
the Christmas meal. In 1919 he wrote, "We had several guests for

44. Ibid., August 1917.
45. Ibid., January 1924.
46. Mann, *The Longing of Circe*, p. 29.

our Christmas dinner, which otherwise would have been rather lonely with only us two."[47]

As the bishop advanced in years his birthdays became diocesan occasions when Churchmen and friends from all over the state showered him with tokens of affection. He described this shower on his eightieth and last birthday. "The Bishopstead rooms became a paradise of flowers. There were some cheques for me to devote to the Cathedral debt, and there were various articles for my own use. Cards, telegrams, and letters rained by the score, by the hundred. The postmen and messenger boys delivered them with sympathetic glee."[48]

During his last seven years as diocesan, Bishop Mann had the assistance of a loyal and loving coadjutor, John Durham Wing, who did much to lighten the burdens of the aging prelate. In his final years Bishop Mann necessarily curtailed his activities, but he remained the chief pastor to his people until very near the end. He was working on a Lenten Pastoral Letter when an attack of general debility forced him to take to his bed. He was weakened further by attacks of sciatica. He did, however, keep his diary almost to the end, with its timely comments, its flashes of wit, and its Christian stoicism. In its last entries he wrote:

"January 24. The day opened for me most unpleasantly, with a stroke of sciatica, which grew worse and worse through the day and the night. Of course there is nothing to be done except to bear it.
January 25. I was able, with Mrs. Lackey's assistance, to answer my mail. [Mrs. Lackey was his secretary.]
January 26–31. Still wrestling with the sciatica."

It was in this wrestling that death took him, February 8, 1932, at 7:45 in the evening. The bell of All Saints' Church, Winter Park, announced the bishop's death to the community by solemnly tolling eighty times, "one for each year of his life."[49] Affectionate admirers of the bishop stopped their activities when they learned of his death.

47. *Bishop's Diary, Palm Branch*, January 1920.
48. *Palm Branch*, May 1931.
49. Orlando *Sentinel*, February 9, 1932.

A lively party was in progress at the Winter Park Women's Club for the parishioners of St. Mary-Margaret's Roman Catholic Church, but on hearing the tolling of the bell of nearby All Saints' Church, the pastor, the Rev. Father Fox, explained that Bishop Mann had just died. The whole gathering stood in reverent silence until the bell had ceased to toll, whereupon Father Fox offered a prayer for the repose of the soul of the departed.[50]

Bishop Mann's body was placed before the altar of the Bishopstead chapel, where it remained until the morning of February 11, the day set for the funeral. At nine o'clock in the morning the bishop's brother, the Rt. Rev. Alexander Mann, D.D., Bishop of Pittsburgh, celebrated a Requiem Eucharist in the chapel. Immediately thereafter, the body was taken to Orlando and borne into the cathedral by eight clergy of the diocese. The Burial Office was read by Bishop Wing assisted by Bishop Frank A. Juhan of Florida, Bishop Nathaniel S. Thomas of Wyoming (retired), and Bishop Albion W. Knight, Coadjutor of New Jersey. Nearly all the clergy of the diocese and many visiting priests were present and in procession. Interment was made at Watkins, New York, the officiating clergy being Bishop Wing, Bishop Burleson, and Bishop David L. Ferriss of Rochester.[51]

Cameron Mann's old friend, Bishop Burleson, described the simple rites at little St. James's Church in Watkins. "It was fitting and beautiful," he said, "that at the end his body was brought back to the church built by his father, where he himself served his first rectorship. From that place, hallowed by many memories, we carried him forth with the Church's blessing to rest in the quiet cemetery on the hillside, overlooking the town and the blue lake beyond, by the side of his father and his own two sons, and amid other kinfolk."[52]

There can be no more appropriate memorial to Bishop Mann than his own words, written long years before his death, but so indicative of the faith that was in him: "Precious above all things

50. *Palm Branch*, February–March 1932.

51. Orlando *Reporter-Star,* February 11, 1932; *Palm Branch*, February–March 1932.

52. Burleson, "Memorial Sermon," p. 64.

is the Easter joy, and happy the man who carries it in his heart, for its song is the song of victory. Victory over the shabbiness and the littleness of life; victory over its weakness and its wickedness, over its pain and its death. Victory, not only *over* death and in *spite* of death, but *because* of death. The great Fear and the great Shadow become a pillar of fire, glowing with the light of immortality."[53]

The American episcopate has seen many great bishops, many perhaps greater than Cameron Mann, but few have equaled his humanity, his learning, his faith, and his sweetness. The bishop's memorial plaque in the cathedral bears a suitable quotation from his beloved Herbert: "His virtue and his worth shall be/Another monument to Thee." To this might be added the request that he put into the preface of his *Concordance to the English Poems of George Herbert*: "Sancte Herberte, Ora Pro Me."

53. Ibid., p. 65.

XIII

The Wing Episcopate

A LTHOUGH JOHN DURHAM WING ACCEDED TO ALL EPISCOPAL authority at the death of Bishop Mann, he was not formally enthroned in his cathedral until Friday, May 13, 1932. The colorful service of installation was a welcome contrast to the period of mourning after the death of Bishop Mann. A large and representative congregation from nearly all parts of the diocese gathered in the cathedral at eleven o'clock for the service.

Many of the diocesan clergy were in the procession together with the lay members of the Standing Committee and the Cathedral Chapter. The music for the service was provided by the cathedral choir. Prior to his enthronement, the new diocesan solemnly promised "well and faithfully to rule and govern the Church in this Diocese" and to "observe the rights and privileges of both Clergy and People, the laws of the State and the statutes and ordinances of the Cathedral." After appropriate prayers, the dean conducted Bishop Wing to the Episcopal chair, promising obedience in the name of the Diocese of South Florida. The Te Deum was sung, and the bishop began the celebration of the Holy Communion. The Rev. William P. S. Lander, president of the Standing Committee and rector of Holy Trinity Church, West Palm Beach, preached the installation sermon. At the conclusion of the service a luncheon

233

in the bishop's honor was served in the chapter house by the Church Service League of the cathedral.[1]

The new bishop's most immediate task was to improve the shaky condition of diocesan finances. There was not only a serious lack of funds for the mission and parochial fields of South Florida, but there was also an equally crippling lack of money to fund the domestic and foreign program of the National Church.

In 1932, after critical scrutiny, the General Convention at Denver approved a budget of $4,225,000. From this amount the National Council subtracted $275,000, since it planned to leave some vacancies in the mission field unfilled because of the pinch of the depression. The remaining $3,950,000, which would come from the normal missionary quotas of each diocese, was accepted by the bishops of the whole Church as a matter of honor, and each agreed to put on a strenuous campaign to obtain the quota in his diocese. Bishop Wing accepted the assessment of $31,448 for South Florida months before his enthronement.[2]

The diocesan campaign for the National Church apportionment was launched with a series of teaching missions set up to reach every parish and mission in the diocese. Visiting clergymen from all parts of South Florida brought news of what the Church was seeking to accomplish in foreign field, in the American insular possessions, in rural areas, and among the Indians, mountaineers, foreign-born, and underprivileged. The teaching mission was headed by an energetic young priest who had just assumed the rectorship of Holy Cross Church, Sanford, the Rev. Henry I. Louttit. After the teaching mission was completed, a special Whitsunday offering was taken in every church in the diocese to be applied to the missionary apportionment of South Florida.[3]

Despite a tremendous effort on the part of the clergy of the diocese, the campaign failed to reach its goal. Only $16,563 of the quota of $31,448 was raised.[4] Two years later the churches of the diocese raised just slightly more than $11,000 for their national

1. *Palm Branch*, May–June 1932.
2. Ibid., April 1932.
3. Ibid.
4. *Diocesan Journal*, 1932, p. 79.

missionary quota. Of this amount only $3,000 was given to the program of the National Church. The rest remained within the diocese even though South Floridians received $7,000 from the National Council for their own missionary work.[5] The collapse of the boom, plus two hurricanes and a national depression, had caused South Floridians to be frugal, even niggardly, with their Church.

Although disappointed that his diocese did not fulfill its financial obligations to the National Church, Bishop Wing was not despondent. His first episcopal address in 1932 began in a tone of pessimism but ended on a note of optimism. "The future of the Diocese," he declared, "is bright with promise. In spite of all our financial difficulties, our poverty, our lack of material resources, we are making progress. Once again, man's extremity is proving God's opportunity. Following last Eastertide the same report came from all over the Diocese: smaller offerings—larger congregations; less money—more devotion; and the Church's Altars thronged with eager worshippers."

The clergy and laity had much confidence in their new diocesan. He was the first bishop to be *elected* by his people, and he thus enjoyed a position of strength that none of his predecessors had possessed. In his six years as coadjutor, he had acquired a thorough knowledge of ecclesiastical administration. He was Bishop Mann's associate and confidant; he held the reins of authority over the missions of the diocese; and all of the Church's work among the Negroes came under his supervision. These two programs, missions and Negro work, continued to hold his interest throughout his episcopate.

In the same year that the new bishop was enthroned, 1932, he pointed out to the diocesan convention held in All Saints', Lakeland, that federal statistics showed that sixty-eight per cent of the inhabitants of South Florida were, in the language of the Prayer Book, "unchurched," that is, they did not belong to any religious body. This was the largest percentage of unchurched people in the entire Province of Sewanee. However, the proportion of confirmed Episcopalians to the total population was 172 per 10,000—the highest in the province. In his mind these two figures proved that the Diocese

5. John Durham Wing, *Episcopal Address* (South Florida), 1934, p. 52.

of South Florida had a rare opportunity for growth and missionary work. It was plain that he planned to make the most of this opportunity.[6]

It was also plain that the new bishop intended to accelerate the work of the Church among young people. The year after Bishop Wing assumed his duties as coadjutor, he founded, along with Morton O. Nace, a young layman from Trinity Parish in Miami, the organization of diocesan youth known as the Young People's Service League. This organization affiliated with the young people of the Province of Sewanee under the same name. Within two years there were twenty active leagues in the parishes and missions of the diocese. In addition to supporting their local churches, the young people contributed money that they had raised themselves to various league projects on the diocesan, provincial, national, and international levels. An annual Lenten study program on the worship and doctrine of the Church was also initiated. With the help of the diocesan Board of Religious Education, the Young People's Service Leagues of South Florida held their first session of summer camp at Pine Island in Dade County, in 1928. The camp, named Camp Wing-Mann in honor of the two bishops of South Florida,[7] brought together for a fortnight the future leaders of the diocese for a program of study, worship, and fun. Bishop Wing was so enthusiastic about the value of the camp that he declared before the Diocesan Convention in St. Luke's Church, Fort Myers, in 1929: "The Camp must be made a permanent institution, and to this end the Young People must have a permanent camp site, buildings and equipment."[8] As a result of the bishop's continuous prodding, this aim was accomplished several years later.

Work with college-age students also interested Bishop Wing. He instituted this work in the diocese soon after becoming coadjutor and heartily cooperated with Bishop Juhan of Florida in his plan to appoint the Rev. Neville E. Johnson the first Episcopal chaplain to the more than two hundred young Churchmen studying at the University of Florida. Since half of the Episcopalians came from

6. Ibid., 1932, p. 31.
7. Ibid., 1929, p. 35.
8. Wing, *Bishop Coadjutor's Address*, 1929, p. 57.

South Florida, the diocese agreed to pay half of the chaplain's stipend and to provide for half the operational budget of Weed Hall, the new Episcopal student center. The building, an old house, was situated across University Avenue from the campus. It was equipped as a club house and reading room. A part of the building was fitted as a chapel where weekly celebrations of the Holy Communion and other services were held.[9] Bishop Wing cooperated further with Bishop Juhan on a similar plan for Florida State College for Women at Tallahassee, now Florida State University. An old house near the campus was acquired as a club room, and the services of a student worker, Miss Hope Baskette, were obtained. Miss Baskette did much counselling among students, instituted a study program, and equipped a makeshift chapel. The center of worship, however, was in St. John's Parish downtown, and was under the direction of the rector, the Rev. W. Jeffrey Alfriend.[10] In spring 1931, a new student center, Ruge Hall, a memorial given by John G. Ruge of Apalachicola in honor of his wife, was completed. The new building, in Tudor-Gothic style, provided a lounge, a study room, a kitchen, and an apartment for student worker or clergyman, as well as adequate chapel accommodations.[11] It is the oldest permanent student center attached to the university. The local clergy in DeLand, Winter Park, and Lakeland were also encouraged to minister to the spiritual and intellectual needs of the college students attending Stetson, Rollins, and Florida Southern. When Bishop Wing became the diocesan, he pressed the work among college students with even greater determination.

One of the foremost problems haunting the Diocese of South Florida during the depression years was that of the low salaries of its clergy. The list below, which compares clerical salaries for the years 1932 and 1934, is representative of the larger and smaller parishes and missions in South Florida.[12] It shows that many churches were forced to cut rather than raise the stipends of their priests between these two years.

9. Bishop Wing's "Scrapbook," vol. 1, 1926.
10. Ibid., 1928.
11. *Palm Branch*, January 1931.
12. *Diocesan Journal*, 1933 and 1935, *Parochial Reports*.

PARISHES	SALARIES	
	1932	1934
Bradenton, Christ Church	$1,790	$1,740
Key West, St. Paul's	1,500	1,800
Leesburg, St. James's	1,200	1,200
Miami, Trinity	4,200	3,600
Orlando, Cathedral	3,000	3,000
Palm Beach, Bethesda	5,000	5,000
Tampa, St. Andrew's	3,600	3,000
Tampa, House of Prayer	1,700	1,000
West Palm Beach, Holy Trinity	5,000	3,000
MISSIONS (with resident clergy)		
Cocoa, St. Mark's	$1,500	$1,500
Delray Beach, St. Paul's	500	——
Homestead, St. John's	360	240
Sarasota, Redeemer	1,800	1,500
Bartow, Holy Trinity	no amt. listed	600
West Palm Beach, St. Patrick's	1,200	1,020

In addition to having their stipends cut, the mission clergy were often forced to cover ever larger territories with no travel allowances provided.[13]

The problem of low salaries was often compounded by the vestries' erratic method of paying the clergy. In many churches priests received no stipend for several months. In some parishes, for example St. Edmund's, Arcadia, and House of Prayer, Tampa, the congregations had such difficulty paying the clergy that they reverted to mission status. Bishop Wing constantly reminded the laity of their duty to provide for their clergymen. At the Diocesan Convention of 1934 he took up the problem in his episcopal address: "A priest, by the very nature of his calling, has cut himself off from every prospect of making money, and must give the whole of his time to his vocation—supplying the spiritual needs of his flock. For his support he must depend upon the contributions of the faithful. He neither asks nor expects for his labors large financial return; his is not a bargaining spirit—so much service for so much cash—but at all times is he willing to spend and be spent. . . . He is, however,

13. Ibid., 1935, p. 65.

entitled to a living and to a reasonable assurance that he will get it. It would certainly appear most natural to expect that only as his mind is set free from carking care and the fret of anxiety as to his material needs [can] the pastor . . . do his best work for his people."[14]

Bishop Wing warned the convention delegates that the first financial duty of their congregations was to pay their minister's salary in full. "For if," he declared, "there is taken from the minister's stipend wherewith to meet any other obligation, such debt is being paid, not with the congregation's money, but with the minister's."[15]

One of the ways in which the diocese helped the debt-ridden churches pay off their indebtedness was permitting the sale of surplus properties. In 1934 the trustees of the diocese authorized the sale of three lots in St. Cloud, the proceeds being applied to the debt of the local mission. That same year All Saints', Winter Park, received permission to sell certain properties bequeathed to the parish in Orange and Indian River counties, the returns of the sale to be applied to the church debt. The proceeds of the sale of the property of the dormant mission in Yalaha, Lake County, were applied to the permanent improvement of nearby St. James's Church, Leesburg. In Winter Haven, the vestry was authorized to transfer certain property for the settlement of indebtedness.[16] During the period 1934–36, the trustees of the diocese liquidated all church property in Thonotasassa, Ocoee, Orange Lake, and Zellwood, the funds generally going into the diocesan mission program. In 1936, St. Mark's Church, Cocoa, was the beneficiary of the sale of the property of dormant Grace Church on Merritt Island, as well as the proceeds from the Clement property at Georgiana.[17] Sales of this kind did much to lighten the financial burden of many struggling parishes and missions during the years of the depression.

Not all churches, however, had surplus real estate to tide them over during the lean years. Funds were so short that the diocesan

14. Wing, *Episcopal Address* (South Florida), 1933, p. 40.
15. Ibid., p. 41.
16. *Diocesan Journal*, 1935, p. 28.
17. Ibid., 1936, p. 27; 1937, pp. 29–31.

mission program had to be drastically curtailed. During the Diocesan Convention which met in St. Petersburg in 1936, Bishop Wing appointed a Diocesan Mission Survey Committee to evaluate the missions of the diocese. The committee divided the aided churches into two broad categories: "Growing Missions" and "Static Missions." The committee also made some bold and painful recommendations so that the limited mission funds of the diocese could be better utilized. Certain growing missions, it declared, had been on the diocesan dole too long and "should be self supporting." These missions were All Saints', Fort Lauderdale; Christ Church, Coconut Grove; St. Agnes's, Miami; St. Mark's, Cocoa; and Good Shepherd, Lake Wales. Certain static missions, after careful study, were branded as "Retrogressive Missions," that is, they were churches "which either are closed or should be as they seem to meet no need." These included St. John's, Kissimmee; St. John's, Orlando; St. Edmund's, Arcadia; Christ Church, Fort Meade; St. Saviour's, Zephyrhills; St. Bartholomew's, St. Petersburg; All Saints', Tarpon Springs; Holy Spirit, Safety Harbor; and St. Stephen's, New Port Richey. The committee also recommended that three archdeacons be appointed to direct the mission work (under the bishop) in each of the three deaneries, and that the diocesan Department of Missions pass on all mission grants on the "basis of accomplishment and prospects . . . rather than on the present basis of allowing each work approximately $300 per year." In addition to recommending that certain retrogressive missions be closed the committee suggested that new work be commenced in the metropolitan Miami district, Mount Dora, Winter Garden, and the Lake Okeechobee region, where the diocese "could wisely invest its mission funds for early returns in the near future."[18]

Not all of the recommendations of the committee were carried out, but the publication of its findings caused some of the stronger missions to become self-supporting and some of the retrogressive missions to become more lively. New work, within a few years, was begun in nearly all of the areas suggested by the committee. It is interesting to note that the committee was chaired by a young priest who was destined to succeed Bishop Wing as diocesan, the Rev.

18. Ibid., 1937, pp. 97–102.

Henry I. Louttit of West Palm Beach, and that three other future bishops served in its ranks, the Rev. William L. Hargrave of Cocoa, the Rev. Martin J. Bram of Sanford, and the Rev. John B. Walthour of Tampa.[19]

The need for such scrutiny in the allocation of funds for the missions program was made apparent by Bishop Wing before the same convention that set up the committee. He stated that the income of the parishes and missions of South Florida had declined from a maximum of nearly $375,000 in 1926 to a minimum of approximately $187,000 seven years later, a loss of fifty per cent.[20] Other statistics, however, were more encouraging. Between 1926 and 1936 there were quite amazing signs of growth. The total baptized membership in the diocese grew from 12,207 to 17,854—an increase of forty-six per cent; the communicant list grew from 8,121 to 12,203—an increase of fifty per cent; and the Sunday school enrollment increased from 3,600 to 6,500—a gain of eighty per cent.[21] These statistics indicated that the Episcopal Church had not lost its appeal in the state of Florida.

Holy Cross Church in Miami presents an excellent example of a parish which wrestled with the problems of debt during the depression, yet continued to grow. On the last Sunday of the year 1935, Bishop Wing solemnly consecrated the now debt-free church building before a large congregation that taxed its seating capacity to the fullest. Seventeen years before, when the church was a small mission in what was then the village of Buena Vista, the Rev. Charles R. Palmer was appointed priest-in-charge by Bishop Mann. Holy Cross grew continuously through boom and depression. When it was consecrated, it was a strong parish with over 600 communicants, and with a parish house, a rectory, and a church school building. During the Rev. Mr. Palmer's tenure he baptized 543 persons, presented 500 for confirmation, solemnized 142 marriages, and officiated at the burial of 234 persons.[22]

A further sign that the gloom of the depression years was abating

19. Ibid., p. 97.
20. Wing, *Episcopal Address* (South Florida), 1936, p. 46.
21. Ibid.
22. *Palm Branch*, January 1936.

showed up in an anonymous limerick pasted in Bishop Wing's scrapbook. The bishop is made to say after the tenth anniversary of his consecration a verse that illustrates with humor the despair and hope of the era:

> The bishop: "Ten years have I served you.
> And hurricanes oft have unnerved you;
>   The fruit flies have stung,
>   And depressions have wrung—
> But I trust ne'er from hope have I swerved you."[23]

Perhaps 1935 was the turning point for the Church in South Florida in the depression years. In that year the Church of St. Luke and St. Peter in St. Cloud was declared free of debt and consecrated by Bishop Wing.[24] Through the generosity of the heirs to the estate of the Rev. Dr. W. C. Richardson, the mortgage was lifted from the House of Prayer, Tampa, and plans were made for its early consecration. The debts on churches in South Florida which had expanded their facilities during the boom were being funded for the first time since the crash. It now appeared that there was no church carrying a debt which was beyond its capacity to pay. Some of the more debt-ridden could even see the day when the monies now going for interest and principal might be released for other and more productive purposes.

The Church's work among the Negroes in the diocese continued to show signs of progress. Efforts were made in Leesburg, under the direction of the Rev. Randolph F. Blackford of St. James's, to establish a new mission there, and the Rev. John R. Lewis of St. James's, Tampa, was attempting to revive the dormant Negro congregation in St. Petersburg. Father Lewis, however, was badly hampered by the lack of a suitable place for his people to gather. Bishop Wing declared "that if we could but find the means with which to purchase a lot and put up any kind of a building,

23. Bishop Wing's "Scrapbook," vol. 1, May 1936. The verse was probably written by the Rev. Edgar L. Pennington, the new rector of Holy Cross, Miami, who was also a notorious punster.

24. *Palm Branch*, December 1935.

we would soon have a flourishing Negro congregation in St. Petersburg."[25]

Easter Day, 1935, was a particularly gratifying landmark for Negro work in Miami. On Bishop Wing's annual visit to St. Agnes's Church, he estimated the congregation assembled there to be no fewer than 1,500, with almost as many unable to get into the building. During Evensong, he confirmed 115 candidates, the largest class ever presented in the history of the diocese. The elated bishop could hardly contain himself: "I am inclined to the opinion that this is the largest number of Negroes to be confirmed upon a single occasion in the entire South since the Civil War; and certain that it furnishes an effective answer to the rather silly but frequently heard statement that the Episcopal Church makes no appeal to the Negro."[26]

In 1935 also, some of the churches of the diocese made acquisitions to their properties. Trinity Church, Daytona Beach, and All Saints', Fort Lauderdale, acquired new rectories, and St. John's, Tampa, enriched its interior by installing a handsome altar and reredos. St. James's, Leesburg, and St. Thomas's, Eustis, built new parish houses, and St. James's also installed a new pipe organ. St. Paul's Church in Delray Beach received funds for the erection of a parish house as well.

Another gratifying fact could be noted in 1935. For the first time in many years, the Diocese of South Florida gave more to the National Church than it received. The diocese received $4,554, to be used entirely for Negro work; it gave $5,000. It had been for some time a source of humiliation to many South Floridians that a diocese as large and as strong as theirs should be included among the "aided dioceses," even though the aid received was entirely for Negro work. Bishop Wing particularly rejoiced that "at last we have ceased to be a 'minus' diocese and, as such, in a certain sense, a financial liability to the General Church, and become an asset." Looking back on that memorable year, the bishop observed: "I am sure we are justified in feeling some measure of encouragement. If we have not altogether emerged from the woods, we can at least

25. Wing, *Episcopal Address* (South Florida), 1936, p. 50.
26. Ibid., 1935, p. 51.

begin to see our way out. If we have not accomplished all that we had hoped for, at least we have accomplished some of it. There are signs of promise on the road before us."[27]

In addition to pressing the work of the Church among the Negroes of South Florida, the new bishop gave his blessings to the missionary labors of Deaconess Harriet M. Bedell among the Seminoles. The deaconess had already had a remarkable career before she came to the Everglades. Born in Buffalo, New York, March 19, 1875, she exhibited an interest in the Church and in charity work during her girlhood. She graduated from the New York State Normal School in 1894 and taught for a number of years in the Doyle School in her native city. After attending a moving mission service in her home parish, St. Mary's-on-the-Hill, she decided to become a teaching missionary. With this vocation in mind, she entered the New York Training School for Deaconesses in 1906.[28]

Deaconess Bedell's first assignment was among the so-called blanket Cheyenne Indians of Oklahoma. For ten years she taught and doctored among these primitive folk, riding thousands of miles on horseback to reach her charges.[29] In 1916, the deaconess was transferred to Alaska, where she served as a missionary and teacher to the Alaskan Indians in Nenana, a village some 100 miles south of the Arctic Circle. She soon won the confidence of the villagers and became an integral part of the community. She not only taught school, but also acted as a medic for the village and the area around it. She often drove a dog team over terrain regarded by her charges as too rough for passage in order to take medical aid to the sick during the Alaskan winters. A strong, natural bond grew between Deaconess Bedell and the Alaskans, a bond so natural that the outside world did not understand it. A visitor to the mission once took the deaconess to task for receiving the Holy Communion at the same time as the Indians instead of ahead of them. Stunned by the conversation, she hurried to her quarters and slashed out these

27. Ibid., 1936, p. 51.

28. William and Ellen Hartley, *A Woman Set Apart: The Remarkable Life of Harriet Bedell* (New York: Dodd, Mead & Company, 1963), pp. 1–15.

29. Ibid., pp. 25–119.

words in her diary: "This is the Place [the altar] where all are certainly equal. With God, there is neither Jew nor Gentile, black or half-breed, Indian or white man! In this Great Mystery when He comes to us, there is no room for bigotry. When will people learn?"[30]

When Miss Bedell began her work among the Seminoles in 1933, she had spent over a quarter of a century in the blinding summer heat of Oklahoma or in the sub-zero temperatures of the Arctic. In her new assignment the climate and terrain were different, but the hardships were just as great.

The deaconess set up her headquarters at Everglades in Collier County, naming her establishment Glade Cross Mission, the name given the first Seminole mission by Bishop Gray. Many of her efforts here were begun with the help of D. Graham Copeland, the manager of the Collier County Operating Company, and were continued with the aid of the Collier family.[31] She also had a monthly grant from the National Council of the Episcopal Church and some support from Bishop Wing.

Many Floridians did not fully understand the complicated social structure of the Seminole nation and the part of it that Deaconess Bedell was trying to reach. There were two tribes of Seminoles: the northern tribe located on the northwestern shore of Lake Okeechobee, called the Cow Creeks; and the southern tribe, the Mikasukis, who inhabited the vast area between the southwestern shore of the lake and the Gulf of Mexico. Of the two, the northern tribe was by far the more advanced. The Cow Creeks consented to live on a reservation and to have a school. The Florida Baptists ministered to the Cow Creeks with some degree of success. The southern tribe, however, was another matter. The Mikasukis lived in the vastness of the Big Cypress Swamp in little villages ten to fifteen miles apart. They still refused to swear allegiance to the United States government; they would not consent to schools; and they were suspicious of every advance made to them by the white man until they could understand why the advance was made. It was to this group that

30. Ibid., p. 143.
31. Ibid., pp. 210–13.

Miss Bedell directed her labors. No Christian body had attempted to reach the Mikasukis since the Episcopalians abandoned the project on the retirement of Bishop Gray. The deaconess noted that some of the elderly members of the tribe still had memories of the bearded patriarch and his workers.[32]

Miss Bedell soon discovered that many of the Indians were on the verge of starvation as the depression had halted nearly all commercial intercourse between the white and red races. Her approach to the Seminoles, however, was not through charity, but through an effort to help them help themselves. She hoped they could become self-supporting and economically independent. She encouraged the Indians to develop their arts and crafts and to sell their artifacts outside the Everglades. The Glade Cross Mission soon became both a wholesale and a retail center for Seminole products. Bookends, dolls, pot-holders, baskets of all sizes, Seminole clothing, plaques, broom-holders, aprons, miniature canoes, and palmetto place mats were only some of the items that the Indians brought in for sale. The best-made items were most in demand; thus the native artists were encouraged to use their talents to the fullest. Within a year, the imaginative Churchwoman arranged a retail outlet for these handicrafts in such Miami establishments as Burdine's and the Red Cross Drug Store. In addition to her program of economic assistance, the deaconess developed a program of medical aid for the Indians. It was not long before she won the confidence of the entire tribe.[33]

Miss Bedell soon discovered that she needed an establishment closer to the Indians and so obtained funds to open a branch of the mission at Immokalee on the property acquired by Bishop Gray. The settlement had not changed much since his time. "Immokalee is still a gathering place for the Indians. It was so named by Bishop Gray. It means 'My Home.' A small white town, or rather trading post, is near the village and the Indians come in from the glades to sell their alligator, deer and coon hides. As nearly always several families may be found there, and trips are necessary back and forth

32. *Diocesan Journal*, 1940, p. 141.
33. Miami *Herald*, August 18, 1935.

from Everglades, we re-established the Mission there, but retain the headquarters in Everglades."[34] To make the trips back and forth, the deaconess was given a secondhand Model A Ford. Within the first year, she drove some 20,000 miles in her efforts to reach the Mikasuki Seminoles. She also traveled by dugout canoe and on foot to reach the more isolated villages. A unique feature of the Immokalee branch was the sickroom Miss Bedell had built in the Seminole village. This cheekee, or Indian hut, was described to the readers of the *Palm Branch*. "It will be 30 by 20 feet, and the roof, now finished, is of palmetto leaves. The wall will be built half-way, then screened. A small room will be partitioned off for my personal use, leaving a room 20 by 20 feet for the care of the sick. . . . We will care for the Indians in their own way, but under sanitary conditions. They are used to sleeping on hard platforms, so I am planning to have pads or quilts rolled up in canvas bags, in readiness for the sick when brought in. Clean linen, proper food, doctor's care, will be possible. The nurses will be their own people, under my direction." If further medical help was needed for any of the deaconess's patients, the services of Dr. M. S. Pender of Everglades were obtained.

The first patient that occupied the hospital was a woman about one hundred years old. "She was sick," the deaconess wrote, "and I had to keep her all night. However, I sent the family, except one to remain with her, to the Indian village near the Mission. We made a comfortable bed for her on a cot, but she said it was too soft and wanted to sleep on the floor; so of course we put a quilt on the floor, and she went to sleep."[35]

The public took a keen interest in the medical aspect of Miss Bedell's work. In the summer of 1934, for instance, the Miami *Daily News* carried this story. "Seminole Indians at Immokalee have been having a siege of measles. There were eight cases among the twenty-six Indians at the camp. . . . The recovery is largely due to Deaconess Bedell. She obtained medicine for them from the white contract doctor for the Indians at Everglades. The Indians

34. *Palm Branch*, October 1934.
35. Ibid.

THE SOUND OF BELLS

at Immokalee so appreciated the work she had been doing for them that they are building her a cheekee, so that she may live among them and teach them the arts whereby they can make money as well as treat them in cases where their ailments do not require deeper medical attention." The *News* also observed that the deaconess was apparently "the only representative of a religious organization which is displaying an interest in the Seminoles."[36]

The Indians appreciated the economic and medical assistance given them by the missionary and showed their warmth and appreciation for her by attending in great numbers the annual Christmas Feast she gave for them. The Christmas Feast of 1935 was typical of the ones that followed. The Rev. Harold Bache of All Saints', Fort Lauderdale, conducted a brief service through an interpreter; a tree was decorated and a great feast eaten. Then Miss Bedell distributed gifts to her flock: checkers and dominoes for the children, trinkets and rattles for the babies, blankets for the women, and boxes of shotgun shells for the men.[37] These parties received good coverage in the newspapers of the state and did much to bring the work of the mission before the public.

The deaconess was often asked about conversions: how many might be forthcoming, and when? Her replies to these inquiries were hopeful but guarded. She periodically reported in the *Palm Branch* and in the *Diocesan Journal* that a few families were ready for baptism, but that the rite had to be delayed until the Indian Council (the legislative branch of the tribe) had given its consent. Although Miss Bedell was given permission by the Indian Council to preach and teach to the Mikasukis and even to officiate with the medicine men at funerals, there is only one record in the diocesan journals of the Council's consenting to a baptism. Elizabeth Osceola, great-great-granddaughter of Chief Osceola, was baptized August 12, 1942. Deaconess Bedell was one of her sponsors.[38] The reasons for the Indians' resistance to baptism were perhaps best summed up by Deaconess Bedell's biographers, William and Ellen Hartley. In essence the Seminoles said, "We believe what you say.

36. Miami *Daily News*, August 3, 1934.
37. Miami *Herald*, December 29, 1935.
38. *Palm Branch*, October 1942.

We believe in your Holy Spirit and the message of Jesus. But we are Seminoles. We, who are Old Tribe Mikasukis, refuse to engage in white ceremony. We accept your teaching. The Jesus man was good. He spoke truly. But don't ask us to accept your rites. Why are they so necessary? Only the way of living is of importance."[39]

Not all of Deaconess Bedell's efforts were confined to the Seminoles. In 1937, she took over the work at Goodland on Marco Island begun by a missionary of the Church Army. There she opened a small chapel, taught Church school, and founded a recreation hall for the young fisher folk of the area. Statistically, she had far more success among the islanders than among the Indians. Numerous baptisms and confirmations were recorded through the years at Marco.

The deaconess was required by canon of the General Convention of the Episcopal Church to retire in 1943 at her sixty-eighth birthday. Still active and vigorous, Miss Bedell complied with the canon and received a modest monthly stipend from the Church Pension Fund. But her retirement was only official. With as much energy as before she continued her work among the Seminoles at both Everglades and Immokalee as a "parochial missionary" of St. Stephen's Church, Coconut Grove. She also continued her work with the Marco Islanders.

Seventeen years after her official retirement, the redoubtable old deaconess was forced to give up her unofficial labors by no less than a natural catastrophe. In September 1960, some months after her eighty-fifth birthday, Hurricane Donna tore through the Everglades with devastating effects. Taken by friends from the mission at Everglades to Ochopee, a settlement on higher ground, the old lady rode out the storm. When the winds subsided, the deaconess must have received a frightful shock. Her home and the missions at Everglades and Immokalee had been almost totally destroyed, and the tiny chapel and the recreation hall on the island were irreparable wrecks. After checking on the welfare of her Seminoles, the deaconess agreed to accept Bishop Louttit's invitation to stay at the diocesan home for the elderly, Gray Inn at Davenport. There she cared for

39. Hartley, p. 258.

the sick, spoke before Church and civic groups, and prepared Sunday school lessons.[40] She died January 8, 1969.[41]

In her long and useful service to the Church and to mankind, Harriet Bedell touched all sorts and conditions of men. Perhaps an excerpt from the following letter written by a Jewish couple at the crossroads of their spiritual life illustrates in some way the catholicity of her ministry: "I hope this little contribution of baby blankets for the Indians will help your work. I am sorry—no, not sorry—that I mentioned our problem. But we have returned again to the synagogue and Morris is now contributing a tenth of his income to charitable work. He wants this small part to come to your Indian work."[42]

In her enthusiasm for her work among the Indians, Harriet Bedell shared her concern, her charity, and her compassion with others. Through sharing with all, she taught all who met her how to share.

During the late 1930s, steady progress was made towards the acquisition of a permanent summer camp for the young people of the diocese. Since its beginning in 1928 the camping program had been seriously handicapped by the lack of perdurable facilities. In 1937, Bishop Wing appointed a diocesan committee whose specific task was to raise money for permanent camp buildings. The Rev. Messrs. Henry I. Louttit, William F. Moses, and Martin J. Bram, and Messrs. Morton O. Nace of Tampa, Albert E. Booth of Cocoa, and William E. Tylander of Fort Pierce[43] energetically conducted a drive to fund a permanent camp to which nearly all of the parishes and missions of South Florida contributed.

The work of the committee received a tremendous boost when John Sears Francis gave a large acreage on Trout Lake, near Avon Park, for a site. During the winter of 1939 construction began, and by the summer of that year the main building (consisting of a kitchen and dining room, and commodious enough to serve the additional purpose of an assembly hall and chapel), a pump house,

40. Ibid., pp. 267–75.
41. *Diocesan Journal*, 1969, p. 91.
42. Hartley, p. 245.
43. *Diocesan Journal*, 1938, p. 12.

caretaker's quarters, and several large cabins for the campers were completed. The committee insisted that the new facility retain the name Camp Wing-Mann, but changed the spelling to Wingmann. Over $16,000 was spent on the buildings. The camp was equipped to accommodate 130 campers in each session. When Bishop Wing dedicated Camp Wingmann on June 24, 1939, the plant stood in need of a permanent chapel, an infirmary, and proper classrooms and recreational facilities.[44] These were, however, gradually added. Through the years, Camp Wingmann has not only provided camping and teaching accommodations for young people; it has also served as a comfortable site for conferences of clergy and laymen.

44. Wing, *Episcopal Address* (South Florida), 1940, p. 54.

XIV

World War II

THE WORLD WAS IN AN ERA OF DIPLOMATIC AND ECONOMIC confusion when John Durham Wing assumed the episcopal authority of the Diocese of South Florida. Japan was preparing to defy the League of Nations by her aggression in Manchuria; Benito Mussolini was formulating plans for an African Empire in Ethiopia; and Adolf Hitler, who was emerging as the most powerful man in Germany, was bent on wiping out every vestige of the Versailles Treaty. In addition to these diplomatic problems, international trade was rapidly declining in the face of protective tariffs and an unstable currency brought on by the depression, the war debts, and German reparations. The bishop and his people watched these newly sown seeds of chaos slowly mature into a harvest of worldwide strife and discord.

When Germany's attack on Poland provoked a declaration of war from Great Britain and France on September 3, 1939, there was little doubt where the sympathy of most Florida Episcopalians lay. Bishop Wing, like most of his flock, was an ardent Anglophile. When he heard the news of the outbreak of war, he was attending a camp session at the Episcopal Conference Center in Kanuga, North Carolina. He quickly left by car for Orlando.[1] As the months

1. *Bishop's Diary, Palm Branch*, September 3, 1939, p. 103.

passed the bishop watched the fortunes of war turn against the Allies. He, like many, voiced considerable anxiety lest European resistance to Hitler collapse altogether. He increasingly came to believe that America's first line of defense was the British Navy and spoke out privately and publicly on this matter. In the Orlando *Morning Sentinel* he stated, "It is most disturbing; and to my mind demonstrates the appalling danger of our own country if we allow Great Britain to fall. Would that the President and Congress and all loyal Americans could be convinced that patriotism and wisdom demand that every possible legal aid should go to Great Britain and go quickly! Regardless of one's personal opinion of Britain, or where one's sympathies may lie in the present struggle, it would certainly seem to be true that the British Fleet stands between us and the menace of Hitlerism." Hence, he declared, "Aid to Britain at this time is aiding our own defense. . . . This is not 'war-mongering,' and of the man who says it is it may well be asked: 'Would you rather send your guns or your sons?' "[2]

If Americans were not quite ready to send their guns, American Episcopalians were certainly ready to send their prayers and their money to help the Mother Church finance her world-wide mission program. The General Convention eagerly offered assistance when asked for help. The Rt. Rev. William T. Manning, Bishop of New York, issued an appeal to South Floridians through the columns of the *Palm Branch*: "A most moving call, and a most sacred opportunity, come now to us in the Episcopal Church in the situation which is facing our mother Church of England and her vast missionary undertakings. The English Church is nobly carrying on and is doing her utmost to meet the situation but it is not possible for her to support adequately the great missionary work which she has been doing in many parts of the world while her people are giving their lives and their substance in this appalling conflict in which all that we hold sacred is at stake. . . . The scope of this missionary work includes more than two million Christians, 2,000 native clergy, 20,000 native teachers, 4,000 foreign clergy and teachers, and 500 doctors and nurses." Bishop Manning urged every Churchman to

2. Orlando *Morning Sentinel*, July 3, 1940.

take part in a national drive to raise "at least $300,000 as Aid-For-British-Missions."[3]

The survivors and descendants of the British immigration were particularly interested in the British Mission campaign. No one's enthusiasm, however, exceeded that of the Negro communicants of the diocese. An example of this enthusiasm can be found in the columns of the monthly magazine of St. Agnes's Church, Miami, a congregation made up largely of West Indians. "More than ever," the paper declared, "the missionary work of the Church of England needs aid from the Church in the United States. These outposts of Christian Civilization are witnesses to righteousness in a world of evil. They must continue to be so." The article went on to explain the financial plight of the Anglican mission program: "Rising taxes and decreased income make normal giving to the Church impossible for the British people. They do give with amazing generosity, but they can not give enough. Thus the Episcopal Church has another opportunity to uphold Christian Democracy by aiding British missions in all parts of the World."[4] A few months later, in an address to the Negro clergy of the diocese, the Anglophilic vicar of St. Agnes's, the Rev. John Culmer, referred to Adolf Hitler as a "Charlie Chaplin moustached madman . . . intoxicated with the iniquitous toxin of race superiority."[5]

Within a few months the parishes and missions of the diocese contributed over $4,000 to the needs of the Mother Church.[6] Many South Floridians made supplementary gifts to the Presiding Bishop's Fund for World Relief, which among its other projects was attempting to answer an Anglican request for some 3,000 American Prayer Books to distribute to British prisoners of war in Germany, since use of the Prayer Book of the Church of England was forbidden in the camps.[7]

Pro-British feelings were also expressed in the Bundles-for-Britain movement. As the Germans intensified their attacks on the British

3. *Palm Branch*, February 1941.
4. *St. Agnes's Herald*, Miami, May 1942.
5. *Palm Branch*, September 1942.
6. Ibid., September 1941.
7. Ibid., March 1942.

Isles in the summer of 1941, hundreds of female Episcopalians in South Florida joined massive knitting sessions in which wool sweaters, scarfs, socks, and other clothing were produced for British servicemen with amazing rapidity. In many localities the knitting sessions were held at the Episcopal parish houses, or churches served as collection stations for the finished products. The columns of almost every local newspaper and parish bulletin abound with the exploits of these industrious women.

Among the many slanted editorials, stories, poems, and articles found in the *Palm Branch* during the two years preceding American entry into the war, none better illustrates the aversion that most Episcopalians shared for Nazi racism than the following. "A 'High Hat' young Nazi officer was brought down in England, badly wounded, and taken to a hospital; when he was recovering he declaimed loudly on the superiority of the German race and the purity of his own Aryan blood. 'See what a quick recovery I am making from a really bad wound,' he said. 'You ought to,' replied the doctor, 'I have put a good two pints of the best Jewish blood into you.' "[8]

So absorbed were Floridians in the European war that they paid scant attention to the activities of Japan. Taking advantage of British and American preoccupation with Europe, Japan began to consolidate its position in the Far East. Following the fall of France, Japanese military forces occupied French Indo-China and Thailand. The United States government, disturbed by these acquisitions and by the continued advance of Japan in China, demanded that these annexations cease. In December 1941, behind a facade of diplomatic conversation, the Japanese Navy struck at the American fleet in Hawaii by air and inflicted heavy damage. The news of the Japanese attack reached Floridians on the warm winter Sunday afternoon of December 7. The next day, still stunned, they listened to their radios as President Roosevelt asked Congress for a declaration of war. Following the president's broadcast, special services of intercession were held in most of the parishes and missions of the diocese.

The war had a profound effect upon the State of Florida. The

8. Ibid., January 1941.

most immediate change was the disruption of the tourist industry and all its affiliated businesses. War regulations which discouraged travel were particularly hard on the coastal resort centers. This brief economic regression was soon offset, however, by the government's decision to convert the state into a gigantic training area for army and navy flying personnel. Thousands of soldiers and sailors came to South Florida to man these new training centers. Within a few years there were forty airfields in operation in the state, the majority of them located within the boundaries of the diocese. To the parishes and missions near the bases, the presence of the servicemen was both an additional burden and a challenge.

The war disrupted the parish ministries of a number of clergy. By the spring of 1943, there were seven South Florida priests on duty in the armed forces of the United States. The Rev. Messrs. Charles W. Adams of All Saints', Tarpon Springs, Andrew D. Milstead of St. Luke's, Fort Myers, and Edgar L. Pennington of Holy Cross, Miami, were serving as navy chaplains; while Randolph F. Blackford of St. John's, Homestead, Henry I. Louttit of Holy Trinity, West Palm Beach, and John B. Walthour of St. Andrew's, Tampa, were serving as chaplains in the army, Mr. Walthour as chaplain of the United States Military Academy at West Point. Another priest, the Rev. Leonard C. Bailey, formerly of St. Edmund's, Arcadia, was listed in the diocesan journals as "U.S. Army."[9] The absence of these clergymen from their cures not only deprived their congregations of forceful leadership during a very difficult period, but it also deprived the diocese of considerable administrative and executive talent. The Rev. Edgar L. Pennington, for example, held the office of diocesan secretary, deputy to the General Convention, and editor of the *Palm Branch*. The Rev. Henry I. Louttit was assistant diocesan secretary, a member of the executive board of the diocese, chairman of the Department of Religious Education, and an active member of the board of managers of Camp Wingmann.[10] The positions of these wartime clerics were quickly filled by able replacements, but their leaving the diocese necessitated considerable diocesan reorganization. The

9. *Diocesan Journal*, 1943, p. 4.
10. Ibid., 1941, pp. 8–14.

Rev. William F. Moses of Lakeland took Dr. Pennington's position as diocesan secretary, while the Rev. W. Keith Chidester of Winter Park replaced him as editor of the *Palm Branch*. The Rev. William L. Hargrave and the Rev. William F. Moses replaced Chaplains Pennington and Walthour as delegates to the General Convention. Mr. Morton O. Nace of St. Andrew's, Tampa, took Chaplain Louttit's place as the assistant secretary of the diocese, and the Rev. John H. Soper of Sarasota replaced him as chairman of the Department of Religious Education.[11]

To care for the thousands of Episcopalians in military service, the General Convention of the American Church set up the Army and Navy Commission which operated throughout the war under the chairmanship of the Rt. Rev. Henry Knox Sherrill, Bishop of Massachusetts. The duties of the commission were manifold. It provided money for chaplains' discretionary funds for emergency situations, granted funds to aid parishes near camps in carrying on work among the members of the armed forces, paid the pension premiums of chaplains for the duration of the war, bought portable altars and communion equipment for chaplains, issued a *Prayer Book for Soldiers and Sailors* and the Church War Cross to every serviceman. The Presiding Bishop, the Rt. Rev. Henry St. George Tucker, asked Bishop Wing for an additional $2,500 for South Florida's proportionate share in this work. The bishop in turn appealed to the churches of the diocese, and the response was gratifying. By May 1942, the parishes and missions of South Florida had contributed $7,798.25 to the Army and Navy Commission Fund.[12] Bishop Wing also set up a diocesan Army and Navy Commission with the Rev. Frank E. Pulley of Holy Cross Church, Sanford, as chairman. The Rev. Messrs. Charles H. Bascom of Titusville, Richard I. Brown of Avon Park, Russell S. Carleton of Bartow, and Mason A. Frazell of Lake Worth, as members of the diocesan commission, did much to help the churches near military installations assist servicemen spiritually and socially during their assignments within the confines of South Florida.[13] On each Third

11. Ibid., 1943, pp. 8–12.
12. *Palm Branch*, May 1942.
13. *Diocesan Journal*, 1942, p. 12.

Sunday in Lent, much publicized as Army and Navy Commission Day in every congregation, the communicants of the Church in the diocese were asked by the commission for funds "to meet the spiritual needs of our sons in the service."[14]

Many parishes of the diocese received minor grants from the Army and Navy Commission. In 1943, these grants totaled over $1,200. The funds, with additional money from the women's guilds and vestries, were spent in a variety of ways. The endeavor at St. Luke's Church, Fort Myers, was typical. There, the Rev. Frank A. Shore, a former rector of the parish who became priest-in-charge when the Rev. Andrew D. Milstead enlisted as a navy chaplain, did excellent work among the servicemen stationed at the various bases around the city. In addition to visiting the bases and counselling the servicemen, the priest and a group of patriotic ladies opened the guild hall every Monday evening from seven to ten for dancing and other entertainment. Refreshments were served throughout the evening. The capacity crowds present week by week attested to the appreciation of the servicemen for this effort on their behalf.[15]

In Fort Pierce, the Rev. William L. Hargrave, newly arrived from Cocoa, and B. F. Ivey, a layman of St. Andrew's Parish, established a junior officers' club in the parish house. Care for the several hundred young officers of the army and navy stationed at the Amphibious Training Base nearby became a major activity of the parish. The club project, however, was not entirely an Episcopalian undertaking, since it was liberally aided by Baptist, Methodist, Christian, Presbyterian, and Jewish congregations.[16]

Servicemen who attended parochial endeavors such as those in Fort Myers and Fort Pierce were usually well chaperoned by the ladies of the parish. These women were careful to see that no undesirable young women were admitted to corrupt the all-too-easily corruptible morals of the soldiers and sailors. The ladies were usually generous in their invitations to attend the services of their local parish. If the men did attend church, it was quite common for them to be asked home to Sunday dinner by hospitable

14. *Palm Branch*, March 1943.
15. Ibid., December 1942.
16. Ibid., October 1944.

parishioners, a reward which may have drawn many a homesick, hungry lad to divine service.

On the west coast, the St. Petersburg *Independent* reported that at the instigation of the Rev. Evan A. Edwards of St. Peter's, a former World War I chaplain, a large recreation center was turned over to servicemen for their pleasure. The hall was equipped with piano, victrola, and various other recreational facilities. There were a few rules which set this club apart from other more parochial and ecumenical endeavors: there were to be no hostesses—the club was for men only; "No Smoking" signs were forbidden; and all volunteers were required to agree not to ask their guests to attend church. "They'll always be welcome," the brusque priest explained (probably to many a raised eyebrow), "but I went through the last war and I know how men feel on the subject. When the time comes that they need the Church it will always be there for them. In the meantime, they have the recreation room to use as they see fit. There are no strings attached to these facilities."[17]

The work of the diocese at the Seamen's Church Institute in Tampa went on during the war under the direction of the kindly and indefatigable F. Barnby Leach. Although this priest did not underestimate the perils under which the wartime army and navy worked, he felt that the American public overlooked the dangers under which the "real merchant sailors" labored. He gave a general description of the hundreds of merchant seamen who visited the institute during the rough days of 1942–43, expressing a poignant appreciation for their nautical fraternity: "The sailors are brought very close together by their dangerous calling. One will give another his last penny if he needs it. They will drop everything while at sea to rush to the aid of another ship. It doesn't make any difference how bad the situation is, or how far they have to go, it is the unwritten law of the sea, and the men follow it, never to refuse help to another less fortunate." Most seamen, the director stated, had no home and no family; the sea was their home. "When ashore these men have no place to go except to saloons and like places." For these men, Mr. Leach explained, "the Seamen's Church Institute was opened." The institute provided the same services during

17. Quoted from the *Independent* in *Palm Branch*, October 1942.

the war as it did in peace. Here the seamen could gather, meet friends, have meals and a clean bed, pick up long-delayed mail, and "last, but not least, worship God."[18] If concern for the lonely, the unwanted, and the unfortunate is a Christian virtue, then this Tampa parson and his labor were of exceeding great virtue.

The work of erecting new church buildings and improving old ones was drastically curtailed during the war. Under the rules of the War Production Board, priorities were given to military construction so that all building unrelated to the war effort was brought to a halt. Some congregations, however, were given permission by the board to finish work projects that had been begun on the eve of the conflict. In early 1942 a new church in a combined Spanish-English style was completed for the congregation of All Saints', Winter Park; an addition to the parish house of Bethesda-by-the-Sea doubled its capacity; the new St. Christopher's Church in Fort Lauderdale was occupied; the Emma C. Thursby Memorial Parish Hall of St. Mark's Church, Cocoa, was finished, equipped, and dedicated; and the work on the new rectory of St. Andrew's Church, Lake Worth, was completed. Renovation projects were also accomplished for Christ Church in the city of Miami.[19] Thursby Hall was given to St. Mark's Parish as a memorial to Emma Cecilia Thursby, the celebrated Mozart vocalist of the last decades of the nineteenth century, by her sister, Miss Ina Thursby. The building proved to be of great benefit to the parishioners of Cocoa, and the civic-minded rector of St. Mark's, the Rev. William L. Hargrave, insisted that the entire community and the servicemen of the Banana River Air Station enjoy the advantages of the hall as well.[20]

Since most congregations could not expand their facilities during the war, they took advantage of this period of affluence to pay off their debts. St. Agnes's, Miami, under the rectorate of the Rev. John E. Culmer, gradually raised over $77,000 and freed itself of

18. *Palm Branch*, November 1943.

19. Ibid., March 1942; Wing, *Episcopal Address* (South Florida), 1942, p. 53.

20. "Program: The Dedication of Emma Cecilia Thursby Memorial Hall," Parish Records, St. Mark's Church, Cocoa; *Cocoa Tribune*, April 24, 1941.

mortgage and other major debt in 1942; St. Mary's Church, Daytona Beach, paid off its capital indebtedness in the same year;[21] and in Orlando, St. Luke's Cathedral began an effort to sell $40,000 in bonds so that the massive boomtime debt could be retired. Three years later, the cathedral congregation paid off the bonds and cast off its indebtedness.[22] The cathedral was consecrated by the bishop on October 21, 1945.[23] By the end of 1944, St. Andrew's, Tampa, had paid off its long-standing mortgage on the church; Holy Cross, Sanford, had cleared the debt on the church, parish house, and rectory; and St. James's, Leesburg, St. Patrick's, West Palm Beach, and Grace Church, Ocala, had retired the mortgages on their rectories. Redeemer Church in Avon Park, through a generous benefaction, paid the debt on its parish house.[24]

Although there was a dearth of construction in the diocese as the war progressed, this did not seriously impede the growth of the Church. Sometime in 1941, a group of Episcopalians organized a mission in the lakeshore town of Pahokee under the name of the Holy Nativity; and in Miami, near the federal housing project for Negroes, Liberty Square, the congregation of St. Agnes's Church purchased a lot for another mission which was organized as the Church of the Transfiguration. The fact that both congregations worshipped in rented halls did not damp their spirits.[25]

The most encouraging reports during the war years came from the Miami area. Across Biscayne Bay at the beach, a group of Church people petitioned the bishop and were granted permission to organize All Souls' Church, with parish status. This congregation grew rapidly under the leadership of the Rev. J. Mitchell Taylor, formerly of Fort Pierce. Since the new congregation could not build a church, the Adams estate on Belle Isle was rented and its large

21. *Diocesan Journal,* 1942, p. 53.

22. Orlando *Morning Sentinel,* January 28, 1942, and September 14, 1945.

23. "Program: The Consecration Service, The Cathedral Church of St. Luke, Orlando," Parish Records, St. Luke's Cathedral, Orlando.

24. Wing, *Episcopal Address* (South Florida), 1944, p. 52.

25. Ibid., 1941, p. 58; 1942, p. 53; *Palm Branch,* October 1941.

music room converted into a "very lovely and quite commodious place of worship." The other rooms in the building afforded ample room for the Sunday school and guild organizations. From the time the Adams property was acquired large congregations filled the improvised church. Many baptisms were recorded and a class of forty candidates was presented for confirmation. Within a year, All Souls' applied to the diocesan convention to be received in union as a constituent parish, a request which the convention joyfully granted. A second new congregation was established in the Miami Springs–Hialeah section of the city under the auspices of Holy Cross Parish. Numerous pledges were collected toward the stipend of a priest, and the rector and vestry of the mother parish made themselves responsible for the balance. The rector of Holy Cross, the Rev. Dr. George W. Gasque, who succeeded Dr. Pennington, served this new mission, the Church of the Epiphany, until the offices of another priest could be obtained. The mission later became St. Margaret's Church in Hialeah. St. Philip's Church, Coral Gables, was the third Miami congregation established in 1943. It began as a parochial mission of St. Stephen's and was served by the clergy of that parish. In the early years of St. Philip's, the congregation used the Coral Gables Women's Club as their place of worship. The mission soon showed signs of becoming self-supporting. In 1944, two other mission congregations were organized: St. Martin's, Clewiston, in the Everglades area, and St. Matthias's in the central Florida town of Clermont. The same year two churches which reported themselves free from debt, St. Agnes's, Miami, and St. John's, Tampa, were duly consecrated by Bishop Wing.[26]

In order to help newly formed congregations acquire land and build churches, the diocesan convention in 1941 created the Church Building Fund, with a corpus of $5,000. The parishes and missions of the diocese were urged to contribute to the fund so that needed monies could be loaned or granted to both new and old missions. St. Andrew's, Lake Worth, St. Matthew's, Delray Beach, and the Church of the Transfiguration, Miami, were among the first mis-

26. Wing, *Episcopal Address* (South Florida), 1943, pp. 47–48; 1944, p. 51.

sions to receive aid from the fund.[27] By annual additions put into the fund from the diocesan assessment, the corpus was gradually increased.

During the war years, several new and old missions were admitted into union with the diocesan convention as parishes. In 1945, St. Philip's Church, Coral Gables, barely three years old, became a parish; Holy Comforter Chapel, a parochial mission of Trinity Church, Miami, declared its self-sufficiency; and St. Patrick's, West Palm Beach, followed the example of her sister Negro congregation, St. Agnes's, Miami, and became a parish.[28] One of the reasons for the growth of the Negro missions during the war was that literally thousands of migrant laborers were imported to work in the vegetable, citrus, and sugar industries. Since they came mainly from the Bahamas, Jamaica, and Barbados, and had been raised in the Anglican Communion, it was natural that they gravitate toward the Negro missions of the Episcopal Church.

The congregations in the resort areas of the state also were swelled by the presence of hundreds of thousands of servicemen. Nearly every resort in the peninsula turned its hotel facilities over to the armed forces. No area felt the impact more than Miami. By April 1942, the Army Air Force was using 70,000 hotel rooms in Miami Beach alone. Training activity in these converted resorts reached its peak in 1943, and as the war drew to an end hotels became hospitals, convalescent homes, and redeployment centers.[29] The churches in Dade County not only had to deal with the influx of military personnel and migrant workers, but two of them, St. Stephen's, Coconut Grove, and St. Philip's, Coral Gables, were also often attended by numbers of Royal Air Force cadets stationed at the nearby University of Miami.

Although church attendance and support in the diocese was stimulated by the presence of the servicemen and, in some cases, their families, wartime restrictions and demands on a portion of the civilian population did interfere with churchgoing and church support. There were complaints that gas rationing prevented at-

27 *Diocesan Journal*, 1941, pp. 45, 59; 1942, p. 53.
28. Ibid., 1945, p. 25.
29. Tebeau, p. 417.

tendance at divine services; complaints that civilian defense projects took up too much time to allow for public worship and parochial meetings; and, of course, complaints that heavy taxes and rising prices interfered with church giving. The clergy of South Florida usually countered these complaints and excuses in the manner of the crusty Evans A. Edwards, rector of St. Peter's, St. Petersburg. That cleric urged his congregation to use public transportation for public worship and his parochial officers to put their organizational meeting at convenient times. To those who used the financial pinch as an excuse to cut their almsgiving, the Rev. Mr. Evans declared that the operational budget of the parish was as much affected by rising prices as that of the parishioners; therefore, rising costs should mean an increase in giving. The rector's admonitions must have borne fruit, for the *Palm Branch* reported that during the war St. Peter's had larger congregations than ever before and that there was a marked increase in both parish giving and parish activities.[30]

The seven chaplains from the diocese who went forth to war kept in constant touch with their bishop and their congregations. Their duties varied. Some served in quiet and some in danger. The Rev. Dr. Edgar L. Pennington, who resigned the cure of Holy Cross, Miami, to go into the navy, often wrote Bishop Wing and his friend, the Rev. W. Keith Chidester, who succeeded him as editor of the *Palm Branch*. Chaplain Pennington, who obviously began his chaplaincy before the Church Army Commission was set up, was first assigned to the mammoth Jacksonville Naval Air Station. He described his duties there: "I have celebrated the Holy Communion at the Trade School Auditorium at 7:30 every Sunday Morning. Last Sunday a boy from the Good Shepherd, Rosemont, Pennsylvania, and another from Swampscott, Massachusetts, served as acolytes. A portable altar and rail are provided, and a cross has been promised; but there is no allowance for communion vessels, wine, bread, candles and cruets. . . . At nine o'clock, there is a service in the Cadet Auditorium, which is attended chiefly by the young aviators. All these men have had at least two years of college, and will become ensigns on graduation. At ten o'clock, there is a service

30. *Palm Branch,* January 1943.

in the Auditorium of the Main Station, where more than a third of the Navy personnel is. . . .

"For the present, my office is adjacent to the Trade School Library. We have an unusually well selected lot of books; and the boys are good patrons. Frequently they drop in to see the chaplains, both to find out what Jacksonville hospitality has in store for them and to ask advice. We usually have been notified of a dance or a party at some church; and we are always glad to direct sailors to places where they can spend an evening in pleasant and wholesome surroundings. So far as their problems are concerned, we do our best. These problems cover a wide range; some are very serious; all are serious to the boys concerned." Father Pennington ended his letter by appealing to South Floridians for "games, books, magazines, pictures, scrap-books, music, and other things which might please and amuse the sailors. There are dozens of barracks and other sleeping quarters where reading matter is welcomed; there are lounges for the men temporarily off duty in most of the principal buildings; there are usually some three or four hundred men under medical treatment. Whatever might entertain or instruct the men will certainly be appreciated; and the chaplains are glad to distribute the same."[31]

In June 1943, the Rev. Richard I. Brown of the Church of the Redeemer, Avon Park, became the eighth clergyman to enter the military service as a chaplain. In training with the 112th Infantry Regiment, which was preparing for the European theater, Chaplain Brown reported a unique experience, but one which soon lost its uniqueness in combat areas: "We had one Communion service in the field that was very interesting. I got separated from my baggage, so I had no vessels nor vestments. I borrowed a cup and a plate from the mess sergeant and celebrated in uniform. We had nine men who received. I found it very impressive, and so did they."[32]

The recently ordained Charles W. Adams of the Dunedin field was sent to Greenland as the only navy chaplain. He wrote Bishop Wing that he had "a large parish indeed" and described the terrain at his new assignment: "This is a beautiful country: deep fjords,

31. Ibid., October 1941.
32. Ibid., November 1943.

rolling hills, plenty of snow and ice, and an ice cap ages old. The sun at this particular season just comes up enough to give us a long slanting look far to the south. Except for the cold, Greenland is a choice bit of Heaven and earth."[33]

Diocesan clergy were always glad to hear news of the parishioners in the armed forces, and Episcopal chaplains were often quite considerate in writing local rectors concerning their former charges. For instance, a chaplain in North Africa sent the Rev. William L. Hargrave of Fort Pierce news of one of his young parishioners. "It was my pleasure to welcome Brian K. McCarty, a member of your parish, at a recent celebration of the Holy Eucharist and to administer the Communion to him." He also added some encouraging words: "I venture to say that the percentage of Episcopalians carrying out their religious obligations faithfully is exceeded by that of no other body—including the Romanist." One East Coast priest took issue with these glowing words. He wrote from a staging area in the combat zone in the South Pacific: "I fear that there are still Atheists in foxholes, all propaganda to the contrary notwithstanding. I celebrate early every Sunday morning with two or three usually in attendance." This could have been an isolated situation, however, since the same chaplain later reported celebrating "several well-attended Communion services" and hearing "a few confessions."[34]

South Florida's chaplains were not negligent in writing home news of the local boys to whom they had ministered. The Rev. Henry Louttit, formerly of Holy Trinity Church, West Palm Beach, wrote from the Pacific the names of the following men with whom he had made contact: Capt. William Hunter and Lt. David Walker, St. Andrew's, Tampa; Capt. Jack Hayes, St. Bartholomew's, St. Petersburg; Brig. Gen. Sumter L. Lowry and Major Edmund McMullen, St. John's, Tampa; Capt. Leonard Lewis, Holy Trinity, West Palm Beach; and Pfc. James Topakian, St. Luke's Cathedral, Orlando. Chaplain Charles W. Adams reported from Greenland that a Key Wester had called on him when he learned that the chaplain was from South Florida. "We had a good chat together and I found he was acquainted with some of our clergy,

33. Ibid., March 1944.
34. Ibid., March and July 1944.

in particular, Father Dimmick [of St. Paul's, Key West]."[35] These contacts and the reports of them seem almost inconsequential today, but they meant much to the men concerned and perhaps more to their families.

One young South Floridian, Gordon B. Knowles of Bradenton, who remained in touch with his rector, reported a rather exciting European tour. Father Frank M. Brunton forwarded the story to the *Palm Branch*: "After fifteen months overseas on a tank-landing ship, his vessel was sunk in the English Channel and Gordon was in the water for three hours before being picked up by an English destroyer." When the sailor returned to Bradenton on leave both Knowleses, Gordon Junior and Gordon Senior, who were lay readers at Christ Church, officiated one Sunday at Morning Prayer.[36]

Most Churchmen in the service were particularly grateful to receive from their local clergy the Church War Cross. One parishioner from St. Paul's, New Smyrna Beach, wrote his pastor apologetically: "I'm ashamed for not having written to you much sooner than this to thank you for the nice medal you gave to —— to send me. I really do appreciate your thoughtfulness and it makes one feel good to know that one is remembered when one has been gone so long. The medal is attached to my dog tags which are always worn around my neck."[37] This letter was typical of the hundreds received by the parochial clergy in thanks for either the War Cross or the *Prayer Book for Soldiers and Sailors*.

The South Florida chaplains were keen for news from their clerical friends at home and for every issue of the *Palm Branch*. One overseas priest wrote joyously: "Had a letter from Glad Rogers not long ago, and one from Hal Bache." Another asked that the diocesan periodical be sent regularly. A young priest in the Pacific, obviously a little homesick, wrote to Bishop Wing, "I miss you all in the diocese very much, and think of you constantly with gratitude and appreciation. I am always proud to tell my fellow Chaplains and Churchmen among the line officers that I am canonically resi-

35. Ibid., July 1944.
36. Ibid., October 1944.
37. Ibid., March 1943.

dent in the Diocese of South Florida. And I am hoping and praying for the day when I will return to my diocese."[38]

Two clergy from the diocese received special commendations for work they did in hospitals in the Pacific zone of operations. Chaplain Henry I. Louttit, stationed in a combat area, was highly commended by the commanding general of the 31st Infantry Division for his part in establishing and operating a camp for casuals. "It befell Chaplain Louttit's lot to administer to the welfare and spiritual needs of these men, which duties were performed in a manner so exceptional as to call forth his commanding General's commendation." With the commendation Father Louttit received the Bronze Star.

Chaplain Edgar L. Pennington, after eighteen-months duty at the Naval Mobile Hospital in Auckland, New Zealand, received not only the praise of his superiors, but the especial praise of a New Zealander, Bishop Simkin of Auckland. Bishop Simkin wrote Bishop Wing expressing his appreciation and that of the clergy and people of Auckland "of the benefit we have all received from his [Pennington's] sojourn amongst us." The letter continued: "Nothing I can say will adequately express the value of his ministrations, preaching, and the real link he has forged between the Church here and the Church in your land. I trust I shall not be guilty of exaggeration in my remarks but I cannot sufficiently express all that the clergy of my diocese and myself feel toward him."[39]

Every parish and mission in the diocese held special services of intercession during the war. Prayers at the Sunday Eucharists were offered for the general safety of all soldiers and sailors, but during the week additional solemn celebrations were held with special intentions for servicemen from the particular local churches. Lent was a particularly prayerful and abstentious season during the years of the conflict, a time of quiet but intense patriotism. The 1943 Ash Wednesday bulletin of Trinity Church in Vero Beach was similar to the bulletins of other churches in South Florida. In it

38. Ibid., March 1943 and March 1944. Mr. Rogers and Mr. Bache were rectors of Lake Wales and Cocoa.
39. Ibid., October 1944.

the clergyman bade his flock come to the Ash Wednesday celebrations and "pray for our Country, our Army and Navy, our loved ones and for Victory and Peace."[40] In St. Gabriel's Church, Titusville, the British-West-Indian-born vicar, Charles H. Bascom, not only prayed for our Army, our Navy, Victory, and Peace, and the President of the United States, but for "King George and all the Royal Family" as well. The vicar, usually a strict old-line Anglican, also held a special weekday celebration of the Holy Communion in which he invited the parents of non-Episcopalian servicemen to participate. One ardent Presbyterian lady, Mrs. J. J. Parrish, boasted that she "helped pray back my own two sons and half the boys of Titusville at those weekly communions."[41]

The Church of the Ascension, Clearwater (rector, the Rev. A. Peter Carroll), honored its parishioners in active service on Septuagesima, February 1943. Similar services and ceremonials occurred from time to time throughout the diocese. Following the processional and the national anthem, the names on the honor roll were called. As each name was read a relative or friend responded by standing. The honor roll was then solemnly dedicated. A color guard and detachment of fifty men from the Technical School Squadron, Army Air Force, stationed at Clearwater, participated in the service.[42]

Although all the churches had special patriotic services, none equalled the extravaganza held at Bethesda-by-the-Sea in Palm Beach. On February 14, 1943, over forty civic and patriotic organizations and a coast guard band, each carrying its flag or banner, attended the fourth annual ceremony of the Massing of the Colors, held under the auspices of the Palm Beach Chapter, Sons of the American Revolution, at four o'clock on Sunday afternoon. The mayors of Palm Beach and West Palm Beach were present as well as representatives of the army, the navy, and the coast guard. The service was said by the Rev. Tage Teisen, D.D., rector, and the Rev. Frank R. Alvarez of Pahokee. After an address by Bishop

40. "Lenten Program, Trinity Church, Vero Beach, Florida, 1943," Bishop Wing's "Scrapbook," vol. 3.

41. Personal recollection, author.

42. *Palm Branch,* March 1943.

Wing, the climax of the service occurred: "All flags and other standards were massed before the altar, while the huge congregation joined in saluting the flag and in singing the Star-Spangled Banner, thus bringing to a close a very striking and impressive service."[43]

The fighting came no closer to the peninsula of Florida than the German submarines that ranged its coasts. But Floridians watched with keen interest the young men who were being prepared within the boundaries of the state for the conflict. The war for these young men was often a time of hedonism, sporadic drunkenness, and irresponsible behavior, but behind the follies of youth the observers noticed that there were also indications of great soul-searching and idealistic enthusiasms. Perhaps Floridians saw in these youths something of their own sons and daughters exiled from home by war, which might help explain the indulgence, the hospitality, and the affection they extended to their transient guests. Churchmen in South Florida gladly bore their share of caring for these youthful strangers, and perhaps thereby occasionally "entertained angels unawares."

There were moments of bereavement in every church in the diocese, moments when news arrived that a parishioner or military visitor had been killed in action. Memorials in almost every church bear witness to these costly sacrifices. For the families who suffered these losses the clergy offered the comforts of religion and the parishioners their concern and sympathy. Episcopalians who lived through the war years still recall the rich but sad phrases of the "Prayer for the War-Bereaved" with feelings of grief: "Redeem, we pray Thee, the pain of their bereavement, that knowing their loss to be the price of our freedom, they may remember the gratitude of the nation for which they gave so costly a sacrifice. . . ."[44]

There were some moments of great gladness in each parish as well as great sadness. News of victory often brought a special service of thanksgiving during wartime, and there were still joyous parochial services marking weddings, confirmations, and baptisms.

43. Ibid.; West Palm Beach *Post-Times*, February 14, 1943.
44. "Prayer for the War-Bereaved" [authorized by the bishop for use in the Diocese of South Florida], *Palm Branch,* November 1944.

There were also numerous droll stories that were passed about throughout the diocese by word of mouth or by the press. Perhaps the most amusing concerns Christ Church, Bradenton. On October 14, 1943, the following news item appeared in the Orlando *Morning Sentinel* and in many other newspapers in the state: "A moonshine liquor still, complete with a ten gallon boiler and copper worm but no mash, was found yesterday in the bell tower of Christ Episcopal Church in downtown Bradenton. The discovery was reported by the Rev. Frank M. Brunton, rector, who said Frank Middleton, sexton, found it when he was sent into the tower for an inspection of the church bell and rope. The rector said he had no idea how and when the still was secreted in the tower which had not been inspected for three or four years."

The incident brought gales of laughter in its wake. It also brought the good-natured suspicion of the fundamentalist sects who were always mistrustful that Anglicanism was too close to Rome and that Episcopalians, sometimes referred to as "Whiskeypalians," were too close to intemperance. The rector and his congregation endured a flood of genial joshing from fellow Bradentonians and from clergy and laymen all over the diocese. Even the bishop joined in the ribbing. He sent Father Brunton a copy of a clipping from the Orlando paper with an attached note dripping with amiable sarcasm: "I note the rector *says* he has no idea how and when the still was secreted in the tower. Oh yeah!" The banter of the bishop was more than the reverend rector could bear. He took vengeance on his prelate and other friends in rhyme:

> The crowd with me have had their say,
> They've razzed and razzed and razzed away,
> Since in the church was found one day
> A still!

> I thought that folks would tired grow,
> Or have compassion on my woe,
> Still ever on the jeerings go—
> And Still!

> And Now the Bishop joins the cry—
> The camel's back is broke, and I

Shout back to you a rude reply,
"Be Still!"[45]

A more sober event that delighted many of the old-timers of
the diocese occurred in Jacksonville. A Jacksonville newspaper
dated July 13, 1944, reported that "the S.S. *William Crane Gray,*
newest Liberty ship to be built by the St. John's River Shipbuild-
ing Company, was launched . . . bearing the name of the late
Bishop of the Episcopal Diocese of South Florida." The sponsor
and cosponsor of the ship were Bishop Gray's nieces, Mrs. Louis
W. Strum and Mrs. J. Hilton Holmes, who smashed the traditional
bottle of champagne across the bow of the ship. The S.S. *William
Crane Gray* went into service immediately carrying military cargo
to the European theater.[46]

The phenomenal growth of the Church's work among Negroes
not only in Miami but on the entire east coast necessitated closer
supervision than the bishop could give. After consultation with the
diocesan executive board and acting with its approval, Bishop
Wing appointed the Rev. John E. Culmer Archdeacon of Negro
Work, an appointment which turned over the supervision of all
Negro clergy and congregations to Father Culmer. The archdeacon,
from 1944 to the date of his retirement, gave "this important work
the oversight its prominence and consequence deserve." In addition to his duties as Archdeacon of Negro Work, Father Culmer
continued his cure as rector of St. Agnes's Church.[47]

One of the great problems faced by the clergy involved in Negro
work was the task of ministering to the large number of migratory
laborers who came to Florida from the British West Indies. Because
the workers were transient, it was hard to plan services and ministrations for them. The clergy usually visited the camps when the
migrants appeared for their seasonal employment. Conditions were
more stable in the eastern Glades, however, near the vegetable-
growing areas around Canal Point. Here the Rev. J. daCosta
Harewood of St. Patrick's Church, West Palm Beach, worked regu-

45. *Palm Branch,* November 1943.
46. Jacksonville *Florida Times-Union,* July 13, 1944.
47. Wing, *Episcopal Address* (South Florida), 1944, p. 49.

larly, in addition to fulfilling his parochial duties in the city. Father Harewood was ably assisted by a parishioner of St. Patrick's whom Bishop Wing licensed as a lay reader, Reginald C. Somerville, himself a Jamaican. The result of their labors was seen in the spring of 1944, when, at the United States Sugar Corporation village of Azucar, Bishop Wing confirmed nine young men.

The Rev. Charles H. Bascom, vicar of St. Gabriel's, Titusville, a St. Lucian by birth, ministered to a colony of Bahamians housed in the abandoned Whispering Hills Country Club. At celebrations of the Eucharist he was pleased to find that the migrants knew all the responses by memory and many of the eucharistic and evening hymns as well. Among the other clergy ministering to the migrant colonies, the Rev. Messrs. Frank Brunton of Bradenton, Bartlett Cochran of Daytona Beach, and Sidney Mason of Pahokee were particularly zealous in their duties.[48]

During the war years there was a pronounced effort to soften the somewhat rigid racial customs and legal practices that had followed in the wake of Reconstruction in the South. It has generally been acknowledged that the Episcopal Church was a leader in this endeavor and that the Diocese of South Florida led the Church. The meeting of the Diocesan Convention which was held in May 1943, in Christ Church, Bradenton, provides an example of South Florida's pioneering spirit. The capable and dynamic vicar of St. Agnes's Church, Miami, the Rev. John E. Culmer, was elected one of the four delegates from the diocese to the General Convention to be held at Cleveland, Ohio, the following October. The election of Father Culmer caused what amounted to almost a national sensation. Nearly all Florida newspapers, church periodicals, and national dailies carried the item or made editorial comments. For example, the Norfolk, Virginia, *Journal & Guide* carried the headline: "South Names Florida Rector Clerical Deputy" with the subheadline "Colored Priest to Represent P.E. Diocese." To be elected a deputy to the General Convention, the paper explained, is an honor coveted by every Episcopal clergyman. The Negro priest, one of sixteen nominees, was elected on the fourth ballot. "When the Rt. Rev. John D. Wing, bishop of

48. Ibid.

the diocese, announced the election of the Rev. Mr. Culmer, it was greeted with thunderous applause." The election came within two hours after St. Agnes's Church had been admitted as a parish in full union with the diocese. This event was also history-making, because St. Agnes's was the first Negro church for more than a quarter of a century to receive such status in the jurisdiction. The paper also reported that during his thirteen years at St. Agnes's, Culmer prepared 1,250 candidates for confirmation, and that the church acquired holdings to the amount of $250,000.[49] It was at this time also that Bishop Wing began to voice his dissatisfaction with the practice of holding separate banquets for Negro and white delegates to the annual diocesan conventions.

As the war drew to a close, the Episcopalians of South Florida celebrated each new victory with enthusiasm and thanksgiving. When the war ended in September 1945 the diocese took stock of itself. Numerically the Church had not only held her own but had shown a remarkable increase. At the war's beginning in 1941 there were 16,605 communicants in the diocese; when the war ended in 1945 there were 20,387, an increase of approximately 19 per cent.[50] This increase was accomplished without the assistance of many of the younger and more energetic clergy and laity who were out of the diocese in the armed forces. Actually Bishop Wing was forced to call willing clergy out of retirement and to bring in clergy from other dioceses to staff his churches.

The war years had taken a heavy toll of the mental and physical stamina of the bishop. During the war he had a heart flare-up, which probably helped convince him that he could not carry on alone. As the conflict drew to a close, he gave in to the wishes of his clerical and lay friends and agreed to ask the Diocesan Convention for a suffragan.

At a special convention held in the cathedral on February 7, 1945, the Rev. Henry Irving Louttit, Major, United States Army Chaplains' Corps, was elected Suffragan Bishop of the Diocese of South Florida. Other clergy nominated for the office were the Rev. Edgar L. Pennington, Chaplain, U.S. Navy, and former rector

49. Norfolk, Virginia, *Journal & Guide*, May 22, 1943.
50. *Diocesan Journal*, 1941 and 1945, *Parochial Reports*.

of Holy Cross, Miami; the Rev. William F. Moses, rector of All Saints', Lakeland; the Rev. Rex Wilkes, rector of St. Stephen's, Miami; the Rev. William P. S. Lander, formerly of Holy Trinity, West Palm Beach, now rector of Good Shepherd, Rosemont, Pennsylvania; and the Rev. Thorne Sparkman, rector of St. Paul's, Chattanooga, Tennessee. The results of the balloting were as follows:

| | FIRST BALLOT | | SECOND BALLOT | |
	Clerical	Lay	Clerical	Lay
Louttit	20	56	27	64
Pennington	5	19	0	10
Moses	7	13	3	10
Lander	1	3	2	1
Sparkman	3	6	3	6
Wilkes	14	21	12	16

Chaplain Louttit was thus elected on the second ballot with more than the required majority in both orders.[51]

The choice of Henry Louttit as suffragan-elect by the special convention did not come as a surprise to the people of South Florida. The sentiment of the diocese was largely for obtaining the new bishop from within its boundaries, and young Louttit was one of the brightest and most capable clerical luminaries of his time. Although by birth an upstate New Yorker, he had spent all of his ministerial life in the diocese. His role as a staff member, a teacher, and later a director of the diocesan camp provided him with an affectionate and devoted following of young people and their parents in all parts of the peninsula. Chaplain Louttit was on assignment in the Pacific when he accepted his election. With the war rapidly nearing its end, South Floridians anxiously awaited his homecoming and consecration.

By unanimous vote of the delegates, the Special Convention which elected Bishop Louttit resolved itself into the Twenty-third Annual Convention of the Diocese, in order to cooperate with the request of the government to suspend as many conventions as possible for the duration of the war. At this meeting St. Philip's, Coral

51. *Diocesan Journal*, 1945, pp. 28–29.

Gables, Holy Comforter, Miami, and St. Patrick's, West Palm Beach, were received into union with the convention as parishes.[52]

The consecration of Henry Louttit to the episcopate was an elaborate and exciting affair for the diocese, especially as it was the first time a bishop had been consecrated within its borders. Bishop Gray was consecrated in Nashville, Bishop Mann in Kansas City, and Bishop Wing in Chattanooga. There was some disappointment in the fact that the Presiding Bishop, Rt. Rev. Henry St. George Tucker, could not act as consecrator because of previous appointments, but equal rejoicing when he appointed Bishop Wing to act as consecrator in his stead. The Presiding Bishop ordered that the service take place May 23, 1945, in the bishop-elect's old parish in West Palm Beach.

The rector and vestry of Holy Trinity, thinking it scarcely fitting that the service be held in an unconsecrated church, began a quiet campaign to raise the money necessary to pay off the mortgage resting upon the building. Their effort was successful, the mortgage was liquidated, and the church was solemnly consecrated by Bishop Wing on April 29, the Fourth Sunday after Easter. Chaplain Louttit, home on leave, was present in the chancel, and a joyful congregation occupying every available seat joined heartily in the service.[53]

The bishop-elect's consecration had all the ritual and color of the Anglo-Catholic tradition, but the deft hand of Bishop Wing was there to stay any attempt at ritualistic excess. The service occurred before a packed congregation and in the presence of over fifty diocesan clergy. For Bishop Wing the occasion was particularly joyful in that he had made the bishop-elect both deacon and priest, and in consecrating him to the episcopate Bishop Wing perhaps became the only bishop in the American Church to confer all three degrees of Holy Orders on the same man. The Rt. Rev. Spence Burton, S.S.J.E., S.T.D., Bishop of Nassau, and the Rt. Rev. Reginald Mallett, D.D., Bishop of Northern Indiana, were the coconsecrators. The preacher for the occasion, Bishop Penick of North Carolina, caught the mood and the imagination of those present

52. *Palm Branch*, March 1945.
53. Ibid., June 1945.

when he said, "It is an immeasurable privilege, as well as a stagger-ing responsibility[,] to enter upon the episcopal office at any time, particularly so at the high noon of opportunity in such a day as this." In his charge to the ordinand, Bishop Penick said, "You have not come to the Kingdom at a time of ease and prosperity and peace, when ordinary leadership is enough. You have come when the forces of destiny are joined . . . and the scales of judgment balanced. You will be a mender of broken things."[54] The new bishop, on a thirty-day leave at the time, had seen enough death and destruction and sacrifice in the Pacific to know the truth of the preacher's words. But he was not destined to play only the role of the mender; he was to be a builder as well.

On May 7, approximately two weeks before the consecration of Bishop Louttit, Germany surrendered unconditionally to the victori-ous Allies. The following August the Japanese sued for peace. When the war ended, Bishop Louttit took up residence in West Palm Beach. He was put in charge of the missions of the diocese and eagerly awaited the opportunity to begin his work.

54. Ibid., July 1945.

XV

The Postwar Years

THE END OF THE WAR BROUGHT SOUTH FLORIDA EPISCOPA-
lians to their churches in droves for services of thanksgiving.
As the servicemen began to return home, many churches planned
parties of welcome. Typical of these social affairs was the party held
in the parish house of St. Paul's Church, New Smyrna. The women
of the church prepared a "Welcome Home Dinner" at which some
hundred parishioners turned out to honor the returnees. A large
and unusual welcoming sign made of hibiscus blossoms formed a
background for the high table. The dinner ended with a talk by
Marvin White, a former Sunday school superintendent under whom
many of the veterans had studied.[1]

The welcome that Holy Cross Church in Miami gave its returning servicemen was more practical. A parochial committee was
formed to assist the veterans in establishing themselves in business,
and a parish credit union was proposed for that purpose. The parish
also planned to use the war bonds which the vestry and parishioners
had accumulated during the conflict for beginning a new Sunday
school building.[2]

In the midst of the joyous victory celebrations the diocese was

1. *Palm Branch*, September 1946.
2. Ibid., June 1944.

saddened by the loss of one of its great pioneers. On September 13, 1945, a month after the surrender of the Japanese, the Hon. Thomas Picton Warlow, Chancellor of the Diocese of South Florida, died in his eighty-first year. Born in India of British parents in 1865, Judge Warlow came to Orlando in 1884 as a member of the English colony. He aided in organizing St. Luke's Church and remained a communicant thereof until his death. Appointed deputy chancellor of the missionary district by Bishop Gray, he held that office until 1933 when he was elected chancellor of the diocese.[3] Judge Warlow's death was but another reminder of the debt that the Church in South Florida owed the early British settlers. During his years as chancellor "he gave to that office of his time, and of his great ability with faithfulness and enthusiasm, performing its duties with zeal and joyousness of heart up to the very end."[4]

Some of the chaplains returned to the diocese at the end of the war; some did not. The Rev. Henry I. Louttit returned as suffragan bishop; the Rev. Richard I. Brown, who entered the army from Avon Park and Sebring, became rector of St. Luke's, Fort Myers, after his discharge; and the Rev. Sidney M. Hopson, who resigned the charge of St. John's, Tampa, to serve in the army, came back to South Florida as the supply priest for Holy Cross Parish in Miami. Chaplain Andrew D. Milstead, formerly of St. Luke's, Fort Myers, remained in the navy, while the Rev. John B. Walthour continued his duty as chaplain of the United States Military Academy at West Point. South Floridians who returned to minister in other dioceses were the Rev. Randolph F. Blackford and the Rev. Edgar L. Pennington (Alabama), and the Rev. Charles W. Adams (Los Angeles).[5]

From the diocese eight candidates for the ministry had been mustered into the armed forces. By May 1946 all but one had been discharged and had notified Bishop Wing of their intention to continue their preparations for the priesthood. One of this number, Arthur Joy Lively of Holy Trinity, Bartow, was a former minister of the Disciples of Christ, and as such had served as a chaplain in

3. Orlando *Morning Sentinel*, September 14, 1945.
4. Wing, *Episcopal Address* (South Florida), 1946, p. 50.
5. Ibid., p. 47.

the United States Army. While stationed at the Bartow Army Air Field he decided to apply for admission as a postulant for the Anglican priesthood. There were six non-veteran candidates and postulants for Holy Orders from the diocese as well.[6]

After the war the National Council of the Episcopal Church embarked on a campaign to raise $5,000,000 to help rebuild the Church's overseas hospitals, schools, orphanages, colleges, and church buildings destroyed or damaged in the war. This effort was known as the Reconstruction and Advance Drive. The mission programs in China, Japan, and the Philippines were to be the primary recipients of these funds, but the missionary endeavors of the Church in Liberia, Central and South America, and other places untouched by the war were to be strengthened and expanded with financial aid as well. The National Council also planned to increase the tempo of its work among American Negroes and among the servicemen in the armies of occupation. The Diocese of South Florida was given the quota of $50,000. When the National Council expanded its goal to $8,800,000, an additional $20,000 was added to the diocesan total. Bishop Wing put his enthusiastic new suffragan in charge of the fund-raising.[7]

Bishop Louttit visited nearly every parish and mission in South Florida on behalf of the program. His enthusiasm was contagious. Throughout the drive for funds he maintained that, if congregations were told about the plans and given the opportunity to participate, they would respond with generosity. He proved to be right. The first parish to complete its campaign was St. Peter's, St. Petersburg. There the Christmas offering was designated for the fund, and because of adequate preparation $5,564.51 was received—more than ten per cent above their quota. Early in the campaign also the treasurer of St. Matthias's, Clermont, sent a check for $25 paying the share of that tiny mission in full. This was closely followed by a check of $150 from the treasurer of St. Peter's, Plant City, which also paid its entire quota.[8] There was real sacrificial giving among Negro communicants of the diocese. One Negro clergyman reported

6. *Palm Branch*, May 1946.
7. Ibid., December 1945, January 1946.
8. Ibid., March 1946.

the case of an aged widow in his flock who "has so little that we did
not think of asking her to give, but she insisted on making a contribution which, though small, undoubtedly meant deprivation for
her." A group of Negro Bahamians working near Titusville and
constituting an unorganized mission under the pastoral care of the
Rev. Shelby Walthall voluntarily gave ten dollars.[9] One of the
greatest successes in the effort was reported from Sarasota. There,
the Rev. John H. Soper and his campaign chairman visited a list
of "special givers," while the newly organized chapter of the Brotherhood of St. Andrew canvassed the remainder of the parish. Within
a short time the suggested quota of $1,500 was surpassed and over
$3,100 was sent to the diocesan treasurer. By using the same tactics,
All Saints' Church, Winter Park, raised the splendid sum of $3,293
against a quota of $2,000. By September 1946 the Diocese of South
Florida had sent over $72,000 to the National Council—a remark-
able figure, as many of the churches of the diocese were engaged in
building and expanding their own parochial facilities.[10]

As the veterans began to return to civilian life they faced a number of political and social problems that had been swept under the
legislative tables in Tallahassee during the war years. The rapidly
expanding population in the southern portion of the peninsula
brought demands for more and better roads and recreational facilities as well as for reapportionment of the state legislature and educational reforms on the secondary and university levels. A returning
veteran and Churchman, Daniel T. McCarty of Fort Pierce, entered the political arena and addressed himself to some of these
pressing problems. Young McCarty promised educational and political reforms without a significant raise in taxes, as well as a war on
inefficiency and corruption. His first attempt to win the governor's
chair in 1948 ended in failure, but a better-planned campaign four
years later engendered such enthusiasm that he was elected governor
in 1952. His untimely death in September the following year prevented the initiation and implementation of his program.

No South Florida politician had ever been so closely identified
with the Episcopal Church. Dan McCarty had been active in St.

9. Ibid., June 1946.
10. Ibid., September 1946.

Andrew's Parish in Fort Pierce since boyhood. While attending the University of Florida he served on the vestry of the student chapel and was elected senior warden. Returning to St. Lucie County after the war, he was elected to the parish vestry in 1945 and shortly thereafter began a term as senior warden. In 1947 he was the principal speaker at the diocesan convention banquet in Tampa, where his theme, "The Church in Our Times," was widely acclaimed by his hearers. At his death, Bishop Louttit, assisted by the Rev. J. Saxton Wolfe, rector of St. Andrew's, conducted the funeral rites from the Fort Pierce church, while simultaneous memorial services were being held in the cathedral in Orlando and in St. John's Church in Tallahassee.[11]

In the five years between the end of the war and Bishop Wing's retirement at the close of 1950, it was apparent to even the most casual observer that the peninsula was gradually moving into another period of accelerated growth, a period not unlike that which followed World War I. South Florida Episcopalians had high hopes that their church would share in the coming era of prosperity. Their hopes were not disappointed. During this half-decade new missions began to appear throughout the diocese and old missions began to grow into self-supporting parishes. In 1945 two almost dormant congregations were brought to life as organized missions: St. Mark's, Haines City, and St. Mary's, Stuart. In April 1946 the dormant mission of All Saints', Enterprise, became an organized congregation. During the 1946 convention two mission congregations reached parish status: The Church of the Good Shepherd, Lake Wales, and St. Paul's Church, Delray Beach.[12] The following year two other missions reached self-sufficiency and became parishes: St. Andrew's, Lake Worth, and St. Bartholomew's, St. Petersburg.[13]

During this time new work was started in a number of cities in the diocese. In Tampa, St. Andrew's Parish organized a church school in the Palma Ceia area. A well-located piece of land was purchased with aid from the diocesan building fund and within a year St. Mary's, a parochial mission of St. Andrew's Parish, had

11. Ibid., November 1953.
12. Wing, *Episcopal Address* (South Florida), 1946, p. 52.
13. *Diocesan Journal*, 1947, p. 67.

been organized. Also with diocesan aid, the House of Prayer in the same city began construction of a combination church and parish house on property it was given in the north Tampa area, and as a result St. Francis's Church came into being. Across the bay in St. Petersburg a new Negro mission under the patronage of St. Augustine was being organized, and in the spring of 1947 a new congregation, St. Francis's, was formed in Miami Shores. This mission later became the Church of the Resurrection. Plans were also being made to start a new mission for Negroes on the property purchased by St. Agnes's Church in the Liberty City section of Miami.[14]

This same period saw much building by the missions of the diocese. The trustees made grants totaling $7,000 from the diocesan building fund. This money, expended on a partnership basis with the National Church and the congregations involved, made it possible to replace the vicarage of St. Matthew's Church, Delray Beach, which had been destroyed by fire; to complete a church building started long before for St. Ann's, Hallandale; to renovate St. Peter's Parochial School, Key West; and to erect a church building for St. Cyprian's, Homestead. A grant from the same fund made it possible for the Church of the Nativity in Pahokee to purchase a new vicarage. Thus, by expending $7,000 from diocesan funds, the missions of South Florida eventually acquired properties valued by the trustees at approximately $25,000.[15] Much of the expansion and construction in the mission field during the postwar years was carefully supervised by the administratively talented suffragan bishop.

The new suffragan did not limit his attention to the mission field. He was also concerned with education and social service. At Bishop Louttit's suggestion an important project in the field of Christian social relations was begun. A two-week session of summer camp for underprivileged boys and girls between the ages of ten and fourteen was held at Camp Wingmann in the first two weeks of August 1947. The session was named in honor of St. Francis. Its purpose was to provide "the normal opportunities for a good time that childhood deserves, regardless of church affiliation" in, of course, a

14. Henry Irving Louttit, *Suffragan Bishop's Address*, 1947, p. 59.
15. Ibid., pp. 59–60.

Christian environment. Camp scholarships were provided by various parishes, welfare organizations, and civic clubs who cooperated with camp authorities in seeking out deserving children who would profit from the experience.

Many of the children came to camp with only one change of clothing for the two-week period. Some had no underclothes except those they wore to camp. Any number came with no sheets or blankets. Few brought toothbrushes, combs, washcloths, or soap. The camp staff had anticipated some shortages, however, and when the children arrived they found a supply of the above-mentioned articles, sent by several branches of the Women's Auxiliary at the staff's request. By the end of the first week of camp the supply of clothing was totally exhausted so an S.O.S. had to be sent out to nearby parishes for more.

The *Palm Branch* reported that "a fine spirit of love and cooperation" permeated the two-week session. Some counsellors gave up their vacations to render their services and many took special courses in college to equip themselves to understand the children better. As a result of their efforts one hundred seventeen campers enjoyed two weeks of wholesome fun that they would not have had otherwise. Welfare organizations, children's homes, family service bureaus, and civic organizations interested in the welfare of children were loud in their praise of the diocese for making this experience possible.[16] Camp St. Francis has been in continual existence since its first session in 1947. For several years All Souls' Parish, Miami, and the Miami Beach Kiwanis Club sponsored the largest group of children attending the camp.

The bishop also envisioned a new role for the defunct Cathedral School. He suggested that the school's board study the possibility of establishing an Episcopal day school under the joint auspices of St. Luke's Cathedral, Orlando, and All Saints' Church, Winter Park. The success of such an experiment, he pointed out, might lead to the establishment of similar Church day schools in the larger centers of population and serve as a "means of strengthening the Church and expanding the faith."

Bishop Louttit also began to press for the establishment of a

16. *Diocesan Journal*, 1947, pp. 95–96; *Palm Branch*, October 1947.

home for the aged as a successor to Bishop Gray's abandoned Church Home and Hospital. The assets of that defunct institution had been absorbed by the Trustees of St. Luke's Hospital, an ephemeral facility operated in DeLand during the Florida boom. The hospital trustees had sold their property to secular authorities in DeLand, but the board remained a legal entity. During the depression the hospital trustees refused again and again to deliver their corporate assets to the impoverished diocese because they entertained hopes of sometime opening a home for the elderly. In his address before the Convention of 1947 Bishop Louttit tried to come to grips with this situation. He spoke frankly: "For many years we have discussed the St. Luke's Hospital Fund and the need for an old people's home in the Diocese. If there be a need for such an institution, and we believe there is, we should act. Let us plan either to open a home for the aged scaled to the funds on hand, or raise the necessary money that the work may be established on a larger basis."[17]

As a result of Bishop Louttit's prodding, the Board of Managers of the Cathedral School was requested by the convention to study the bishop's suggestion to open a day school under joint auspices and to make appropriate recommendations at the next convention. A request was also made that the Board of Trustees of St. Luke's Hospital prepare a definite plan for the next convention, either to start a home for the aged within the limit of the funds now on hand or to inaugurate a campaign to raise the needed additional funds to begin this work.[18] The book value of the St. Luke's endowment, according to the current report, was approximately $160,000,[19] a sizable basis on which to begin the new endeavor.

In the midst of its attempt to keep pace with the rapid growth of the peninsula's population, expand its educational facilities at the colleges and universities, and establish a home for older people, the Diocese of South Florida was stunned to learn that its energetic suffragan had been elected Bishop of Western New York at a special convention held in Buffalo on October 14, 1947. The election

17. Louttit, *Suffragan Bishop's Address*, 1947, p. 58.
18. *Diocesan Journal*, 1947, p. 36.
19. Ibid., pp. 109–10.

of Henry Louttit to that see should not have come as a surprise. He was a native of Buffalo, and a number of clergy and laity from that diocese had watched with considerable interest and admiration his vigorous approach to solving the diffused problems of South Florida. While proud that Western New York had recognized his worth and ability, the people of South Florida hoped that Bishop Louttit would remain in the diocese "among us who know and love him best."[20] Letters, telegrams, and phone calls poured into the diocesan office in Orlando urging him to decline his election. When he did so, there was a great feeling of relief throughout the diocese, a feeling perhaps best expressed by Bishop Wing, in these words: "It is quite beyond my power of expression to voice either my own deep sense of gratification or that of our clergy and people over Bishop Louttit's decision to decline his election to the Diocese of Western New York in order that he might continue to exercise his Episcopate in South Florida."[21] Not long afterwards Bishop Wing, whose health was rapidly declining, requested a coadjutor. At the 1948 convention held at All Souls', Miami Beach, Henry Irving Louttit was elected Bishop Coadjutor of South Florida on the first ballot.[22]

As the population of the state increased so did the building of churches and church facilities. The journal of 1948 reported a new chapel finished at Camp Wingmann and the erection of new church buildings in Deerfield. In the Tampa area the new missions of St. Mary and St. Francis continued to grow and build. A new mission was formed at Wauchula under the patronage of St. Ann. New rectories were acquired by St. Paul's, Delray Beach; St. James's, Ormond Beach; the Good Shepherd, Dunedin; St. Timothy's, Daytona Beach; and St. John's, Tampa. New parish houses were finished for St. Timothy's, Daytona Beach, Christ Memorial Chapel, Hobe Sound, and Grace Church, Ocala. Additions were finished to the parish halls of St. Stephen's, Coconut Grove, and St. Mary's, Dade City. A rectory was also acquired for the Church of the Epiphany in Miami Springs—the mission that later moved to Hia-

20. *Palm Branch*, November 1947.
21. Ibid., December 1947.
22. *Diocesan Journal*, 1948, pp. 31–33.

leah and changed its name to St. Margaret's. All Saints' Church in Fort Lauderdale purchased more land at the site of its new church and thereby made the property one of the finest in that rapidly growing city, while St. John's, Tampa, and Holy Trinity, West Palm Beach, began campaigns to secure funds for new or enlarged parish houses.[23] Never in the history of the diocese had more building projects been planned or completed.

The Department of Missions under the leadership of the Rev. William L. Hargrave began to press the local mission congregations to raise the salaries of their clergy. The department suggested stipends of $3,000 plus housing for married priests and $2,400 plus housing for single clerics. Father Hargrave noted that of the twenty-two clergy currently working solely in missions, only ten received stipends of $3,000.[24]

Many of Florida's returning veterans took advantage of the educational benefits of the G.I. Bill and enrolled in the colleges and universities of the state. Seeing this, Bishop Wing increased his support of the already established student programs at the two state universities and encouraged the organization of student-Church activities at the private institutions in his diocese. These activities were usually under the supervision of the Episcopal college organization, Canterbury Club.

At Ruge Hall, the Episcopal student center at Florida State University, the Rev. G. P. Reeves, a cleric in deacon's orders, was appointed as the first full-time chaplain. When Mr. Reeves was advanced to the priesthood some months later, he reported more frequent communions and better attendance at daily Evensong and Compline. During his first year at Ruge, 514 services were held in the chapel with a total attendance of 9,902 and two confirmation classes were presented. Ruge Hall was the oldest and for many years the only student center on the Tallahassee campus. Because it had a resident chaplain, a regular and frequent schedule of worship, and an advantageous location, Ruge Hall was "coming more and more to be thought of in terms of its being in some sense 'The University Chapel.'"

23. Wing, *Episcopal Address* (South Florida), 1948, p. 43.
24. *Diocesan Journal*, 1948, p. 94.

The college program at the University of Florida, like that at Florida State, was jointly sponsored and financed by the Dioceses of Florida and South Florida. The Rev. Morgan Ashley, chaplain at Weed Hall, the Episcopal student center in Gainesville, reported that nine per cent of the 9,000 students at the university were Episcopalians and that 474 services had been held for them during the period from spring 1948 to spring 1949. The chapel had an active chapter of the Brotherhood of St. Andrew, an acolytes' guild, an altar guild, a choir, and an inquirers' class.[25] The program of the Church received a boost when a new student center was opened during the fall term, 1950.[26]

With the help of diocesan funds, the parish churches located near the other college campuses took the lead in establishing programs for the returning G.I.s. For example, the 69 Episcopal students at Florida Southern College in Lakeland were invited by the rector and vestry of All Saints' to form a Canterbury Club. The activities of the club included worship, fellowship, and intellectual endeavors.[27] At John B. Stetson University in DeLand, the Rev. LeRoy D. Lawson of St. Barnabas's Church reported some 112 Churchmen registered in that institution. Of that number, 90 were members of the Canterbury Club. For them a monthly corporate communion was celebrated, followed by breakfast in the parish house. Discussion groups and social evenings were also held monthly and frequent dinners were served.

In nearby Daytona Beach, the Rev. M. Bartlett Cochran, vicar of St. Timothy's Church, carried on the only work in the diocese for Negro college students at Bethune-Cookman College. He reported that there were 27 Episcopal students attending that institution and that his ministrations to them were very similar to those of the clergy at other colleges. Father Cochran, however, made a real effort to incorporate the worship and social activities of his students with those of the regular flock at St. Timothy's. At the University of Tampa a Canterbury Club was organized and a room for it was provided on the campus by the university. Local parishes

25. Ibid., p. 95; 1949, p. 97.
26. *Palm Branch,* December 1950.
27. Ibid., November 1946.

took turns in monthly corporate communions for the club, followed by breakfast. The student Churchmen were under the direction of the Rev. Clarence W. Brickman of St. John's Parish.

At Rollins College in Winter Park, the Rev. James L. Duncan of All Saints' reported a group of 125 students and 25 members of the faculty who belonged to the Episcopal Church. The Rollins Canterbury Club met monthly for supper and discussion. The Rollins faculty members were as interested in the club as the students and their assistance at the meetings resulted in enthusiastic attendance. A monthly corporate communion followed by breakfast was also included in the program of the club.[28]

The work at the University of Miami was carried on largely by the clergy of St. Philip's, Coral Gables, and Epiphany, Miami Springs. The interest of the university administration in the spiritual life of the students was shown by the designation of Tuesday night as Religious Activity Night. This aspect of the students' life was thus placed on a par with other campus activities. There were 420 members of the Episcopal Church in the student body. A large and active Canterbury Club was in operation, but the part-time chaplain, the Rev. G. L. Gurney, felt that the work of the Church would be more effective if the ministering clergyman did not also have parochial duties. Father Gurney reported that the Canterbury Club had tripled in size in a year and that members had as an annual goal the raising of $500 for the building of a chapel and recreation hall. The completion of such a student center for the University of Miami was but a dream, however, in the closing years of Bishop Wing's episcopate.

A shortage of capital prevented the completion and expansion of the diocesan mission program and of other projects such as the establishment of a home for the aged. The 1949 diocesan convention did attempt to improve the financial picture. It passed resolutions asking the diocese to raise the necessary capital funds for these efforts. The campaign for capital funds was put under the direction of the Rev. James L. Duncan, chairman of the Department of Promotion and newly elected rector of St. Peter's Church, St.

28. *Diocesan Journal*, 1948, p. 95; 1949, pp. 97–98.

Petersburg. Under the mandate from the convention, the Department of Promotion asked thirty-two people to become members of a fund drive committee and sought their counsel and advice. After several meetings concrete plans were made.

The plans provided for a capital funds drive to be known as the Advance Work Campaign. The three-year campaign would begin Easter, 1950, and last until the following Whitsunday, with renewed solicitation during this same period for the next two years. The goal was set at $330,000 to be divided as follows:

		TOTALS
Home for the Aged:		
Endowment	$110,000	
Renovation and equipment	50,000	$160,000
Diocesan Mission Expansion	100,000	100,000
Buildings at		
University of Florida	15,000	
University of Miami	50,000	65,000
Expenses of Campaign	5,000	5,000
		$330,000

According to Father Duncan, grants for missions would be made on a part-gift, part-loan basis. The loans were to be repaid after the mission congregation became self-supporting. The home for the aged would be run on a "pilot" basis in one of the buildings of the old Cathedral School. Since for many years college work in the state had been supported by both dioceses, the cleric hoped the Diocese of Florida would make a significant contribution towards the Miami student center.[29]

Campaign brochures were prepared for distribution throughout the diocese. Bishops Wing and Louttit, with the assistance of the Department of Promotion, made a direct appeal to the communicants of the diocese during the appointed period for the Advance Work Program. Plans called for clergy and area campaign chairmen to draw up a list of some three hundred persons who could give

29. Ibid., 1950, pp. 93–94.

$1,000 over a three-year period and another list of six hundred persons who could give $500.[30]

In the midst of this campaign for funds Bishop Wing suffered another heart attack. Financial pressure and the urgent problems of diocesan growth and pastoral care undoubtedly aggravated his unsteady coronary condition. Although the attack occurred some months before the 1950 diocesan convention, the bishop was forbidden by his physicians to attend it. In his address, which was read for him from the pulpit of Holy Trinity Church, West Palm Beach, he announced his intention to retire at the end of the year.[31]

30. Ibid., 1951, pp. 85–86.
31. Wing, *Episcopal Address* (South Florida), 1950, pp. 43–44.

XVI

John Durham Wing
Third Bishop

THE EPISCOPATE OF JOHN DURHAM WING DIFFERED FROM those of his two predecessors in a number of striking ways. In the first place, there was a gradual shift to a more elaborate ceremonial in most of the churches of the diocese; and in the second, there was a marked tendency to put more emphasis on Negro work and to give Negro Churchmen a proper share of their privileges and their responsibilities as communicants. The Wing episcopate was also one of distinct contrasts. It began at the nadir of the bust that followed the Florida boom and ended in the early post-World-War-II years of unparalleled growth and development. Then, too, the personality and background of Bishop Wing, vividly reflected in his tenure, contrasted sharply with those of Bishops Gray and Mann. Unlike his predecessors, John Wing was not a born Churchman, he was not the son of a clergyman, and he was not educated in a Church college. He was a convert, and as a convert he knew what aspects of the Episcopal Church had attracted him and what aspects would attract others. He was also more aware than his predecessors of those features of the Church that might be changed in order to make it more inclusive, more catholic in its appeal and its mission. The third Bishop of South Florida was not a typical Episcopalian, or a typical bishop, or a typical Southerner. He was perhaps unique among prelates in the South in the quarter of a century that the diocese was under his care.

The future bishop was born in Atlanta, Georgia, November 19, 1882. His parents, John Durham and Sallie Peeples Wing, were devout Baptists and reared their son in that denomination. John Wing was educated in the secondary schools of Atlanta, at the University of Georgia, and at the College of William and Mary, in Williamsburg, Virginia. While at the University of Georgia, he majored in English literature.[1]

Bishop Wing's conversion to the Episcopal Church was unusual. He was brought up in a family where the King James version of the Bible was read often. Sometime after he left the University of Georgia in 1903, he read an article in a distinguished New York periodical which stated that the Book of Common Prayer, the works of William Shakespeare, and the King James translation of the Bible were the most influential works in the English language. Familiar as he was with the Bible and Shakespeare, Wing had never even heard of the Book of Common Prayer. He bought a copy, studied it thoroughly, and decided to seek confirmation in the Episcopal Church.[2]

Soon after his confirmation, John Wing was sent to England by the Pittsburgh Plate Glass Company, by whom he was employed. In the two years of his stay in the British Isles, he saw the English Church at work with all its strengths and weaknesses. He was drawn to the restrained ceremonial of the great cathedral and collegiate churches, to the musical settings of Anglican liturgical worship, and to the all-embracing nature of the English Church which made it truly the Church of England in a way the Episcopal Church could never be the church of the United States. He also realized that ceremonial and liturgical worship lost much of their value if they were not properly understood, that comprehensiveness often meant vagueness in doctrine and ritual, and that the Catholic aspects of English Christianity were often obscured by a too rigidly hierarchical social structure.

Soon after his return from England, Wing offered himself as a

1. Orlando *Morning Sentinel*, March 7, 1960.
2. *Palm Branch*, March 1960.

postulant to the Rt. Rev. Cleland Kinlock Nelson, Bishop of Atlanta. The bishop sent him to the Episcopal Theological Seminary
in Alexandria. He was ordained by Bishop Nelson to the diaconate
in 1909 and to the priesthood the following year. He began his
ministry at the Church of the Holy Comforter in Atlanta, a mission
with fewer than a hundred communicants. In 1912 he was called to
be rector of the Church of the Incarnation in the same city. In
1913, while rector of this parish, he was elected secretary of the
Diocese of Atlanta, an office which he held for only one year, however, as in 1914 he severed his ties with the diocese when he accepted a call as rector of Grace Church in Anniston, Alabama.[3]

During his clerical tenure of four years in Atlanta, John Wing
became fast friends with the distinguished Southern Churchman
Cary Breckinrige Wilmer, rector of St. Luke's Church. It was Dr.
Wilmer who had helped prepare him for confirmation and later
guided him to the threshold of the priesthood. Although Dr. Wilmer
was rector of the largest and most prestigious parish in the city of
Atlanta, he was hardly the typical early-twentieth-century society
clergyman. He began his career in the mission field as priest-in-
charge of Grace Church, Ocala, when that church was still a part
of the old Diocese of Florida, and later served as superintendent of
the Colored Orphans Asylum in Lynchburg, Virginia. Dr. Wilmer's
concern for Negroes lasted all his life. As a prominent member of
the Southern Interracial Commission, he became a leader in attempting to further better relations between the races. Wilmer combined a keen mind with serious social concern. He was a polished
and powerful preacher as well as the possessor of a potent and
drawing personality. On his frequent visits to the rectory on Pied-
mont Avenue Wing felt the full influence of Wilmer's views, which
were later reflected in the social attitudes and concerns that distinguished Wing's episcopate.[4]

The tie between John Wing and Dr. Wilmer was not merely
ecclesiastical; it was destined to be filial as well. During John's
many visits to the doctor he met and soon fell in love with Wilmer's
stepdaughter, the attractive Mary Catherine Ammons. The old

3. *Diocesan Journal*, 1960, p. 69.
4. Interview with Mrs. John D. Wing, April 7, 1968.

rector was delighted by the ripening romance, but refused to permit the young couple to marry until John's parochial stipend reached one hundred dollars per month, a figure which Dr. Wilmer deemed minimal for the proper support of his daughter. John Wing and Mary Ammons were married in 1913.[5]

The Wings did not remain in Anniston long. Although he had been priested less than five years, John Wing in 1915 was called to Christ Church, Savannah, the mother parish of the Diocese of Georgia, where he became well known as an informative and provocative preacher and was much in demand as a speaker for civic and charitable enterprises. His views on race and Churchmanship were considerably advanced for the citizens of the oldest city and the members of the oldest church in the state of Georgia. While the Wings were in Savannah the United States entered World War I. John Wing guided his parishioners through the hectic years of the war and the even more hectic years of the peace that followed it. As a measure of the esteem in which he was held he was elected to represent the Diocese of Georgia as a deputy to the General Convention in 1919 and 1922. Wing's tenure as rector of Christ Church ended in 1923 when he succeeded the Rev. W. J. Loring Clark, D.D., as rector of St. Paul's Church in Chattanooga.[6]

In 1924 the National Council of the Episcopal Church chose a number of forceful preachers to lead a nationwide campaign to buttress the mission program of the National Church in each diocese. John Wing was appointed to preach in the Diocese of South Florida. In June of that year he conducted mission conferences and preached in Orlando, Tampa, Lakeland, DeLand, and West Palm Beach.[7] The campaign was a success, and the zeal and directness of the preacher became indelibly impressed upon the minds of a large number of South Floridians. When the Rt. Rev. Cameron Mann asked the diocesan convention for a coadjutor the following year, it was not surprising that the rector of St. Paul's was one of the thirteen clerics nominated. A large number of parochial clergy received nominations as favorite sons, but John Wing and the Rt.

5. *Palm Branch*, March 1960.
6. *Diocesan Journal*, 1960, p. 69.
7. Ibid., 1925, pp. 21–22.

Rev. Theodore Payne Thurston, Missionary Bishop of Oklahoma, took early commanding leads. The Chattanooga cleric led on the first ballot and was elected on the seventh.[8]

The consecration of John Durham Wing took place in St. Paul's Church, Chattanooga, on the feast of St. Michael and All Angels, September 29, 1925. The *Chattanooga News* gave a colorful account of the procession: "Promptly at ten o'clock a.m. the procession which had formed in the Parish House entered the Church, led by a crucifer and large vested choir. The processional hymns were 'Rise crowned with light' and 'The Church's one foundation.' Following the Choir came the Vestry of St. Paul's Church, and lay representatives of the Diocese of South Florida, members of the faculty and trustees of The University of the South and the University of Chattanooga, theological students of Sewanee and the Du-Bose Training School. Then came another crucifer and the clergy of South Florida and those of Tennessee and Atlanta who were present in vestments. The master of ceremonies was Dr. A. H. Noll of Memphis. . . . Another crossbearer headed the third section of the procession, consisting of the participating bishops, the bishop-elect with Dr. C. B. Wilmer and the Rev. Charles T. Warner as his attending presbyters; the presenters, Bishop Mikell of Atlanta and Bishop McDowell of Alabama; the coconsecrators, Bishop Reese of Georgia and Bishop Gailor of Tennessee; and finally the consecrator, the Rt. Rev. Cameron Mann, D.D., bishop of South Florida."

Bishop Mann as consecrator celebrated the Holy Communion. The musical setting for the service was Mozart's *Mass in C*, and the preacher for the occasion was the Rt. Rev. James M. Maxon, D.D., Bishop Coadjutor of Tennessee. The offering at the service was placed at the disposal of the new bishop for work in the Diocese of South Florida.[9] The following day, the Rt. Rev. John Durham Wing confirmed his first confirmation class. It consisted of thirty candidates from his old parish, St. Paul's. In early November the Wings moved to Florida and occupied the rambling old rectory near the Church of the Good Shepherd in Maitland on the out-

8. *Palm Branch*, May 1925.
9. *Chattanooga News*, September 29, 1925.

skirts of Winter Park. About the same time Bishop and Mrs. Mann moved into the newly completed Bishopstead in Winter Park.[10]

Bishop Wing took over the administration of the rapidly expanding mission field of the diocese as well as the supervision of work among the Negroes of the diocese. He was young for a prelate, not quite forty-three, and he brought a fresh approach to the problems of South Florida and a vigor that the aging Bishop Mann did not have. John Wing needed all his physical and mental resources, for the growth engendered by the Florida boom was spiraling to its height. Within a year the bishop coadjutor visited almost every parish and mission in South Florida, confirming, preaching, soliciting funds for diocesan and national mission programs, and urging the stronger missions under his jurisdiction to become self-supporting parishes. The growth was phenomenal, the pace was hectic, but the rewards were rich. Two new missions were organized: Good Shepherd, Lake Wales; and St. Alban's, Auburndale. Five missions became parishes: St. Andrew's, Fort Pierce; St. John's, Homestead; St. Lucia's, Stuart; St. Edmund's, Arcadia; and The House of Prayer, Tampa.[11]

Negro work occupied much of the coadjutor's time and thought. He was concerned not only with the spiritual welfare of his black flock but with their social welfare as well. During the revival of the Ku Klux Klan and its anti-Negro activities in the state in the 1920s, Bishop Wing brought the full weight of his office and forceful personality against this secret organization. He considered the Klan "in its principles, methods and organization, absolutely inconsistent with the Christian religion . . . a menace to good government and a disgrace to our civilization." He urged that all good citizens express open indignation at being restrained in the free use of streets during Klan parades "in the interest of men who are ashamed to let their faces be seen."[12]

Shortly after his arrival in Florida, Bishop Wing was appalled by what he believed to be a Klan-inspired lynching in Ocala. He held a conference with Clark Forman of Atlanta, Secretary of the

10. *Palm Branch*, December 1925.
11. *Diocesan Journal*, 1926, p. 13.
12. *Palm Branch*, December 1925.

Southern Interracial Commission, to draft a petition to the Governor of Florida, John Martin, urging a swift and energetic investigation of the incident.[13] He also publicly supported officials and newspaper editors throughout the South who took stands against the KKK and lynching. When Julian Harris, the editor of the Columbus, Georgia, *Enquirer-Sun*, won the Pulitzer Prize for his crusade against lynching, the bishop wrote: "I devoutly hope that editors of other representative Southern newspapers emulate your good example and wage with you continued warfare against those evils which degrade our Southern civilization."[14] Bishop Wing used the columns of the *Palm Branch* to attack the practice of lynching and to correct some misunderstandings about it. In an article in the May issue, 1936, he pointed out that of the 168 lynchings which had occurred in the South in the previous 36 years, only fifteen per cent were reported as due to assault on white women, and only ten per cent for attempted assault; and only this twenty-five per cent involved white women in any way. "Lynchings are mostly racial exploitation," the article said, "and in most cases can be traced to economic, political or other such reasons. Ninety per cent of the victims of lynch law are Negroes who represent only one-tenth of the nation's population." The article further stated that mob violence was "anti-Christian" and that the "social teachings of Christ are of the utmost power in averting the spirit of mob activity." At his private urging the Women's Auxiliary of the diocese went on record supporting a federal anti-lynching law.[15]

Another social concern of Bishop Wing's was the brutality in the Florida prison camps. In the fall of 1932 a North Dakota farm boy, Martin Tabert, was murdered by whipping in a road camp. Sometime later, Arthur Mailefert, a New Jersey lad, badly bruised and with a chain around his neck attached to a rafter, died by torture in a sweat box. About the same time a heavily shackled Negro prisoner in the Orange County stockade was shot and killed while trying to escape. Using these three events as examples of prison cruelty, the bishop brought the whole prison farm system to the

13. Wing, *Bishop Coadjutor's Diary, Palm Branch*, February 1926.
14. Columbus, Georgia, *Enquirer-Sun*, May 16, 1926.
15. *Palm Branch*, February 1936.

attention of the public in a forceful article published in the Orlando *Sunday Sentinel* entitled "Convict Trial." He put the responsibility for these cruelties on all the citizens of Florida and insisted that legislation be introduced so that the camps might be run by "humane and conscientious guards." The article produced considerable public outcry for prison camp reform. One concerned reader suggested that provision be made "whereby Bishop Wing and like-minded citizens could visit these camps at all times and investigate them as to their sanitary condition, food supply and moral tone, and hear complaints of these unfortunate people in the absence of guards."[16]

Bishop Wing was an ardent anti-prohibitionist, not because he condoned excessive drinking, but because prohibition forced on a society a set of morals which many of its members abhorred. Prohibition attempted to legislate morality, and this he condemned as "an unwarranted and dangerous interference with man's political and intellectual freedom." In a sermon preached in St. Bartholomew's Church, St. Petersburg, in October 1927, he also opposed legislation prohibiting the opening of movie theaters in Florida on Sunday evenings, legislation which was being pushed by the ministers of numerous Protestant sects on the grounds that movie-going profaned the Sabbath and interfered with evening church attendance. Said the bishop: "If the church, through its teachings and the lives and examples of its ministers and lay people, cannot win souls to Christ and induce them to perform their solemn duty to God by attending the services of His church, then we certainly admit defeat if we resort to the power of the secular arm, which has nothing to do with the church and never should have."[17]

In his relations with Negro communicants Bishop Wing was far ahead of his time. During diocesan conventions he made sure that the Negro delegates sat where they desired instead of being relegated to the back of the host church. He thought that inequality before the altar was blasphemous and would not tolerate it. The Ven. John E. Culmer, Archdeacon for Negro Work, recalled that back in 1933, when the diocesan convention was meeting in Miami, Bishop

16. Orlando *Morning Sentinel*, October 20–21, 1932.
17. *St. Petersburg Times*, October 17, 1927.

Wing called off the diocesan banquet because blacks were not permitted to eat in the establishment where the dinner was to be held. In lieu of the banquet, the bishop invited the whole convention to Evensong in St. Agnes's Church, and "the large outpouring of convention delegates" almost filled the building.[18] The bishop's action took considerable moral courage for this era. It did not, however, end the practice of having segregated diocesan banquets at other conventions.

Bishop Wing was a Southerner to the core, but as a Southerner he saw the contradiction between Christianity and segregation. During his episcopate he not only worked quietly to remove the racial restrictions against Negroes in hotels where the diocesan conventions were held and in restaurants where diocesan banquets took place; he also became the chief pastor of his black flock in fact as well as in title. In his unassuming way he was politically and socially one of the great liberals in the Church, but his liberalism was not theoretical or philosophical, it was rooted and grounded in the Christian faith. Because of this he was respected by both white and black Churchmen. He was a member of the Florida Council on Inter-Racial Cooperation and twice was elected its chairman.[19] He received with pride the notice of his election as a charter member of the Southern Regional Council whose purpose was "the improvement of economic, civic, and racial conditions in the South." As a leader in these progressive organizations he made frequent addresses before ministerial unions in the cities of the state to promote better race relations.[20]

The pastoral care that Bishop Wing gave the black Churchmen of the diocese was deeply appreciated by them. They gathered around him on his visitations to congratulate him on a sermon or to wish him well. It was not uncommon for crates of vegetables from Negro parishioners in the south to arrive at the Bishopstead in Winter Park. On one occasion during a visitation to a number of congregations in the Lake Worth–Biscayne area, when it was observed that the bishop looked haggard and tired, a group of Negro

18. *Diocesan Journal*, 1960, p. 101.
19. Jacksonville *Florida Times-Union*, October 31, 1945.
20. *Diocesan Journal*, 1945, pp. 38, 51.

Churchmen took up a collection and sent him a check wherewith to buy a "comfortable chair for relaxing."[21] In 1944, some six years before the bishop retired, a further indication of the people's affection was shown when a window dedicated as a thanksgiving for his episcopate was placed in St. Patrick's Church, West Palm Beach.[22]

Bishop Wing had a splendid reputation as a preacher. In his sermons he combined reverence for tradition with evangelical zeal. He rarely read a sermon, but preached from brief notes. He was well prepared and at times dramatic when he wanted to emphasize a point. He was capable of almost drawing his listeners from their pews by a gesture or a whisper. He often preached at diocesan conventions in other states, at high school graduations, and at college commencements. The texts were always biblical and the expositions always related to modern situations. The bishop was a "relevant" preacher long before the term came into favor in ecclesiastical circles. His grasp of national and international affairs made him a popular preacher on college campuses and at civic gatherings. For example, he preached at Evensong in the Cathedral of St. John the Divine to 600 members of the New York Police Square Club in October 1934. In his sermon, reported in the *New York Times*, he referred to policemen as "soldiers of peace." He listed as obstacles endangering the peace of the world "the dreadful threat of war hanging like a thunder cloud over the earth," governmental and economic insecurity, "defiant lawlessness," the struggle between labor and capital, and the question of race relationship, which, he said, was "an ever-present problem in the South." The bishop rejoiced in the opportunity to face these problems head on. "We are at one of the great turning points of history," he declared. "Let others 'mourn for the return of the old order while men of courage press onward in spite of all obstacles."[23] Bishop Wing preached another widely acclaimed sermon at the baccalaureate service of Florida A. & M. College in May 1927.[24]

One of Bishop Wing's favorite confirmation texts was from St.

21. Interview with Mrs. John D. Wing, May 8, 1967.
22. *Palm Branch*, October 1944.
23. *New York Times*, October 15, 1934.
24. Tallahassee *Democrat*, May 23, 1927.

Paul: "Put on the whole armor of Christ." After he preached in Sebring using this text the local editor commented, "Bishop Wing, in that wonderful way of his, talked with the people."[25] The bishop was not a great scholar and his sermons did not reflect the deep scholarship of Bishop Mann, nor did they emulate the rambling zeal of Bishop Gray. John Wing did not have time for deep reading, yet he was careful to keep himself well-informed about the problems of his time. He seemed to synthesize the best theological, social, and political thought of his period and express it in a way that laymen not only understood but enjoyed. He was by nature an eclectic and his sermons vividly bore witness to the fact. Amazingly, Bishop Wing was rarely criticized for preaching too long, but was instead often criticized for not preaching long enough.

The bishop's ability as a preacher was matched by his ability as an executive. Before he attended a meeting of the Standing Committee or the Department of Missions, he carefully acquainted himself with the problems under discussion and addressed himself to a sensible solution. One clergyman said that Bishop Wing never "presided over a diocesan convention, he ruled it." Another member of the cloth who occasionally disagreed with the bishop complained that "he was too arbitrary." Archdeacon Culmer, who seldom disagreed with him, described John Wing in the chair of the diocesan convention in this way: "It is interesting to watch Bishop Wing preside. He does it with consummate skill. Humorous, alert, tolerant, firm and sure of himself. An Old Timer [the archdeacon] harks back to other years and notes, with admiration, how the Bishop has grown perhaps faster than the convention."[26]

Interested in liturgics and in putting the liturgy to beautiful but singable music, Bishop Wing created a new diocesan Department of Church Music in 1935. He appointed Charles M. Gray, the organist and choirmaster of St. Peter's Church, St. Petersburg, as its first chairman and made a place for him on the executive board of the diocese.[27] During his first year as diocesan, Bishop Wing noted with

25. Sebring, Fla., *American*, April 12, 1929.
26. *St. Agnes's Herald*, May 1942.
27. *Diocesan Journal*, 1935, p. 63

near alarm that the two hymns almost always used for episcopal visitations were "Onward Christian Soldiers" and "The Church's One Foundation." As time passed he grew tired of these same hymns, and on one occasion was reported to have asked a clergyman, "Do you know that there are other hymns in the hymnal?" He used the columns of the *Palm Branch* to plead with the choirmaster to sing other hymns during visitations.[28] Bishop Wing insisted on choosing hymns for ordinations, possibly because he feared the ordinand might also pick unduly familiar ones. When a would-be deacon or priest objected to the bishop's choice he would reply with both humor and firmness, "You may think that this is *your* ordination, my son, but it is really *mine*."

Another habit that often galled the episcopal spleen was what Bishop Wing called "The Error of Reverend." The bishop was fond of explaining that contrary to popular belief among journalists "Reverend" is not a title but a descriptive adjective. "It is just as absurd to say 'Reverend Brown' as 'Honorable Coolidge.' The correct usage is the Reverend Mr. Brown, or the Rev. John Brown, or (in case the said minister has a Doctor's degree) the Reverend Dr. Brown. Naturally, it follows that a clergyman is never correctly addressed as 'Reverend.' " The bishop was fond of quoting a poem by a long-suffering priest, perhaps Bishop Wing himself, who expressed his indignation at being called "Reverend" in this way:

Call me "Brother" if you will.
Call me "Parson" better still.
Or if, perchance, the high-church frill
Doth your heart with longing fill,—
Though plain "Mister" fills the bill,—
If that title lacketh thrill,
Then even "Father" brings no chill
Or hurt or rancor or ill-will.
To no "D.D." do I pretend,
Though "Doctor" doth some honor lend.
"Preacher," "Pastor," "Rector," "Friend,"—
Titles, almost without end,—

28. *Palm Branch*, March 1938.

Never grate and ne'er offend;
A loving ear to all I bend.
But how that man my heart doth rend
Who blithely calls me "Reverend."[29]

The bishop was a great advocate of good manners both inside
and outside church. The breach of church etiquette that angered
him most was the departure of communicants from the celebration
of the Holy Communion before the benediction or "without even
returning to their pews for a prayer of thanksgiving," a practice
that was particularly common among the occasional churchgoers
who attended the festival services on Easter and Christmas. Leaving
like this, the bishop thought, was the equivalent of leaving one's
host's dinner table without so much as a "by your leave, thank
you, or goodbye." The custom exhibited a shocking lack of reverence for "the presence of our Lord at the Altar," and Bishop Wing
waged an unrelenting war against it in the *Palm Branch* and in
sermons and talks whenever the opportunity presented itself.[30]

Bishop Wing was a High Churchman in his theological views, but
he did not push an elaborate ceremonial during his tenure as diocesan. He wore cope and mitre only in certain parishes where these
vestments would be appreciated and understood, and during festival
celebrations in the cathedral or the services of the diocesan conventions. He had what he called two "traveling kits" for his visitations,
one "Protestant" and the other "Catholic." The "Protestant kit,"
consisting of the rochet and chimere or traditional "magpies," was
used when he visited most of the parishes and missions of his jurisdiction, while the "Catholic kit" was reserved for the more advanced
parishes such as St. Paul's, Key West, St. Stephen's and St. Agnes's,
Miami, and St. Patrick's, West Palm Beach. Toward the end of his
episcopate he wore cope and mitre more frequently for visitations,
when the clergy requested it. Bishop Wing quietly encouraged the
use of eucharistic vestments, especially those of plain linen, the re-
verencing of the sacrament when it was on the altar, and the reservation of the sacrament for the sick.

29. Ibid., May 1926.
30. Ibid., July 1944.

In his relations with other Christian bodies he was distant. He was opposed to the practice of "open communion" with Protestant bodies because their doctrine of the Eucharist was at variance with the Anglican doctrine and because the practice was expressly forbidden by rubric. He also forbade the use of intinction as a means of administering the Holy Communion. Bishop Wing stood aloof from such Pan-Protestant organizations as the Florida Council of Churches and local ministerial associations, not because he was opposed to cooperation with other Christian bodies, but because he was an ecclesiastical conservative even though he was a social liberal. As an Anglican prelate he believed that he could not take part in Protestant communion services or exchange pulpits with Nonconformist divines. He encouraged his clergy to remain aloof too, not only on the above grounds, but also because they were sometimes asked by their colleagues in the local ministerial associations, who often ignored racial injustice and poverty, to cooperate in such projects as closing bars.

The bishop treasured his home life. It was as quiet and as normal as could be expected with his diocesan travel obligations. During his limited time at home, Mary Wing did her best to shelter her husband from the burdensome ecclesiastical pressures that beset him in the office and on the road. She belonged to few church, civic, and social organizations because she felt they interfered with her attempt to create for herself and her family a calm Christian household. She, too, treasured their home life. Her time was taken up with the oversight of the Bishopstead and the care of their four children. Having been reared in the rectory of bustling St. Luke's Church in Atlanta, she knew the demands that Church people put on the time of their clergy and she was determined to make the best of the cherished hours that the bishop was able to spend with his family.

A remark made by the Rev. Martin J. Bram, a frequent visitor at the Bishopstead, at the celebration of the twentieth anniversary of the bishop's consecration, illustrates the closeness of the Wing family: "We know that if our Bishop were permitted to say anything here, he would insist that without the love and devotion of Mrs. Wing and his children he could hardly have kept up the pace.

We join him in this insistence and sincerely extend our gratitude and affectionate regard to Mrs. Wing and the children."[31]

The Wing children grew up at the Bishopstead. Mary, the eldest, married Douglas Carter and settled in Winter Haven; John Durham, Jr., became a priest and held cures mainly in the East; Breckinridge Wilmer became a physician and returned to practice in Orlando; and Sally, the youngest, married David C. Wilson and moved to Morristown, New Jersey.

When Bishop Wing retired in 1950, he and his wife moved into a small bungalow on Lincoln Circle in Winter Park. In the ten years before his death he took a keen interest in the affairs of the diocese but in no way interfered with the running of it. The new diocesan was a frequent visitor to Lincoln Circle, and the warmth and affection that existed between the young bishop and the old continued to grow over the years. With the Wing children grown and living away from Winter Park with families of their own, the relationship between Bishop Louttit, orphaned at an early age, and the Wings became almost filial. Henry Louttit spoke of their loving relationship in this way: "For nearly thirty years, he was not only my father in God, but in truth a father to me."[32] Bishop and Mrs. Wing were also close to Bishop Louttit's new suffragans, Martin Bram and William F. Moses, and to William L. Hargrave, who had returned from Charleston, South Carolina, as the executive secretary of the diocese.

Bishop Wing was sometimes accused of inflexibility in regard to Churchmanship. These charges, however, were largely groundless. One of the aspects that drew him to the Church was its moderation. He understood the nature of the Church far better than most of the clergy and laity who were born in it. Ceremonially he was a moderate Prayer Book Anglo-Catholic, but he believed that there was an Anglican *via media* in ritual just as there was in theology. Most Southern bishops have been quoted at one time or another as saying, "I am a Catholic, but I am not a ritualist." This could not be said of John Wing. He was a Catholic and a ritualist as well. He had no fear of ritualism, but he had very high standards. He

31. Ibid., September 1945.
32. Ibid., March 1960.

disliked the excesses of the zealous Anglo-Catholics because these were often "apings" of Rome; on the other hand, he was apprehensive about the excessive liberties that some of his evangelical clergy took with the liturgy of the Prayer Book. When a clergyman was "too Roman" or "too Protestant" in his conduct of services, he might be called on the episcopal carpet and gently rebuked. The rebuke, however, was generally the result of the cleric's inflexibility, not the bishop's.

Some accused Bishop Wing of having a "depression mentality," a charge that was not entirely groundless. He began his episcopate at the height of the Florida boom, but not long after his consecration came the bust, followed by the crash of 1929 and the years of the depression. These violent economic contrasts made him cautious with the finances of the diocese, but, if this caution slowed the launching of some of the postwar expansion programs, it also provided the sound financial basis for the growth of the diocese after the bishop retired. During the quarter of a century that Bishop Wing was in office, from 1925 to 1950, it was difficult for any man to escape being marked by the turbulent economic extremes of the era. One of the bishop's greatest accomplishments was that he held his diocese and his people together and kept the Church on the offensive in this difficult time. "When even stout hearts quit," said one veteran clergyman, "our Diocesan kept our courage high."[33]

During Bishop Wing's tenure the diocese made remarkable gains. When he became coadjutor in 1925, the population of the part of the state that constituted the diocese was approximately 680,000. In 1950 when he retired the total population of those same counties was 1,668,000, an increase of 147 per cent. During the same years the number of communicants increased 227 per cent, or 80 per cent more than the population increased.[34] When John Durham Wing was consecrated, the Diocese of South Florida was only two years away from being a missionary district; when he retired it was one of the strongest and most unified dioceses in the entire South.

The quiet decade that the Wings spent together after his retirement was not a healthy one for the bishop. The twenty-five years

33. Ibid., September 1945.
34. Ibid., March 1960.

of his episcopate had made enormous demands on his mental and physical resources. Bishop Wing's heart condition caused his wife and family much anxiety, and in spite of watchful eyes, there were flare-ups from time to time. The coronary problem was complicated by a gradual decline in health, and in the winter of 1959 he was hospitalized for surgery. Just as he was recovering from the effects of the operation he was forced to return to the hospital with a kidney infection. It was from this immediate sickness that he died at 3:30 a.m., February 29, 1960, in the Orange Memorial Hospital in Orlando.[35]

Robed in his episcopal vestments, the bishop was laid in state in the chancel of St. Luke's Cathedral. His coffin was covered with his cope and mitre. The clergy of the Orlando area kept watch until the funeral, which was held at eleven o'clock on the morning of March 3. The Rt. Rev. Henry I. Louttit celebrated the requiem assisted by Bishops Hamilton West of Florida and Spence Burton, S.S.J.E., of Nassau. Three other bishops were in attendance. The officiant at the burial service was the son of Bishop Wing, the Rev. John D. Wing, Jr., rector of St. John's-on-the-Mountain, Bernardville, New Jersey. He was assisted by the Rt. Rev. William F. Moses, Suffragan of South Florida, who read the lessons. Committal was in Palm Cemetery at Winter Park.[36]

In many ways John Durham Wing towered above his episcopal contemporaries in the South. His high standard of worship, his ability as a preacher, and his social and Christian concern for his black communicants put him in a category almost by himself. No prelate understood the background, the failures, the accomplishments, and the hopes of the Anglican Communion better than he. Bishop Wing comprehended its genius, and his episcopate was a witness to its appeal.

35. *Diocesan Journal*, 1960, p. 69; *Palm Branch*, March 1960. The date listed for the bishop's death in the *Journal* memorial is March 6. It is incorrect.

36. Orlando *Evening Sentinel*, March 3, 1960; *Palm Branch*, March 1960.

XVII

The Louttit Episcopate

T HE RESIGNATION OF THE RT. REV. JOHN DURHAM WING, D.D., LL.D., as Bishop of the Diocese of South Florida became effective at midnight, December 31, 1950, when the bishop coadjutor, the Rt. Rev. Henry Irving Louttit, D.D., acceded to all canonical and legal authority. On January 25 Bishop Louttit knocked on the doors of the west portals of his cathedral in Orlando and was conducted to his throne in the sanctuary of the still unfinished church. Bishop Wing presided at the colorful ceremony and handed his pastoral staff to the young man whom he had ordained deacon and priest and consecrated bishop. The enthronement formally marked the end of an era and inaugurated a new ecclesiastical reign.

The new episcopate would witness such advances, such growth in communicant strength and congregations, that even the sizable number of new parishes and missions reported at Bishop Louttit's first convention as diocesan gave but a slight indication of the phenomenal growth to come. Four mission congregations petitioned the 1951 convention held in St. Mary's, Daytona Beach, to be admitted into union with it as self-supporting parishes: Holy Trinity-by-the-Sea, Daytona Beach; Holy Trinity, Melbourne; Trinity, Vero Beach; and St. Mary's, Stuart. During the previous year many new congregations had been formed: Incarnation (Liberty City), Miami; Trinity-by-the-Cove, Naples; St. Ambrose's, Fort Lauderdale; St. Martin's, Pompano Beach; St. David's-by-the-Sea, Cocoa Beach; Glades Cross, Everglades; St. Raphael's, Fort Myers Beach; Messiah, Winter Garden; and St. Thomas of Canterbury, South Miami. Once again the number of confirmations exceeded the figures of any previous year; almost 1,600 persons received the rite of confirmation in 1950.[1]

Bishop Louttit's first convention also reported considerable building among the parishes and missions of the diocese. Probably the most noteworthy building, the only Episcopal church of colonial design in South Florida at that time, was constructed by the newly established congregation of Trinity-by-the-Cove in Naples. The *Palm Branch* described it as "beautifully located near Pirates Cove in one of the more newly developed parts of Naples . . . a commodious and lovely parish church."[2] All Souls' in Miami Beach was in the midst of a campaign to raise funds to erect a church and parish house on its new site in the center of the city. The completed plans called for a church to seat 400 people, a parish house, Sunday school rooms, and the usual administrative offices. The property already had an adequate rectory and was large enough to provide parking facilities for the growing congregation. It was hoped that the new church would be in use by Christmas, 1951. Several months before the convention, the newly organized mission of the Incarnation in Liberty City with the help of the diocese secured a frame building which was moved to its property. Plans were implemented to renovate the building and to make necessary additions so that it could be used as a church.

Expanding churches in the diocese were fortunate to receive aid from the National Church for some construction. Early in 1951 the National Council made available to the dioceses as loans a sum of money held in the Advance and Reconstruction Account for eventual use in China. Because of the turbulent political situation in

1. Henry Irving Louttit, *Episcopal Address* (South Florida), 1951, pp. 47–48.

2. *Palm Branch*, April 1951. The editor erred in calling Trinity-by-the-Cove a parish; it had only recently been organized as a mission.

China the money could not be spent for construction there, so the Council thought it wise to lend the funds to dioceses in the United States where growing populations demanded new churches. The Diocese of South Florida, which had vigorously supported the Advance and Reconstruction Campaign, borrowed $90,000.

From this fund the trustees and executive board of the diocese loaned $35,000 to the Church of the Resurrection, Miami. Construction quickly began on the first unit of its new plant, a parish house and certain Sunday school rooms, on the property that the mission had acquired in Biscayne Park. The congregation planned to use the Parish house for worship until a church could be constructed. $10,000 was loaned to St. Martin's Mission in Pompano Beach, and construction began on a combination church and parish house. A third loan of $25,000 was made available to the newly organized Church of the Epiphany in the Hialeah–Miami Springs area of Dade County. The balance of the fund was earmarked for St. Ambrose's Mission on the St. Petersburg Beaches.

With aid from the diocesan Advance Work Fund, St. Michael's Mission in Orlando was able to obtain a local mortgage to erect a combination church and parish house. In Volusia County St. James's, Ormond Beach, and St. Mary's, Daytona, began new parish houses. During the previous year St. Andrew's, Lake Worth, made considerable additions to its parish house, and the Ascension, Clearwater, purchased property across the street from the church with plans to use the large house on it for educational and social purposes. New rectories were acquired by the congregations in Fort Lauderdale, Kissimmee, and Brooksville.[3] All of this activity reported at Bishop Louttit's first convention reflected a growing Church in a growing state.

The most important matter to come before the 1951 convention was the election of a suffragan bishop. After Bishop Wing announced his proposed retirement to the diocese in April 1950, a special convention was called for the following September in Orlando. This body appointed a committee to receive nominations for suffragan. The Rev. Richard I. Brown of Fort Myers, chairman of the committee, reported to the regularly scheduled conven-

3. Ibid.

tion in Daytona that the following names had been received: the Rev. Martin J. Bram of Holy Trinity, West Palm Beach; the Rev. Clarence W. Brickman of St. John's, Tampa; the Rev. Mark T. Carpenter of All Saints', Fort Lauderdale; the Rev. Don H. Copeland of St. James's, South Bend, Indiana; the Rev. William L. Hargrave of Holy Communion, Charleston, South Carolina; and the Rev. William F. Moses of All Saints', Lakeland. Opportunity was given for nominations from the floor, but as none were made, balloting began by order, the clergy and laity voting separately. The first ballot showed the Rev. Martin J. Bram far ahead of the closest contender, the Rev. Mark T. Carpenter, with a plurality of both clerical and lay votes. On the second ballot Father Bram received the majority of the votes cast by both orders. Upon motion the election, which was characterized by extraordinary charity and good will, was made unanimous.[4]

Father Bram had been ably prepared for his new position. Born in New York City, September 25, 1897, the suffragan-elect attended public schools there. In 1926 he received his B.A. degree, *magna cum laude,* from Hobart College in Geneva, New York. The following fall he entered Virginia Seminary at Alexandria where he received his B.D. degree in 1929. Although a native New Yorker, Bram chose to be a postulant and candidate from the Diocese of Delaware because its bishop, the Rt. Rev. Philip Cook, had been vicar of his church when he was a boy. Bishop Cook ordained Bram deacon in June 1928, and priest in 1929. Father Bram began his clerical career as rector of St. Philip's Church, Georgetown, Delaware. In 1933 he came to South Florida as rector of the Church of the Holy Cross, Sanford. While in Sanford he married Mabel Harris Bowler. In 1941 he accepted a call to be rector of St. Andrew's, Tampa, where he remained until 1945 when he became rector of Holy Trinity, West Palm Beach.

During his years in South Florida Father Bram served as a member of the Board of Managers of the Cathedral School, as a member and for ten years president of the Standing Committee, and as a member of the Trustees of the Diocese and of the Executive Board. He was secretary of the diocesan Board of Examining

4. *Diocesan Journal,* 1951, pp. 35–36.

Chaplains from 1936 until his election and for three years served
as president of that board for the Province of Sewanee. He ran
Camp St. Mark for four years and for five years was director of
the annual adult conference held at Camp Wingmann. Four times
he was elected a deputy to the General Convention.[5] Seldom does
any one parish give two successive rectors to the episcopate; however, this case was even more unusual as the careers of these two
friends, Bishops Louttit and Bram, were so similar. Both attended
Hobart College, joined Kappa Sigma Fraternity, were members of
Phi Beta Kappa, went to Virginia Seminary, and were rectors at
Sanford and West Palm Beach.

Martin Bram was consecrated on St. Matthew's Day, September
21, 1951, in his parish church, Holy Trinity, West Palm Beach.
The consecrator was Bishop Louttit; the coconsecrators were
Bishops C. Avery Mason of Dallas and Spence Burton of Nassau.
The Rt. Rev. Francis Eric Bloy, Bishop of Los Angeles, flew from
California to preach the sermon.[6] At his consecration Bishop Bram
was presented with a cope and mitre and a gift of money for other
vestments from the diocesan Women's Auxiliary, and with a pectoral cross and chain, a complete set of episcopal robes, and a wrist-
watch from his former parishioners at Holy Trinity.[7] The new
suffragan and Mrs. Bram took up residence in Orlando.

Soon after Martin Bram's consecration both bishops turned their
attention to the Advance Work Campaign. Three important projects hinged on its successful conclusion: missionary expansion, the
establishment of a home for elderly people, and the construction of
a student center at the University of Miami. The bishops hoped
that by the end of 1953 the congregations of South Florida would
raise half the $330,000 originally set as the goal for the campaign,
but actually by that date only $130,000 had been raised, a figure
which included an individual gift of $26,000 from Mrs. Flagler
Matthews of Palm Beach.[8] The diocese, however, continued its

5. *Palm Branch*, May 1951.
6. Ibid., October 1951.
7. Martin Bram, *Suffragan Bishop's Address*, 1951, pp. 55–56.
8. Louttit, *Episcopal Address* (South Florida), 1954, p. 68. By 1955,
when the diocese quietly abandoned the campaign, approximately $148,000

missionary expansion using the $90,000 loan from the National Council for church construction, saving the bulk of the $130,000 collected in the Advance Work Campaign to complete the Miami Student Center and to acquire property for a home for the elderly.

The delegates to the 1950 diocesan convention had been so impressed by the urgency of the Church's work at the University of Miami that there was talk of raising $50,000 to build a student center and of employing a full-time chaplain on the campus.[9] Although the student center was not built for several years, a priest was engaged. The Rev. William Ward took up his duties as full-time chaplain in time for the fall term, 1950. At the next convention he reported his impression of the bustling campus and its cosmopolitan students: "Within the past five years the University of Miami has grown to be the largest educational institution in the State of Florida—with a total enrollment of over 11,000 students. Of these 650 indicate affiliation with the Episcopal Church. Our people come from 31 states, and from Brazil, Cuba, Costa Rica, the Canal Zone, France, Honolulu and the Netherlands. Half of this number come from Florida. It is interesting in breaking down these figures to note that the Roman Catholics claim the largest percentage of students and faculty, some 2,400—with the Jewish faith numbering 2,100."

The chaplain painted a vivid picture of his handicaps: "Cramped as we are, *without any facilities whatsoever*, it is a problem as to what we can do about religious activities for our students. For formal programs we have been given the use of St. Philip's Parish House in Coral Gables—for other activities we 'camp around' wherever we can—and adapt our program accordingly. It is not difficult to understand that the Church cannot make any headway on this campus so remote from any parish. *We must have a building.* The Methodists have just allocated $100,000 towards a building. The Roman Catholics and the Presbyterians (both of whom have assigned new full-time workers since my appointment), are

had been raised, which included an additional gift of $12,000 from Mrs. Matthews. *Diocesan Journal*, 1955, pp. 115–18.

9. *Diocesan Journal*, 1950, p. 90.

ready to build. Hillel is to build a second building on a more suitable site."[10]

Within a year Father Ward had his wish. A student center costing approximately $65,000 was constructed with funds from the Advance Work Campaign as a memorial to the late Bishop Cameron Mann. Included in the new building were a student lounge, a library, a chaplain's office and residence quarters, a covered patio, and a temporary chapel. The building was formally dedicated by Bishop Louttit in April 1952.[11]

In the summer of 1951 the diocese, through the corporation known as the Board of Trustees of St. Luke's Hospital, bought the Holly Hill Hotel in Davenport, Florida, located some four miles north of Haines City. This frame building, purchased fully equipped for the sum of $35,000, became a long-dreamed-of home for older people.[12] Within a year there were twenty-six guests in the facility, twenty-three women and three men. The home was appropriately called the William Crane Gray Inn for Older People, or in its shortened form, Gray Inn. The trustees of St. Luke's Hospital then turned over its assets to the newly established Board of Trustees of Gray Inn with the stipulation that the assets be used only for the care of older people. According to the new suffragan bishop, life at the inn was similar "to that of any Christian family. The day begins with breakfast at 8 o'clock, followed by Morning Prayer read in the chapel on week days, dinner at 12 Noon, and supper at 5:30 p.m. . . . Most of our guests are active and occupy their time with needle work and light duties in connection with the operation of the Home. These duties, such as having charge of the linen room, flower arrangements, library, Altar, and ground beautification, etc., are offered to various guests at their request." Committees were formed to promote numerous other activities designed to keep the guests constructively busy. Social occasions were provided by church groups in such neighboring cities as Kissimmee, Winter Haven, Lakeland, and Haines City. These consisted of movies, teas, rides, visits to places of interest, concerts, and entertainment in

10. Ibid., 1951, pp. 97–98.
11. *Palm Branch*, June 1952.
12. *Diocesan Journal*, 1952, p. 115; also *Palm Branch*, October 1951.

private homes. A station wagon was purchased to furnish transportation for shopping, church, and movies. The worship and social activities of Gray Inn were under the direction of a resident retired priest, the Rev. Warren C. Cable.

The inn contained twenty-six bedrooms, sixteen with private bath and steam heat and ten in the older part of the building with two community baths and a gas heater. Shortly after the inn was acquired four new baths were added in the old wing so that those ten rooms were supplied with either private or connecting baths. The heating system was extended as well, and an elevator, which proved to be a great comfort to the more infirm residents, was given to the inn through a gift of Mrs. W. D. McCreery of All Saints', Winter Park. The dining and kitchen facilities were sufficient to accommodate approximately fifty guests, but as there were room accommodations for only about half that number the diocese started a building fund to construct an additional twenty bedrooms, an adequate infirmary, and a chapel.[13]

Christmas at Gray Inn gave the nearby church people and civic groups an outlet for their holiday altruism. A Christmas tree was given and trimmed by the women of St. Mark's. The Carl Floyd family of Haines City brought a movie and served refreshments following it. On another night the girls' choir from St. Paul's, Winter Haven, sang carols, while the ladies of St. Paul's served ice cream and cake to all, leaving two large jars of cookies for the guests. The residents were also treated to a Christmas concert by the Haines City High School Glee Club. Members of the Women's Auxiliary throughout the diocese showered the Inn with what were called "White Christmas Gifts"—sheets, pillow cases, and towels.[14] Under the leadership of Bishop Bram, the entire diocese came eventually to share in this endeavor of Christian social relations.

With the successful completion of the student centers at the Universities of Miami and Florida, the purchase of Gray Inn, and the steady advance of new mission churches in the diocese, the Advance Work Campaign lost much of its momentum. There were several reasons for this. During the immediate postwar years and

13. Bram, *Suffragan Bishop's Address*, 1953, pp. 63–64.
14. *Palm Branch*, January 1953.

the early 1950s most of the parishes and older missions of South Florida which were engaged in construction or expansion projects of their own saw the continued demand for funds by the National Church and the diocese as an impediment to local growth. Even so, the churches of the diocese contributed approximately $125,000 to the Advance and Reconstruction Fund of the National Church and to the Presiding Bishop's Fund for World Relief, and in most cases the diocese oversubscribed these projects during a period of four years. When the most important tasks of the diocesan Advance Work Campaign had been accomplished, even though they constituted only half the number of projects planned, the local congregations naturally turned their thoughts and their funds to their own needs. Besides, they knew that the General Convention was planning to embark on another campaign for capital funds in the near future. Early in 1954, "without too much prior warning" from the National Council, the goal of this "Builders for Christ" campaign was announced to be $4,500,000. The Diocese of South Florida's share was over $61,000,[15] and in addition the diocese contracted to raise $3,500 to help equip the Protestant Radio Center in Atlanta.[16]

In early 1954 Bishop Bram suffered a heart attack brought on by the strain of keeping pace with the constant growth of the diocese. It was evident to Bishop Louttit that he needed additional help while his suffragan was recovering and even after Bishop Bram was well enough to return to his duties. In an effort to lessen the pressure on Bishop Bram and himself and to make the diocesan office more efficient, Bishop Louttit engaged an old friend and colleague, the Rev. William L. Hargrave, who returned to the diocese from South Carolina where he was rector of the Church of the Holy Communion, Charleston. Father Hargrave became executive secretary of the Diocese of South Florida, administrative assistant to the bishop, and actuary of the diocese. He was also installed as canon to the ordinary in the Cathedral Church of St. Luke. The new executive secretary was admirably qualified for his position. He had a firsthand knowledge of the diocese from his years in Cocoa,

15. Louttit, *Episcopal Address* (South Florida), 1954, pp. 67–68.
16. *Diocesan Journal*, 1955, pp. 117–18.

Fort Pierce, and Miami, and he retained an intimate command of its administrative problems from the many terms he had served on the important committees of the diocesan conventions. He was also a graduate in law. It was his responsibility to handle matters of property and finance, to manage Camp Wingmann, to free the bishop from the business affairs of the diocese, and to represent him at various meetings of boards and committees.[17]

Work among the Negroes of South Florida was given the same care and attention under Bishop Louttit that it had enjoyed during the episcopate of Bishop Wing. The Ven. John E. Culmer continued as Archdeacon for Negro Work, and his annual reports to the diocesan conventions showed a steady if unspectacular growth in black communicants. In his report to the 1951 convention Archdeacon Culmer stated that the Diocese of South Florida ranked fourth in the nation in number of Negro communicants and that it had by far the largest number in the South. Ten priests and one deacon served the two parishes and eighteen missions. Of the 25,199 communicants in South Florida some 4,655 were black; and of the 38,061 baptized persons, 5,611 were black.[18] A glance at the parochial reports for the year indicates that Father Culmer, as rector of St. Agnes's Church, Miami, presided over the largest parish in the diocese.

The Negro Episcopalians of South Florida resented the continued legal segregation of the races, and during the early years of the Louttit episcopate, many Negroes expressed opposition to the practice. Since the majority of South Florida's black clergy and laity originally immigrated from the British West Indies where segregation was not practiced in either church or state, they were more vocal than their counterparts in other dioceses. As Episcopalians they naturally looked to their Church for support in their fight against injustice.

Resentment against legal segregation began to show itself during the period of idealism that accompanied the entry of the United States into World War II. To many Negroes the war was being waged abroad to stamp out racism, while at home the same sort

17. Louttit, *Episcopal Address* (South Florida), 1954, pp. 66-67.
18. *Diocesan Journal*, 1951, p. 99.

of racism, although less brutal, was sanctioned in the practice of legal segregation. Negro Episcopalians felt that continued segregation in their own country was almost blasphemous. A report in the columns of the 1942 *St. Agnes's Herald*, the parish paper of Archdeacon Culmer's church, expressed strong opposition to the practice of dividing the races during diocesan banquets. The convention banquet that year was held at the Orlando Country Club with Bishops Frank A. Juhan of Florida and Campbell Gray of Northern Indiana as the speakers. Father Culmer noted with sarcasm, "The colored delegates did not *choose* to attend." Instead, the Negroes banqueted at the Hungerford School in splendid segregation. The archdeacon described the affair. "We had a jolly good time, the after dinner speeches were too long and in some cases too serious for the occasion, and in some of the speeches, there was an undertone of awareness that even the Church of God has not yet attained unto her ideal of Christian Democracy and all inclusive Catholicity. . . . There are still some walls of Jericho which Christian trumpeters have not yet been able to *make* fall down [but] they are tottering."[19]

White Churchmen of the time had varied views about race. There were a few, mostly clergymen, who favored immediate integration. There were some moderates who saw the injustice of segregation but pleaded for time to prepare the people for the change to integration. They considered themselves "Christian Realists" and believed that the Kingdom of God and integration would come *gradually*—"in the fullness of time." The vast majority of white communicants were happy with the status quo. They either favored segregation or refused to sanction integration on the grounds that it would create enormous social problems. In the conventions Archdeacon Culmer led the integrationists for many years, while the moderates were led by the compassionate rector of All Saints', Lakeland, the Rev. William F. Moses. The champion of the segregationist cause was an indomitable vestryman from St. John's, Tampa, General Sumter Lowry.

No man realized the wrongs of segregation more fully than Archdeacon Culmer, yet he knew that South Florida had progressed

19. *St. Agnes's Herald*, May 1942.

further in racial relations than the other Southern dioceses: "Although we shepherd and feed in different pastures—some of them not so green—our annual meeting in Diocesan Convention demonstrates to others, and should be a source of satisfaction to us, that at least, on the diocesan level, we are not totally disobedient to the divine injunction that 'there shall be one fold and one shepherd.' "[20]

The most tender racial nerve in the diocese was Camp Wingmann. For almost two decades the diocese had promised to embark on a project of building a camp for the Negro youth of the Church, and at one point a prominent Negro layman from Daytona Beach agreed to donate property to the diocese once funds had been obtained for building. Nothing was done, for two reasons: first, since the camp facilities near Avon Park were not really completed until the early 1950s, all available funds were channeled there; and second, the Negro congregations were in no financial position to take on a project of such magnitude without help. Negro youths, therefore, had no camp, nor were they encouraged to use Camp Wingmann for a segregated session. They found this particularly galling since Camp St. Francis, a session for white underprivileged non-Church children, had been held under diocesan auspices for several years. A segregated session at Camp Wingmann would have fulfilled at least the legal ideal of "separate but equal" facilities.

When the first and only session for Negroes, Camp St. Peter, was finally held in the summer of 1953, the campers were not permitted to use Camp Wingmann. A Boy Scout camp near Princeton, called Camp Rocky Pine, was rented instead. The session was directed by the Rev. Elisha S. Clarke, Jr., vicar of St. Matthew's Church, Delray Beach. The camp was coeducational and its routine was similar to the routine of sessions at Camp Wingmann. Each day began with matins and a celebration of "Low Mass" and ended with compline. The campers enjoyed a varied athletic program under the Rev. John J. Jarrett, Jr., vicar of the Church of the Incarnation, Liberty City, Miami, and an academic program consisting of courses on the catechism, church music, and altar work was also offered. Ninety-four boys and girls were present from nine

20. *Diocesan Journal*, 1952, p. 109.

congregations. The Rev. Theodore Gibson served as the camp chaplain.[21] Although Camp St. Peter was a success in its first year, the diocesan Department of Camps and Conferences decided to cancel the session the following year. The department could not find adequate facilities for the camp, and it was financially impossible to build a separate Negro camp north of the Camp Wingmann property even though the construction would be aided by money released from the "St. Alban's Fund," which the diocese had acquired when the property of old St. Alban's School in Miami was sold by the trustees several years earlier.[22]

It became unnecessary to construct a separate camp, however, when the United States Supreme Court decision in 1954 outlawed school segregation. Many thoughtful Churchmen began to see the significance of the court's voice in ecclesiastical as well as in social affairs. They felt that, if it was now illegal as well as undemocratic to segregate children in school, it would certainly be unethical, to say the least, to segregate them in a Church camp. This was probably not the majority opinion among the laity as a whole, but it was the opinion of most of those who assembled to face the problem at the Diocesan Convention of 1955. At this convention the Church in the Diocese of South Florida did not join the state in its efforts at procrastination, but spoke out clearly and firmly for the decision of the court.

Bishop Louttit tackled the issue of segregation in his opening address when from the pulpit of All Saints' Church, Fort Lauderdale, he delivered one of the most powerful sermons ever preached in the history of the diocese, taking as his text *Galatians 3:27–28*, "For as many of you as have been baptized into Christ have put on Christ. There is neither Jew nor Greek, there is neither bond nor free, there is neither male nor female; for ye are all one in Christ." The bishop began by asking several probing questions: "What has the Christian faith and the Christian Church to say of racial antagonism? of unreasoned prejudice? of unjust discrimination? of enforced segregation?" He then proceeded to answer these questions before a spellbound congregation. It was during this

21. *Palm Branch*, May 1953; October 1953.
22. *Diocesan Journal*, 1954, pp. 125–26.

convention that the Rev. Clifton H. White of All Saints', Lakeland, moved that the Department of Camps and Conferences "be instructed to authorize each Camp Director and Conference Head to accept enrollments at Camp Wingmann, without respect to race or color." The motion was carried. Archdeacon Culmer, speaking for his flock, called Bishop Louttit's sermon "one of the boldest, most courageous, most fearless and straightforward messages on the subject of desegregation it has been our good fortune to hear anywhere."[23]

The following summer, Camp Wingmann was integrated. There were only 18 Negro children enrolled out of a total of 580 in all the sessions. "Because of the splendid character of all our children, white and negro, a good spirit prevailed," the *Palm Branch* reported.[24] The integration of Camp Wingmann brought a Vesuvian eruption from a group of conservative Churchmen under the leadership of the colorful and plainspoken Sumter Lowry of St. John's Church, Tampa. The segregationists pointed out that the integrated sessions of the past summer were attended by only eighteen black children, while the one segregated session the previous year was attended by ninety-four. This proved, according to them, that the Negro children and their parents *preferred* their own session. In short, segregated sessions would bring more children of both races under the wholesome influence of the Church during the summer.

Integration obviously was by no means a settled question. The following year, 1956, when the Diocesan Convention met in the Church of the Redeemer in Sarasota, the segregationists made a last desperate effort to secure racially divided sessions of the camp. Although General Lowry was not a delegate his spirit permeated a group of his followers. A. Pickens Coles of the general's home parish presented a resolution that the integration of the camp be rescinded and that the directors be instructed "to open enrollments to white and negro persons . . . at separate camp sessions held for each race." Mr. Coles also cleverly moved that the motion be presented without debate and that the vote be taken by secret ballot. There was much excitement. Bishop Louttit ruled that the convention vote first on

23. Ibid., 1955, p. 143.
24. *Palm Branch*, October 1955.

the motion pertaining to the method of balloting. The motion for a secret ballot was soundly defeated. Mr. Coles then moved that the resolution be presented without debate. The motion was carried. The delegate from Tampa again presented the first part of his resolution, whereupon the chancellor of the diocese, the Hon. Lawrence Rogers of Kissimmee, moved that the motion be laid on the table. It was moved that a record vote be taken. The motion was carried. The motion to table the Coles resolution was carried by an overwhelming majority; it was never reintroduced.[25]

Most Episcopalians were opposed to extremes. The thinking laity were probably gradual integrationists who did not want to uproot violently the social traditions of their Southern heritage or undermine the fabric of public education. They pleaded moderation to both the black and the white extremes. To Negro communicants of South Florida "gradual integration" seemed a long time in coming, and it was not uncommon for them to express their impatience. Often this impatience was laced with humor.

An amusing story, perhaps apocryphal, about the white "gradualists" in the neighboring Diocese of Florida circulated freely in South Florida. At an integrated clergy conference held at Camp Weed on the northern Gulf Coast, a number of white clergy were urging the black rector of St. Michael and All Angels Church in Tallahassee, the Rev. David H. Brooks, who was standing on the dock, to join them in swimming. Father Brooks politely declined. Again the clergymen, splashing merrily in the water, enthusiastically repeated the invitation, but again it was politely declined. Finally one good-natured cleric called to the black priest from the water, "David, if I were drowning, would you jump in and save me?" "Yes," replied Father Brooks after a moment of thought. "Gradually."

Through the 1940s and the 1950s Father Culmer led the Negroes of South Florida in demanding their civil as well as their ecclesiastical rights. His address before the Diocesan Convention of 1955 concerning the Supreme Court decision is an example of the moderation, realism, and Christianity that were in him: "Perhaps some of you would like to know what Negroes are thinking. And I

25. *Diocesan Journal,* 1956, pp. 39–44.

answer: The Negroes' thinking on this subject is as varied as that of white neighbors. There is no set pattern. There are some who want to see immediate implementation of the Supreme Court's Order; while others, like myself, must know that where there is determined resistance, change, of necessity, must be a gradual process.

"It is not a question of whether the Negroes want this change. But it is a question of whether or not we, as law-abiding, peace-loving, Godfearing citizens of the United States whose highest court, constituted of nine good men (all white men), some of the ablest of them proud sons of the South, shall uphold the majesty of the law.

"I crave your indulgence while I again repeat the prophetic words of an astute southern statesman, a Kentuckian by birth, a great secretary of state, Henry Clay by name:

" 'Years of close observation and study have led me to the conclusion that the stability of this nation depends upon the perpetuation of two institutions—the Supreme Court of the United States and the Protestant Episcopal Church.' The Supreme Court of the United States has spoken; can the great Episcopal Church afford to hold her peace?"[26]

Father Culmer was obviously a powerful speaker, which enhanced his remarkable career as a church and civic leader in South Florida. He was born in Savannah Sound, the Bahamas, and received his B.D. degree from Bishop Payne Divinity School, his LL.D. from Bethune-Cookman College, and his D.D. from Virginia Seminary. His D.D. was bestowed upon him as "one of the nation's great humanitarians." He was the author of several books including *A Manual for Catholic Worship*, *The Responsibility of the Negro*, and *Born in a Washtub*. He also contributed regularly to the Miami *Times*. Father Culmer spoke out courageously against racial injustice throughout his life. But with his death in 1963 an era ended: it was time for resistance less passive than his to racial segregation.

Even before Archdeacon Culmer's death the mantle of racial leadership passed to a group of more aggressive clergy and laity. The impatient Negro communicants of the diocese came under the

26. Ibid., 1955, p. 146.

influence of the Rev. Theodore Gibson, rector of Christ Church, Miami. Father Gibson and his followers took a prominent part in the actions of Negro rights groups. He demonstrated vigorously against continued segregation in public institutions and places of business and, like other Negro and white Churchmen, suffered arrest for his part in the demonstrations. But he had the pleasure of seeing the barriers of public segregation come crashing down under continuous pressure. These more aggressive Episcopalians accomplished much, but much of what they did accomplish was built on foundations laid by John E. Culmer and men like him.

It is impossible to chronicle the founding and development of every new mission and parish during the Louttit episcopate, there was so much new growth. The following chart shows the astonishing number of new missions formed in the diocese during the decade of the 1950s.[27]

CHURCHES ORGANIZED DURING THE 1950s

Mission	Convention Year Organized	Year Mission Became Parish
Anna Maria, Annunciation	1953	
Belleair, Epiphany	1954	
Belle Glade, St. John's	1954	
Boca Raton, St. Gregory's	1954	1960
Boynton Beach, St. Cuthbert's	1953	
Boynton Beach, St. Joseph's	1954	1957
Brooksville, St. John's (reorganized)	1950	
Clearwater, Good Samaritan	1956	1961
Cocoa Beach, St. David's	1951	1958
Crystal River, St. Ann's	1959	
Englewood, St. David's	1957	
Everglades, Glades Cross	1951	
Fort Lauderdale, Intercession	1958	
St. Ambrose's	1957	1959
*St. Christopher's	1951	
St. Mark's	1954	1959
Fort Myers, St. Hilary's	1959	
Fort Myers Beach, St. Raphael's	1951	1966

27. *Diocesan Journal*, 1950–1969, *passim*. Those missions with asterisks were in existence earlier as unorganized missions.

Hallendale, *St. Ann's	1951	
Homestead, St. Cyprian's	1959	
Indian Rocks, Calvary	1954	1962
Indiantown, Blessed Sacrament	1959	
Jupiter, Good Shepherd	1958	
Key West, Holy Innocents'	1957	
Lakeland, St. David's	1954	1957
Lake Placid, St. Francis's	1957	
Lake Worth, St. Francis's	1953	
Largo, St. Dunstan's	1958	1966
Maitland, Good Shepherd (reorganized)	1956	
Marathon, St. Columba's	1954	
Miami, Holy Angels (Norwood)	1956	
*Incarnation	1951	
St. Aidan's ⎫ united to form	1954	
St. Jude's ⎬ St. Paul's, 1965	1954	
St. Faith's (Perrine)	1955	1964
St. Matthew's	1959	
St. Simon's	1957	
Miami Springs, All Angels' (Holy Family)	1958	1962
Mount Dora, St. Edward's	1956	
Mulberry, St. Luke's	1953	
Naples, Trinity-by-the-Cove	1951	1955
Okeechobee, Our Saviour	1952	
Opa Locka, St. Kevin's	1955	
Transfiguration	1958	
Orlando, Christ the King	1954	
Emmanuel	1954	
Holy Family	1956	
St. Michael's	1950	1953
Palm River, St. Cecilia's	1956	
Pine Castle, St. Mary of the Angels	1958	1963
Pompano Beach, St. Martin's	1951	1954
St. Petersburg, *St. Augustine's	1951	
St. Bede's (parochial mission)	1952	1954
St. Giles's (Pinellas Park)	1958	
St. Matthew's	1958	1959
St. Thomas's (parochial mission)	1952	1954
St. Vincent's	1955	1959
St. Petersburg Beach, Advent (now St. Alban's)	1951	1953

Sanibel Island, St. Michael's	1959	
Sarasota, St. Boniface	1955	1961
St. Wilfred's	1959	
South Miami, St. Thomas's	1951	
South Patrick Shores, Holy Apostles		
(Satellite Beach)	1958	
Tampa, St. Chad's	1954	
St. Clement's	1957	
St. Francis's (formerly a		
parochial mission)	1951	1960
Temple Terrace, St. Catherine's	1958	
Valrico, Holy Innocents'	1957	
Wauchula, St. Ann's	1950	
West Hollywood, Holy Sacrament	1956	
West Palm Beach, Grace	1956	1961
Holy Spirit	1954	1956
Winter Garden, Messiah	1951	
Winter Park, St. Richard's	1957	
Zephyrhills, St. Elizabeth's	1957	

Much of this missionary expansion was made possible through the generosity of Mrs. Flagler Matthews, who established the Henry Morrison Flagler Memorial Fund in memory of her grandfather in 1949. The original corpus was $50,000 to be used for loans to new missions at no interest. Several years later an additional $100,000 was placed into the memorial to be loaned to missions, on a revolving basis.[28]

The extraordinary growth of the Church in St. Petersburg during this era provides a typical example of the Church's development throughout the diocese. In May 1946 when Bishop Louttit attended his first diocesan convention as suffragan, in St. Petersburg, there were only two congregations in that city: St. Peter's, a large and active church of 1,350 communicants, and St. Bartholomew's, a struggling mission of 135 communicants. Seven years later when the 1953 convention assembled in the same city, St. Peter's reported a congregation of 1,547, and St. Bartholomew's had become a strong parish of 480 communicants.

28. *Palm Branch*, June 1949; interview, the Rt. Rev. William L. Hargrave, October 10, 1972.

As a result of the missionary efforts of these two churches in the intervening years, four new congregations were established. In 1946 St. Peter's, in cooperation with the diocese and the National Church, helped St. Augustine's mission in the Negro section of the city find adequate land to build an attractive church. In 1950 the Church of the Advent was established on St. Petersburg Beach, sponsored by St. Bartholomew's. This mission quickly attained self-sufficiency, and three years later when it was admitted by the diocesan convention as a parish of 168 communicants it possessed a large and attractive building on a well-located lot. In 1952 St. Peters's, under the direction of its missionary-minded rector, the Rev. James L. Duncan, helped establish two more new missions: St. Thomas's and St. Bede's. St. Thomas's, which reported 122 communicants at the 1953 convention, became self-supporting almost immediately. Land was purchased on Snell Isle, and the congregation busied itself with plans for a church. St. Bede's, technically a parochial mission of St. Peter's, rapidly approached self-support. The congregation erected on its large property in north St. Petersburg a building designed to serve as a church and parish house, together with an attractive vicarage. While in 1946 only three clergymen were at work in the St. Petersburg area, there were six resident in 1953, with St. Augustine's served by the vicar of St. James's, Tampa.[29] Two other new missions, St. Matthew's and St. Vincent's, started in the late fifties, reached parish status. A third mission, St. Giles's in Pinellas Park, was organized in 1958. When the decade of the fifties ended all of the churches in the St. Petersburg area with the exception of St. Augustine's and St. Giles's had reached parish status. The following statistics, taken from the parochial report of 1960, illustrate the remarkable progress of the Church in the St. Petersburg area:[30]

CHURCHES	1946	1953	1959
St. Bartholomew's	135	480	749
St. Peter's	1,350	1,549	1,839
St. Augustine's	22	30	26
St. Bede's		127	532

29. Louttit, *Episcopal Address* (South Florida), 1953, p. 55.
30. *Diocesan Journal*, 1960, *Parochial Reports*.

St. Thomas's		122	497
Advent (now St. Alban's)		168	391
St. Matthew's			202
St. Vincent's			329
St. Giles's			44
Totals	1,507	2,476	4,609

Although the growth of the Church was not so marked in the rest of the diocese as it was in St. Petersburg, it was nonetheless astounding. Struggling old congregations became self-supporting, vibrant new churches became parishes, and missions popped up by the dozen, according to the parochial reports of every diocesan convention during the amazing first years of the Louttit episcopate.

XVIII

Growth and Division

THE PROBLEMS WHICH CONFRONTED THE TWO BISHOPS DURING the dynamic growth of the diocese in the first half of the fifties drained Bishop Bram of much of his physical energy. Within two years of his consecration a coronary thrombosis incapacitated him for several months, but he recovered and resumed a full schedule of activity. His work during the last years of his life was particularly strenuous and his schedule exhausting. On February 8, 1956, he attended a pre-Lenten clergy retreat at the Good Shepherd Monastery in Orange City. The following morning he rose at six for the service of Lauds and returned to the chapel for the service of Prime followed by a celebration of the Eucharist. Bishop Bram died of a heart attack while sitting on the steps of the chapel waiting for Prime to begin. In the previous service he had just said the somber words of the ninetieth psalm: "The days of our age are threescore years and ten; and though men be so strong that they come to fourscore years, yet is their strength then but labour and sorrow; so soon passeth it away, and we are gone."

Bishop Bram did not attain even threescore years; he was fifty-eight when he died. He was buried from the cathedral on the morning of February 11. The Rt. Rev. John D. Wing read the burial office, and his old friend Henry Louttit celebrated the requiem. Interment was made in Glen Haven Cemetery, Winter Park, with the Rev. Canon William L. Hargrave reading the office. Bishop Bram was survived by his widow, Mabel B. Bram.

Martin Bram was sorely missed. In addition to assisting Bishop Louttit with the grueling rounds of administrative work, he met an ever-increasing number of confirmation visitations and speaking engagements. He was also chairman of the Department of College Work, editor of the *Palm Branch*, and chairman of the Executive Committee of Bishop Gray Inn. No man missed him more than Bishop Louttit: "The personal loss to me will be even greater because our association began as fraternity brothers at Hobart College, continued as classmates at Virginia Seminary, and after a few brief years while he served in the Diocese of Delaware, continued through the years as we served as Priests and finally as Bishops in the Diocese of South Florida. In the early years, soon after ordination, we always took our vacations together, many times we have made our retreats together."[1]

The Diocesan Convention of 1956 meeting in Sarasota filled the vacuum caused by Bishop Bram's death by electing the Rev. William Francis Moses, host rector, as suffragan. A total of twelve men were nominated for this office. The election came on the sixth ballot when Father Moses received 54 clerical and 137 lay votes. Other leading contenders were the Rev. James L. Duncan and Canon William L. Hargrave. The election was made unanimous the following morning.

Father Moses was a moderate progressive in his political and racial views and a moderate Catholic in his views on Churchmanship. He was born in Atlanta, Georgia, February 6, 1898, and attended public school in his native city. He received his higher education from The Georgia Institute of Technology and The University of the South, where he obtained a license in theology. He was ordained both deacon in 1924 and priest in 1925 by Bishop Mikell of Atlanta. He married Cornelia Chaffee in 1923, and to them were born three children: Frank, Carol, and Cornelia. The bishop-elect started his ministry in the Diocese of Atlanta, with charges in Cedartown and Cartersville. Later he took the cure of the

1. *Diocesan Journal*, 1956, p. 72; *Palm Branch*, March 1956.

church in Sheffield-Tuscumbia, Alabama. He came to the Diocese of South Florida as rector of All Saints', Lakeland, in 1930, and continued there until 1952 when he became rector of Redeemer Church, Sarasota. In addition to serving as a member of the Executive Board of the diocese, secretary of the Diocesan Convention, an examining chaplain, and a representative to the Anglican Congress, he was six times elected a clerical delegate to the General Convention.[2] In his spare time, Father Moses was an avid reader of detective stories and an even more avid fisherman.

The former rector of Redeemer Church, Sarasota, was consecrated suffragan in his old parish on St. Luke's Day, October 18, 1956. The Rt. Rev. Henry Knox Sherrill, Presiding Bishop of the American Church, was the consecrator and the Rt. Revs. Henry I. Louttit and John D. Wing were the coconsecrators. All of the bishops who participated in the two-hour service were attired in "post-Reformation vestments," making the consecration uniformly colorful or uncolorful depending on one's point of view. At the close of the service the new bishop was vested in cope and mitre and gave his blessing.[3]

During the 1950s Episcopalians in South Florida showed a great deal of interest in education, an interest which led to the founding of several Episcopal schools. These schools were divided into two general types: parish day schools which were sponsored by a particular parish and usually offered instruction in the elementary grades, and independent schools which were private corporations in no way tied to a particular church. Instruction at the independent schools was generally offered on the junior-senior high school level and was geared specifically for college preparation. The independent Episcopal schools were not supported by the diocese but by tuition fees and private contributions.

In the fall of 1951 the cathedral parish in Orlando, in conjunction with other Episcopal churches in the area, opened an elementary day school on the property of the old Cathedral School. In 1953, when John W. Shank, Ph.D., became headmaster of the institution, he extended the grades through the ninth and broadened

2. *Palm Branch*, June 1956.
3. Ibid., November 1956.

the range of academic courses. The clergy of the cathedral offered instruction in religion and with their colleagues in other Episcopal churches took charge of the chapel services.[4]

Shortly after the Cathedral School was reopened, St. John's Church in Tampa founded a day school in its parish buildings along the same lines as the Orlando institution. Within a year there were five parish day schools operating in the diocese with 306 pupils.[5] By the mid-sixties the number of day schools in the diocese had grown to 38, offering instruction to 3,027 pupils. The following list shows the number of students and the instruction offered at each school.[6]

EPISCOPAL DAY SCHOOLS	PUPILS	GRADES
Boynton Beach, St. Joseph's	77	kdg.–gr. 6
Cocoa, St. Mark's	129	kdg.–gr. 6
Coconut Grove, St. Stephen's	139	4–5 kdg.,–gr. 6
Coral Gables, St. Philip's	28	nur. 4–5–kdg.
Delray Beach, St. Paul's	22	4–5 kdg.
Dunedin, Good Shepherd	21	kdg.
Ft. Lauderdale, St. Ambrose's	62	4–5 kdg.–gr. 3
Ft. Lauderdale, St. Mark's	136	4–5 kdg.–gr. 6
Kissimmee, St. John's	20	kdg.
Lake Worth, St. Andrew's	16	4–5 kdg.
Leesburg, St. James's	17	kdg.
Longwood, Christ Episcopal	25	kdg.
Melbourne, Holy Trinity	170	kdg.–gr. 6
Merritt Island, St. Luke's	38	nur. 4–5 kdg.
Miami, Holy Family	20	kdg.
Miami, St. Faith's	120	4–5 kdg.
Miami, St. Simon's	37	4–5 kdg.
Ocala, Grace	220	4–5 kdg.–gr. 6
Orlando, Cathedral	166	kdg.–gr. 9
Orlando, Christ the King	110	kdg.–gr. 6
Ormond Beach, St. James's	164	4–5 kdg.–gr. 6
Pinecastle, St. Mary's	52	4–5 kdg.
Plant City, St. Peter's	35	kdg.
Pompano Beach, St. Martin's	37	4–5 kdg.
Punta Gorda, Good Shepherd	25	nurs. 4–5 kdg.

4. *Palm Branch*, May 1953.
5. *Diocesan Journal*, 1954, p. 151.
6. *Palm Branch*, December 1966.

St. Petersburg, St. Alban's	35	4–5 kdg.
St. Petersburg, St. Thomas's	63	4–5 kdg.
Sanford, Holy Cross	39	kdg.
South Miami, St. Thomas's	180	nur. 4–5 kdg.–gr. 6
Tampa, St. Christopher's	37	4–5 kdg.
Tampa, St. Francis's	54	kdg.–gr. 4
Tampa, St. Mary's	208	4–5 kdg.–gr. 6
Tampa, St. John's	289	4–5 kdg.–gr. 6
Titusville, St. Gabriel's	40	kdg.
Valrico, Holy Innocents'	21	4 yr. kdg.
Venice, St. Mark's	29	nurs. 4–5 kdg.
West Palm Beach, Holy Spirit	57	kdg.–gr. 3
Winter Park, Bishop Wing	89	kdg.–gr. 3
Total	3,027	

By the fall of 1966 there were also four independent Episcopal schools in operation: St. Andrew's, a boarding school for boys in Boca Raton; St. Ann's, a boarding school for girls in Boca Raton; Berkeley Preparatory School, a coeducational college preparatory day school in Tampa; and St. Edward's, a coeducational day school with grades two through nine in Vero Beach.[7] In 1968 Trinity Preparatory School, a coeducational institution with grades seven through twelve, opened its doors near Orlando.

Many people have argued that the day school movement in the South began as a direct result of the 1954 Supreme Court decision outlawing segregation in the public schools. It would be difficult to substantiate such a charge against the Church school movement in the Diocese of South Florida, which was motivated by two basic aims: to provide quality education and to bring Christian concepts into the process of learning. Obviously the high court's decision engendered support for the parish day schools, both inside and outside the Church, and obviously more day schools were founded after the 1954 decision than before it. But Negroes were enrolled in some of these schools, even if they were not enrolled in large numbers.

One of the great events of the Louttit episcopate was the meeting of the General Convention of the Protestant Episcopal Church at Miami Beach in October 1958. Between October 5 and 17, thou-

7. Ibid.

sands of Episcopalians converged on the city from all parts of the United States, its territories, and its missionary jurisdictions. The opening service, attended by over 15,000, was held in the new Exhibition Hall. The convention headquarters were set up in the recently opened Deauville Hotel, with its hall seating 3,600 persons. The House of Deputies and the House of Bishops held joint and separate sessions there, while the Triennial of the Women's Auxiliary met in the more lavish Fontainebleau. It was at this triennial that the Women's Auxiliary changed its name to the Episcopal Churchwomen.

The task of arranging for a meeting of such magnitude was enormous. Fifty-nine hotels were put under contract to house the visitors; some fifty breakfasts, luncheons, and dinners were scheduled; meeting rooms were provided for scores of committees; and temporary chapels were set up in a number of locations for various services of worship. Episcopal supervision for the General Convention was given to the suffragan, Bishop Moses. Brig. Gen. Lewis B. Rock was appointed General Chairman on Arrangements, with a budget of $50,000 and a free hand to pick his own staff. The Rev. Don H. Copeland of St. Stephen's was made Chairman of the Executive Committee, and Lewis E. Cooke was appointed Convention Manager. Hundreds of persons in the Miami area worked untiringly to make the convention a smooth and successful affair.[8] The man largely responsible for securing Miami Beach as the site for the 1958 triennial was the Ven. John E. Culmer, Archdeacon for Negro Work. As a South Florida delegate to the 1955 convention in Honolulu, he assured skeptical members of the Committee on the Time and Place of the Next Convention that they would find Miami Beach as free of racial discrimination as New York, San Francisco, Detroit, or any of the other cities that were being considered.[9]

The problems of growth and development that bore down on Bishops Louttit and Bram continued to haunt Bishops Louttit and Moses. Time and time again, young, vigorous, and promising mission congregations appealed to the diocese for financial aid so that they could secure suitable land while it was still available and

8. *Diocesan Journal*, 1959, pp. 76, 136–38; *Palm Branch*, October 1958.
9. Interview with the Rt. Rev. William L. Hargrave, July 15, 1972.

proceed with plans for permanent building. Each time the bishops had the unhappy responsibility of writing to say that all funds for that purpose were already in use. To come to grips with the interrelated problems of expansion and finance, the two bishops and Canon Hargrave decided to embark on another diocesan fundraising campaign. The firm of Ward, Dreshman, and Reinhardt, Inc., was engaged to organize and direct the campaign.

This drive, known as the Episcopal Church Development Fund Campaign, was put under the vigorous leadership of Gen. Charles H. Gerhardt of Winter Park. The aim of the drive was to secure a minimum of $770,000 over a three-year period;[10] the goal was later changed to approximately $1,240,000. The first year over $496,000 was collected by the intrepid general and his co-workers,[11] and in the second year the fund reached slightly over $1,000,000 in cash and pledges.[12] Towards the conclusion of the campaign Mrs. Flagler Matthews made a special gift of $100,000 to erect a chapel as a memorial to her grandfather, Henry Morrison Flagler, for the student center of the University of Miami. This relieved the diocese of the $65,000 that was allocated for the project in the Episcopal Church Development Fund.[13] The chapel was completed and dedicated in the spring of 1959. Despite the generosity of Mrs. Matthews the full goal of the Episcopal Church Development Campaign was never quite realized as some parishes and missions were not able to honor their pledges. Nearly all of the money raised, almost a million dollars, was poured into loans for mission expansion in the diocese, college work, theological education, and a conference center at Camp Wingmann. The diocese also made a large donation to the National Church for work overseas.[14]

The monies raised through the Episcopal Church Development Fund permitted the congregations of the diocese to continue their expansion through the late fifties and early sixties, although it was almost impossible for diocesan authorities to keep pace with the

10. *Palm Branch*, November and December, 1956.
11. Louttit, *Episcopal Address* (South Florida), 1958, p. 65.
12. *Diocesan Journal*, 1959, p. 126.
13. Ibid., 1960, p. 157.
14. Ibid., 1961, p. 111.

fantastic growth of population in the southern peninsula. The resources of the diocesan, the suffragan, and the executive secretary were sorely taxed by the administrative and spiritual problems of the burgeoning area. In the summer of 1961 Bishop Moses and his wife left for several weeks on a much needed vacation of travel and relaxation in England. On July 26 the suffragan suffered a severe heart attack and was placed in St. George's Hospital, London. The news of Bishop Moses's illness was transmitted to South Florida by the Rev. James L. Duncan, who was in London en route home after an exchange of parishes in South Africa.[15] On July 31 the bishop's physician called by his hospital room and found him resting comfortably, but when the doctor looked in a short time later he found that the bishop was dead.[16]

Because of the complications of Anglo-American regulations governing the transportation of the remains, the body was cremated. The ashes of the bishop were flown to Atlanta where interment took place with Bishop Claiborne of Atlanta officiating at the committal. Simultaneously in the cathedral in Orlando a requiem was celebrated by the diocesan before a congregation gathered from all over South Florida. Mrs. Moses and her family chose to be at the requiem rather than at the interment of the ashes.[17]

Churchmen throughout the diocese mourned the loss of William Francis Moses. He was missed because so many people from all walks of life treasured his friendship. His genuine warmth, his concern, and his capacity to make people feel comfortable in his presence, along with his devotion to his calling and his sweet good humor, made him well and widely loved. This man never expected to be a bishop, particularly at his comparatively advanced age; he was nearly fifty-nine at his consecration. He brought to the episcopate all the warmth, graciousness, and inner spiritual strength that had adorned his priesthood.

South Florida was again faced with the problem of choosing a suffragan. She had had two suffragans within ten years, and both had fallen victims of heart attacks. Bishop Louttit had not only

15. *Living Church*, August 6, 1961.
16. Ibid., August 13, 1961.
17. *Palm Branch*, September 1961.

lost valuable co-workers; he also had lost the affectionate association of two close friends. It was clear to all that the care and administration of the diocese were too much for only two men.

Even before the death of Bishop Moses, the administrative structure of the diocese was under serious examination. At the 1960
convention a study committee returned a recommendation that the
diocese be divided into three areas, each under the supervision of
an archdeacon: the Central Archdeanery, composed of the deaneries of Orlando, Daytona Beach, and Lakeland; the East Coast
Archdeanery, composed of the deaneries of Miami, Fort Lauderdale, and Palm Beach; and the Gulf Coast Archdeanery, composed
of the St. Petersburg, Tampa, Sarasota, and Fort Myers deaneries.

Bishop Louttit accepted the general recommendations of the
study committee, but he was strongly opposed to the use of archdeacons. He preferred to use suffragans. At the special diocesan
convention called in Orlando prior to the General Convention
which was meeting in Detroit in mid-September 1969, the delegates
concurred with Bishop Louttit's revision.[18]

After the permission of the General Convention for the election
of two suffragans was secured, another special convention was called
in Orlando, October 19–20, for the purpose of electing them. There
was little doubt as to who they would be, even though the balloting
was prolonged. The first ballot showed that the Rev. James L.
Duncan, the dynamic rector of St. Peter's Church, St. Petersburg,
and Canon William L. Hargrave, the industrious and efficient executive secretary, had commanding leads. In the first election,
Father Duncan was elected on the fifth ballot; in the second, Canon
Hargrave was elected on the third.[19]

On December 20 the Rev. James L. Duncan was consecrated in
his former parish in St. Petersburg. The consecrator was the Rt.
Rev. Arthur Carl Lichtenberger, D.D., Presiding Bishop of the
Episcopal Church, and the coconsecrators were the Rt. Rev. Henry
I. Louttit and the Rt. Rev. John Vander Horst, D.D., Bishop of
Tennessee. The preacher for the occasion was the Rt. Rev. Albert

18. Ibid., September 1961.
19. Ibid., October 1961.

Rhett Stuart, D.D., Bishop of Georgia. The following day Canon Hargrave was also consecrated by the Presiding Bishop, in the Cathedral Church of St. Luke in Orlando. His coconsecrators were Bishop Louttit and the Rt. Rev. Walter H. Gray, D.D., Bishop of Connecticut. The preacher for the service was the Rt. Rev. Thomas H. Wright, D.D., Bishop of East Carolina.[20]

The suffragans had long associations with the diocese, although both were natives of North Carolina. James L. Duncan was born in Greensboro, September 11, 1913. His father was a Scot, and both his parents were Roman Catholics. He first attended an Episcopal service at thirteen and was immediately drawn to the Church. During his college days at Emory University in Atlanta, where he received both his B.A. and M.A. degrees, he came under the influence of that strong personality, the Rt. Rev. Henry Judah Mikell, Bishop of Atlanta. Young Duncan's decision to study for the priesthood was no doubt encouraged by the bishop. He spent three years in St. Luke's Hall at The University of the South. The future bishop was ordained deacon in 1938, awarded his B.D. in 1939, and ordained to the priesthood the same year. His first parish was St. Peter's Church in Rome, Georgia. While rector of St. Peter's he met and married Evelyn Burgess. The Duncans had three children: Mary Ann, John Robert, and James, Jr. After Evelyn Duncan's death in 1967, the bishop married Mrs. Elaine Gaither.

In 1945 Duncan was called to be rector of All Saints' Church, Winter Park; five years later he became rector of one of the oldest and largest parishes in South Florida, St. Peter's Church, St. Petersburg. As rector of St. Peter's, he demonstrated his administrative skill by presenting a parochial program with clearcut objectives for all ages. He also foresaw the potential growth of St. Petersburg and arranged for a survey of the city by the National Council research unit. As a result of that survey, St. Peter's Church engaged in one of the most spectacular missionary programs of any parish in the South, founding six missions under Father Duncan's direction. The rector's concern for the spread of the Church through a planned missionary program was to stand him in good stead when he became

20. Ibid., January 1962.

suffragan. Father Duncan was also active in diocesan affairs. He was president of the Standing Committee from 1954 to 1961 and was instrumental in the development of Suncoast Manor in St. Petersburg, one of the largest and best-planned retirement centers in the state.[21]

Bishop Hargrave was born in Wilson, North Carolina, November 10, 1903. He graduated from the Atlanta Law School in 1924 and went to live in booming Miami where he was employed by the Miami Bank and Trust Company and associated with J. P. Simmons, an attorney. It was at this time that he met Henry I. Louttit, as both men were communicants of Trinity Church, Miami, and active in its worship and affairs. Bishop Hargrave's decision to enter the priesthood was not a sudden one. After wrestling for several years with the idea, he made a firm commitment and entered Virginia Seminary in the fall of 1929. While still in seminary he was ordained to the diaconate in 1931 by Bishop Wing and the following year was advanced to the priesthood. Young Hargrave's first mission was St. Mark's Church, Cocoa, where he also had the cure of St. Luke's, Courtenay. The ease and attentiveness with which he discharged his duties made him one of the most popular figures in Brevard County. Within a few years he had made St. Mark's into a strong parish and had also founded St. Philip's Church, a Negro mission congregation on Merritt Island. While in Cocoa he married Minnie Frances Whittington. The Hargraves had four children: Frances, Betty, Sarah, and William III.[22]

In 1943 Father Hargrave accepted a call as rector of St. Andrew's Church, Fort Pierce, and two years later he became rector of Holy Comforter, Miami. In 1948 the Hargraves moved to Charleston, South Carolina, where he became rector of Holy Communion Church and chaplain to Porter Military Academy. He became acting president of the academy in 1952 and was instrumental in saving that almost bankrupt institution. It was while he was acting president of Porter, in 1953, that he accepted a call from Bishop Louttit to become executive secretary of the Diocese of

21. *Living Church*, November 5, 1961; *Palm Branch*, November 1961, December 1967.
22. *Palm Branch*, November 1961.

South Florida. He was later appointed actuary of the diocese and made canon to the ordinary.

One of the canon's chief concerns as executive secretary was establishing and financing new missions. He personally established new work in Mount Dora, Pine Castle, and Winter Garden, serving as a mission priest to these churches. Canon Hargrave's legal training was used to great advantage by the diocese in many knotty problems of administration and finance. Archdeacon Culmer on several occasions paid tribute to the dogged canon by referring to him as "the man who keeps the diocesan machinery working." He did indeed. His capacity for retaining facts and figures was phenomenal. Few men brought to the office of bishop such a remarkable knowledge of the life and work of the diocese and few men offered that knowledge with more warmth and charity.[23]

Following their consecrations, the new suffragans spent several months under Bishop Louttit's direct supervision. After this period Bishop Duncan was assigned to the East Coast Archdeanery and Bishop Hargrave to the Gulf Coast Archdeanery, while Bishop Louttit retained the general supervision of the diocese and of the Central Archdeanery. Thus it was that the lines for the forthcoming partition of the diocese were laid with the consecrations and assignments of the suffragans.[24] Bishop Duncan made his headquarters at Trinity Church, Miami, while Bishop Hargrave moved his office to St. Peter's Church, St. Petersburg. His position as executive secretary was later filled by J. William Werts, a layman who had served as the canon's assistant for several years.[25]

The growth of the state which staggered the imagination in the first decade of the Louttit episcopate continued into the second. In this growth the Church not only managed to keep abreast of the state's increase in population, but what is even more remarkable, exceeded it. Over forty missions were founded in the sixties despite the slowdown at the end of the decade caused by a slight

23. Ibid.; interview with the Rt. Rev. William L. Hargrave, July 15, 1972.
24. *Palm Branch*, November 1961–January 1962.
25. Ibid., July 1963.

recession and a shortage of missionary funds.[26] The list below tells its own story.

CHURCHES ORGANIZED DURING THE 1960s

MISSION	YEAR ORGANIZED	YEAR MISSION BECAME PARISH
Bradenton, St. George's	1964	
Bushnell, St. Francis's	1962	
Cape Coral, Epiphany	1963	
Carol City, St. Anthony's	1960	
Clearwater, St. John's	1967	
Cocoa, Gloria Dei	1965	
Dunedin, St. Alfred's	1964	
Dunnellon, Faith	1965	
Ft. Lauderdale, Atonement	1967	
Holly Hill, Holy Child	1963	
Hollywood, St. James's	1962	1969
Immokalee, St. Barnabas's	1967	
Islamorada, St. Adrian's	1966	
Key Biscayne, St. Christopher's	1960	
Lake Worth, Holy Redeemer		
Lantana, Guardian Angels' (moved from Lake Worth)	1962	
Lehigh Acres, St. Anselm's	1962	
Marco Island, St. Mark's	1967	
Margate, St. Mary Magdalene's	1960	
Melbourne Beach, St. Sebastian's	1964	1969
Miami, Ascension	1966	
Miami, St. Andrew's	1964	1969
Miami, Todos Los Santos	1962	
Miami, Venerable Bede (University Chapel)	1960	
Naples, St. Paul's	1968	
North Miami Beach, St. Bernard's (called St. John the Divine)	1964	
N. Port Charlotte, St. Nathaniel's	1964	
Ocala, St. Patrick's	1962	
Orlando, St. Christopher's	1967	
Palm Bay, Our Savior	1962	
Palm Beach Gardens, St. Mark's	1963	
Palmetto, St. Mary's	1966	
Plantation, St. Benedict's	1960	1967
Pompano Beach, St. Nicholas's	1960	1969

26. *Diocesan Journal*, 1960–1969, *passim.*

Port Charlotte, St. James's	1962
Port St. Lucie, Holy Faith	1965
Ruskin, St. John the Divine	1963
St. Petersburg, Holy Cross	1960
Tampa, St. Anselm's Chapel	
(University of South Florida)	1963
Tavernier, St. Simeon's	1960
Titusville, St. Titus's	1967
West Palm Beach, St. Christopher's	1966

During the 1960s thousands of exiles from Fidel Castro's Cuba swelled the population of southern Florida. Over 364,000 persons registered in the Cuban refugee program in Miami alone, confronting the people of the Miami area with the gargantuan task of resettling these exiles in Dade County and in other areas of the state and nation.

The Rev. Frank L. Titus of Holy Cross Parish, Miami, and a band of sympathetic helpers began to work among the refugees in July 1961. The labor soon grew to such an extent that the diocese and the National Church became interested in the endeavor. Property was rented in the heart of the refugee area, and the Episcopal Latin American Center under the direction of the Rev. Max I. Salvador, an exiled Cuban priest, was opened on Northwest Seventeenth Avenue. The center operated an extensive social welfare program for the refugees in addition to organizing a mission under the name of Todos Los Santos (All Saints'), which attracted over 100 persons to its Sunday services.

Father Salvador was assisted in his efforts by Mrs. Carmen Ibáñez, a Spanish-speaking social worker. Refugees were interviewed and counselled for resettlement, taught classes in English conversation, and provided food and clothing for emergency relief. The center also made an effort to find jobs for them in the Miami area. It arranged transportation for Cubans who the Missionary Bishop of Cuba, the Rt. Rev. Romualdo González, said needed to flee the country, sometimes for their lives. Many of these people arrived with little more than the clothes on their backs. Often their transportation had to be paid for. Their planes and boats had to be met, and temporary homes had to be found for unaccompanied children.[27] As the number of refugees increased so did the work of the Miami center. The expenses of the center were met by funds raised by Episcopal congregations in greater Miami, grants from the diocese, and gifts from the Presiding Bishop's Fund for World Relief. The Rev. A. Rees Hay later assumed the direction of the Cuban refugee work on the diocesan level and did much to coordinate the efforts of local congregations, women's groups, and philanthropic organizations.

By the beginning of 1963, the congregations of the diocese were donating over $1,500 per month to Cuban families in need. In the first four months of that year some 158 families were given counselling and financial assistance, while some 350 families were provided with food, clothing, and blankets. The student resettlement program and classes in conversational English were perhaps as helpful to the refugees as the physical relief they were given. During 1963 about 500 Cubans were taught the basics of the English language by dozens of volunteers—high school teachers, college professors, businessmen, and housewives. The center placed twenty-two Cuban college students in American colleges and universities during the fall term of 1962; within a year the number had more than doubled.[28]

In September 1961 Bishop Louttit had expanded the Church's work among the refugees to include the Tampa area, where the Rev. Luis Arcacha, another exile, was put in charge of the program. At the outset services were held in St. Andrew's Church, but it soon became evident that this location was inconvenient because of its distance from the Spanish-speaking community. With the cooperation of the Rev. G. Ralph Madson, Father Arcacha selected the House of Prayer as a better site and began holding services there. Attendance continued to be disappointing, however, probably because in Tampa, unlike Miami, there was not a large core group of refugees who had been affiliated with the Episcopal Church in Cuba.[29]

As the Cuban crisis passed, and as the two suffragans came to

27. Ibid., 1962, pp. 195–97.
28. Ibid., 1963, pp. 105–6.
29. Ibid.

feel at home with their people on the east and west coasts, it became increasingly clear that Bishop Louttit was steering the diocese towards a three-way division. He had already set up the administrative structure of the three archdeaneries. Now he gradually turned over full episcopal authority to his suffragans on the east and west coasts, while he himself retained full authority in the Central Archdeanery. It was evident that the majority of Churchmen in South Florida favored a future partition along these general lines of demarcation.

There were a number of reasons for this sentiment. First, many Episcopalians felt that the diocese was too large in area and population for proper pastoral and administrative supervision; second, they believed that the creation of smaller jurisdictions would result in greater participation by individuals and congregations within their limits; and third, they assumed that smaller dioceses would be easier to accommodate at conventions. Some also feared that the administrative costs of the one old diocese would spiral if it continued its phenomenal growth. Then, too, many of the old-timers longed for the days of Bishops Mann and Wing when the annual conventions were smaller and warmer affairs—real gatherings of the "diocesan family."

There was some opposition to a division as well, since many regretted the loss of contact with close associates from other parts of the state that partition would bring; some believed that division would result in a loss of power and prestige in the National Church; and others felt that separation would increase rather than diminish administrative costs. Lastly, there was the question of what to do with the diocesan facilities, the ecclesiastical loaves and fishes, such as Camp Wingmann, Gray Inn, and the monastery in Miami.

There was no doubt that serious thought was needed. With this in mind, at the 1966 Convention the bishop appointed a committee under the chairmanship of the Rev. William H. Folwell to study the division of the diocese. The Folwell Committee met often and long. After three years of careful deliberation it made a number of recommendations to the 1969 Diocesan Convention.

The committee proposed a division of the diocese along the broad lines of the three archdeaneries. Parochial property (land and buildings) would be divided on the basis of geographical location, and all monies owed on mortgages on these properties would be assumed by the diocese receiving them. All liquid assets (cash and marketable securities) and all debts of the old Diocese of South Florida would be divided into three equal portions. The institutional property connected with the Diocese of South Florida was to be divided in the following manner. The title of the Monastery Gardens in Dade County would be conveyed to the new southeast diocese, but the monastery was to be operated by a non-profit corporation named St. Bernard's Foundation, which would assume responsibility for all indebtedness. This arrangement was changed subsequently to give each diocese equal ownership and responsibility. Because of its location, the title to Camp Wingmann was to be retained by the central diocese, but it would be governed by a joint committee from the three dioceses and the cost of operating it would be divided three ways. Bishop Gray Inn and the newer Bishopscourt in Lakeland, the diocesan facilities for the elderly, would remain in the hands of the autonomous non-profit corporation entitled the William Crane Gray Inn for Older People, composed of a group of thirty-nine trustees, thirteen from each diocese. Each diocese was to give a token amount of $2,000 per annum to Gray Inn to keep it before the convention and the people.[30]

The recommendations of the Folwell Committee were adopted by the Diocesan Convention of 1969. The Special General Convention of the National Church, which met in early September at South Bend, Indiana, the same year, approved the division of the Diocese of South Florida. The three archdeaneries were thus free to organize themselves into new dioceses. This organization was done at a special or primary convention for each.

The Primary Convention of the Diocese of Southeast Florida was held October 8, 1969, at Holy Trinity Church, West Palm Beach. Bishop Louttit celebrated the Holy Communion and presided at the organizational meeting. At that time "the congregation and clergy located in Monroe, Dade, Broward, Palm Beach, Martin, Glades, and Hendry Counties in the State of Florida" organized and constituted themselves as a diocese. The Rt. Rev. James Duncan was

30. Ibid., 1969, pp. 136–47.

elected Bishop of Southeast Florida on the first ballot, and Bishop Louttit relinquished the chair to the new diocesan. The convention responded with a standing ovation. Trinity Church, Miami, was chosen as the cathedral.[31]

The Primary Convention of the Diocese of Southwest Florida was held in the Bath Club, North Redington Beach, on October 16, 1969. At that meeting it was resolved that "those congregations and clergy located in Hernando, Pasco, Hillsborough, Pinellas, Manatee, Sarasota, Charlotte, DeSoto, Lee, and Collier Counties" organize and constitute themselves as the Diocese of Southwest Florida. The Rt. Rev. William L. Hargrave was elected diocesan on the first ballot. He announced that St. Peter's Church, St. Petersburg, would be the new cathedral.[32]

The continuing diocese, that is, what was left of the old Diocese of South Florida, was composed of congregations and clergy located in Marion, Sumter, Lake, Orange, Polk, Hardee, Highlands, Okeechobee, Osceola, St. Lucie, Indian River, Brevard, Seminole, and Volusia counties. This remnant met in special convention at the cathedral church in Orlando on December 3, 1969, and changed its name to the Diocese of Central Florida. At that meeting Bishop Louttit, who had previously announced his intention to retire, presided as diocesan for the last time. When he called for nominations for a new bishop some eight names were submitted. The Rev. William H. Folwell, the energetic and open-minded rector of All Saints', Winter Park, was elected easily on the second ballot.[33] Father Folwell had been vicar of Plant City and Mulberry, chaplain at St. Martin's School, New Orleans, and rector of St. Gabriel's, Titusville, before moving to Winter Park.

The bishop-elect was born in Port Washington, New York, October 26, 1924. He received his high school education in Miami, Florida, and in 1947 was awarded the B.C.E. degree from the

31. *Annual Reports of the Diocese of South Florida Together with the Reports and the Journals of the Special Meetings of the Diocese of Central Florida, the Diocese of Southeast Florida, and the Diocese of Southwest Florida* (n.p., 1969), pp. 150–51.

32. Ibid., pp. 224–26.

33. Ibid., pp. 108–11.

Georgia Institute of Technology. Upon graduation he was employed by the City of Miami as a member of the Traffic Engineering Department. In 1949 he married Christine Elizabeth Cram; they had three children: Ann, Mark, and Susan. Young Folwell decided to study for the priesthood and entered Seabury-Western Seminary, Evanston, Illinois, where he received the L.Th. degree in 1952, and the same year was ordained both deacon and priest. The following year he was awarded the B.D. degree from Seabury-Western.

In the Diocese of South Florida, Father Folwell served as president of the Florida Episcopal Schools Association and as a member of the Standing Committee. He was chairman of the Division of Camps, a member of the Executive Board of the diocese, and a deputy to the General Convention. In 1966, Bishop Louttit made him an honorary canon of the cathedral. In addition, he was chairman of the important Committee to Study the Division of the Diocese.[34] Despite his involvement in so many diocesan affairs his parishioners recall his pastoral concern as the dominant characteristic of his ministry amongst them.

34. *The Episcopal Church Annual*, 1971, p. 239.

XIX

Henry Irving Louttit
Fourth Bishop

W HAT OF THE MAN WHO PRESIDED OVER THE DIOCESE OF
South Florida during the last two decades of its fantastic
growth? Henry Louttit was no ordinary man. Born in Buffalo, New
York, January 1, 1903, he was orphaned at an early age. Many of
the material joys of his boyhood were obtained by his own hard
work, and so was his later education. He has said often, not entirely
jokingly, "I never realized the Episcopal Church was supposed to
be the affluent church until I left Buffalo and enrolled at Hobart."
At Hobart College his quick mind and youthful energy brought him
a membership in Phi Beta Kappa and a B.A. degree in history in
1925. Throughout his undergraduate days Henry Louttit was torn
between two callings, the priesthood and the law. Finally he entered
law school but soon thereafter realized that he was destined to be a
priest. After a year in the construction business in booming Miami,
the young college graduate became a postulant under Bishop Wing
and enrolled at the Virginia Seminary in Alexandria. Awarded the
B.D. in 1929, he was ordained to the diaconate during his senior
year at seminary and priested by Bishop Wing in 1930. The young
cleric's first assignment was tiny All Saints' Church, Tarpon Springs,

but after a brief time there he returned to his home parish, Trinity Church, Miami, as curate.[1]

In 1930 the Rev. Henry I. Louttit became rector of Holy Cross Parish in Sanford, where he remained until 1933, when as a young man of thirty he was called as rector of one of the most prestigious (and debt-ridden) parishes in the diocese, Holy Trinity Church, West Palm Beach. While in West Palm Beach he married Amy Cleckler of Atlanta. Three children were born to the couple: two sons, Henry, Jr., and James, and a daughter who died in infancy. Father Louttit's cure at Holy Trinity was interrupted by the war and his enlistment in the United States Army as a chaplain. He spent much of the war with the 31st Infantry Division in the Dutch East Indies, where he was awarded the Bronze Star. During the war years Mrs. Louttit taught school in Palm Beach County. In 1945, shortly before his discharge from the 31st Division with the rank of lieutenant colonel, Chaplain Louttit was elected suffragan.[2]

Henry Louttit was the first suffragan elected by the Diocese of South Florida. Three years later he was elected coadjutor. These two titles were little-known in Florida and were frequently confused and abused by news reporters of press, radio, and television. The bishop no doubt winced many times at being referred to as the "sufferin' bishop" or as the "bishop co-agitator."

Because of Bishop Wing's illness Bishop Louttit carried much of the load of the diocese from the time he became coadjutor. He visited its parishes, helped found its missions, and headed its fund-raising drives. It must have been with some relief that he assumed full authority in January 1951, and was able to ask the next convention for his own suffragan.

In 1954, as chairman of the Armed Forces Department of the National Council of Churches, the bishop, with four clergymen from other denominations, took time off to tour the air force bases in the Far East and to report on the spiritual welfare of their personnel. On his return the former chaplain must have caused con-

1. Interview with the Rt. Rev. Henry I. Louttit, July 16, 1967; *Palm Branch*, October 1965.

2. Interview with Bishop Louttit, April 7, 1968; *Palm Branch*, October 1965.

siderable discomfort in the higher echelons of the Department of Defense when he told the press that the "problem of morality among the military is staggering" and supported his statement with observations from the tour. Bishop Louttit's courage and frankness in this matter brought him a citation from the commanding general of the air force, Nathan F. Twining, for "outstanding service performed on the tour."[3]

Bishop Louttit was often in the news, partly because of his outspoken stand on integration. His remark made to an Orlando civic club, "You can have all the prejudices you want, but don't label them Christian," was widely quoted. In the same speech he summed up his approach to integration: "The racial problem will not be solved by laws . . . but by Christian people acting as Christians."[4]

The demands of his office in the fast-growing Diocese of South Florida forced Bishop Louttit to sacrifice much of the time most men would spend with their families and in recreation. "I'm not saying this just to be funny," he once replied to a question concerning his hobbies, "but I honestly don't do anything but church work."[5] There was a gentle hint of this almost total involvement with diocesan affairs in an interview with Mrs. Louttit reported in the "Florida Magazine" in January 1957. She described the bishop as "quite a mean hand with the hoe and the rake, if memory serves me correctly." Her husband, however, had long ago turned over the garden to their elder son, Henry, Jr., once called Bo, "way back when I was optimistic enough to think there would be confusion over two Henrys in one household." Mrs. Louttit said wryly that her principal activity was "waiting for the bishop to return."[6] In such "activity" she probably remembered and followed her mother's example, for her father was a Methodist minister.

When he was able to be home, Bishop Louttit tried to spend most of his time with his family. Recreation included boating and swimming in front of their home on Lake Virginia and an occasional trip together. Bishop Louttit followed an early-to-bed, early-to-rise

3. Ibid.

4. "Florida Magazine," Orlando *Sentinel*, January 27, 1957.

5. Ibid.

6. Ibid.

routine whenever possible. Early-to-rise, his wife once explained with a trace of regret, generally meant that he was up and reading at four a.m.: newspapers, periodicals, history, theology, biography, and, of course, fiction. The bishop used these early morning hours to stay abreast of the social and intellectual world around him.

By nature Bishop Louttit was a student and a preacher, yet he found himself bogged down by the administrative demands of his office. He seldom had time to read through a book or to polish a sermon thoroughly; nonetheless he was a powerful preacher. By his own admission the bishop had compensations for his intellectual sacrifices, principally his satisfaction in watching the Church grow. He spoke out forcefully on the great social issues that were current in his episcopate. Considering his own intense feeling he had an amazing tolerance of the opinions of others, but this tolerance did not prevent him from standing for his own convictions. Henry Louttit possessed both warmth and gentleness, virtues which an innate shyness, the pressures of his office, and the weight of family tragedy sometimes conspired to hide.

Throughout his episcopate there was a constant but muffled controversy over the increase of ritualism in the services of the Church. Although Bishop Louttit considered himself a moderate in ceremonial matters, there is little doubt that he leaned toward a more elaborate service. There was a marked decline in the number of Low churches in the diocese in the first decade after his accession because the bishop generally brought in clergy with High Church views to fill the numerous openings in the new churches. The bishop listened to complaints from both sides about the extent of ritualism in the Church, but usually refused to interfere with the High or Low Church proclivities of his clergy. He was fond of pointing out that it was not the bishop's function to dictate the type of service in a parish, as the latitude within the Episcopal Church permitted a rector to conduct a comparatively informal service or one with much solemn ceremony. He felt that the ceremonial of a parish was one of the externals of the Church and "that externals are unimportant." What mattered to him was the Church itself, "and the task God has given her to do."[7]

7. Ibid.

Undoubtedly the most publicized event of Bishop Louttit's last decade as diocesan was his controversy with the Rt. Rev. James A. Pike, the eristic and erratic former Bishop of California, who had resigned his see but not his office. In the fall of 1966 Bishop Louttit led an attempt to indict Pike for heresy at the annual meeting of the House of Bishops which convened October 30 in Wheeling, West Virginia. Most of the bishops strongly disagreed with Pike's doctrinal views but they did not believe that he was a conscious heretic, while Bishop Louttit regarded Pike as little more than an apostate in bishop's clothing and was determined to drive him from the episcopate. The Louttit presentment, which had been previously circulated, was thought by many to be ill-prepared. The Presiding Bishop, the Rt. Rev. John E. Hines, wished to block a heresy trial by keeping the presentment from the floor, for he knew the ensuing discord, confusion, and scandal would cause great damage to the Church. A compromise was reached. Bishop Louttit withdrew his presentment, and the House of Bishops issued a statement blistering Bishop Pike for his "offensive" and "irresponsible" utterances. Although little of what Bishop Louttit set out to accomplish came about, both prelates received national, and even international, publicity from the controversy.[8]

The outreach of the Church was broadened during the Louttit episcopate. On the parochial level much work was done with alcoholism, the largest branch of mental illness in the state. The bishop encouraged a number of clergy to study this problem under trained direction, and some became efficient and compassionate counsellors to the victims of the disease. The Church also reached out to minister more efficiently to the elderly. The capacity of Gray Inn was tripled, and another home, Bishopscourt, was founded in Lakeland. Church retirement centers, which permitted couples to spend their riper years in an atmosphere of comfort and Christian concern, were begun in St. Petersburg and Daytona Beach.

The diocese under Bishop Louttit's leadership strongly supported The University of the South at Sewanee, Tennessee. Regular allocations were sent to Sewanee by many parishes and missions, and

8. *Time*, October 21 and November 4, 1966; *Living Church*, October 9 and November 13, 1966.

special drives were made to help complete All Saints' Chapel for the college and to expand the facilities of the seminary. The diocese provided funds to build a number of apartments for married seminarians and their families. The bishop encouraged support of college projects within the diocese as well. Student centers were built at the University of South Florida and at Stetson, and new work was begun in the many junior colleges which sprang up during the fifties and sixties.

Much effort was spent during Bishop Louttit's episcopate among the thousands of West Indian migrant laborers who came annually to Florida to do seasonal work on truck farms and citrus groves. Special clergymen were hired to work among the migrants, and parochial clergy gave them the sacraments of the Church. Both clergy and laity brought pressure to bear on employers to provide adequate housing and sanitary conditions in the migrant camps.

Naturally not all of Bishop Louttit's projects were received with enthusiasm. There was some opposition to the purchase of the Old Spanish Monastery Gardens in North Miami Beach in the spring of 1965.[9] Even though the property housed a new mission, many felt that the $350,000 mortgage which the trustees of the diocese indirectly assumed could be employed better in the underfunded missionary program of South Florida. Another of the bishop's projects which engendered only lukewarm support was his attempt to establish an Episcopal college as one of the colleges of Stetson University, a Baptist institution in DeLand. Property was acquired and over a period of several years money was raised, but nowhere near enough to construct the necessary buildings or to provide an adequate endowment. The project was abandoned soon after Bishop Louttit's retirement.

Two great sorrows marred the bishop's private life, the loss of an infant daughter and his wife's illness. The drain of the latter on his emotional, physical, and spiritual energies must have been enormous. On February 9, 1960, Amy Louttit suffered a massive cerebral hemorrhage. She rallied from the hemorrhage so quickly that it was possible later in the month for surgeons to operate and tie the aneurism. After that operation, however, Mrs. Louttit never re-

9. Personal recollection, author.

gained lucidity.[10] For over eight years she lingered, unable to recognize family or friends. She died in Winter Park, April 25, 1968, at the age of fifty-two.[11]

In 1970 Bishop Louttit married Mrs. Elizabeth S. Harms, the widow of a friend and parishioner from Holy Trinity, West Palm Beach. The Louttits have made their home in Orlando.

Henry Irving Louttit presided over the Church in South Florida for almost a quarter of a century during a period of unbelievable growth for both the Church and the peninsula. Most of his years as diocesan were lived in the whirlwind engendered by this growth, yet with his energetic and determined leadership the Diocese of South Florida managed to outpace the whirlwind. When he laid his crozier by on January 1, 1970, he must have looked back over those chaotic and exciting years with some satisfaction. He had divided his jurisdiction into three parts, and had left each of the new dioceses that he helped bring into existence stronger numerically and financially than the old Diocese of South Florida which he had inherited on New Year's Day, 1951.

10. *Palm Branch*, March 1960.
11. Orlando *Sentinel*, April 26, 1968.

Appendixes

APPENDIX I

CLERGY CANONICALLY RESIDENT IN THE
MISSIONARY JURISDICTION OF SOUTHERN FLORIDA
AT THE TIME OF THE PRIMARY CONVOCATION
HELD IN HOLY CROSS CHURCH, SANFORD, FEBRUARY 21–22, 1893[1]

*Rev. John J. Andrew	Orlando
*Rev. C. W. Arnold	Daytona
Rev. Juan B. Baez	Key West
*Rev. Wm. H. Bates	Sanford
Rev. J. S. Beekman	Halifax
*Rev. C. F. A. Bielby	DeLand
*Rev. B. F. Brown	Titusville
*Rev. S. B. Carpenter	Sanford
*Rev. Joseph Cross, D.D.	Tampa
*Rev. James H. Davet	Zellwood
*Rev. Charles M. Gray	Ocala
*Rev. Curtis Grubb	Pittman
*Rev. Gilbert Higgs	Key West
*Rev. S. Kerr	Key West
Rev. Lyman Phelps	Sanford
Rev. H. H. Ten Broeck	Bradentown

1. *Convocation Journal*, 1893, p. 2. Those present at the convocation are marked with an asterisk.

*Rev. E. L. Turquand	Enterprise
*Rev. J. H. Weddell	Thonotosassa
*Rev. C. S. Williams	Sanford
*Rev. R. B. Wolseley	Daytona

APPENDIX II

LAY DELEGATES TO THE CONVENTION[2]

St. Luke's, Orlando	*L. C. Massey
	L. C. Vaughan
	*A. Haden
	H. W. Greetham
Holy Cross, Sanford	*E. K. Foster
	*B. F. Whitner
	*A. C. Dowdney
Grace Church, Ocala	*Walter Hawkins
St. Gabriel's, Titusville	Geo. Robbins
Christ's Church, Longwood	*F. H. Rand
St. Mark's, Cocoa	*F. C. Cantine
St. James's, Zellwood	*H. P. Burgwin
St. James's, Ormond	*E. W. Amsden
All Saints', Lakeland	*J. W. Emerson
Courtenay Mission	J. H. Sams
St. Edward's, Lane Park	Rowland Frick

2. Ibid.

Bibliography

DIOCESAN AND GENERAL CONVENTION PUBLICATIONS

Atwill, Edward Robert. *Episcopal Address,* bound with *The Journal of the Twelfth Annual Convention of the Protestant Episcopal Church in the Diocese of West Missouri,* 1902. Kansas City: Union Bank Note Company, 1902.

Bishop's Diary. The official diary of the bishops of the Missionary Jurisdiction of Southern Florida and of the Diocese of South Florida, sometimes titled *Report* or *Journal,* published in both the *Palm Branch* and the *Diocesan Journal.* (The authors and years are: William Crane Gray, 1893–1913; Henry Irving Louttit, 1951–1969; Cameron Mann, 1914–1932; John Durham Wing, 1932–1950.)

Bishop Coadjutor's Diary. Published in the *Diocesan Journal* and the *Palm Branch.* (The authors and years are: Henry Irving Louttit, 1949–1950; John Durham Wing, 1925–1931.)

Bram, Martin J. *Suffragan Bishop's Address,* 1951–1955, bound with *The Journal of the Annual Convention of the Diocese of South Florida,* 1951–1955.

Burleson, Hugh Latimer, D.D. "Memorial Sermon to the Late Bishop Mann." Appended to *The Journal of the Tenth Annual Convention of the Diocese of South Florida,* 1932.

Coxe, Arthur Cleveland. *Episcopal Address,* 1874, 1876, 1881, bound with *The Journal of the Annual Convention of the Protestant Episcopal Church in the Diocese of Western New York,* 1874, 1876, 1881.

Diocese of Florida. *The Journal of the Proceedings of the Annual Councils of the Protestant Episcopal Church in the Diocese of Florida,* 1839, 1854,

1867, 1873, 1880–1894. (The printers and places of publication are: 1839, Knowles and Hutchins, Tallahassee; 1854, 1867, 1873, Office of the Florida *Sentinel*; 1880–1884, Ashmead Bros., Printers, Jacksonville; 1885–1886, Church and Home Office, Jacksonville; 1887, 1892–1894, Da Costa Printing and Publishing House, Jacksonville; 1888–1891, Church Publishing Company, Jacksonville.)

Diocese of Missouri. *The Journal of the Forty-Third Annual Convention of the Protestant Episcopal Church in the Diocese of Missouri,* 1882. St. Louis: Woodward, Tiernan and Hale, Printers, 1882.

Diocese of South Florida. *The Annual Reports of the Diocese of South Florida Together with the Reports and the Journals of the Special Meetings of the Diocese of Southeast Florida, and the Diocese of Southwest Florida. N.p.,* 1969.

Diocese of South Florida. *The Journal of the Annual Conventions of the Church in the Diocese of South Florida,* 1923–1968. 46 vols. (The printers and places of publication are: 1923, 1932–1945, Carl W. Hill, Printer, Tampa; 1924–1931, Paragon Press, Montgomery; 1946–1952, The Commercial Press, Lakeland; 1953–1957, Printing Press Co., Fort Myers; 1958–1968, n.p.)

Diocese of South Florida. *The Journal of the Special Conventions of the Diocese of South Florida,* 1925, 1945, 1951, 1957. (The printers and places of publication are: 1925, The Paragon Press, Montgomery; 1945, Carl W. Hill, Printer, Tampa; 1951, The Commercial Press, Lakeland; 1957, Printing Press Company, Fort Myers.)

Diocese of Western New York. *The Journal of the Annual Convention of the Protestant Episcopal Church in the Diocese of Western New York,* 1874, 1876, 1881. (The printers and places of publication are: 1874, 1876, Buffalo: Printing House of Matthews and Warren; 1881, Buffalo: *Morning Express* Printing House.)

Duncan, James L. *Suffragan Bishop's Address,* 1962–1969, bound with *The Journal of the Annual Conventions of the Church in South Florida,* 1962–1969.

General Convention of the Protestant Episcopal Church in the United States of America. *The Journal of the Proceedings of the Bishops, Clergy, and Laity of the Protestant Episcopal Church in the United States of America,* 1892, 1901, 1913. (The printers and places of publication are: 1892, Printed for the Convention, Baltimore; 1901, Alfred Mudge and Sons, Printers, Boston; 1913, Sherwood Press, New York.)

General Convention of the Protestant Episcopal Church in the United States of America. *The Memorial of the Diocese of Florida for Cession of Territory to the General Convention of the Protestant Episcopal Church.* Baltimore: Printed for the Convention, 1892.

Gray, William Crane. *Episcopal Address,* 1893–1914, bound with *The Journal of the Annual Convocation of the Protestant Episcopal Church in the Missionary Jurisdiction of Southern Florida,* 1893–1914.

Hargrave, William L. *Suffragan Bishop's Address,* 1962–1969, bound with *The Journal of the Annual Convention of the Church in the Diocese of South Florida,* 1962–1969.

Louttit, Henry Irving. *Bishop Coadjutor's Address,* 1949–1950, bound with *The Journal of the Annual Convention of the Church in the Diocese of South Florida,* 1949–1950.

Louttit, Henry Irving. *Episcopal Address,* 1951–1969, bound with *The Journal of the Annual Convention of the Church in the Diocese of South Florida,* 1951–1969.

Louttit, Henry Irving. *Suffragan Bishop's Address,* 1946–1948, bound with *The Journal of the Annual Convention of the Church in the Diocese of South Florida,* 1946–1948.

Mann, Cameron. *Episcopal Address,* 1915–1931, bound with *The Journal of the Annual Convocation of the Church in the Missionary Jurisdiction of Southern Florida,* 1915–1922, and with *The Journal of the Annual Conventions of the Church in the Diocese of South Florida,* 1923-1931.

Mann, Cameron. *Episcopal Address,* 1902–1913, bound with *The Journal of the Annual Convocation of the Protestant Episcopal Church in the Missionary District of North Dakota,* 1902–1913. Fargo: Roy T. Post, 1902–1913.

Missionary Jurisdiction of Southern Florida. *The Journal of the Annual Convocations of the Church in the Missionary Jurisdiction of Southern Florida,* 1893–1922. 30 vols. (The printers and places of publication are: 1893, *Sentinel* Steam Print, Orlando; 1894–1896, Edwards and Broughton, Printers, Raleigh, N.C.; 1897–1905, M. D. Cushing, Printer, Tampa; 1906–1919, 1921–1922, Carl W. Hill, Printer, Tampa; 1920, The Record Press, Boston.)

Moses, William Francis. *Suffragan Bishop's Address,* 1957–1961, bound with *The Journal of the Annual Convention of the Church in the Diocese of South Florida,* 1957–1961.

Reports of the Actuary to the Trustees of the Diocese of South Florida, October 4, 1932, and March 18, 1958, Diocesan Office, Winter Park.

Tyler, John P. *Episcopal Address,* bound with *The Journal of the Annual Convocation of the Protestant Episcopal Church in the Missionary District of North Dakota,* 1914. Fargo: Roy T. Post, 1914.

Weed, Edwin Gardner. *Episcopal Address,* 1886–1894, bound with *The Journal of the Proceedings of the Annual Council of the Protestant Episcopal Church in the Diocese of Florida,* 1886–1894.

Wing, John Durham. *Bishop Coadjutor's Address,* 1925–1931, bound with

The Journal of the Annual Convention of the Church in the Diocese of South Florida, 1925–1931.

Wing, John Durham. *Episcopal Address,* 1932–1950, bound with *The Journal of the Annual Convention of the Church in the Diocese of South Florida,* 1932–1950.

UNPUBLISHED PARISH RECORDS

All Saints' Church, Lakeland.
Bethesda-by-the-Sea, Palm Beach.
Holy Trinity Church, Conway (on deposit, Diocesan House, Winter Park, Florida).
Holy Trinity Church, Fruitland Park.
Holy Trinity Church, Melbourne.
Holy Trinity Church, West Palm Beach.
St. Andrew's Church, Tampa.
St. Gabriel's Church, Titusville.
St. James's Church, Leesburg.
St. Luke's Church (Cathedral), Orlando.
St. Mark's Church, Cocoa.
St. Mary's Church, Daytona Beach.
St. Paul's Church, Key West.
St. Peter's Church, Narcoosee (on deposit, Diocesan House, Winter Park, Florida).
Trinity Parish, Miami.

PUBLIC DOCUMENTS

Collier County Tax Roll, Episcopal Cemetery (on deposit, Diocesan House, Winter Park, Florida).
State of Florida. *Acts and Resolutions Adopted by the Legislature of Florida, Regular Session,* 1893. Tallahassee: *Times-Union* Legislative Printers, 1893.
State of Florida. *Third Census of the State of Florida,* 1905. Tallahassee: Capital Publishing Company, 1906.
U.S. Bureau of the Census. *The Tenth Census of the United States,* 1880. Vol 2. Washington: Government Printing Office, 1880.
U.S. Bureau of the Census. *The Eleventh Census of the United States,* 1890. Vol 1. Washington: Government Printing Office, 1890.

AUTOBIOGRAPHIES, DIARIES, LETTERS

Cadman Papers. A collection of letters, newspapers, and documents pertaining to the English colony at Narcoosee. In the possession of W. H. R. Cadman, Harding Street, Orlando, Florida.

Fairbanks, George R. Fairbanks Collection, a collection of Florida letters, manuscripts, and articles. Robert M. Strozier Library, Florida State University.

Gray, William Crane. "The Journal of William Crane Gray, 1858–1860." 4 vols. Unpublished. In the possession of The Very Reverend Francis Campbell Gray, former Dean, the Cathedral Church of St. Luke, Orlando, Florida.

Minutes of the Bucket and Dipper Club. In the possession of Mr. and Mrs. Alfred P. Bosanquet, Fruitland Park, Florida.

Stapylton Papers. In the possession of Lady Gillett, c/o John Gillett, Esq., Gulworthy Farm, Tavistock, Devon, England.

Wing, John Durham. "Scrapbook." 3 vols. A personal collection of newspaper clippings, photographs, and comments. Diocesan Library, Winter Park.

NEWSPAPERS

Chattanooga News
Cocoa Tribune
Columbus, Georgia, Enquirer-Sun
Jacksonville Florida Times-Union
Key West Citizen
Kissimmee News Leader
Kissimmee Valley Gazette
Kissimmee Osceola Gazette
Lakeland Sun
Leesburg Commercial
London Times
Miami Daily News
Miami Herald
Miami Times
New York Times
Norfolk, Virginia, Journal and Guide

Orlando Daily and Weekly Record
Orlando Morning Sentinel
Orlando Record
Orlando Reporter-Star
Orlando Sentinel
Orlando South Florida Sentinel
Sanford Journal
St. Petersburg Independent
St. Petersburg Times
Sebring American
Tallahassee Democrat
Tampa Tribune
Washington, D.C., National Tribune
West Palm Beach Palm Beach Post
West Palm Beach Post-Times

UNPUBLISHED MANUSCRIPTS

Gray, William Crane. "Status of Work Among Negroes." Attached to The Journal of the Annual Convocation of the Protestant Episcopal Church in the Missionary District of Southern Florida, 1914.

Hiller, G. Irving. "Trinity Church, Miami, Florida." Appended to Vestry Notes, Trinity Church, Miami.

Leonard, Paul A. "The Growth of the Episcopal Church in South Florida, 1892–1932." Master's Thesis, University of Florida, 1950.

O'Neal, William R. "The Protestant Episcopal Church." Diocesan Library, Winter Park.

Parkhill, Harriet Randolph. "Our Work Among the Seminoles." Diocesan Library, Winter Park.

Rand, Elizabeth. "Memories of the Church in the Early Days in Florida." Diocesan Library, Winter Park.

Robinson, Corinne. "The Cathedral School—A Diocesan Institution." Diocesan Library, Winter Park.

Robinson, Corinne. "The Church Home and Hospital." Diocesan Library, Winter Park.

Vaulx, J. J. "A History of Holy Trinity Church." In the Parish Register, Holy Trinity Church, West Palm Beach.

PERIODICALS

The Belfry of Grace Church. Ocala, Florida, May 19, 1935.

The Churchman.

The Living Church, March 29, 1921; October 9, November 13, 1966.

The Palm Branch (the official organ of The Women's Auxiliary of the Missionary District of Southern Florida; it became the official organ of the bishop on the accession of Cameron Mann.)

St. Agnes's Herald, Miami, May 1942.

Time, October 21, November 4, 1966.

ARTICLES

"The Church Home and Hospital." *Orange County Historical Quarterly*, March 1967.

"Consecration of Christ Church, Coconut Grove, May 25, 1930." Bishop Wing's *Scrapbook*, vol. 2.

"A Florida Girl." *Cornhill Magazine*, December 1893, pp. 162–85.

"Florida: The State of Orange-Groves." *Blackwood's Magazine*, September 1885, pp. 316–32.

Gray, Fannie C. "Letter from England." *Palm Branch*, January 1898.

Hall, Kathryn E. "History of the Episcopal Church of Bethesda-by-the-Sea." *Chronicles, The Church of Bethesda-by-the-Sea, 1889–1964.* West Palm Beach: Distinctive Printing, Inc., 1964.

"Lenten Program, Trinity Church, Vero Beach, Florida, 1943." Bishop Wing's *Scrapbook*, vol. 3.

Mann, Cameron. "A Parting Word." *The Spectator*, August 1, 1908, p. 164.

Pennington, Edgar Legare. "Cameron Mann, Bishop and Doctor." *The Angelus*, a publication of Grace and Holy Trinity Church, Kansas City, Missouri, February 1932.

Pennington, Edgar Legare. "The Episcopal Church in South Florida, 1764–1892." *Tequesta*, March 1941, pp. 47–88.

"Program: The Consecration of the Church of St. Luke and St. Peter, St. Cloud," Bishop Wing's *Scrapbook*, vol. 2.

"Program: The Consecration Service, The Cathedral Church of St. Luke, Orlando, Florida, October 21, 1945." Parish Records, St. Luke's Cathedral, Orlando.

"Program: The Dedication of Emma Cecilia Thursby Memorial Hall." Parish Records, St. Mark's Church, Cocoa.

BOOKS

All Saints' Church: The History of the Parish. Winter Park, Florida: Orange Press, 1947.

Blackman, William F. *A History of Orange County, Florida: Narrative and Biographical*. DeLand: E. O. Painter Printing Co., 1927.

Bulletin of The University of the South: Annual Catalogue 1966–67. Sewanee: The University Press, 1966.

Burke's Landed Gentry, 1885, 1895. London: Harrison and Sons, 1885, 1895.

Crockford's Clerical Directory, 1894. London: Oxford University Press, 1894.

Cushman, Joseph D., Jr. *A Goodly Heritage*. Gainesville: University of Florida Press, 1965.

Cutler, H. G. *A History of Florida, Past and Present*. Chicago: The Lewis Publishing Company, 1902.

Davidson, James W. *The Florida of Today: A Guide for Tourists and Settlers*. New York: D. Appleton and Company, 1889.

Drane, Herbert J. *A History of All Saints' Church, Lakeland, Florida*. N.p., 1919.

The Episcopal Church Annual, 1965, 1971. New York: Morehouse–Barlow Company, 1965, 1971.

Fries, Kena. *Orlando in the Long, Long Ago and Now*. Orlando: Ty Cobb's Florida Press, 1938.

Gore, E. H. *From Florida Sand to City Beautiful: A Historical Record of Orlando, Florida*. Orlando: n.p., 1947.

Grismer, Karl H. *The Story of St. Petersburg: The History of the Lower Pinellas Peninsula and the Sunshine City*. St. Petersburg: P. K. Smith and Company, 1948.

Hanna, Kathyrn Abbey. *Florida: Land of Change.* Chapel Hill: University of North Carolina Press, 1941.

Hardy, Iza Duffus. *Down South.* London: Chapman and Hall, Ltd., 1883.

Hardy, Iza Duffus. *Oranges and Alligators: Sketches from South Florida Life.* London: Ward and Downey, 1887.

Hartley, William and Ellen. *A Woman Set Apart: The Remarkable Life of Harriett Bedell.* New York: Dodd, Mead and Company, 1963.

Hoag, Amey R. *Thy Lighted Lamp, A History of Holy Trinity Church, Melbourne, Florida.* Eau Gallie: Undersea Press, 1958.

The Living Church Annual and Church Almanac, 1903, 1913, 1921. Milwaukee: The Young Churchman, 1903, 1913; Milwaukee: Morehouse Publishing Company, 1921.

Lloyd's Clerical Directory, 1898: A Treasury of Information for the Clergy and Laity of the Protestant Episcopal Church. Chicago: edited and published by Frederic E. J. Lloyd, 1898.

Mann, Cameron. *The Longing of Circe and Other Poems.* New York: privately printed, 1922.

Mann, Cameron. *October Sermons: Five Discourses on Future Punishment.* New York: Thomas Whittaker, 1888.

Mann, Cameron, comp. *A Concordance of the English Poems of George Herbert.* Boston: Houghton Mifflin Company, 1927.

Marie Louise, Princess. *My Memoirs of Six Reigns.* London: Evans Brothers, Limited, 1957.

Muir, Helen. *An Outline History: St. Stephen's Episcopal Church, Coconut Grove, Florida.* Miami: n.p., 1959.

National Cyclopaedia of American Biography, Vol. XIII. New York: James T. White and Company, 1906.

O'Neal, William R. *Memoirs of the Pioneer.* Privately printed for the Orlando *Sentinel Star* by the Florida Press, Incorporated, 1932.

Parkhill, Harriet Randolph. *The Mission to the Seminoles.* Orlando: *Sentinel* Printers, 1909.

Pennington, Edgar Legare. *The Beginning of the Episcopal Church in the Miami Area.* Hartford: Church Missions Publishing Company, 1941.

Quintard, Charles Todd. *Doctor Quintard, Chaplain C.S.A. and Second Bishop of Tennessee.* Sewanee: University Press, 1905.

Rerick, Rowland H. *Memoirs of Florida.* 2 vols. Atlanta: Southern Historical Association, 1902.

Rhodes, James Ford. *A History of the United States.* New York: Macmillan Company, 1920.

Sewell, John. *Memoirs and History of Miami, Florida.* Miami: Franklin Press, Inc., 1933.

Silver, James W. *Confederate Morale and Church Propaganda.* Tuscaloosa, Alabama: Confederate Publishing Company, Inc., 1957.

Stowe's Clerical Directory of the American Church, 1917, 1926–1927. 1917: Minneapolis: edited and published by the Rev. Andrew David Stowe; 1926–1927: Minneapolis: edited and published by G. Stowe Fish.

Stowe's Clerical Directory of the Protestant Episcopal Church in the United States of America, 1953. New York: Church Hymnal Corp., 1953.

Straub, William L. *History of Pinellas County, Narrative and Biographical.* St. Augustine: *Record* Company, 1929.

Tebeau, Charlton W. *A History of Florida.* Coral Gables: University of Miami Press, 1971.

Trinity Episcopal Church, Miami, Florida. Germantown, Pa.: Arman L. Davis, 1942.

Vickers-Smith, Lillian D. *A History of Fruitland Park, Florida.* DeLand: O. E. Painter Printing Company, 1925.

Weigall, T. H. *Boom in Florida.* London: John Lane, Bodley Head Limited, 1931.

White, J. W. *White's Guide to Florida and Her Famous Resorts.* Jacksonville: Da Costa Printing House, 1890.

Winter Park, Florida, 1888. Boston: Rand Avery, Printers, 1888.

Year Book: St. Luke's Cathedral, 1935. N. p., 1935.

Index

369

Moses, Cornelia Chaffee, 331
Moses, William F., suffragan bishop
(South Florida), 250, 275, 308,
312, 319, 335; background, 331–
32; consecration, 332; death, 337,
338; elected suffragan, 331
Moultrie Creek, Treaty of, 63
Mount Dora, 144, 171–72, 240; St.
Edward's, 326; Trinity, 172
Mulberry: St. Luke's, 326
Mulford, Joseph N., priest, 2, 87
Mundy, H. H., 158

Nace, Morton O., 236, 250, 257
Naples: St. Paul's, 342; Trinity-by-
the-Cove, 310, 326
Narcoosee, 43–44; St. Peter's, 17, 44,
56, 124
Nashville, Tenn.: Church of the
Advent, 14, 119
National Recovery Administration
(N.R.A.), 205
Nelson, Cleland K., bishop (Atlanta)
294
Negro work, 137, 243, 283; after
hurricane of 1926, 186–88; be-
ginnings, 100–106; during boom,
165–66; during depression, 198–
200; during World War I, 147–48;
during World War II, 272–74;
and resentment of segregation,
318–20; and salaries of clergy, 106;
and schools, 106
New Smyrna: St. Paul's, 17, 278
North Miami: St. John's, 342
North Port Charlotte: St. Nathaniel's,
342
Noyle, W. A., priest, 50

Oaklawn: Trinity, 17
Ocala: Grace, 16, 22–23, 172, 203–
4, 286, 294, 333, 357, 358; St.
James's, 102–3; St. Patrick's, 342
Ocoee: Grace, 17
Okeechobee: Our Saviour, 326
Old Doctor (Seminole), 70–71
Opa Locka: St. Kevin's, 326;
Transfiguration, 326

Orange City, 17, 330
Orlando, 6, 19, 21; Cathedral, 15, 16,
21–22, 32, 33, 34, 93, 107–8, 167–
69, 194, 197, 238, 261, 333, 339,
357, 358; Christ the King, 326;
Emmanuel, 326; St. Christopher's,
342; St. John's, 107, 240; St.
Michael's, 311, 326
Ormond: St. James's, 17, 193, 286,
311, 358
Otey, James H., bishop (Tennessee),
113, 116, 117
Owen, Ruth Bryan, 160–61

Pahokee: Nativity, 261, 269, 283
Palatka, 6
Palm Bay: Our Savior, 342
Palm Beach, 2, 165; Bethesda-by-the-
Sea, 17, 25, 141, 164–65; St.
Edward's (R.C.), 165
Palm Beach Gardens: St. Mark's, 342
Palm Branch, 26–27, passim
Palmer, Charles R., priest, 185, 241
Palmetto: St. Mary's, 342
Palm River: St. Cecilia's, 326
Parish day schools. See Schools,
parish day
Parkhill, Harriet Randolph, 25, 26, 97
Payne, Henry E., priest, 187
Payne's Landing, Treaty of, 64
Peck, Arthur S., priest, 169–70
Pell-Clarke, Leslie, 15, 91, 96
Penick, E., bishop (North Carolina),
276–77
Pennington, Edgar L., priest, 256,
257, 262, 264, 265, 268, 275, 279
Phelps, Lyman, priest, 357
Phillips, Robert T., priest, 153, 180
Pierce, Charles C., priest, 211
Pike, James A., bishop (California),
353
Pine Castle: St. Mary's, 326, 333
Pine Island, 17
Pinellas: St. Bartholomew's. See St.
Petersburg, St. Bartholomew's
Pittman: St. John's, 17, 357
Plant, Henry B., 5, 6
Plantation: St. Benedict's, 342

Plant City: St. Peter's, 280
Pollard, T. T., priest, 203
Pompano Beach: St. Martin's, 310,
311, 326, 333; St. Nicholas's, 342
Population, state of Florida, 6, 7
Port Charlotte: St. James's, 343
Port Orange: Grace, 17
Port St. Lucie: Holy Faith, 343
Porter, John F., priest, 102
Prayer Book for Soldiers and Sailors,
257, 267
Presbyterians, 178, 314
Presiding Bishop's Fund for World
Relief, 317, 344
Protestant Radio Center, Atlanta,
317
Punta Gorda: Good Shepherd, 6, 17,
25, 187, 333

Q<small>UINTARD</small>, C<small>HARLES</small> T., bishop
(Tennessee), 14, 15, 119

R<small>AILROADS</small>, 5, 6, 80
Rand, Anna, 26
Rand, Elizabeth H., first editor, *Palm
Branch,* 26
Rand, Frederic H.: first treasurer, 18,
19–20, 61, 91, 153, 154, 358
Reconstruction and Advance Drive,
280–81, 310–11, 316, 317
Reed, Sir Edward, 28
Reeves, G. Paul, bishop (Georgia),
287
Richardson, William C., priest, 153
Rickert, Alfred A., priest, 93
Robins, George, 107, 358
Robinson, Corinne, 26, 92–93, 127
Rock, Lewis B., 335
Rogers, Lawrence, chancellor, 323
Rollins College, 170, 237, 289
Roman Catholics, 170, 178, 314
Roosevelt, Franklin D., 161
Royal Air Force, 263
Ruge Hall, Florida State University,
237, 287–88
Ruskin: St. John's, 343
Russell, James T., priest, 164–65
Rutledge, Francis H., bishop
(Florida), 7, 104

S<small>AFETY</small> H<small>ARBOR</small>: Holy Spirit, 240
St. Bernard's Monastery. *See* Spanish
Monastery Gardens
St. Cloud: St. Luke's, 59, 237, 242
St. Edward's School, Vero Beach, 334
St. Luke's Cathedral, Orlando. *See*
Orlando, Cathedral
St. Luke's Hospital, 179, 195, 285,
315
St. Petersburg, 6, 174; Holy Cross,
343; St. Augustine's, 283, 326, 328;
St. Bartholomew's, 17, 48–49, 58,
59–60, 173, 240, 281, 327, 328;
St. Bede's, 326, 328; St. Giles's,
326, 328, 329; St. Matthew's, 326,
329; St. Peter's, 49, 157, 174, 280,
327, 328, 338, 341, 347; St.
Thomas's, 326, 328, 329, 334; St.
Vincent's, 326, 329
St. Petersburg Beaches: St. Alban's
(Advent), 326, 328, 329, 334; St.
Ambrose's, 311
Salvador, Max I., priest, 343–44
Sams, J. H., 358
Sanford, Henry S., 20, 22
Sanford, 6; All Souls' (R.C.), 170;
Holy Cross, 15 16, 22, 141, 169–
70, 312, 334, 357, 358
Sanibel: St. Michael's, 327
Sarasota, 143, 157; Redeemer, 175,
238, 332; St. Boniface, 327; St.
Wilfred's, 327
Satellite Beach: Holy Apostles, 327
Sayers, Dorothy, 1
Schools: boarding, 334; independent,
334; parish day, 333–34
Seamen's Church Institute, 180, 200–
202, 250–55
Sebring: St. Agnes's, 172, 205
Seminole Wars, 63–64
Sewell, John 81–82
Sherrill, Henry K., Presiding Bishop,
257, 332
Shore, Frank A., priest, 182, 258
Smith, G. I., priest, 84
Soper, John H., priest, 257, 281
Southern Florida School for Boys,
98, 99–100